THE GREAT UNIVERSAL EMBRACE

ARMS SUMMITRY—
A SKEPTIC'S ACCOUNT

Kenneth L. Adelman

SIMON AND SCHUSTER
New York   London   Toronto   Sydney   Tokyo

Simon and Schuster
Simon & Schuster Building
Rockefeller Center
1230 Avenue of the Americas
New York, New York 10020

Designed by Irving Perkins Associates
Manufactured in the United States of America

1   3   5   7   9   10   8   6   4   2

Library of Congress Cataloging in Publication Data

Adelman, Kenneth L.
The great universal embrace: arms summitry—a skeptic's account/
Kenneth L. Adelman.
p.   cm.
1. Nuclear arms control—United States.   2. Nuclear arms control—
Soviet Union.   I. Title.
JX1974.7.A3   1989
327.1′74′0973—dc20   89-36340
CIP

ISBN 0-671-67206-1

ACKNOWLEDGMENTS

To ALICE MAYHEW, who helped conceive and publish this book, go first thanks. As conceptualizer, editor and cheerleader, she really *is* the best. George Hodgman cheerfully helped edit and keep this project on track.

To Joyce and Don Rumsfeld go special thanks for helping shape my intellectual framework. Not just by themselves but by assembling in the "poverty program" of O.E.O., nearly twenty years ago now, a group of splendid minds and splendid people—Ellen and Don Murdoch, Lynn and Dick Cheney, Shana and Don Lowitz, and Marcia and Frank Carlucci. I worked with the ever-kindly Don Lowitz later when he became one of America's arms negotiators, a role to which he gave his last full measure of devotion. Each of these people has given intellectual nourishment and cherished friendship throughout most of my adult life.

We joined another extended family when leaping into the foxhole beside Jeane Kirkpatrick at the U.S. Mission to the United Nations, where we banded and bonded with the Sorzanos and Gershmans. All superb folks, challenging, even inspirational.

Back in Washington, I was honored to work under Ronald Reagan—for whom I have much affection, as this book makes evident—and with so many outstanding colleagues in government that I cannot possibly list them. Unlike many (or most) in a similar position, I genuinely *liked* my colleagues. And I continue to learn from them, as we stay in steady touch.

On Capitol Hill, Senator Dan Quayle led a band of serious-minded Senators who met frequently and quietly with me to deepen our knowledge on security and arms control. The group also included Warren Rudman, Malcolm Wallop, and Pete Wilson; from our fivesome, I learned much about not only practical politics but also statesmanship.

Since we ventured to Africa in the early 1970s, Lyse and Lawson Mooney have opened vistas of art and of life that we had altogether missed. Lawson has, among his many talents, one for being an unabashed cheerleader and dearest friend.

Each of these individuals—to say nothing of my parents and family—has contributed something to this book and so much more to our lives. Each is special.

But none is so special as Carol. Everyone should have such a staunch friend, steady support, wise critic, and engaging companion.

Some years ago, Don Rumsfeld inscribed a photo by writing that our girls, Jessica and Jocelyn, should forever be grateful that their mother had dominant genes. Watching them mature into such marvelous people, I'm grateful for that too.

This book is dedicated
in loving memory
to

Donald R. Murdoch

He just couldn't have done it if he had any quit in him at all.

CONTENTS

THE GREAT UNIVERSAL EMBRACE

In 1932, the Spanish Ambassador to the Geneva Disarmament Conference told this fable in response to the new Soviet foreign minister, Maxim Litvinoff, grandly proposing "total and general disarmament":

> *"When the animals had gathered, the lion looked at the eagle and said gravely, 'We must abolish talons.' The elephant looked at the tiger and said, 'We must abolish claws and jaws.'*
>
> *"Thus each animal in turn proposed the abolition of the weapons he did not have until at last the bear rose up and said in tones of sweet reasonableness: 'Comrades, let us abolish everything—everything but the great universal embrace.'"*

INTRODUCTION

Why this topic? Because concerns about relations between the superpowers and about nuclear weapons have filled our thoughts and aroused our passions for the past forty years. The specter of nuclear war is hanging over our civilization, and we search for ways to make it less haunting, if not to make it vanish altogether.

Why now? Because we've come to romanticize United States–Soviet summits and idolize arms accords in a way that is both dangerous and inaccurate, and because we hear the sound of Cold War ice cracking. When George Bush sits down across the table from Mikhail Gorbachev—surely the most imposing, impressive person on the world stage today—he will face the same man we see Ronald Reagan meeting on these pages. For the most part, they will discuss the same issues.

Yet everything outside that room will be different. Indeed the watchword of our times, at least in this realm, may have first been uttered by Dorothy: "Toto, I have the feeling we're not in Kansas any more." A sweeping transformation in big-power politics began during the Reagan administration, a change which may eventually be considered Reagan's main historical legacy.

Why the skepticism? Our hopes for productive arms accords have soared with the presence of a "new thinking" Soviet leader (after a string of "no thinking" ones); with the signing of an INF Treaty; with the growth of greater trust and stronger economic incentives. But prospects for a meaningful arms accord are actually worse than ever. Traditional arms control has reached a dead end, for reasons you'll read about in this book.

This is not particularly sad. Greater security and fewer nuclear weapons—the goals arms control has generally failed to achieve —will, alas, be achieved.

The same factors which *hurt* chances for traditional arms control actually *help* chances for a safer world. Benefits commonly ascribed to—but seldom delivered by—traditional arms control can now be advanced in other ways and with more success.

To wit: for thirteen years in Vienna, armies of diplomats gathered to negotiate conventional arms reductions before utterly failing. Had the West achieved total success, however, the Soviets would have reduced the number of their troops in Europe by 11,500. Yet as that negotiation was closing down, Gorbachev announced troop cuts of a half million—*forty-three times* the West's goal at the table. Of these, 240,000 are to be taken out of Europe, more than twenty times what we sought.

Why me? Because I was fortunate enough to participate in three summits during nearly five years as Arms Control Director, from early 1983 until the INF Treaty was signed at the end of 1987. My position on the front lines merely reinforced my view that arms control is not what it's cracked up to be.

I write both to share my special experiences at the Reagan–Gorbachev encounters and to pass along my reflections. This can be important; as William Gladstone said, "How little do politics affect life! One single good book influences people a good deal more." Let's hope so.

But people can be influenced only if they can understand. Most works in this realm boggle the mind, if they don't terrify the reader beforehand. It is simple for experts to be complicated, yet difficult for them to be simple. I am told that Enrico Fermi was brilliant enough to teach Physics 101 in a way college freshmen could understand; lesser intellects were not. This book is designed to meet the Fermi standard.

Regardless of the book's merits, there can be no doubt of its necessity. This struck me during a two-day speaking swing in southern California in the summer of 1984, which also revealed the vast variety of views and emotions this topic provokes.

My first stop was at Asilomar conference center outside Monterey. When I arrived, the more than 800 participants had been whipped into passion against the Reagan administration's handling of arms control. Before then, the Soviets had walked out of the Geneva talks; everything seemed dead in the water; and the participants were claiming it was all our fault.

I played into the critics' hands by confining my speech to the threat of chemical, not nuclear, weapons. These chemical weapons were actually killing people. H'mong peasants in downtrodden parts of Laos and Thailand were dying excruciating deaths; some choked on their own blood; some had their skin burned off. Hence, the civilized world had to fight chemical weapons before they became the poor man's weapon of mass destruction.

I had become moved after witnessing the effects of chemical weapons while visiting victims' families at the Ban Vania refugee camp in northern Thailand. The cruelty inflicted upon these poor people, matched by the indifference of supposedly "concerned citizens" of the world, got my goat. I had spent much of my two years as the Deputy United States Permanent Representative to the United Nations—Ambassador Jeane Kirkpatrick's number two—striving to spark diplomatic action on this dire problem.

But members of the World Affairs Council of Northern California didn't want to hear about it.

They wanted to hear about the *potential* tragedy of nuclear holocaust rather than the *ongoing* tragedy of chemical weapons. From the time my speech ended (around 8:00 PM) until 10:30, when the chairman kindly closed the session (with more than thirty people still standing at microphones waiting to pelt me with more questions), I responded to their inquiries and accusations.

"This is 1984, and your talk was an exercise in Newspeak and Doubletalk. Your agency is a transparent camouflag [sic] of rearmament—amounting to 1.6 trillion in five years. How seriously do you expect us to take you?" read one card I was handed.

Another asked about chemical weapons but in its own way: "Do you deny that the U.S. is producing and selling chemical weapons (ranging from tear gas to nerve gas) to Third World nations to help in their struggles against civilian 'dissidents?' " Of course I denied we sold nerve gas; it wasn't true. Besides, what did that have to do with Soviet's furnishing chemical weapons which were being used to exterminate defenseless H'mong people?

Still somewhat irritated, I arrived the next day at the Orange County World Affairs Council. There I found a group of kindred souls, the kind who had packed the house years before to hear Barry Goldwater as introduced by John Wayne.

After delivering my speech about controlling nuclear weapons —the kind I should have given the night before—I faced questioners wondering: "Why do we bother negotiating with the Russians?" "Haven't they cheated on every agreement they ever signed?"

After that session, we took a limousine—the driver bragged how his company had seven stretch limos with hot tubs; too bad we had not ordered one, he added—and proceeded along to Marina del Rey. The next day, in that swanky community by the sea, we gathered for a World Affairs Council meeting at the Yacht Club. The cocktail conversation initially centered on tennis camps; someone had just visited a new one in Sweden. Others asked about its facilities, the quality of its instructors, and so forth, before jotting down the name.

Then we moved on to the boats. One group thought it best to send their ships and crews ahead, while they flew later to join them in the Caribbean for the cruise. Another favored staying with their boats all the way from California to the Caribbean.

What did I think? Though known for having strong opinions on most topics, I was at a loss on this one.

During dinner, the conversation continued in a similar vein until the Council president was stricken with what appeared to be guilt. He jingled his glass to call our head table to order. With a pained look on his bronzed forehead, he moved us on to heavier topics.

"Ambassador Adelman, we all know how vital verification is to sound arms control. Now then," he went on, gazing at the expanse of yachts outside the picture window, "with these sea-launched cruise missiles, or SLCMs, coming along, verification may prove difficult. Tell us about this. We're all concerned about it."

"You all are familiar with SLCMs, or sea-launched cruise missiles," I began somewhat mischievously. "They're pilotless airplanes which can hold nuclear weapons and are carried on ships. And they're small, so small that several SLCMs could fit in your garage."

As I inhaled to continue my response, one nice lady blurted out, "Not in *my* garage! You should see my garage!" she said with a dramatic gesture. "Why, Phil and I have so much junk stashed in our garage that we simply cannot fit anything else in there."

"Have a garage sale then," someone suggested.

"No! Don't just have a garage sale," another volunteered. "Combine it with a bake sale . . ." The conversation veered away from SLCM verification, never to return.

With enough time and effort, I could walk each of the three remarkably different California crowds through my thesis that arms control has little to do with survival. But it takes a book to show why we are now entering an age when formal arms control is becoming counterproductive. And why we'll be better off without it.

This book is neither a kiss-and-tell nor one of the more common kick-and-tell accounts; it settles no scores. Nor does it claim to be a treatise on "arms control in the Reagan years," since much of this material comes from memory. The conversations give the flavor of what transpired; besides, they are substantively sound.

Moreover, my material is not organized chronologically. It begins in October of 1986 with Reykjavik, one of the most momentous and revealing events of the Reagan era. Here was the superpower summitry at its worst and its best, with the two world leaders making historic mistakes and historic advances.

We then step back to the January 1985 reopening of the arms talks where, in two summit-like days, we launched negotiations which led to the successful conclusion of one treaty and set the framework for the arms efforts continuing to this day.

Gorbachev makes his first on-stage appearance in Chapter 3, during the November 1985 summit in Geneva, where we in the Reagan administration first meet him. Next comes treatment of two rancorous issues of the Reagan years—getting into the INF Treaty and getting out of the SALT II Treaty—in Chapters 4, 5, and 6—which also describe the December 1987 Washington summit. The book concludes with Chapter 7 about the May–June 1988 Moscow summit and my musings on the future of United States–Soviet relations and arms arrangements. That's where I lay out why I've become a skeptic about arms summitry but an optimist about entering a safer world, which is the point of it all.

CHAPTER 1

THE REYKJAVIK SUMMIT

WAKE RONALD REAGAN AT THREE A.M. and whisper "Reykjavik," and he would beam. So would George Shultz, who considered it among his shining moments in office. They would only regret that what the President discussed there was not consummated, due to Gorbachev's keen desire to gut the Strategic Defense Initiative (SDI).

Yet mention Reykjavik to most foreign affairs types in the United States and nearly anyone in Europe, and you get snickers at best and shock at worst. They would only be consoled by appreciating that what Reagan discussed there was *not* consummated. Thank goodness for SDI! These people would place Reykjavik on the shelf of unforgettable and controversial summits, alongside Munich 1938, Yalta 1945, and the Kennedy-Khrushchev session in Vienna, 1961.

Since those two days in the supposedly haunted Hofti House, foreign policy sages have turned Reykjavik into a dirty word. Richard Nixon writes in his recent book, *1999:* "No summit since Yalta has threatened Western interests so much as the two days at Reykjavik." Nixon singled out President Reagan's agreeing to eliminate ballistic missiles and then all nuclear weapons without consulting the Joint Chiefs or Allies. "No deeper blow has ever been dealt to allied confidence in the United States than by the incorporation of the nuclear-free fantasy into the American negotiating position at Reykjavik."

Why the opposite appraisals of Reykjavik? Because of the extreme dangers it aroused and the substantial contributions it made. Here was pure, undiluted summitry—a veritable case study of how top-level meetings can go terribly wrong and how they can accomplish much good.

19

Moreover, here was pure Ronald Reagan. At every other session with Mikhail Gorbachev, he was carefully scripted, surrounded by advisors, and boxed in with other engagements.

Not at Reykjavik. This man, feared as a wild cowboy about to fire off nuclear weapons, was here unmasked as more of a visionary about to bargain away nuclear weapons. The last thing we advisors wished to do on nuclear matters at Reykjavik was to "let Reagan be Reagan." This too helped make Reykjavik among the most intriguing episodes of the Reagan years.

And, in his own peculiar way, Reagan was right. Not about his previously shrouded but strongly held antinuclear bias, but about the future of arms control. All this ponderous babystepping with mind-cluttering numbers and systems and types and categories had long blocked progress toward real reductions in nuclear weapons and real increases in world safety. Indeed, traditional arms control largely led to more nuclear weapons and less safety over the years.

At Reykjavik, Reagan tried to break out of the traditional procedures, with the encouragement if not complicity of Mikhail Gorbachev. It was the right goal but the wrong approach, at least according to the way I recommend in my last chapter.

For all these reasons, we begin our peek into the world of summitry and of arms control in that barren land at that extraordinary time.

· · ·

I could not afford to get to Europe, even on cheap Icelandic Airlines fares, during college. So, unlike millions of students, I had not been to Reykjavik before.

But I felt the usual summit-time thrill when we landed on that drizzly Thursday evening in early October 1986, soon after Air Force one arrived. Not that I expected peace to break out. More than twelve years in government taught me that in summitry there is less there than meets the eye. It was just that I felt special being in the middle of this world drama featuring two real stars. Top officials sometimes pooh-pooh high-level meetings—"What can the boss do that we can't do?"—but try to exclude them and see how blasé they act.

We were met on the tarmac by our assigned driver and limo and whisked away. En route I asked him to point out some sights, which he was delighted to do.

After a few minutes' drive across desolate plains, we arrived in downtown Reykjavik. Our fellow pointed out a Gothic church, a bite-size structure with scaffolding all around. The construction work, he told us proudly, would be completed over the next year or two.

"How long has the church been in renovation?" I asked.

"Since 1946," he said soberly.

Beginning to relish his role as a tour guide, the driver proceeded to circle the 4 twelve-story buildings, the only such skyscrapers in the country, and crisscross the metropolitan area, which spans six miles end to end. Everything reminded me of the model city in Walt Disney World; Reykjavik was less crowded, and everyone moved slower.

Nothing much happens in Reykjavik. Nothing at all happens quickly there. The "dawdling is worse in Iceland than in Peru," wrote the great explorer Richard Burton in 1872 after visiting both. Now Reykjavik, which Burton found reeked of decaying fish, has 80,000 dwellers in a country of 120,000 tranquil souls. A perfect foil for the frantic madness of a superpower summit.

On the summit's third day, bone-tired and increasingly irritable, I felt the need to get outdoors again. So I asked a driver, another one, to show me around a bit more.

This kindly elder took me to the outskirts, asked me to step out of the car, and pointed to a barren hill over yonder with three teensy houses barely visible against the gray soil. "Look at that," he said staunchly. "In the 1950s, that hill had nothing."

"And just look at it now," I said, to please. Later I thought back that Reykjavik, where people point with pride at the most minuscule developments on their stark hills, was thereby ideal to host arms control negotiations.

The hills of Reykjavik are indeed barren. The Hofti House, where President Ronald Reagan and General Secretary Mikhail Gorbachev met, featured a huge and crude portrait of American astronauts in full garb stomping around the foothills outside the capital. Until our summit meeting that area was best known, though only in selected circles, as the astronauts' training ground. Iceland's hills resemble moonscape more than any other spot on earth.

Repeatedly during those exhausting days, I gazed at that monstrous painting of astronauts tromping around the hills of Iceland hoping to ascend to the weightless world beyond. As I looked, I wondered what kind of world beyond the two men were discussing a floor below.

A summit. A meeting of the two most powerful people on earth. Negotiations over nuclear weapons, which can leave the world in smithereens. All this taking place right there, in Reykjavik, while its good citizens plod along their humdrum routines. Normal human drudgery and superpower glitz mingling for one fleeting moment in history.

The invading press corps, several thousand strong, did not know what to make of it. Reykjavik, the capital of a NATO ally but unlike any other NATO capital. When a CBS reporter assigned to do "background pieces" on the country arrived a week before opening day, he immediately called the President's and Prime Minister's offices to schedule an appointment at some point.

"Yes," each of the personal secretaries told the newsman in his first call. "Would you want to come over now? Would that be convenient?"

Not yet unpacked, let alone equipped with any information about the country, he held off. Could he make an appointment for later? Sure, that would be fine. Anytime would be fine, except when Reagan or Gorbachev landed. Then, the Icelandic officials would have to be at the airport for arrival ceremonies. Yes, so would the reporter. So they agreed not to do it then.

It was bizarre—the place, the timing, the main participants, even the subject matter. But it was captivating. A summit is like Cleopatra: alluring and exciting to be involved with, yet exceedingly treacherous. Reykjavik more so than most.

Something like it never could happen again, never would happen again, and never should happen again. But if it *is* ever to happen, it is nice to be a part of it.

Reykjavik was unique. Granted, the Geneva summit in November 1985 was special as the first time Ronald Reagan and Mikhail Gorbachev met each other, the first summit for each, the first U.S.-Soviet summit in six and a half years, the first revolving around the Strategic Defense Initiative (SDI), and so forth. Geneva was the summit you should have, if you must have a summit. It was nicely prepared, nicely scheduled in advance, nicely handled, and nicely reported.

It was *nice*—the two men chatting amicably by the fireplace, Gorbachev telling how he adored Reagan's movies (the sure pathway to his affection), the two teams working comfortably, all orderly and nice. Seeing the two leaders of opposing camps chatting together quenched our subconscious thirst for real humans to be the movers and shakers of history, rather than for impersonal forces as Marx and Toynbee would have it.

Geneva had to turn out well. Both leaders then shared an overriding goal: to steer U.S.-Soviet relations on a steadier course than before. Reagan wished to prove he could do it better in his second term than he had in his first, which was marked by "megaphone diplomacy." Gorbachev wished to prove he could do it better than the old Gromyko gang. Both men, though confident by nature, were not too sure of themselves in Geneva. They had to feel their way with each other and with summitry. Destined to succeed, Geneva succeeded.

Reykjavik was something else, less a run-of-the-mill summit and more a come-as-you-are affair. It was everything a summit should not be. It was not nicely prepared, nicely scheduled in advance, nicely handled, or nicely reported.

Reagan and Gorbachev felt they knew it all then—summitry, each other, nuclear weaponry, all of it. Each was riding high, and it showed. Hubris got the best of them.

At the time of the Reykjavik summit, in October 1986, Gorbachev had switched a lot of heads, thereby placing an impressive number of his own supporters in office. He even managed to boot upstairs that living Russian monument, Andrei Gromyko, to make room for the international affairs neophyte but personal loyalist Eduard Shevardnadze as Foreign Minister.

Gorbachev was the new, energetic force in the old and expended Soviet Union. He was "communism with a human face," to use Czech reformist leader Jan Dubcek's phrase, and an appealing one at that. Sure, the KGB had besmirched Gorbachev's smiling face by nabbing American journalist Nicholas Daniloff, but Reykjavik helped Gorbachev finesse even that one. After all the strong talk in Washington about not trading a Soviet spy for an innocent American newsman who was nabbed on trumped-up charges, Gorbachev got his trade.

Reagan was smiling then, too. He had every reason to smile. His popularity had risen to astonishing heights. He had the Midas touch: he felt he did; he read that he did. Seemingly, he had not a care in the world.

The twin blows of the initial Iran revelations and loss of the

Republican Senate loomed just over the stark Icelandic horizon, less than three weeks away, with the Iran-contra connection coming out three weeks farther down the road. Neither was anywhere in sight then.

At Reykjavik the world was theirs, Gorbachev's and Reagan's. Five thousand newsmen to catch a glimpse, to watch their every move.

Both succumbed as they started wheeling and dealing, undoubtedly beyond what either of them had anticipated. Meetings take on a momentum and a mood of their own; Reykjavik surely did. It was one of unbridled confidence right up to the end.

When the big boys started to wheel and deal, the staff aides watched with bated breath. At Reykjavik, we all felt a keen sense of unpredictability and of suspense—granted, not sensations to be relished in superpower bargaining over nuclear weapons, but stimulating nonetheless. A clear playing field with confident players makes for long passes.

The world will long remember that suspenseful Sunday afternoon in windblown Reykjavik during which Reagan and Gorbachev passed papers back and forth to eliminate this or that— who knows which?—category of nuclear weapons.

But the world has little noted nor much cared about the substantial progress we made during the last twenty-four hours there on the real meat of arms control, progress that made the INF Treaty possible, progress that breathed life into the then dormant strategic talks.

Without the big boys leaping into a world of weightlessness, a world without nuclear weapons, Reykjavik would have been hailed far and wide. As it turned out, it was ridiculed—nay, castigated—far and wide.

For there was something amiss about Reykjavik. Maybe it was the isolation of the place. Maybe the times. Maybe the participants. Maybe all of us, the President's advisors, let him down. Or maybe it was the subject matter. As my predecessor at the Arms Control and Disarmament Agency once quipped, arms control thinking drives out sound thinking. At Reykjavik, though, visionary talk drowned out sensible talk.

Preparations

How did it happen? We went through the motions of preparations but somehow missed the boat. In fact, the way Reykjavik began foreshadowed the way it was to end.

I first heard about the place—I could not have named the capital of Iceland and certainly could not have spelled it before then —when called into the nicely decorated White House office of National Security Advisor John Poindexter. He shut the door— John was forever shutting doors—and handed me Gorbachev's "personal" letter to the President. I had read much of their previous correspondence and came to expect platitudes of hopes and dreams, challenges and opportunities, risks and openings. (Any historian looking for nuggets in this stack of letters is hereby warned.) But this one looked and felt different, at least to me.

And it was different. Gorbachev had written a longer-than-usual and nastier-than-ever letter. He carried on about nefarious American behavior, the fuss we made over the Korean airline KAL 007 shoot-down, Afghanistan, and especially Daniloff. That affair had dimmed Gorbachev's sparkle; the American people and particularly the press did not like the Soviets jailing one of their own in a KGB prison to exchange for a true-Red Soviet spy. The affair ignited passions in Americans but apparently not much in Ronald Reagan.

I no longer recall the particulars, only the surging anger I felt sitting on Poindexter's white couch with him patiently smoking his pipe watching, waiting for me to finish. Gorbachev's message offended to the end. Then came the kicker: one paragraph, one sentence, as I recall, suggesting he and Reagan meet somewhere halfway, London or Reykjavik were mentioned, to pave the way for a Washington summit.

I figured there had been some mistake. The last paragraph might have come from a defective Soviet word processor that stuck a paragraph intended for the President of Bolivia or Sierra Leone on a letter going to the President of the United States. No, John assured me coolly, it was a real offer. His fellows (who? one wonders) had checked it out. Moreover the President wanted to accept. Right away.

"Now? Under these conditions?"

"Yeah." After some tempering, the President agreed to hold off his final acceptance until the Daniloff affair had been finessed.

Thus was the die cast. A hasty acceptance of a hasty offer for a hasty meeting. The President simply was eager to go. What prompted him—whether summit glitz; the pleasure he expected from dealing with Mikhail Gorbachev (an offshoot of the "Stockholm syndrome" for a rampant anticommunist); pervasive "Nancyism" or the soft inclinations of his wife, as conservatives contended; the cold calculation that the meeting would help the Republicans in the coming midterm elections (or that refusing Gorbachev's offer would open him to criticism); or the President's real sense that the moment was ripe for arms control—I cannot say.

Still, it was strange. It was strange of Gorbachev to propose the meeting then, in the midst of an unresolved and seemingly unresolvable episode. (Most diplomatic endeavors seem unresolvable until they are resolved.) Strange of him to propose it at the close of such a nasty letter. Strange to propose it in a week or ten days' time. (Usually the foreplay is the best part of a summit, perhaps like anything in life.) Strange to propose it in London or Reykjavik rather than in Washington, where he and Reagan had already agreed to meet. And strange to have a summit in order to prepare a summit. After all, that's what a secretary of state and a foreign minister are for, to set up summits.

To be fair about it, maybe it all seems stranger now than it did then. Maybe if Reykjavik had not ventured off into weightlessness—like those astronauts tromping around the outskirts of Reykjavik—if both sides had stuck to the script, none of this would seem so strange now. Reykjavik might have ended with Reagan appearing his politically masterful, gutsy self and with Gorbachev his public relations masterful self, adept at covering the Daniloff tracks fast and clean.

The dangers were there right from the start. They should have been analyzed and discussed. That did not happen then, or any time since. Reagan's acceptance brought to mind Sir John Slessor's observation that any foreigner would be fascinated "to watch the way even the most capable Americans shy off any attempt to formalize or regularize the governmental system."

Poindexter made me pledge absolute secrecy—another thing John was constantly doing—and plunge ahead with the planning. It would not be much, though.

The Soviets were not coming to Reykjavik to engage in tough negotiations. That we knew. Besides, our arms control positions were already set in concrete, chiseled in a letter Reagan had written Gorbachev the previous July. All we needed to do at Reykjavik was explain the letter.

Not that this was an easy task. The President's letter was convoluted, to put it mildly, partly a product of diarrhea of the computer by a staff aide and partly a result of the President's own thinking then.

Usually in arms control, Reagan "kept aloof from all details, drew magnificent plans, and let others find magnificent means," as Horace Walpole said of British statesman William Pitt. Not in this case, however. During the summer of 1986 when the policy was being set, Reagan conceived and refined his two favorite themes—sharing SDI with the Soviets once it became ready and moving toward eliminating nuclear weapons.

These two ideas sprang from Reagan's irrepressible optimism, however they might clash with his long, strong antipathy toward the Russians. Here was a man singularly endowed with an ability to hold contradictory views without discomfort. Besides, Reagan never thought of Gorbachev as a *real* Russian leader. Sure, he was part of that cruel regime, but yet apart from it—nice, direct, and unstodgy. And he seemed to share Reagan's feeling that somehow, someday, we had to escape the nuclear threat.

The policy-setting letter—since then, like most hotly contested arms control schemes, relegated to the dustbin of history —was carefully massaged that July. The scores of "draft letters" became part of a masterful exercise in shuttle diplomacy done by Bob Linhard of the National Security Council staff, who scurried between various government agencies. His boss, Poindexter, resisted gathering all the main players around one table—the President, Vice President, Secretaries of State and Defense; Chairman of the Joint Chiefs, Director of Central Intelligence, Arms Control Director, and the negotiators—for fear it would become another free-for-all.

During those times, NSC meetings had a way of aggravating everyone, addling everything, and accomplishing all too little. Anything the State Department recommended would instantly become suspect to the Defense Department. A proposal cobbled together brick by brick might work, Poindexter surmised, whereas one hammered out with everyone present surely would fail. And Poindexter was inclined to work outside the formal system, as we have learned since.

His was not a foolish approach in this case, given Poindexter's predicament. And, for a change, the NSC had something to work with. The Defense Department, customarily comfortable with just saying no, offered a rather novel notion: the elimination of all ballistic missiles.

Somehow, the idea took hold in the Pentagon corridors—among civilians, that is, since the military never liked it. Secretary Caspar Weinberger once explained that the Soviets were so far ahead in ballistic missiles that we could never catch up. So why not ban them?

A weightier reason came from the fact that ballistic missiles stood at the heart of the strategic threat. They have pinpoint accuracy, are unrecallable—once sent, they are gone—highly explosive, and potentially vulnerable when based in silos. ICBMs, intercontinental ballistic missiles, constitute the sole strategic system that targets its own kind. Our ICBMs target their ICBMs; this can quickly prompt a "use 'em or lose 'em" push during a crisis.

So runs the theory. Putting the idea into play at the arms control table was deemed relatively risk-free; no Soviet leader would or could seriously entertain it. And it made a marvelous debating point to counter the Soviet claim that SDI was designed to further our first strike capability. Without ballistic missiles, there could be no such capability, with or without SDI, since there would be no fast-flying, accurate, and highly potent weapons. If they persisted to lambast SDI after hearing our no-ballistics offer, their arguments would be seen as primarily propagandistic.

It was logical, but it was wrong.

Regardless of the merits, the White House bought the no-ballistic missile proposal. It gave our negotiators something to work with. The Defense Department would incorporate this idea in a new proposal, and the State Department could get SDI on the table by our pledging not to deploy SDI for some years if the Soviets made concessions on the rest.

Though the Joint Chiefs of Staff opposed the zero-ballistic notion, they let it pass. It was a foolhardy scheme to scrap the forty-year-old strategic triad (strategic forces on land, at sea, and in bombers) with a stroke of the pen, but why fuss over yet another arms control scheme? Serious military men had more serious things to do. None of these arms control proposals ever came to anything; none of them had any relation to the real stuff of military power: guns, tanks, planes, boats, missiles. Besides, the various reiterations of the President's July letter moved this notion to the back burner; zero ballistics would be discussed after SDI had been deployed and deep cuts had been agreed upon and completed in strategic weapons. Like never.

All this was crammed together in one extensive, nearly unintelligible letter. Reading over various versions, I thought of the challenge to diagram some of the unending Buckminster Fuller–like sentences. I pitied the poor clerks in the Kremlin condemned to translate all this into Russian.

When we gathered in the Oval Office to discuss the final, final version—without staff and without the negotiators—Poindexter's foreboding turned true. Chief of Staff Donald Regan—then claiming that no sparrow could land on the White House lawn without his okay—had not seen the letter before. Indeed, he was unaware of its existence.

"What is the President writing Gorbachev for?" he asked rather angrily at the outset. Most of the others knew of the letter's existence and had a vague notion of its contents (though they too would have had trouble diagramming its sentences, or even paraphrasing them). Among those assembled, the President knew its substance best.

Unfortunately, though, the group did not dive into the substance. The meeting dove into the pros and cons of the Anti-Ballistic Missile (ABM) Treaty, Shultz pro and Weinberger con. The Chiefs took the position, since presented in public, that we are better off with the ABM Treaty than without it, even though the Soviets were violating it. This somewhat convoluted argument holds that the Soviets are better poised to break out of the ABM restrictions than we are; although true, it does not say much for our military preparedness which is, after all, part of the Chiefs' responsibility.

I tried valiantly to change the topic, but with scant success. I made the simple point that the ABM Treaty was the supreme law of the land, whether we liked it or not. Thus the President, indeed all of us, were sworn to uphold it, unless we chose to give six months' notice and withdraw, which no one was advocating. I tried to dilute the zero-ballistics idea—knowing any frontal assault would fail—by transforming it from a subject of serious negotiations to one possible pathway for both countries way, way in the future.

Again, to no avail. The first positive arms control proposal from the Pentagon was not about to be stricken by the Arms Agency Director. Besides, by then the President had warmed to the idea, seeing this not as a clever debating point, but as a mighty step toward his personal penchant for a nuclear-free world.

It was a done deal. Even my passionate calls on the secure line to White House Chief of Staff Don Regan about the dangers of such a scheme proved fruitless. He may not have cared as much about the down sides as I did.

After that Oval Office session, which ended abruptly as the President and Secretary of State George Shultz scooted off to welcome some visiting dignitary, the rest of us retreated into Poindexter's office. Joint Chiefs of Staff Chairman William Crowe expressed more apprehension about the whole approach than before, but he softened his criticism by saying the Chiefs would like to see how the Soviets react.

"It's clear how they'll react," I said. "They'll reject it out of hand." Crowe concurred, and CIA Director Bill Casey burst into laughter. He was pleased to know the risks were low.

Here he was right. The letter did no harm; it had a half-life of a few months—well within the bell-shaped curve for any arms proposal—and then vanished. The harm came later, as the letter helped set up Reykjavik. Even Bill Casey would not laugh about that.

LUNGING FOR THE CAPILLARIES

Meanwhile, after the startling announcement of a meeting at Reykjavik, the hordes of arms control experts began busily to work away. Word processors spewed out reams of papers on where we stood and why, the usual paperwork masking the real action. Though nothing came of all this bustling—a word Dr. Johnson defined as horseback riding aboard ship—such busywork is standard.

And it is revealing. A summit, including its preparation, furnishes real insight into how government works. Just as psychotherapy teaches that a personal crisis reveals the strengths and weaknesses of an individual's psyche, so a political crisis reveals the strengths and weaknesses of that system or group.

Those outside government may not consider a summit a type

of crisis, but those on the inside do. It is a time of high stress, a time of high stakes. Those fretting U.S. giveaways in arms control fret more than ever. Those pushing for "breakthroughs" in arms control push most forcefully then.

Papers fly back and forth on the sundry issues. How much give is there in our position? Where's the give? In return for what?

Little if any of this goes anywhere—arms control has had scant bearing on national security—but somehow everyone plays as if the stakes could not be higher. After all, the President is clearly engaged in the arms control process, the press is mesmerized by it, the Allies pore over each comma, and the Congress kibitzes endlessly about what should and should not happen. So arms control gains a momentum of its own, not only in the big game of strategic arms control, but also in the smaller arenas.

NUCLEAR TESTING AND OTHER NONSENSE

Take talks over nuclear testing, for instance. Here is a near nothing—halting nuclear testing would actually increase the number of nuclear weapons and make future nuclear arms less safe—but still it has long been advanced. No one advocates stopping the testing of ships or guns or planes—indeed, we would never purchase a car that had not been fully tested—but some think we would be wise to stop testing the final guarantor of our national security (and that of friends and allies around the world): nuclear weapons.

Void of any national security benefit whatsoever, a test ban has managed to stay a hot topic on the arms control agenda since the Kennedy-Khrushchev deal in 1963 (which was actually an environmental move; after moving all nuclear testing underground, there were more tests than before).

Due to pressure from the arms control community, the Congress, and the press, even the Reagan administration felt compelled to "do something" about nuclear testing. That's when we can get in most trouble, when we feel we must "do something" in arms control.

Pressure for new arms control initiatives is unrelenting, coming from as many political and diplomatic sources as it does. We need to adopt some new scheme or other, it is advocated; we need, in essence, to negotiate with ourselves, since the Soviets had until then come up with few new serious notions.

Actually, most arms ideas peddled as "new" have been pushed and rejected before. It is like that story of Dean Rusk cabling Ambassador John Kenneth Galbraith in India to tell him that, insofar as the arguments he mustered in an elaborate diatribe on Vietnam were coherent, they had already been considered and rejected.

This is why any administration needs experienced people in arms control, unlike some other realms of foreign policy. Otherwise, the President stands as easy prey for the professional arms control pushers.

So in the Reykjavik run-up, bids went out for innovative ideas on nuclear testing. First prize went to the Arms Control and Disarmament Agency notion to propose reducing the number and/or yield of nuclear tests in proportion to reductions in nuclear weapons (ballistic missile warheads in particular).

I pushed the idea. It had a ring of symmetry to it. It would allow nuclear tests, though reduce the numbers of them. It had a spin of public affairs about it, highlighting as it did our first priority of START (Strategic Arms Reduction Talks). And it had an air of improbability about it: the chances of consummating and implementing cuts in nuclear warheads during our administration was slight, at best. As Ollie North would have said, here was a neat idea.

But it was wrong. After even a moment's reflection, anyone could see that it made little practical sense. With fewer nuclear weapons, the United States would need to test more, not less. Precisely because we maintained a vigorous testing program were we able to reduce the total number of nuclear weapons in the U.S. arsenal by 25 percent and the total megatonnage (bang) by a whopping 75 percent since the 1960s. Without testing, the scientists and the military would have made more weapons to assure the same number worked.

But things happening as they do, just as I became disenchanted with this scheme—having by then given it more than a moment's reflection—others in the administration became enchanted with it. The State Department was forever accommodating to anything new proposed in arms control. The Defense Department must have been looking the other way. Anyway, the President bought it and proceeded to unveil it with a flourish before the United Nations General Assembly.

After this September 1986 speech came the October Reykjavik

summit—nonsummit, planning meeting for the summit, pre-summit summit, whatever it was then called. The arms controllers became itchy and began looking around for something even newer. The Soviets had not responded to the UN proposal, since it had just been made, but why wait for them?

Sundry schemes came forth. The arms controllers ground out decision memos and "talking points" for their bosses while themselves hustling from meeting to meeting. The perpetual motion in those presummit days can best be captured in the words of World War II General Joseph Stilwell:

> Washington [was] a rush of clerks, in and out of doors, swing doors always swinging, people with papers rushing after other people with papers, groups in corners whispering in huddles, everyone jumping up just as you start to talk, buzzers ringing, telephones ringing, rooms crowded with clerks all banging away at typewriters.

The good General had a solution for all this chaos:

> Someone with a loud voice and a mean look and a big stick ought to appear and yell, "Halt, you crazy bastards. Silence, you imitation ants. Now half of you get the hell out of town and the other half sit down and don't move for one hour." Then they could burn up all the papers and start fresh.

Of all the schemes that the arms controllers devised, my favorite was to have the "six continent" (or some such name) nations —Tanzania, Sweden, Mexico, India, Finland, and someone else— help verify nuclear testing treaties. No matter that neither we nor the Soviets have ever wanted others prying into our bilateral deals. No matter that, as a group, they were not the staunchest of our friends. (Sweden, so conscience-stricken today, had allowed the Nazis to cross their territory during World War II while prohibiting the Allies from doing so and could not even manage to keep Soviet attack submarines out of their own territorial waters.) And no matter that the lack of Soviet agreement to solid verification measures could not be helped by Mexico or Sweden or Tanzania.

Yet it lived, right up to a White House meeting immediately before we left for Reykjavik. There, Fred Ikle of the Pentagon serenely suggested that this approach would hurt rather than help our verification capabilities. Since no one could contend his point, the proposal was shelved—no doubt to arise another day in another administration when arms controllers scour the shelves to find something new on nuclear testing.

All's well that ends well, one might reasonably conclude. But not necessarily. For killing dumb schemes takes staff resources, paperwork, and the time and energy of high-level officials, who have all too little time for substance as it is because of their endless ceremonial occasions.

Conservatives contend that arms control deludes the public or saps the will of the West by lulling us into a false sense of security, but this is not the worst of it. Rather, its main liability is the staggering drain on presidential and other top-level time for matters of little or no relevance to keeping the peace or strengthening the nation.

The numbers speak for themselves. To take one year—1983, the year I joined the Arms Control and Disarmament Agency— the President presided over eight National Security Council meetings on arms control. In addition, he met with advisors in the Oval Office or the Situation Room six times. Thus, fourteen presidential meetings were conducted that one year devoted exclusively to arms control, even though no arms control progress at all was made that year. Meanwhile, the high-level Senior Arms Control Policy Group—whose initials produced the indecorous label "sack-pig" (SACPG)—met eighteen times that same year in the Situation Room with the President's National Security Advisor presiding.

The time consumed by all this is staggering. In 1985, for instance, the President called two separate NSC meetings on the Mutual and Balanced Force Reduction (MBFR) talks, and yet another on the same topic in 1986—three presidential meetings on talks that made no progress whatsoever for thirteen years and have never shown any prospect of doing so. The two sides disputed even the title of these talks for all these years, with the Soviets leaving out the "B" since they wanted mutual force reductions but no balance.

The President surely spent more time on this MBFR Kabuki dance than he ever did on the overall military balance in central Europe, on what NATO must do to keep deterrence strong. He undoubtedly spent more time working out proposals on the nuclear arms talk in Geneva—many of which the Soviets never even addressed—than he did on deciding how to maintain the overall strategic balance.

In 1983 or 1984, the President presided over a full NSC meeting on whether to include SLCMs (sea-launched cruise missiles) in the START accord—an issue undecided to this day—but none I was aware of on the shape of the navy into the twenty-first century, a navy largely determined by decisions made during his administration. Likewise the President called an NSC meeting on whether to include ALCMs (air-launched cruise missiles) in our arms proposals, but none on the future of strategic bombers.

This may be passed off as poor staff work during the Reagan administration, but it seemed unavoidable. The congressional obsession with arms control feeds the press, who ask about it at the daily White House and State Department briefings. This feeds the White House staff and the President. To hold an NSC meeting on arms control shows that the President really cares; not so with more critical topics involving long-range defense planning. As the Shah went down the tubes, and with him huge U.S. interests in the critical Persian Gulf, Secretary of State Cyrus Vance was diving into the capillaries of SALT II.

MODEST EXPECTATIONS

So our presummit scurrying was in full force to prepare for Reykjavik. Still, we did not expect much—in the words of Lady Bird Johnson, a "howdy and hello" session wherein Gorbachev and Reagan would greet each other, express sorrow over the Daniloff "misfortune," pledge to avoid this type of "misunderstanding" in the future, and "rededicate" themselves to arms talks (when substance remains unchanged, it becomes more important to stress rededication and acceleration). In essence, we expected the usual platitudes, without effect but without harm either.

But this was not to be. Reykjavik would explode on the world scene in a way that beckoned yet defied accurate explanation. A year later, when headlines alleged that clean-cut American Marines escorted KGB agents around the U.S. embassy in Moscow as part of a "honey trap" for sex and money, European papers claimed to have found the key to unlock the mystery of Reykjavik. The Italian *La Stampa* wrote in April 1987, "The marines . . . offered Gorbachev the opportunity to go to Reykjavik with a perfect knowledge of U.S. disarmament plans." Soon conservative *Il Tempo* echoed the theme: "The Soviets knew our cards at the Reykjavik poker game" because of "the espionage network at the U.S. embassy in Moscow."

Partially true; the Soviets did have "a perfect knowledge of U.S. disarmament plans" going into Reykjavik. But so did everyone else—at least anyone who bothered to watch the President deliver his speech to the United Nations General Assembly a month before, in September 1986. None of our "cards at the Reykjavik poker game" was facedown. Despite all the bureaucratic tail chasing, we planned no new initiative. We had no real fallback position. We wouldn't need anything to fall back to.

For the Soviets were not going to *do* anything at Reykjavik. That we knew. Former Ambassador to the United States Anatoly F. Dobrynin told us so, as did all our sources in Moscow, who spoke with one voice on how Gorbachev merely wanted to hear the President out on his "novel" proposals for SDI outlined in his July 25 letter. There might be some "exploration" of INF, but probably not.

State Department and intelligence "experts" echoed this prognosis. They explained that Gorbachev had to consolidate his power at home and could not turn his attention to foreign affairs until he had done so. He wanted to show motion but to have no real movement. That was why the Soviets requested an arms control experts' meeting in Moscow the prior August, to show motion without accomplishing much. And that was why they requested regional dialogues that fall, more talk to show some motion. Reykjavik would take it another rung up the same ladder. Winston Churchill may have thought Russia was a riddle wrapped in a mystery inside an enigma, but we had it all unwrapped.

PREPPING THE PRESIDENT

Before heading off, we met with the President one final time. For some reason—who makes these decisions and why?—the meeting was held in the Roosevelt Room, the lovely pastel room across the hall from the Oval Office adorned with portraits of Teddy and Franklin Delano.

Present that day were the President, Vice President, Secretaries of State and Defense, National Security Advisor, White House Chief of Staff, Director of Central Intelligence, Chairman of the

Joint Chiefs, Director of ACDA and our arms negotiators, the Attorney General, the Secretary of Energy, and a few others. This too is an arms control trademark, more high-level talent chasing fewer results than in any other human endeavor. Much of government is populated with dalmatians, who bark loudly atop the fire engine but contribute nothing to putting out the fire; arms control is most richly endowed thus.

This particular presidential meeting got off to a rocky start. Admiral Poindexter read his notes, written by some technical type. He framed the key issue of Reykjavik the way SAT tests frame analogies: Spaghetti is to clouds as a kangaroo is to . . . His wording went something like "Mr. President, if the Soviets move on START but continue to link START to SDI, should we express a willingness to discuss new definitions on testing, development, and research under the ABM Treaty in the context of their accepting the basic START principles but excluding SCLMs?"

This kind of thing is hardly Ronald Reagan's strong point. Those assembled offered their wisdom on this smoldering question while the stewards poured coffee and tea. Occasionally the "principals" glanced up from their papers, no doubt wondering if the words they were reading made more sense to others.

Having finished this series of statements—who knows what it was about? Who knows what was decided?—the President raised the issue of the Intermediate-Range Nuclear Forces (INF), commonly called Euro-missiles. He wanted to push for the complete elimination of INF missiles, because this had been our position since 1981, but also because it might lead to eliminating all nuclear weapons. Cap Weinberger was gung ho for that position; Defense had concocted the notion and proposed it with a flourish back then.

Someone gently reminded the President that our position had changed in March 1985 from a "zero-option only" to a "zero-option preferred." We then told the Soviets that they could pick a number, any number (up to our deployment level), and we would settle on that for equal limits. The President knew that, but he seemed not to care much. He wanted to end up at zero. In some mysterious way, he knew we should go for it.

That does not seem possible, Mr. President, he was told, since the Russians insisted on keeping some if not all their missiles in Asia. Okay, he would then threaten to deploy our Pershing II missiles in Alaska to match theirs in Asia.

The more the President talked like this, the more nervous our

INF negotiator, Mike Glitman, became. He was spending his life in secret, cautious talks with the Soviets, always exploring, always probing: If we proposed this, could you think of proposing that? And here was the President tossing out all kinds of notions with seemingly careless abandon. It was the most worried I had seen an arms negotiator since a few years back when, in the presence of our MBFR ambassador, the President eagerly suggested he tell the Soviet ambassador that we knew all about Lenin's plan to conquer the West. Lenin would wait until Western democracies were ripe before plucking them. "Tell your fellow there that they can never do that to us." Standing outside the Oval Office afterward, I asked our diplomat to send me a copy of his report back to the President after he conveyed this to his Soviet counterpart. Somehow I never received it.

The President's stance on INF and installing missiles in Alaska was somewhat tempered by being a bluff. The Air Force, and thus the Pentagon, did not want to deploy any such missiles in Alaska, where frigid territory and lack of protection would make them vulnerable. Besides, fired from Alaska, they could not hit any important Soviet targets, which were far beyond range.

Maybe Reagan did not know it was a bluff. Less likely, maybe the Russians did not know it, either. But the Soviet negotiators continued to make a big fuss over the Alaska option. I recall months later sitting in that magnificent Soviet Foreign Ministry chalet in Moscow seeing Foreign Minister Shevardnadze again worked up over it. "Why, we gave you Alaska," he said emphatically at one point, "and now you use it to threaten us!" Shultz calmly explained that we bought it, fair and square, though admittedly for a few million dollars. Besides, if you Russians don't want us to deploy these things in Alaska, fine, you can sign on to the zero option.

This was precisely the President's view—part of Shultz's appeal to successive presidents was his talent at presenting his boss's views with conviction—and Shultz sensed it during that crowded pre-Reykjavik session in the Roosevelt Room. He then took the conversation back to the main topic, SDI and the July letter. He said that Gorbachev would want to know if this was indeed the President's plan or a product of our overenergized bureaucracy, and if the President was really serious about eliminating all ballistic missiles, or, again, if this was merely a bureaucratic stance.

With this, the President became piqued and launched into a pitch about the Russians still seeking world domination. Lenin's line about communism's world conquest was still their guiding principle. That's why, the President figured, the Soviets had turned down the Baruch Plan to abolish all nuclear weapons, even before they had any. As long as the Soviets stayed expansionist, there was no way to resolve such tough issues.

The President then mused about a possible failure at Reykjavik. He would go out and tell the people that he had done his best, but Gorbachev had refused to go along. We would thus be in fine shape. Had this point sunk into the minds of those gathered there, Reykjavik could have ended upbeat rather than in the doldrums. Don Regan's "shovel brigade" would not have been needed to turn around a dismal ending.

Lastly the President wondered about Gorbachev's latitude. He remembered Nixon telling him how Khrushchev once said, "You have your Congress. I have my generals."

REYKJAVIK BREAKS THE RULES

And so we were off. Not that we were fully prepared—former Secretary of State William Rogers said later that Reykjavik might have turned out okay, but it still seemed like a green football team with an unprepared coach whose best move was the forward fumble—but we *felt* prepared. And the President was taking the arms control brainpower along with him. If anything came up, we were ready for heavy work on a technical level.

But not on a grand level. History furnishes loads of lessons, but none ever seems to get learned. We knew better but did not do better. We just tripped along from one meeting to another without taking time for reflection.

Before each summit, I sent to the President and Secretary of State a marvelous article written by Dean Rusk entitled "The Presidency." The quarter-century-old article wears well, with an interesting story of its own. Rusk wrote the piece when president of the Rockefeller Foundation, early in 1960. Candidate John F. Kennedy was so impressed by its cogent arguments against a summit, especially a hasty and ill-prepared summit, that he became more interested in Rusk for a top post if he won. Kennedy won; Rusk became Secretary of State; and the two of them soon arranged a hasty and ill-prepared summit. So much for the power of pieces in *Foreign Affairs*; they seem not to influence policy making, even that made by the author.

Nonetheless Rusk was right. Summits do move public opinion "by desperate hope and the fascination of the spectacular," which makes for "problems of distinguishing form from substance and of avoiding the slippery slope of relaxed effort which can lead to disillusionment and critical danger." What comes of it? "The result is a persuasive pressure toward the creation of illusions—at worst an illusion of victory, at best the pretense of accomplishment where none was achieved."

The summit setting is not conducive to serious business. "The general atmosphere is that of a football stadium. Is our team winning? Did our man throw him for a loss? Who wins the Most Valuable Player award?" Thousands of newsmen gawking, aides fluttering, and the President negotiating. As Versailles should have proved for all time, putting a president in the role of negotiator-in-chief deprives him of what a negotiator most needs to succeed: the ability to sound out, to hold out, to help out the boss back home with careful analysis. With the President at the table, there is no back home. Again, as Rusk wrote, "The court of last resort is in session."

Add the pressures heaped on an American president to "make progress" by a huge press, eager Congress, and ever-anxious Allies —pressures not placed on the Soviet leader—and you make summitry a disaster waiting to happen.

The harping for a deal never lets up; even the best correspondents keep beating the drum and even at the oddest of times. The Reagan era's most influential reporter, Lou Cannon of *The Washington Post*, wrote during the administration's final days, when nothing at all was happening on START, that the Reagan team was "solidly on track toward a nuclear arms accord that could be one of the most striking foreign policy achievements since World War II." It would come in "a final chapter of his presidency that could be applauded for generations." Most readers, not up on these negotiations, might presume Cannon's analysis had some basis in fact.

Rusk's Cassandra-like warning was issued even before the era of nuclear arms control. Rusk could never imagine a president being expected to negotiate with his Soviet counterpart in an area so laden with technicalities yet significant enough to affect the national security for decades. Especially a president amply endowed with sound instincts and strong feelings but with neither much expertise nor curiosity.

But even before nuclear arms control came thundering in, Rusk found that summits do "not give us effective negotiation; such experience as we have had with summit diplomacy does not encourage the view that it contributes to the advancement of American interests." Reykjavik again proved him prophetic, and in spades.

Granted, the personal aspect of summits matter since personalities matter, particularly to such "people persons" as Reagan and Gorbachev. A summit furnishes a unique opportunity for leaders of the world's main adversaries to size each other up, to discover each other's personal views and feelings. This comes since presidents and general secretaries, as master politicians, are masterful at evaluating people; after all, that's how they got to the top.

Yet this too can be a mixed blessing. The size-up can be seriously wrong, and the top-level discussion can lead to confusion if not added apprehension. That was why in the fifteenth century Philippe de Comines advised, "Two great princes who wish to establish good personal relations should never meet each other face to face but ought to communicate through good and wise ambassadors." Certainly Winston Churchill, who never met Hitler, sized him up better than Neville Chamberlain, who spent hours with the Führer at Berchtesgaden and Munich. "I got the impression," Chamberlain recalled after Munich, "that here was a man who could be relied on when he had given his word." Seldom was a man so wrong. Seldom was his error so costly.

More recent wrong appraisals have likewise been costly. Khrushchev probably left Vienna in 1961 convinced that Kennedy was weak. Worse yet, Kennedy left sensing that Khrushchev sized him up as weak. This impression indubitably contributed to Kennedy calling up U.S. reserves for Berlin and building up U.S. forces for Vietnam soon afterward. Within months the Russians built the Berlin Wall, about which Kennedy heaved, exhorted, and did nothing; even his kindly friend James Reston wrote that the President "talked like Churchill and acted like Chamberlain." Next year Kennedy and Khrushchev had their nuclear showdown over the Cuban missile crisis. No wonder that after Versailles Sir John Wheeler-Bennet wrote how summits can become "the grave of reputations and the womb of future wars."

With such a disappointing if not dismal record, why do presidents keep on having them? Largely because summits have become part of the international landscape. People everywhere take comfort in the two main antagonists sitting together to discuss their differences. Better to jaw-jaw than war-war, quipped Churchill, as if those were the only alternatives.

All presidents adore summits, for the glitz they provide and for the "breakthroughs" they are supposed to yield. For all presidents take pride in their persuasive powers, most deservedly so. It was their power to move and persuade that made them presidents; once in office, that magic multiplies manyfold. They all succumb, even the steely Lyndon Johnson, as he told his aide Richard Goodwin:

> I always believed that as long as I could take someone into a room with me I could make him my friend. And that included anybody, even Nikita Khrushchev. From the start of my presidency, I believed that if I handled him right, he would go along with me. Deep down, hidden way below, he too wanted what was good.

Even though Khrushchev might try a fling at world domination, Johnson said he "knew I could cope with it so long as he and I were in the same room."

This is fine theory, but not real life. Soviet leaders, unlike congressional chiefs or Allied statesmen or most others a president deals with, are not susceptible to persuasion by an American president.

Despite the deck stacked heavily against him, more so in some ways than against any other president, Reagan did well at summits. Holding five meetings with Gorbachev in a thirty-seven-month stretch was a bit much, but still they worked out well, especially the Moscow summit. Perhaps because Reagan, above all, understood that summits resemble show biz more than corporate meetings.

And perhaps because Reagan was a "big game" player. Cannon once compared him with a high school football player. The word around the circuit was "to leave him alone, treat him politely, and pick him up if you happened to block him" since he was ordinarily rather ordinary, "no particular menace when left alone." But if anyone did something "to make him angry, he dominated the field of play. Reagan is like that." He does best when challenged hard and when it counts most.

This trait helps explain the real mystery of the Reagan administration—how, under a president who was allegedly so distracted, inattentive, in many ways ignorant and nondirective, there emerged a successful foreign policy. How much credit goes to Reagan? How much to Gorbachev? How much to luck? To the times?

These are questions that historians have to sort out. But taking an early cut, I would attribute a large chunk of the credit to Reagan. Only under him could two hallmarks of his foreign policy—SDI and the "Reagan doctrine" of aid to those fighting communist regimes—have been launched and sustained.

As for his legendary "management style," reports of Reagan's tuning out, though exaggerated, were frequently justified. They color the view of intellectuals, who assume that great success is a function of great intelligence or great diligence. But this is not the case. At the end of his term, rather than attributing the success of "peace breaking out all over"—from Afghanistan to southern Africa to northern Africa to western Sahara, Cambodia, and the Iran-Iraq border—to Reagan, intellectuals would much rather attribute it to luck or to Gorbachev or to "historical conditions."

Yet Reagan was there when the nation needed him. When it counted, he turned on, was tuned in and toughed it out. When it did not count, he could become a caricature of his laidback image. The work pattern of his presidency resembled that of his acting days, long periods of passivity followed by bursts of intensive, nearly exhausting activity. Hence do movie actors resemble soldiers and, at least in this case, the President himself.

The Reagan experience reemphasizes what historians have long known, that there are a few decisive moments in any presidency that demand decisive leadership. Otherwise, the post can be handled routinely. A full-time president can miss or mishandle those moments and be relegated a failure despite hard work; Jimmy Carter stands out here. A part-time president can be highly successful if he seizes those moments and handles them well; Ronald Reagan stands out here. He surely would be blamed if everything had fallen apart; so why not give him credit when everything came together?

OH, WHAT A SUMMIT

"Hell, this isn't a meeting to prepare a summit. It's a summit," the President said in a resigned way late that fateful Sunday afternoon in Reykjavik. For Gorbachev was eager to wheel and deal, his briefcase bulging with new ideas, quite in contrast with the old days when only we would propose new ideas and they would mostly say *nyet*.

Better than the substance of Gorbachev's proposals was their choreography. Here he truly shone. Stringing out new ideas on strategic arms that "opening day," especially during our all-night session; springing his new INF initiative on Sunday morning; building to the crescendo of negotiating the elimination of some or all nuclear weapons, and ending up with SDI as the stumbling block late Sunday afternoon. It was all beautifully staged and timed.

How were we to know all this lay before us? When walking into a final preparatory session with advisors on the eve of opening day, Reagan passed by a television showing Gorbachev's plane arriving in Reykjavik. "When you stop trying to take over the world, then maybe we can do some business," he said in a John Wayne–like way to the television set.

Actually, we spent most of our first day at Reykjavik not preparing for negotiations with Gorbachev, but conducting active negotiations with the Congress. As it happened, that was the day the Senate and House Armed Services Committees held their conference on the defense budget. The House crammed the bill with arms control amendments fit to kill (to kill us, anyway), making the United States abide by the provisions of SALT II that the Soviets had not chosen to violate; stopping our nuclear testing and antisatellite testing programs; slashing money for SDI; and so forth. These issues were on the table with the Soviets as well as in the bills of Congress. Indeed, the House wanted to write Soviet arms control proposals into American legislation.

After considerable haggling, the then Republican-controlled Senate prevailed on every contentious issue, except the ban on antisatellite testing. Here the House triumphed, which meant prohibiting us from testing this weapon the Soviets had both tested and deployed. This move was to prove harmful the next day.

Faces turned and cameras clicked as the President and General

Secretary shook hands at the doorstep of the seaside Hofti House in Reykjavik. Somehow Reagan, usually endowed with exquisite timing on such occasions, was late bounding out of the doorway to greet Gorbachev. This I took as a bad omen, thinking about omens ever since I had read that Hofti House was reputed to be haunted.

We "experts" killed time that morning, something we had become expert at doing. I read some historical biography at the tiny American embassy; others went out shopping or watched CNN on a special hookup.

Slightly after noon, curious about what was happening, I was told to proceed to the secure "bubble." I headed to this room-within-a-room found in every U.S. embassy around the world. A square, transparent plastic room specially coated to assure that it cannot be bugged, a "bubble" is secure until opened by someone twisting the two big handles of the door. A great *swoosh* of air then rushes out; I always feared the accumulated words *swooshed* out as well, but security folks assured me that this could not happen.

Since the bubble is the sole place approved for secret conversations, I anticipated spending lots of time in the Reykjavik bubble, until I saw it. The Reykjavik embassy contained the smallest bubble ever built. Some administrative officer naturally figured nothing much secret ever happened in Reykjavik, or could happen there. Sound logic, but wrong in this case.

Anyway there we were, in the bubble with a capacity of eight maximum for top-level meetings in the midst of a summit. We began that initial meeting with eight—Secretary Shultz, Don Regan, John Poindexter, Arms Negotiator and Advisor Paul Nitze, Richard Perle of the Pentagon, the NSC's Robert Linhard, Chief Negotiator Max Kampelman, and me—crammed in like 1950s teenagers in a telephone booth. We eagerly awaited the morning's readout, only to have Secretary Shultz begin by telling us he did not have much to say. He was not called in to join Reagan and Gorbachev until the very end. The two leaders spent most of the morning alone, with one interpreter each. The Soviets had previously refused our request for simultaneous translation, so consecutive translation was used; this wasted half the time. Shultz however would tell us what he had heard.

It was not much. Gorbachev monologued most of the time, though he handed Reagan a paper presenting his views. (This happens regularly since the staff—any staff, Soviet or American —is terrified that its "principal" will get it wrong.) Knowing the paper counted for much more than Gorbachev's monologue—it had to have Kremlin blessing and thus was definitive, whereas Gorbachev could have spoken more casually or been misinterpreted—we dived for the paper, letting Shultz talk on in his slow, meticulous manner.

We then heard a noise as the upper handle of the bubble door suddenly turned. Through the plastic, we spotted a burly man leaning over to turn the lower handle. The door opened; the air *swoosh*ed; and the hearty fellow called out, "The President of the United States!"

We were startled but did what comes naturally: we all rose. This caused a considerable commotion; our chairs knocked about, and some of us bumped into each other.

The President seemed taken aback by the racket he caused— he constantly seemed surprised when people treated him as someone special—but quickly broke the moment's awkwardness. "We could fill this thing with water and use it as a fish tank," he quipped, looking around the tiny square room.

By then we were "secure" again. The giant human specimen had turned both handles to keep in the air and the words.

What to do now, in a big-stakes game of musical chairs? Since my chair was closest to the door, I motioned to it and said, "Right here, Mr. President," much to the relief of the others. I then plopped down on the only square foot of unoccupied floor space, leaning solidly against the President's legs and with nearly everyone's shoes touching my legs.

In this cramped condition did we listen to the President and discuss how to proceed. Each time over those forty-five or so minutes one person shifted his weight, all the others had to adjust. Washington wags who claimed that members of the Reagan administration could never work closely on arms control should have seen us then.

We learned that Gorbachev had more in mind than "howdy and hello." It was not clear what, but he did want to move forward. The Geneva proposals were "floating around" in the air somewhere, he told the President. They needed to break the deadlock.

On INF he said nothing new, though he did reconfirm his previous concession not to include the British and French systems in these negotiations. On strategic arms, his position was dramatically new but strictly self-serving—nothing to take seriously in the real world of arms control.

On SDI we faced the same old objections, but here with a new twist. Unlike the first summit, Gorbachev was not foursquare against any and all SDI research. He had become more refined, now handling a scalpel rather than a bludgeon, arguing that we could proceed with SDI research as long as we confined it to the laboratory. Interesting, but nothing to call home about. (Don Regan had already instructed us in Reykjavik not to call home in any case, about anything, at any time, to anyone.)

I came alive, though, when the President told how eager Gorbachev was to negotiate a ban on antisatellite testing. I blurted out, "Tell him it's a done deal. The Congress gave that away yesterday." Gorbachev proposed a mutual ban; Congress enacted a unilateral ban.

Reagan then strained to reconstruct Gorbachev's long peroration, which had consumed all but fifteen minutes of their two-and-a-half-hour session. So while the world waited outside with bated breath, the General Secretary practiced oral reading throughout the morning.

That afternoon, after meeting with us all in the dining room of the Ambassador's residence, the President (as we say in the trade) retaliated in kind. He slowly recited words on our paper, six or seven pages worth single-spaced, that we had prepared for him. While Reagan was rehearsing at the dining room table beforehand, I asked if he had any questions about the technical terms or phrases; he said he did not. The script's second reading, to Gorbachev, consumed more than half the afternoon session. With translation coming after each sentence or so, that must have been every bit as boring as the first.

Amazing how much executive time is eaten up by "principals" reading statements to each other, statements that could have been mailed ahead of time or given to the other's staff for reading.

This bothered me that Saturday. It no longer bothered me that Sunday. By then, the two "principals" had spread their wings and begun talking about eliminating all strategic weapons or all ballistic missiles, and all nuclear weapons. Reykjavik made me gain a keener appreciation for diplomatic formalities, especially those that box in the boss. No wonder a British Foreign Service officer in 1804 told his boss, Lord Harrowby, to respond to a pleading foreign diplomat with "neutral, unmeaning civilities." These are safe.

Government is words, as politics is words. In the big time, like summit time, words matter a lot. That day, while crammed in the bubble, President Reagan related how Gorbachev had erupted when Reagan began to explain that his plan for SDI could be contained in a new agreement superseding parts of the ABM Treaty. Gorbachev fired back that he could not support scrapping the treaty.

In the Ambassador's residence afterward, I asked our interpreter how he translated what Reagan had said. In Russian, the word used evidently meant either "supersede" or "completely substitute for," thus giving rise to Gorbachev's pique. The interpreter tried out other words with me, explaining their sense in Russian. We landed on a more appropriate word for future use and heard no more on this matter from Gorbachev.

Language is marvelous, though tricky. Reading an article or speech translated back into English from a foreign tongue shows the limits of transmitting ideas through words across languages and cultures. A University of Chicago professor's work on "higher education" was translated into Japanese as a treatise on "mental institutions." I once addressed a group of Japanese about arms control, after which the delegation head thanked me by saying I deserved "much clap" for such sagacious remarks. A Chinese academic emoted over my rather pedestrian comments one time; my words had "vividly aroused" the members of his group. I never cared to verify his statement but was grateful at least that they were not visibly aroused.

The classic case comes from the golden if archaic tongue of Zimbabwe's Prime Minister, Robert Mugabe. Schooled in South Africa by Afrikaner teachers, Mugabe waxed eloquent in his maiden speech to the UN Security Council on how he struggled mightily for his nation's independence. He was inspired by a vision that someday he would appear before this "awesome organ," the UN Security Council. After hearing of this, I began asking my boss, Jeane Kirkpatrick, if she were planning to appear before "the awesome organ" or if I should cover for her.

Reykjavik had no such hilarity, but it had its store of surprises. Among them was the appearance of Sergey F. Akhromeyev on the scene. This wiry, compact, and modest man commanded the military might of the Soviet Union and the respect of its top man, Gorbachev.

We knew little about Marshal Akhromeyev as we climbed the circular wooden stairways of the Hofti House around eight that night, after Reagan and Gorbachev had spent much of the day reading out loud to each other. We had heard of Akhromeyev, but none of us had met him or known the Soviet Chief of Staff to be heavily involved with arms control.

Personally I dreaded the evening meeting—arranged by Reagan and Gorbachev for their staffs to "make progress" and report back in the morning—as I came to dread most such meetings. I found them repetitious, unproductive, and excruciatingly boring. Besides, our respective negotiators had been meeting day and night in Geneva with no progress.

Soviet officials, we knew, considered Reykjavik a place for review, not for initiating. Moreover, this summit would be ending the next day, which scarcely gave us time to accomplish much in this intricate business.

The no-nonsense way Marshal Akhromeyev began raised my hopes from their depths. "I'm no diplomat, like all of you," he said in essence. "And I'm no negotiator, like most of you. I'm a military man. So let's not repeat all the familiar arguments. Let's see how much progress we can make tonight. That's what I want, and that's what Gorbachev wants."

You could feel the relief from our side, as we had feared the Soviets' standard fare of endless repetition. We all had experiences with the likes of Ambassador Victor P. Karpov, then head of their Geneva arms team and later my counterpart as chief of the Soviet Foreign Ministry's arms control section.

My personal experience with Karpov began during a lavish Geneva lunch—the only type Victor would attend—in March 1986. Between courses he launched into a long exhortation about the meaning of a "strategic" nuclear system.

"Victor," I interrupted as he was warming up, "I recently rummaged through our files to find that you first made that argument late in 1969. We first rebutted it early in 1970. Now you can give your lines, and I can give mine. Or I can make your arguments and you can make mine. Or, better yet, both of us can skip the whole discussion, unless you have something new to say. I sure don't." Victor smiled his gushing and mocking smile and proceeded on undeterred. I naturally retaliated in kind with the worn U.S. counterpoints.

Akhromeyev wanted none of this at Reykjavik and tolerated none. When Victor launched into a diatribe, Akhromeyev placed a hand on his colleague's arm until he piped down. "Now, where were we?" Akhromeyev asked innocently. Later that night when the Russian propagandist Georgy Arbatov, Director of the USA and Canada Institute, inhaled before unloading some tirade against SDI, Akhromeyev again turned off the set piece.

Not that Akhromeyev negotiated like Americans, though. One of his moves, though rather clumsily done, was bold. Early on he presented Gorbachev's notion that we simply slice each category of existing strategic nuclear weapons in half. This would end the haggling, he told us.

As Mencken said, each problem has a solution that is neat, simple, and wrong. Even if we took the Soviet numbers, though of dubious reliability, they would end up superior in most categories of strategic power since they were ahead then. No American president would or could sign on to Soviet strategic superiority, especially since the Jackson Amendment accompanying SALT I made this illegal.

We passed much of that night's first session arguing against this Gorbachev-Akhromeyev scheme. Ours were not the most erudite of arguments; we merely echoed that Chinese expression, "No problem. We can't do that." No arms accord could leave the United States at a disadvantage. Simple as that, but said countless ways by different Americans over the ensuing six hours.

How can grown people argue over such basic points for so long, especially in a session everyone deems of cosmic importance? Effortlessly, as it turns out.

In any case, Akhromeyev caught the idea that his idea was not going to catch; we would never accept it. So around 2:00 A.M. he wisely suggested that we take a break.

Actually, this was our second recess. An hour or so before then, Ambassador Ed Rowny felt uneasy about a point Akhromeyev raised on how to count nuclear warheads. We retreated upstairs to caucus and met in a small room; everything in Reykjavik is small. Ed made his point vigorously, and he was correct, though its relevance to the discussions that night was somewhat obscure. Nonetheless, Ambassador Paul Nitze, head of our negotiating team then, strenuously disagreed. Paul sounded out other delegation members, who agreed "in principle" with Ed, and then took the issue to Secretary Shultz at 3:00 A.M. The Secretary supported him.

Supported him on what, though? Although the argument was

heated at the time, it was eminently forgettable afterward. Nothing came of the issue; it was not mentioned again in Iceland, nor since, as far as I know.

"There it is," the Austrian Emperor said in *Amadeus* each time an issue, of whatever urgency, came before him. That's needed more in arms control disputes, an ability to simply say, "There it is" and let issues pass away. They always do, given enough time.

We also spent part of that night discussing how to verify sea-launched cruise missiles, small pilotless airplanes that can carry nuclear or conventional armament. This could have been an interesting and important discussion, but it wasn't. Indeed, we whiled away the hours with the Soviets, the propaganda triplets of Arbatov, Falin, and Velikhov in the lead, insisting that we agree "to find a solution" to SLCM verification. We said we could not so agree if there was no "solution." We could agree to "seek a solution"; when Falin at one point proposed such a phrase, I put a note in front of Paul Nitze urging that we buy it. Nitze did, but Akhromeyev demurred.

"Maybe you would seek and not find," Akhromeyev said. True, but if it wasn't there to find, the best we could do is seek. We went back and forth with such inanities until someone suggested that we agree to find a "mutually acceptable solution." Again the Soviets demurred. Every solution must be mutually acceptable; that's what negotiations are about. Why do we need these words?

Clearly we didn't. But since we had proposed them, we dug in. Back to the Falin solution, but that was "no longer" on the table. So let's drop it. No, that wasn't possible. No inclusion of SLCM, no conclusion of START. Finally, as a sign of magnanimity, the Soviets yielded. We would seek a "mutually acceptable solution" after all.

Feeling triumphant, even euphoric at our victory, but with our brains rattled—as evident from this conversation—and worsened by it, we took our break.

When we returned after 3:00 A.M., braced for another round of regurgitation, we were hit with another surprise. Akhromeyev casually opened by saying that they were dropping their new scheme on strategic arms. So much for that, one among thousands of new arms control approaches to come and go over the years. This had a half-life of a half night. No apologies; no explanation. It was gone; good riddance.

Contrary to conventional wisdom, the Soviets can and do

change their positions. In fact, they manage reversals with an ease and grace we lack. For the United States to change a basic position takes an Herculean effort, even by a president. He must win over the Joint Chiefs, explain the switch to Allies worried that arms control is either going nowhere or going too far, and pacify well-organized conservative groups ready to pounce on any "cave-in."

Soviet leaders, unencumbered by the dispersion of power, can turn a deft about-face. That's how they came back to arms talks in January 1985, after walking out the year before because NATO followed through on its policy. Meanwhile, the Soviets threatened "countermeasures," like deploying some ballistic-missile-carrying submarines closer to American shores, only to learn that this prospect pleased the U.S. Navy which could then track Red subs more easily. They installed shorter-range nuclear systems into East Germany and Czechoslovakia, who objected as much as they could.

After their blustering failed to produce thunderclaps, the Soviets acted like a puppy dog. I remember the November morning in 1984, shortly before Thanksgiving, when Secretary Shultz beckoned me into his private office. He showed me a letter from then Soviet leader Chernenko that proposed a Shultz-Gromyko meeting to resume the arms talks. "Look," I said, pointing to one densely written paragraph. "The Soviets are willing to come back to INF, as well as START." We were startled. The Soviets crawling back to INF despite their dogmatic, seemingly irrevocable statements? This we never expected, but they found a way.

Just as they found a way that night in Reykjavik for Akhromeyev to drop a bad scheme and propose a new and good scheme. For the first time ever, they were willing to change their definition of a "strategic weapon." This seemingly arcane matter actually goes to the heart of Western security. (Big issues can be tucked in boring corners.)

Since SALT I began in 1970, the Soviets had defined a strategic weapon to *exclude* Soviet weapons that target Europe and thus threaten our Allies but to *include* American weapons that are deployed in Europe and thus protect our Allies. That night they dropped this one-sided definition; they no longer counted our forward-based systems as "strategic." As if this weren't enough for one night—yielding in minutes what they had pursued time and again for over sixteen years—they likewise discarded their insistence on limiting the number of nuclear bombs on strategic bombers. Instead they agreed to count only the number of bombers, regardless of their load. As yet another bonus, they agreed to the overall totals of a START Treaty: 1,600 ballistic missiles and bombers and 6,000 ballistic-missile nuclear warheads.

Granted, these "accomplishments" addle the brain of the average American. But they titillate the heart of the average arms controller. Defining strategic systems, excluding bomber weapons, and closing on limits is one amazing night's work, indisputably more progress than we achieved in thousands of hours in hundreds of meetings over the previous five years.

Excited about these moves, we wished to nail them down. So we reached for pad and pen to propose language for Reagan and Gorbachev to issue at the summit's close.

We tried to do the same on SDI and the ABM Treaty, only to run up against the same old roadblocks. Karpov was being particularly ornery as he insisted that no settlement in START was possible without settling SDI; no settlement on INF was possible without settling START; and so on. It all became even more complicated. Each negotiation was complicated enough without being tied to the other in some way that required a huge flow chart to portray. INF that night was also an occasion for debate, not discussion, since there was no real give-and-take on either side.

On strategic arms, we had something big to write up, and we did. But we soon found that we had no way to make copies to hand the Soviets. Our delegation, hastily thrown together, had come to the Hofti House with a typist and a typewriter, though somehow they never seemed to be around. We asked for a photocopy machine, but Hofti House had none, and it was not easy to move a copy machine across Reykjavik at four or five A.M. We were in a bind until a nice Soviet staff aide, grinning broadly, presented us with a sheet of old-fashioned carbon paper. Not wanting to become too dependent on the communists for our diplomatic tools, we rang up the embassy and asked them to bring over some American carbon paper. But the staff there had none, so we had to make do on borrowed, low-tech carbon paper from the Soviet delegation.

A DELAYED OBSTACLE

The only other episode that night concerned "sublimits." We insisted then, as we had since 1982, that the overall limits of 1,600/6,000 (the former on what's called "SNDVs," or strategic nuclear delivery vehicles, basically missiles and strategic airplanes; the latter 6,000 limit on warheads) did not suffice. If START was to be "stabilizing," to reduce the risks of nuclear war by reducing the likelihood of a surprise attack, we had to reduce the most "destabilizing" systems. All this is standard in arms control. Indeed, the Soviets had agreed to sublimits in SALT I and II. To help reduce the temptation to use or lose nuclear forces during a crisis, we had to limit land-based missiles more severely than sea-based missiles. For they posed greater dangers.

Strangely, Akhromeyev balked over sublimits. So we argued about this, too, finally "laying down the marker" that we could not conclude a START agreement without them. If the Soviets refused to budge here, we'd bring it up in Geneva. As it was approaching five A.M. by then, Akhromeyev shrugged it off saying either side could raise any issue it wanted in the formal Geneva talks. We moved along.

This part of the discussion could have been forgotten, it was eminently forgettable, had the Soviets not resurrected it regularly thereafter. In classic Soviet style, they later contended that their agreeing to the 1,600/6,000 limits and to what we sought on bomber weapons and on defining "strategic systems" were contingent upon our dropping sublimits.

This Soviet twist on Reykjavik first arose during a Shultz-Shevardnadze meeting in Vienna a few months after Reykjavik. The State Department, so protective of its prerogative as the diplomatic paper holders, had no record available of the Reykjavik talks. That is more typical than one would expect. When Alexander Haig was Secretary of State, he could not locate copies of the Camp David discussions. President Carter had carted off his notes to Georgia. Cyrus Vance and Carter's National Security Advisor Zbigniew Brzezinski had taken their notes to help in writing their memoirs. Lesser lights had not attended the critical sessions. At one point, Haig kindly asked the Israelis for their notes on Camp David.

At Vienna, I had my notes handy. I found where Akhromeyev agreed that either side could raise any issue at Geneva. The Soviets didn't trust our notes and insisted that Akhromeyev had said no such thing. So as it happened, in Vienna we found something new to argue over—not just the substance of sublimits or no sublimits, but also what had happened at Reykjavik over sublimits.

THE ENDLESS NIGHT ENDS

We broke at 6:15 A.M., satisfied though not elated—it hadn't sunk in, all that had been accomplished—and pooped. After bidding Akhromeyev and the others adieu, I headed back to my hotel room, small and stark like the country itself, to shower. At breakfast we talked about everything but arms control.

Around 8:30 or 9:00 A.M., after checking into the temporary White House office and finding my cubbyhole filled with cables —who was writing this stuff? Reykjavik was the only thing happening—we returned to the bubble. Secretary Shultz was already in place when the rest of us arrived, perhaps because he realized there was no reserved seating. He quickly became elated about our night's work, partly on its merits and partly on its presentation.

Even the coolest of negotiators hype their own deeds—probably everyone in life does—giving the impression that our negotiating brilliance, our toughness when we had to be tough, our flexibility when it was okay to be flexible, our agility throughout, had yielded this harvest. Never mind that we came with nothing to offer and had offered nothing; we merely sat there while the Soviets unwrapped their gifts.

I don't believe negotiators, at least not in U.S.-Soviet affairs, ever prompt concessions because of their agility and guile. No Soviet, even a five-star marshal and chief of staff of the Soviet armed forces, wings it in a roomful of Americans. If he were the type to solo, he would not have become a marshal. No Soviet is so awed by American negotiating skill as to suddenly decide to scrap missiles in response. Akhromeyev's leeway, perhaps even Gorbachev's, had to have been circumscribed by the Politburo before they left Moscow.

Secretary Shultz, not then deep in nuclear matters, nevertheless caught the drift. We had triumphed. And once he got it, he couldn't get over it. He repeated the wonders we had done back to us. I recall trying to dampen the euphoria a smidgen but being neither terribly vigorous nor effective. Why temper an effusive secretary of state praising your work? We all began to feel good.

No one then and there put the Reykjavik "breakthrough" in its truer light. The agreed-to 1,600 strategic nuclear delivery vehicle (SNDV) total was still more than *seven times* what the Soviets had during the Cuban missile crisis, when we worried plenty about their nuclear arsenal. The 6,000 warhead total approximated the Soviet number when Reagan took office and was more than *twelve times* what the Soviets had deployed during the 1962 crisis.

So any cut agreed at Reykjavik still left the numbers astronomically high. Perhaps they would not leave our country any safer. CIA Director William Casey never tired of saying in NSC meetings that "deep" reductions in strategic forces of 30 percent or even 50 percent would not necessarily leave us any more secure: the Soviets would still retain enough firepower to do whatever damage they chose to do.

Ambassador Karpov let out a dirty little secret that night. Our 50 percent cuts heralded in START would not cut either side's strategic arsenal in half. He explained how our 2,000 SNDVs would, under START, go down to 1,600; according to his math, this did not constitute a 50 percent decline. Add on a massive number of cruise missiles coming downstream, and the overall number of strategic weapons would rise under this accord. Karpov's discourse was a harbinger of what would surely come if a START agreement reached the Senate for ratification. A lot of people would feel cheated upon realizing the hard numbers did not match the lofty words. But such is arms control.

When the President arrived in the bubble, he too was pleased. Not only was a seat being reserved for him, but he soon heard of our night's work. We touted the results again, explaining that the 1,600/6,000 numbers were some 20 percent or 25 percent below SALT II levels. He was happy, but nothing like Shultz, who positively beamed.

We couldn't be upbeat, though, about INF. That negotiation, once so hopeful, was going nowhere. Throughout the night, we had insisted that the Soviets include their SS-20s in Asia. Throughout the night, Akhromeyev had resisted. They would not include these missiles. INF was a European negotiation and did not encompass Asia; moreover, their SS-20s were needed in Asia to counter the Chinese and American nuclear systems there.

SDI too had been a bust. Although we spent relatively little time on it, whatever we spent was wasted. Gorbachev would probably go at it again with the President.

All this said, we began to chat about one thing or another. I remember my impression instead of the topics. Here we were, crammed in this damn bubble in the middle of a spectacular summit meeting, sitting with the President of the United States, the whole world wondering what was happening, when in fact nothing at all was then happening. We were chatting away as if on vacation in Tahiti.

The President said he was set for the morning; he always seemed set for everything. He had his points in mind: blessing our progress on strategic arms (to reaffirm but not revisit—or for God's sake—reopen, this topic), making a pitch on INF for the record, and entering the wondrous world of SDI.

We urged him to hang tough on INF. Tell Gorbachev that there just could not be a deal, any deal, unless it included Asian missiles. Remind him that the Soviet negotiators had previously agreed to limit Asian SS-20 warheads to 100. We could live with that, but not with Akhromeyev's tough stance. If that reflected Gorbachev's position, they thereby showed they were not interested in INF.

Don Regan wished to give the President a little "downtime" before entering the ring again. We had said our piece. So we moseyed out to the cars and headed off to the Hofti House, where we were to be "on call" in case the President needed our advice. Little did we know.

Soviet Bazaar

But we doubted that he would. We had done our work that night and had made progress. He had merely to sanctify it with Gorbachev and make some statements "for the record" (if anyone could find it later) about INF and SDI.

Meanwhile we indulged in a rare treat, attending a veritable bazaar of the top Soviet leadership. There, on the second floor of the Hofti House, stood the titans of Soviet foreign policy. Each stood poised as if waiting for a conversation bouquet to form around him. Members of the Soviet negotiating team were there, but they attracted few comers. It wasn't their fault, but we'd had our fill of their company over the years.

Longtime Washington master Anatoly Dobrynin still draws. He regaled us with tales, many very funny, about the vagaries of life in both capitals. His conversational bouquet stayed active and full. Deputy Foreign Minister Alexander Bessmertnykh gained his own group, which he deserved. He was strong on Brezhnev's dealings with Nixon and Kissinger and was somewhat interesting on Afghanistan.

The morning passed quickly. When finished with the Russians, we could retreat to the side room, where Don Regan was holding court, joined by courtiers John Poindexter and Larry Speakes. Somehow at Reykjavik, Russian officials became more informative and engaging than the Americans.

Maybe that was just as well; Admiral Poindexter gleefully informed the President on Saturday morning that, in a side conversation with Akhromeyev, he detected Soviet *support* for SDI. Not a good information pickup, as it turned out.

I didn't realize how special this occasion was until I spotted Arthur Hartman looking aghast. He exclaimed how, as U.S. Ambassador in Moscow, he had requested appointments with many of these people for more than a year. There they were, speaking openly to anyone who was kind enough to approach them.

A Tough Cookie

I was drawn to Akhromeyev. There was the attraction of his being (aside from Gorbachev) the heavyweight of the opposing team; he directly commanded all Soviet forces, whereas our Chairman of the Joint Chiefs is principal advisor to the President and Defense Secretary. Akhromeyev was also in the unique position of being a five-star Marshal and new boy on the arms control block.

Moreover, the Marshal, who would retire from active service two years later, had a pleasant bearing and a nice sense of humor. Early that morning I said that it was a shame he had not met with our JCS Chairman, Admiral William Crowe, since Crowe had spent a good part of each day thinking about Akhromeyev. The Marshal chuckled and replied quickly, "Yes, it's a case of mutual attentiveness."

Akhromeyev is somewhat different. A year later, at a lovely dinner Shultz hosted in Geneva, National Security Advisor Colin Powell asked Akhromeyev if any other World War II officers were still serving in the Soviet armed forces. No, Akhromeyev lamented, he was the "last of the Mohicans," explaining that the James Fenimore Cooper book was mandatory reading for every Soviet youngster.

With a bit more prodding, Akhromeyev told of his role in the Great Patriotic War. Born and raised on a farm, he had joined the Red Army when seventeen, on the eve of World War II. He was stationed some sixty kilometers outside Leningrad and told to stay put to fend off approaching Germans. The historic city braced itself for what was to become its nine-hundred-day siege, at the height of which Akhromeyev said some twenty thousand Russians died daily. But he knew little of the staggering misery in Leningrad as he stayed put to hold the road. And hold the road he did, throughout eighteen long cold months, even when temperatures dropped to forty or fifty degrees below zero during those two horrendous winters.

"I never went inside a building during those eighteen months," he said without emotion but to our utter amazement.

"Never?" I asked.

"No. We were told to stay there. We stayed there."

I turned to Secretary Shultz, sitting next to me, and whispered that here was "one tough cookie." Later Akhromeyev said that eight out of ten males born in the Soviet Union the year he was born, 1923, died during the war; only two of the thirty-two boys in his high school class made it through alive.

The Secretary picked up the point and told of the American people's admiration for such stupendous Soviet courage during World War II. This was surely the case. But it was also true that having a commander-in-chief like Stalin builds up one's courage. It was Stalin who said after the war, when asked about the return of Soviet soldiers held in German prisoner-of-war camps, that there were no captured Soviet soldiers. There were only captured Soviet traitors.

ANOTHER REVERSAL WITH MORE TO COME

While we were mingling upstairs, Gorbachev and Reagan were wrangling downstairs. They began early that morning and were scheduled to end at noon. Don Regan was hankering to appear on a Sunday talk show but had the good sense to wait until he knew what had happened that morning.

Amazing things had happened, but not on matters I thought most important. Over the whole weekend, I urged the President to raise regional problems—Afghanistan, Angola, Nicaragua, Cambodia—and questions of human rights. But I was repeatedly told that since Gorbachev had addressed only arms control, we should answer his arguments; then, time remaining, we could bring up the other things. I countered that if Reagan began with regional and human rights issues, he and Gorbachev would end up on arms control; but if Reagan began with arms control, they would end on arms control. Then the truly vital issues would never get discussed. This proved to be the case.

After the President opened on INF, Gorbachev surprised him by saying, in essence, "You want to include our missiles in Asia? Okay. We'll include our missiles in Asia." So no more than four hours after Akhromeyev reiterated his decisive *nyet*, the Soviets turned another deft reversal. "No way" all through the night became "no problem" by the morning.

We first learned of this breakthrough when Shultz emerged to brief us after the morning session. No more bubble cramping for us. Shultz motioned to gather around him right there, in the haunted Hofti House, as the President headed back to the residence for lunch and rest. We knew something was up by the look on Shultz's face. Usually stoic, he was full of exuberance that day, only to revert to utter despair at the day's end.

The Secretary came right out with it: Gorbachev had agreed to include Soviet missiles in Asia. The two leaders closed on the outlines of an INF deal—100 warheads for each side in Europe and another 100 in Asia.

That was fine by us, right along the lines the two arms control teams had tossed around in Moscow a few months before. An INF breakthrough coming on top of START progress was almost too good to be true. In part it was.

"I have it slightly different," the American note-taker broke in. "Mr. Secretary, I think that General Secretary Gorbachev talked about permitting *no* warheads in Europe, rather than one hundred. That's what you and the President agreed to." Shultz silently flipped through the sheets of his yellow legal pad and eventually looked up to say that wasn't what he had written down. He had recorded one hundred in Europe, one hundred in Asia.

This prompted the increasingly anxious note-taker, not accustomed to correcting a secretary of state smack dab in the middle of a summit, to reexamine his notes. The aide found, sure enough, that it was 0/100 that their side had proposed and our side had bought. "Well then, that's it," the Secretary said calmly.

No doubt a tolerable mistake, Shultz's agreeing to 100/100 when Gorbachev had actually offered him and the President 0/100. This was a pressured time during a pressured and wearying weekend. But still Shultz's error made all the substantive difference in the world. The main objection to the INF Treaty later was that the complete removal of U.S. missiles from Europe would further decouple our security from theirs. A hundred U.S. warheads on missiles in Europe, as Shultz believed we had agreed to, would have precluded this objection.

One prominent member of our delegation mused, after Shultz spoke, that perhaps we shouldn't accept the zero in Europe. But the President had "zero" locked in his brain, and all of us had supported the zero option for five long years. There was no walking that back after Gorbachev had accepted it in Europe. We had to take yes for an answer.

Others, including the Soviets, also knew the problem here. The day before, Gorbachev had harangued the President—that is what Gorbachev often does, harangues—about Allied reluctance to have us remove all our missiles from Europe. "You don't want to take all your missiles out, do you?" he asked several times. Reagan did; in fact, he wanted to take them all out of everywhere that weekend.

Once this was ironed out, the ever-creative Richard Perle suggested that we notify our Allies, especially the leaders of the five "basing countries" who were accepting U.S. missiles on their territory, so they wouldn't first hear the news from the radio or the Russians. This was so ordered, though it became technically difficult to do.

Why, I could never understand. Difficult to contact the main Allied leaders when we had the President's celebrated communications apparatus at hand? It brought to mind all the times I sat waiting ten or fifteen minutes for an SDI briefer to fix the Vu-Graph machine so he could tell me how we could shoot down a thousand or so Soviet intercontinental ballistic missiles within 120 seconds of their launch.

Ambassador Ed Rowny made the sound suggestion that we also contact the Japanese leaders. This caused more complications and a good deal of State Department grumbling; the department had grumbled about Rowny ever since he bolted from the SALT II negotiations to oppose the treaty. In government, the source matters as much as the substance of any recommendation.

Later, the Allies became aghast at Reykjavik. It became the code word for U.S. irresponsibility or, more charitably, indifference on Allied security. Among the litany of gripes was that we failed to consult them on matters affecting their security.

Like many such complaints, this was largely wrong, though partly true. On INF, their main concern, we did notify them immediately, from the Hofti House, about the 0/100 offer. Later they would mutter about the zero in Europe, but that was later and only a mutter since they had *all* supported this proposal for years.

On the notion of zero ballistic missiles—including strategic ballistics, which are of some (though lesser) concern to them—they had sat in the UN General Assembly applauding the President when he proposed this concept (though, to be fair, they probably relegated it to another world, just as the Joint Chiefs had). Explicitly placing it in an arms control proposal and fixing a date on it did pull the issue down to earth. Still, they had a warning about this notion and said nothing about it. They seemed genuinely surprised by the zero-ballistics idea being proposed later in Reykjavik, which leads me to conclude that the best way to keep secret an arms control proposal is to have the President announce it on world television before the UN General Assembly; the worst way is to propose it in the closed talks in Geneva.

In any case, Reykjavik proved INF was for real. Gorbachev's move paved the way for the INF Accord, which up to that point had been deemed unattainable.

As we learned about this, another big step in the real world of arms control, I again spotted that monstrous portrait of the astronauts tromping around the hills of Iceland and wondered what had happened on space matters.

Secretary Shultz told us of the sparks flying between Reagan and Gorbachev on SDI: "It's been a slugging match all the way," as had been anticipated.

What was not anticipated was that the two would decide to go into overtime. The summit would not end at noon—the morning session had already lasted until one-thirty—but would go into sudden death overtime. Don Regan couldn't do his Sunday talk show, but there would be another time for that. The leaders would meet again at three. They sensed they were honing the really big issues, which indeed they were, and wanted to see how much they could accomplish.

At this precise moment, I knew Reykjavik had changed. No longer were the President of the United States and General Secretary of the Soviet Union reading staff papers to one another. No longer were they blessing what their arms control teams had worked out.

They would move from headquarters in base camp to the front lines. They would become negotiators-in-chief, with all the dangers that entails, especially for an American president. All the lessons learned since Versailles would be forgotten or ignored. All the sound advice of Dean Rusk went out the window.

President Reagan, aroused by Gorbachev's parroting the old Soviet line from the 1950s about a world without nuclear weapons, wanted to give it his all. Here at last, as Margaret Thatcher had said, was a Soviet leader you "could do business with," one Reagan could talk to, deal with. One who talked his language.

Here came what the world now associates with "Reykjavik." We were told to stand by. We might be needed.

THAT TUMULTUOUS AFTERNOON

Sunday in windblown Reykjavik is a day that will live, though not in infamy, surely in embarrassment. I take it a bit lighter than Richard Nixon and the others, who describe it almost as the nadir of Western civilization. Why the stigma? Why my tolerance?

Granted, the discussions that afternoon should never have happened. They showed gross ignorance of essentials of Western security by the guardians of that security, not just the President but a few of his top advisors as well.

But this aspect of Reykjavik was all talk. None of the talk was matched by action; none of it could have been. As Bertrand Russell once quipped, metaphysicians, like savages, are apt to imagine a magical connection between words and things. Politicians are, too.

Even if a dramatic deal had been struck by the two leaders, it would not have stuck. Even in that inconceivable case, Reykjavik would have turned out like the summit between Wilhelm II of

Germany and Nicholas II of Russia at B'yorko in July 1905; after the two monarchs agreed firmly to restructure the European alliance system, they were so roundly rebuffed back home that they had to take it all back.

Reykjavik took on a life of its own. Still, it was Reagan's doing, and Gorbachev's. Reagan was driven by his dream of a world without nuclear weapons, Gorbachev by his dream of nipping SDI before who-knew-what happened in the program. Gorbachev, as every Soviet leader, has technophobia. He especially feared technology made in the U.S.A. that the Soviets could not implement even if they succeed in stealing.

At Reykjavik, part of the problem was that neither leader had anything else to do but to meet with each other or, less appealing, with their staffs. Summits should always be held in one capital or the other, so that the visiting leader can sight-see and meet with locals. The subsequent summits in Washington and Moscow were much safer; the visitor was kept on a tight schedule, scooting around town and meeting with this and that group. There was no time for extensive negotiating sessions. Whatever serious negotiations took place weren't much and could be kept from "going critical" by extensive extracurricular activities. Any impulsive temptation to go into overtime would be scotched by the all-powerful schedulers.

Another part of the problem was that Reagan unwittingly—the way he does most things—called the Soviets' age-old bluff. Gorbachev was only doing what Soviet leaders had long done, talk about the most complicated topic in the most simplistic and propagandistic way.

Ten months before Reykjavik, on January 15, 1986, he grabbed global headlines with his "megaproposal" advocating the total elimination of nuclear weapons in three stages by the turn of the century. This offer, heralded far and wide, was nearly identical with Nikita Khrushchev's offer in a United Nations speech in September 1959 a quarter century earlier. He too advocated eliminating all nuclear weapons—and all conventional and chemical weapons besides—also in three stages. Gorbachev's plan took a few more years than Khrushchev's, either because he was more ambitious or less honest. (Ironically, Khrushchev's proposal would have come to fruition in 1962, just when he was sneaking missiles into Cuba.)

Nothing much happened with Gorbachev's megaproposal.

Within days it was brushed aside by U.S. negotiators. Everyone in the United States saw it as a vapid propaganda ploy—everyone, that is, except Ronald Reagan, who was surprisingly intrigued by it. That should have taught the rest of us something but didn't. Within weeks Gorbachev's megaproposal was forgotten by Soviet negotiators. It had dropped into the historical memory hole until Reykjavik, where it was renewed with a vengeance.

In a way, Gorbachev got taken at Reykjavik. He was only following the usual Soviet practice of tossing out some grand scheme that sounds marvelous to the unwashed public but is doused by the practical-minded Americans. But Reagan broke the rules. Instead of lecturing the Soviet leaders on how and why these visionary notions were impractical, as had his predecessors, Reagan too took flight.

I have visions of Mikhail Gorbachev sitting there stunned the first time he heard Reagan answer his gibberish about eliminating this or that nuclear weapon with a warm smile, a shake of the head, and the paced response, "Well, that's what I've been saying for ages. But why stop there? Can't we eliminate them all? And why take so long? Can't we do all this quicker?" Gorbachev trumped at the Soviets' own game! Reagan does not play fair.

And part of the problem was, admittedly, us, all the President's men. We did not serve him well, not just then but for months and years before then. We took the easy road, a tempting thing to do when a President holds firm but wrong views. It's still a bad thing to do.

The President's advisors had heard him speak of a world without nuclear weapons, but we just shook our heads and looked at one another knowingly. We'd heard such talk grow since he first mentioned it in a speech to the Japanese Diet in 1983. We dismissed it coming from our president even though we had mocked it coming from the previous president. When Jimmy Carter touted the total elimination of nuclear weapons as a personal goal during his 1977 inauguration address, we knew he wasn't fit to be chief executive.

One afternoon, soon after I had come to ACDA, Secretary Shultz sat us down in his office to tell us how the President really did believe in a world without nuclear weapons. Now, we might disagree, Shultz knew, but there it was, fixed in the President's head. It was important for us to take that seriously. Richard Burt, then in charge of European affairs, and I blurted out that this was a terrible idea. There was no way to squirt perfume over it and say it smelled fine.

To propose that we usher in a nuclear-free world would be to abdicate our postwar responsibilities. We could kiss NATO good-bye and leave Western Europe far less secure. The Soviets would never actually agree to such a scheme. They might propose it but surely didn't want it. If we ever called their bluff, they would recoil in horror (though in less horror than our Allies).

If the Soviets ever did agree verbally, they might never comply. At least we would never know whether they complied. We could never know whether a country nearly 6,000 miles in breadth, of 8.6 million square miles, had scrapped every single nuclear weapon, some so small that they can fit in a backpack and others that can easily be placed in a car. No American president ever could or would scrap the last American nuclear weapon on the hope that the Soviets were doing likewise.

Even if the Soviets agreed, and even if they complied, the world would be more dangerous. With no nuclear weapons, Europe would be made safer for conventional war. The forty-year Soviet superiority in tanks and other conventional armaments in central Europe has been compensated by American, British, and French nuclear weapons. Moscow could never be sure that one of us wouldn't pop one off if the Red Army came hurling across the Volga gap.

This point became implanted in my consciousness a few years back, about the time the President began talking openly of a nuclear-free world. I then appeared before the foreign affairs com-mittee of the British House of Commons to explain where the arms talks stood. But before I could get a word out, the rather jolly Chairman peered at me, finger wagging, and asked, "Ambas-sador Adelman, do you share the President's goal of a world with-out nuclear weapons?" I sidestepped, gingerly answering that indeed the President believed strongly in that goal. "Mr. Ambas-sador, not one single member of this committee shares the Pres-ident's vision," said the Chairman.

I replied, as politely as I could, that I doubted such unanimity among such a diverse group. Could each committee member please state his own position for me and explain why? Down the row they went, from the most conservative member, including Winston Churchill II, to the most leftist Labor M.P. When I heard them all, I tried to reply. How strange it was, I said, that the prosperous states of Western Europe could not pay for a conventional deterrence against the dilapidated countries of Eastern Europe. "Why can't the British pay for defense like the Bulgarians?" I ended my compelling pitch.

"Wonder no more," John Gilbert, a particularly clever Labor M.P., shot back. "Most Britishers don't wish to live like Bulgarians. That's why."

And even if the Soviets did agree to a nuclear-free world, did comply, and never attacked Europe with conventional arms, the world would *still* be more dangerous. The superpowers, by eliminating nuclear weapons, would eliminate some of their super-power-ness. Lesser powers would never relinquish the power and status that can be theirs by having nuclear weapons. China and France would never, never give them up.

Once the United States and USSR left the nuclear club, others would enter it. Less responsible nations would then have even more incentive to possess nuclear weapons, in order to become a mini-superpower. It is startling to realize that the first nuclear weapons test proved successful in all known cases, for us in 1945, for the Soviets, British, French, Chinese, and Indians. This suggests that perhaps it is not as tough to build these things as scientists once supposed.

And even if this difficulty was magically overcome, eliminating nuclear weapons would still be foolish since it would be transitory at best. Nothing known to the human mind, nothing written in books and articles, can be erased from human intelligence. The first casualty in any serious war would be the elimination of nuclear weapons. Scientists from both sides would hurry to make them once again. But now they would have the essential bit of information lacking during the Manhattan Project, namely that it was indeed possible to make them.

Such was the flow of logic—not particularly insightful or novel, but sound nonetheless—we put across to Secretary Shultz that memorable afternoon in his office. Such was the logic that led Winston Churchill, in his last address to Congress, to warn: "Be careful, above all things, not to let go of the atomic weapon until you are sure, and more than sure, that other means of preserving the peace are in your hands." And such was the substance of our arguments—delivered in dribbles and ineffectively at that —to President Reagan over the ensuing years.

It worked fleetingly with the Secretary—why it never stuck

more I cannot explain—but it never stuck at all with the President. He'd hear the arguments, respond to bits, and then reiterate his goal of a nuclear-free world. This vision was combined with a world of defenses in a creative way, one only shared (to my knowledge) by fellow mystic *New Yorker* writer Jonathan Schell. Indeed, in a New York discussion group once, I heard Schell spin out his utopian portrait later written in *Abolition.* I was dumbfounded and said that I had heard such notions from only one other person in my life, the President of the United States.

Reagan is a man of instinct and vision, not logic. In his kick-and-tell memoirs, *For the Record,* Don Regan tells of the President recuperating from a cancer operation in July 1985 by reading a biography of Calvin Coolidge, a president whose portrait Reagan restored to the Cabinet Room wall. Regan tells that one of the things the President most admired about Coolidge was "his successful foreign policy, especially the 1928 Kellogg-Briand Pact renouncing aggressive war." To international affairs types, be they liberal or conservative, the Kellogg-Briand Pact is a laughingstock—a vacuous pledge made cynically by world leaders that was not worth the paper it was written on. A large number of nations signed this empty pledge to renounce war, the more honest ones with qualifications so wide that any war could be driven through, the least honest and hence most aggressive ones with no qualifications at all.

Reagan's cockeyed optimism is among his most appealing characteristics. But its flip side is gross impracticality. I first spotted this aspect of the Reagan makeup on the eve of the 1982 Falklands War. At an NSC meeting then, we heard a report from Secretary Haig on the status of his negotiations between Britain and Argentina. Haig proceeded in his singularly contorted way—"We can buy on to that policy," he told me during the transition period about some approach or other, "but we're not going to put any theological platelets around it"—with his distinctive flourish. He spoke of the difficult negotiations; the more he spoke, the worse the situation seemed. Prime Minister Thatcher couldn't do x, y, or z because of her pride or her Cabinet. The Argentinian Foreign Minister would agree, but the Chief of the Argentinian Air Force would resist, and so on.

When Haig wound down, Reagan sat up. He became all perky, his eyes bright. "Imagine when"—he caught himself—"uh, if, you do settle this, Al. We'll be the envy of all the world!" He smiled an infectious smile, leaned back wholly satisfied, and looked around to see us suddenly happy, too.

Reagan's visionary streak and optimism is not tempered by depth or breadth of knowledge in history or foreign affairs. His talk about arms control would often leap into unbridled idealism, the kind more often associated with advocates of Esperanto as a global language and with World Federalists (who incidentally disagreed so violently among themselves that their movement split into various factions) than with a conservative Republican.

I did not sense the depth of the President's passion for a nuclear-free world, or its tenacity, until Reykjavik. So while Rick Burt and I argued our points with Shultz, neither we nor he effectively marshaled them with the President. We would patronize him and hope his fanciful notions would go away.

Meanwhile, we faced the real world problem of squaring the words of our leader with the policies of his administration. This demanded creative crafting. The ultimate goal of eliminating all nuclear weapons was, as we say in government, "put in its proper context." To wit: We could eliminate them after ending all regional disputes, all oppression, all problems—in essence when the Messiah came to earth (in which case we wouldn't need arms control, either).

Shultz asked for heftier material, studies on "how to" rather than "why not to." He never received them. I wrote a memo or two summarizing the main reasons a nuclear-free world was a fatuous and pernicious notion. But I never took the matter seriously enough to do it more seriously. So Shultz kept raising the topic, we kept dodging, and the President kept believing. We paid at Reykjavik.

It wasn't until *after* Reykjavik that I hammered home the risks of a nuclear-free world more forcefully to the President. Even this consisted of only a few minutes' back-and-forth during a session in the Situation Room. I made my main points, the President rebutted some—we couldn't know that nuclear weapons had kept the peace in Europe for forty years, maybe other things had —while the administration's heavy hitters watched. The Secretaries of State and Defense, the Chairman of the Joint Chiefs, and the National Security Advisor were mere spectators, turning their heads back and forth as if watching a tennis tournament.

No wonder the President figured his beliefs were neither radical nor harmful. None of his advisors responsible for assuring national security voiced strong objections then or at other times in my presence. Why, then, shouldn't Reagan be Reagan?

Apparently some of them even agreed with the President. His closest aide then, the one who most resembled him and spent the most time with him then, certainly did. Don Regan writes that the President's "every action in foreign policy . . . had been carried out with the idea of one day sitting down at the negotiating table with the leader of the USSR and banning weapons of mass destruction from the planet," as if Reagan and Gorbachev had such power. Regan concludes: "If he is remembered, as evidently he wishes to be, as the American President who banished nuclear arms from the world, then he will be a great figure in history indeed. . . ." What malarkey!

THE FOCAL POINT: SDI

The uproar over Reagan and Gorbachev discussing a nuclear-free world was to come later. Our focus at Reykjavik then was on SDI, which had gone from being a Pentagon research program to a conservative cause, entering the pantheon of conservative values alongside prayer in the school and right to life. It had become more hallowed with each Soviet objection. Thus no American official at Reykjavik dared to suggest a compromise on SDI, no matter what he may have thought privately.

During the break between the morning and overtime afternoon sessions, while the President was lunching with Don Regan, Secretary Shultz proposed to Foreign Minister Shevardnadze that they tinker a bit. We'd agree not to deploy SDI for ten years, an idea Shultz had cleared with the President over dinner the night before, in exchange for some Soviet concessions.

This decade deployment delay, like nearly everything in arms control, had a long and contentious history. Before Reykjavik, Gorbachev had been talking about a pledge of no deployment for fifteen to twenty years. Ambassador Dobrynin then signaled they'd drop down to fifteen years or so, as Gorbachev implied in his nasty "invitation" letter. That Sunday in Reykjavik, Gorbachev agreed to ten, no doubt delighted that SDI's father would agree to such a lengthy "temporary" ban. This could then be extended by a subsequent, less fervently pro-SDI president. Gorbachev knew that temporary arms accord is like temporary housing: it lasts a long, long time.

Shultz could give him the ten-year delay if, in exchange, Shevardnadze agreed to eliminate all ballistic missiles in the interval. Shultz admitted he had not mentioned this to the President, folding the elimination of all ballistic missiles into the ten-year period—indeed, he hadn't talked to many folks about it—but he wanted to try it out. Shevardnadze wasn't sure. He, at least, would have to check with his military and his boss.

Shultz's suggestion set the framework for that afternoon's negotiations. The President didn't mind, especially after hearing that it was okay with the NSC staff and the Pentagon representative—afterward Defense Secretary Weinberger minded plenty; he was furious about the whole business—but Reagan was determined to hold his ground on SDI.

Back into the ring Reagan sauntered. Sparks flew over the new Shultz scheme on three points. One was on the offensive side: we asked to eliminate all "ballistic missiles" within ten years. Gorbachev said he wished to eliminate all "strategic weapons" in that time frame. He upped the ante since all strategic weapons include bombers and cruise missiles as well as ballistic missiles. Not for a moment do I believe he would have accepted his own proposal, just as we could never have accepted our offer.

On the defensive side were two issues. First was the type of SDI research to permit. Reagan wanted everything allowed by the "broad interpretation" of the ABM Treaty; Gorbachev wanted SDI research confined to the laboratory. This was to become the deal-buster at Reykjavik, as the Soviet proposal would have stopped half to three-fourths of our then-planned SDI tests. It would thereby have crippled or killed the program.

Second was what would happen after the ten-year period. We advocated a "green light" for SDI deployment, with all restrictions against deploying SDI, even those in the ABM Treaty, lifted. Gorbachev sought a "return to base"—the ABM Treaty ban against deployment after the ten-year period.

Describing the differences on these three issues is to impose order on the free-wheeling discussion then going on downstairs, which was by no means orderly. Meanwhile we stayed upstairs and shot the breeze, asking local embassy staff if they had heard the score of the Washington Redskins' game that afternoon, previewing the upcoming elections with Don Regan, wondering when we'd leave Reykjavik (some feared missing the start of Yom Kippur at sundown that day).

"The door opened. He's coming," another burly Secret Service agent called into the side room where we were sitting, sometime after four. Indeed, "he" bounded in with that jaunty stride.

"Why is he so against SDI?" the President asked to no one in particular as he settled into a big armchair in the corner.

"For two reasons." I spoke before anyone else could respond. "First, they have invested massive resources in their own SDI program over the past fifteen years, far more than we have. They've found there's something to it. The 'something' there is to it can be done better by us than by them, since SDI plays into our strength, high-tech, rather than their strength, brute military force. Second, SDI represents a strategic end run. Rather than matching their new missiles with our new missiles—their SS-24 with our MX, their SS-25 with our Midgetman—SDI discounts the importance of these missiles altogether."

The President still looked miffed. He thought of SDI as apple pie. Everyone should want it; it's good for everyone. It's protection. The rest of this stuff is destruction.

The President then handed over a paper, Gorbachev's redraft of our initial draft, with his three changes. The Soviets wished to confine SDI research to the laboratory, to knock out the "green light" for deployment, and to change the ten years' elimination of "ballistic missiles" to elimination of "strategic weapons." We took his redraft of our draft and redrafted it into yet another draft. In short, we changed Gorbachev's three changes back to our positions.

While this was being retyped, using Russian carbon paper again, we tried to explain to the President and those around him, slowly and carefully, the differences on the offensive side between scrapping all ballistic missiles (as we proposed) and all strategic arms (as they wished). " 'All ballistic missiles' does not include bombers or cruise missiles. They're ahead in ballistic missiles, which are the most dangerous weapons. That's why we want to eliminate them. We're ahead in bombers and cruise missiles. That's why they wish to eliminate them, and we don't." It all gets back to the fable about the animals' disarmament conference.

We walked the President through such argument slowly and carefully, but without much effect. We were down in what he deemed the details while he was thinking big. We were trying to huddle to go over our next move with care, while he was picturing himself racing downfield like mad.

Or maybe it was our fault. For neither Shultz nor Don Regan, who showed more attention to our lesson than the President, grasped the key distinctions either.

Again Regan shows this failure most clearly. His book describes our position as eliminating "strategic nuclear weapons . . . at the end of a second five-year period." That was Gorbachev's proposal, to which we took strong exception. Regan writes how the President could take pride in knowing "that the record would show, no matter what the outcome of the summit, that the United States had offered to go to zero—to dismantle all its strategic nuclear weapons. We were calling the Soviets' bluff." Just the opposite was true. The Soviets were calling *our* bluff. As if these errors weren't gross enough, Regan adds the kicker: "If they accepted, nuclear missiles would vanish from the earth." Even under this, Gorbachev's proposal, which Regan believed was our proposal, the British, French, and Chinese still would retain all their "nuclear missiles." And even the United States and the Soviet Union would retain their thousands of tactical nuclear arms.

After we went over these points carefully, the President fretted about SDI. "Does anyone here think we're proposing this," he asked us, waving our draft counterproposal, "just to get an agreement?" Silence. None of us did.

"Well, what would our old friends say about it? Will *Human Events* knock us for this?" he pressed. Don Regan, forever the courtier, told him no. *Human Events* wouldn't mind a bit. They'd like his tough stance on SDI.

Still, the President wanted to be sure. So he read over the redrafted paper with far more care than he'd taken the previous afternoon. He then proposed a change. The wording, he felt, cast SDI research in a bad light, especially the part about both sides being able to conduct research *as permitted* by the ABM Treaty. Why not say that each side could vigorously conduct research that *was allowed* by the treaty? The tone changed as the words changed. All of us were delighted that Reagan had made a substantive suggestion, and he was most delighted of all.

While the President remained riveted on SDI, his Secretary of State focused on the nuclear reductions. Shultz did not want to risk losing the gains we had made over the preceding twenty-four hours. "Let's not lose it," he said. "We've done some amazing things here," which was unquestionably a good point but one hard to apply at that moment.

During this critical discussion—though nothing ever seemed all that critical to Reagan, who carried a casual if not carefree air wherever he went—Don Regan fussed over the schedule. "We might have to stay here overnight," he offered at some point, for what reason I could not fathom. He had received no more information about what was happening than I had; yet he spoke with the confidence that only comes from having inside knowledge.

Reagan grimaced, more than I ever saw him grimace before. "No, we just can't do that," he said, pain crossing his face. I think he was looking forward to having dinner with Nancy; he may have said something along that line. Anyway, he was determined not to spend another night at Reykjavik. By then he'd had quite enough of this business, enough of Gorbachev, enough of Reykjavik.

That's when Reagan said, "Hell. He doesn't want to set up a summit. He wants to have a summit. Right here." That's when it again struck me that, contrary to everything we had expected, and contrary to much of what we knew was wise, we had entered a full-scale, free-wheeling summit. And like few in history.

THE FINAL ROUND

Down he went again with that shrug of the shoulders and shake of the head that became Reagan trademarks. Back we went again to milling about, the American and Russian delegations by then keeping pretty much to themselves. Not long after the President left, Max Kampelman asked me what the chances were of Gorbachev buying our proposal. I said none. "He wouldn't even buy his own proposal!" Max shook his head, bewildered, an appropriate response.

"Then why do we do this? Why propose something he'd never accept, something even we might not want?" Good question, but that's the nature of the beast. That didn't seem to satisfy Max, though.

As before during these waiting periods, we chatted. Actually the scene resembled a condolence call in that people rambled on about everything but the matter at hand. Apart from my brief exchange with Max, no one mentioned what we had done, what could be happening below, or what to do later. That afternoon, neither Regan nor Poindexter questioned anyone about what all this was really about, though they might well have profited by adding to their knowledge in this high-stakes talk.

At one point I casually mentioned to Don Regan how "our guy" must be getting tired below. Indeed, the President had begun his day at eight or so with our briefing in the bubble, gone into his meetings with Gorbachev until one-thirty, grabbed a quick lunch, and headed back for the second session. The President had worked "without any downtime at all," as his Chief of Staff put it, for ten hours. Regan insightfully added that the President would get drowsy, he might even fade off, if Gorbachev droned on with long polemics, but the President would be fine if Gorbachev proved contentious.

No problem. Gorbachev was being Gorbachev, as contentious as ever. So Reagan was being Reagan, as feisty as he gets when challenged frontally.

Even from reading the transcript afterward, one gets the sense of Reagan's determination to support SDI; how frustrated, even desperate, Gorbachev was hitting against this stone wall; and how terribly confused they both were about who wanted to eliminate what in categories of nuclear weapons.

We kept chatting until another Secret Service agent burst into the room to announce, "The door is opening," and, "He's out"— not "coming out," but "out." We grabbed our coats and briefcases and raced downstairs.

Running down that grand round wooden staircase, I glanced at Reagan and Gorbachev in the foyer and said to Max Kampelman or Paul Nitze (whoever was running beside me), "There's no deal." It was written all over their faces, especially Reagan's, as they stood at the door talking for one last moment. Our stampede came to an abrupt halt, the hordes of experts almost crushing those in front. After the pile-up, the two leaders walked out and we resumed rushing down to leave through a side door in order to watch the ceremonial send-off.

But there was no ceremony. Just a send-off. Seeing the quick good-bye, we realized that we faced a most frightening prospect —a presidential motorcade flying away, police cars screeching, with us left behind. We leapt into action.

Movement with a president is carefully controlled, just how carefully I learned when arranging the President's 1981 trip to the United Nations and reading a draft "elevator manifest" describing who was to ride up one flight with the President and where each accompanying person was to stand during that journey. But this time whatever plans were laid turned to chaos. Or we turned them into chaos.

I grabbed Max Kampelman and shoved him toward the nearest getaway car. Each limo was marked for its proper passenger—it was all laid out in the hefty White House advance book we had been given with strict admonitions to follow it precisely—but there was no time now to search for the right car.

Tugging Max along, I jumped into a support car, only to find myself squashed beside two of Don Regan's aides, courtiers to the courtier. They grumbled, but Max and I stonewalled and stayed. We bolted from the Hofti House compound in the screeching madness of a presidential motor caravan.

Back at the Ambassador's residence, we threw our coats on the floor and grabbed a seat around the dining room table. The President had obviously retreated to his room, disappointed that he and Gorbachev could not go for broke. We were to hear from Secretary Shultz. Everyone leaned over to catch each syllable of Shultz's readout.

Like arms control itself, the report was long on foreplay and short in conclusion. This had been an important meeting. We all had done fine work. We had much to show for our efforts. We had served the President well. We had served him well. Gorbachev wanted to gut SDI. The President wouldn't give in. SDI was the engine driving the arms control process. The President was right to hold.

Then, with genuine emotion, Shultz came to his conclusion: He had never been prouder to work for this president. This was a principled stance, taken by a principled president. He was proud. We should be proud. The nation should be proud.

Fine and nice, but what about the negotiations? Would anything be issued to the press? No. Shultz rose to leave as I shot in: Was another summit scheduled? No. Someone else asked a question, and he too received a no. Shultz had said all there was to say at that moment. He stood, there was warm applause, he nodded and then reached for Don Regan's hand, which he held for an emotion-filled instant, and then turned to leave.

We grabbed our coats and headed for whatever car was nearest. I rode to the international press center with our most experienced negotiator and offered him my opinion: this would help Reagan. Sure, the American people like their president to sit down with the Russians, but they like it even more when he stands up to the Russians. He vehemently disagreed.

Reykjavik *would* help Reagan and the Republicans in the next month's elections. It would also help SDI. Nothing so solidifies American support as virulent Soviet opposition. Anyone claiming that SDI wouldn't work could be asked, "Why, then, are they so insistent on banning it?"

Later that day, Secretary Shultz gave his funereal press conference. He looked worse than he sounded, but he was tired.

Few people realize that the singular element that binds top political appointees in any administration is not necessarily talent or loyalty to the President or concern over the issues; rather, it is utter exhaustion. Each high official takes mental and physical pulverizing over the years. Obviously this affects their judgment when we need them most, in a crisis.

Shultz personified how Reykjavik had been a bust; he looked like he had just been busted. After he finished, Paul Nitze, Art Hartman, and I gave a "backgrounder" in the conference hall; Paul was dejected, Art told how this fit into overall Soviet strategy, and I was rather positive. Reykjavik showed how strongly Reagan felt about SDI, how much Gorbachev feared it, and how the gains we made on nuclear reductions could be pocketed. That was my view, at least, so why not say it?

Don Regan held his own makeshift press conference at the airport while Air Force One, with the President aboard, waited for him. He told how Reykjavik showed what kind of people the Soviets really were, as if we needed a no-agreement summit to teach us. He too looked as if he had been kicked in the stomach by a horse. Later he wrote sympathetically: "It is no wonder that Shultz looked sad and tired; he had been present at one of the most devastating disappointments in history. He had seen total nuclear disarmament in the grasp of his president, then seen it slip away." (He had not seen it there, and if he had seen it "slip away," good riddance!)

I should have expired that evening, having slept poorly on Thursday, our arrival night, and on that busy Friday. On Saturday I pulled my first all-nighter since finals week at college; we had no time even for a catnap. By Sunday afternoon I should have been more exhausted than I felt, but nothing so pumps the adrenaline like a summit.

Someone from the White House Press Office asked me to ride back on the press plane, as I had done after the first summit in Geneva, to do yet more "backgrounders" for reporters whose thirst for inside stories was unquenchable. So I had to stay in

Reykjavik for a few more hours to give the press time to file their stories about the President's speech and the Secretary's press conference.

While waiting, I did a live interview on ABC News, which if I am not mistaken was the first to paint Reykjavik in a rosy light —to say that SDI was a good thing, had not been sacrificed, the President "just said no" when asked to compromise U.S. national security interests (as a good president should), and that all the gains made on INF and on START would be pocketed. Soviet negotiators in Geneva couldn't continue refusing to restrict their missiles in Asia when Gorbachev had agreed that they could be cut. We had achieved something real and lasting at Reykjavik. The interviewer, Peter Jennings I believe it was, seemed startled. Indeed, what I said did contradict the administration line, which was then gloom and doom.

We did not take off until around midnight. I then faced a planeload of raging reporters, who wanted each and every tidbit from the weekend. I tried to feed them as best I could before we landed at Andrews Air Force Base around 3:00 A.M. I arrived home shortly before 4:00 and collapsed, only to be awakened at 5:30 A.M. or so to be asked to go on the *Today* show at 7:10. I sleepily agreed, puttered around unpacking, and then headed out to the car. For the first time ever, our car would not start, even after I pushed it down the hill and jumped in, popping the clutch. So I charged over to a neighbor's, who was delighted to see me at 6:30 A.M., and borrowed his van.

I did the show, trying to appear as upbeat as I could manage feeling as I felt, then headed home in something of a stupor. Somehow I had to get the family car into the shop that morning since we needed it to keep the household functioning. I again imposed upon my neighbor, who obligingly pushed me in the stricken car to the repair shop.

On the way back, my eleven-year-old daughter asked shyly, "Dad, what are you going to do about the freezer?" and I started to lose it.

"What do you mean, do about the freezer?"

It had kaplotzed. So I began to scoop up soggy packages of semifrozen vegetables and place them in a shopping cart to carry to the neighbors for storage.

While moving dripping boxes, I received calls first from Bill Casey wondering what went on "in that place." I filled him in; he wanted to know everything, particularly who supported what and when. He became delighted with the nonresults. "I'm going to issue a press release saying what a triumph it was," Casey told me. "That's kind of unusual for a CIA chief. My guys say it's never been done. But what the hell?"

The packages sogged more; the phone rang more—Jeane Kirkpatrick, then friendly Senators like Dan Quayle and Pete Wilson wanted the scooby. I next spoke to Don Regan to make sure that the President's speech that night would be upbeat. "Be sure to include the point that what the Soviets conceded cannot be taken back. We'll build on Reykjavik in Geneva for years to come."

One last matter to handle. Shultz had asked me to head for Australia to brief Prime Minister Bob Hawke, with whom I had developed a nice relationship over the years. Hawke had stood by the United States on many critical issues, resisting the soft streak of his own Labour party. Having a top administration official brief him right after the summit would show how well plugged in to Washington he was, as he deserved to be.

But after all this, I just could not go off to Australia. I was at my wits' end, physically and mentally beat. My wife was on a business trip; the kids wanted attention; the freezer and car needed tending; and Australia happened to be at the end of the earth. A trip to Sydney that day was out of the question. I'd have to leave at noon on a nonstop flight to Los Angeles, wait a few hours at that airport, then take the longest commercial flight in the world, nonstop Los Angeles to Sydney for more than fourteen hours.

Somehow, it happened. At noon I boarded the United flight to spend one day in the capital of Canberra and then more than twenty hours of flying time back to Washington.

While I was winging to the far-flung corners of the earth, heads were scratching around Washington and Europe about just what had happened at Reykjavik. Some events, like the Glassboro summit of 1967, end when they end, never to be revisited seriously. Others, like Yalta, provoke endless discussion and warrant interminable analysis.

Reykjavik grew like that. After the initial dip came an ensuing soar, and then an eventual crash.

The soar came from the uplifting presidential speech Monday night and the acclaim that went to an American leader, especially one identified with John Wayne, who could stand up to Soviet blandishments.

The administration added to the lift by launching a public affairs effort of unprecedented scale. Everyone participating in Reykjavik was told to go "on the record" and reveal everything. Secretary Shultz canceled all other appointments to meet with the top editorial boards, appear on television and radio, and make the administration's case that, contrary to how he looked and what he said immediately afterward, Reykjavik had in fact been a smashing success.

For a time, it worked. Following Reykjavik came skyrocketing support for SDI. Doubts about whether or not SDI would "work" evaporated in the American body politic; Gorbachev had knocked that out as a contentious issue.

On a more tactical level, Gorbachev made a big mistake at Reykjavik. He objected to the strongest part of the President's scheme on SDI by demanding that we confine SDI research to the laboratory. Even the most fervent SDI opponents in the United States or Europe would not accept that condition. Had Gorbachev broken up Reykjavik over Reagan's "green light" for deployment or his desire to research SDI according to the new interpretation of the ABM Treaty, Gorbachev would have garnered wide support. By tugging on the strongest link in the SDI chain, Gorbachev blew it.

After Reykjavik polls showed that 60 percent or more Americans wanted no restrictions on SDI research, even if that meant no deep cuts in nuclear weapons. The President's priority of SDI over the nuclear reductions was shared around the nation.

The politicians, then in the heat of midterm elections, followed the people, as leaders are wont to do. Even liberal senatorial candidates like Terry Sanford in North Carolina and Tim Wirth in Colorado buried past condemnations of SDI and became fresh converts to SDI research. Conservatives bragged of their longtime support of SDI. When the dust settled, though, it probably made no big difference. The Democrats took the Senate in a cakewalk.

Even during the soar, the ground was being set for the eventual crash. The quantity of administration statements drowned out most qualms about Reykjavik. But the quality of administration statements left a lasting impression: Reykjavik as the scene of riverboat gamblers, rolling for big stakes without understanding much about the game.

Here too Secretary Shultz led the way, saying the day after Reykjavik, "As the agreement-that-might-have-been said, during this ten-year period in effect all offensive strategic arms would be eliminated. . . ." Again, that was the *Soviet* position, not ours, confused even afterward by the U.S. Secretary of State. Worse yet, it came from the sole other American official then in the room with Gorbachev and Reagan.

Don Regan was worse. That same day he said something different and even more inaccurate. "We said to the Soviets, we will do away with all nuclear weapons—nuclear bombs, nuclear shells for field artillery. Everything was on the table. We'll give it away if you will agree to let us continue our search for his [sic] defense," meaning SDI. As if the total elimination of all nuclear weapons was ever negotiable, practical, or prudent. As if we would even consider doing it unilaterally, if only the Soviets allowed SDI research. And as if we needed Soviet approval to conduct our "search for his defense." SDI research, as the administration had been saying daily for three years running, was fully consistent with the ABM Treaty. We would proceed whether the Soviets liked it or not.

The President answered no questions in public. But what he apparently said in private nonetheless became devastating. Senator Sam Nunn left the White House reporting that the President told a congressional group, "We put on the table a proposal to eliminate within ten years all nuclear ballistic missiles and everything else, including bombs." This stunned all those gathered around the Cabinet Room, Republicans and Democrats alike, and rocked European leaders.

A week later, the Soviets entered the public battle. They further confused things as they couldn't get it right, either. On October 22 Gorbachev said, "With all responsibility as a participant in the talks, I state: The President did, albeit without special enthusiasm, consent to the elimination of all—I emphasize all, not only certain—individual strategic offensive arms, to be destroyed precisely over ten years in two stages." Three days after Gorbachev's pitch, his adept Deputy Foreign Minister Bessmertnykh said something different, namely that Reagan told Gorbachev, "If we agree that by the end of the ten-year period, all nuclear arms are to be eliminated, we can refer this to our delegations in Geneva to prepare an agreement that you could sign during your visit to the United States."

So when the dust settled, not one of the top five Soviet or American participants had accurately described the U.S. offer that the President handed Gorbachev on that critical piece of paper.* Reagan, Regan, and Bessmertnykh said that the President offered to eliminate *all* nuclear weapons. Gorbachev and Shultz said he offered to eliminate all strategic offensive arms. Actually he offered to eliminate all ballistic missiles, and only this in exchange for monumental Soviet concessions.

The paper Reagan handed Gorbachev that Sunday afternoon indisputably shows that we offered to eliminate *strategic ballistic missiles* within the decade if the Soviets did likewise and agreed to sweeping testing, development, and even deployment of SDI.

The public debate, far from being dampened by all these statements, only flared up again. The more that came out, the more appalled the security community became as the likes of Richard Nixon, Henry Kissinger, Zbigniew Brzezinski, James Schlesinger, Jim Woolsey, Les Aspin, Brent Scowcroft, and Dick Cheney took to the airwaves to castigate the administration. Their point was simple: Eliminating nuclear weapons was myopic and perilous, while eliminating all ballistic missiles was foolhardy. It would have scrapped the hallmark of U.S. deterrence in the postwar era, the strategic triad, in one fell swoop.

A bit later on, James Schlesinger took the prize for the most astute observation when writing in *Foreign Affairs* how, if nothing more, SDI had performed a useful strategic function: it had blocked whatever offensive reductions Reagan had proposed or agreed to at Reykjavik. The impression began to sink in that the administration did not know what it had done at Reykjavik, nor what it was doing now. Whatever it had done or was doing about eliminating this or that category of strategic systems was mistaken.

Secretary Shultz tried again to salvage the situation. But he ended up deeper in the briar patch. Learning from pollsters that SDI was most appealing as "insurance" and learning from European colleagues that the elimination of all nuclear weapons was horrifying—even scrapping ballistic missiles was foolish—he delivered a speech in Chicago on November 17, 1986, that made more publicity than it did sense:

---

* They may have been somewhat confused, as everyone was, by what Reagan said in private to Gorbachev, or his muttered assent, or his nod, or whatever. If that's the basis of their error in describing what transpired at Reykjavik, that's a grave error in judgment. In our system, as in the USSR's, the papers passed about count for policy much more than spoken words or gestures.

Even as we eliminate all ballistic missiles, we will need insurance policies to hedge against cheating or other contingencies. . . . An agreed-upon retention of a small nuclear ballistic missile force could be part of that insurance.

In order to ensure that the elimination of ballistic missiles takes place safely, each side could retain ballistic missiles. How's that? Even in the annals of arms control speeches, this was destined to become a classic.

The Allies clung to one consolation, that Reykjavik ended without a deal. They were initially pleased by Reagan's willingness to meet Gorbachev and try to push arms control. But they were soon horrified by the near results. Europeans heaved a big sigh of relief that SDI saved the day by blocking an accord.

First grabbing their attention was Gorbachev's INF offer of zero missiles in Europe. Though NATO leaders had regularly mouthed this position since 1981, they did not like it. They had spilled much blood, sweat, and tears to get U.S. missiles into Europe. They didn't really want them all to leave.

Later, as they learned more of the Reykjavik dialogue, they became positively mortified. With one sweep of the arm and motion of the pen, yet without any consultations with them—so their perception ran—an American president could alter the basis of postwar security. For forty years their security had been based upon "extended deterrence." We would threaten to use our nuclear weapons, including our most accurate and powerful ballistic missiles, to discourage the Soviets from *any* type of attack, nuclear or conventional, against them.

Our main European Allies—the British, French, and Germans —were even more incensed that Reagan broached the idea of eliminating all nuclear weapons. They believed these had kept the peace. As Prime Minister Thatcher told Gorbachev in April 1989, "Both our countries know from bitter experience that conventional weapons do not deter war in Europe, whereas nuclear weapons have done so for over forty years." Moreover, the British and French knew their own nuclear forces would engender more public opposition if the "big boys" seemed to be getting rid of theirs. France, which glorifies its *force de frappe* and its mini– "strategic triad," was as always most disdainful.

Europeans soon grasped that their concerns and President Reagan's ran in opposite directions. They cared nothing for SDI—if it were up to them, they'd gut it as Gorbachev wished—but they cared everything about preserving ballistic missiles and clinging to nuclear protection. The President cared nothing for nuclear weapons—if it was up to him, he'd scrap them as the Soviets publicly advocated—but cared everything for SDI.

The Europeans' complaints ran even deeper. Reykjavik reinforced their age-old anxiety mixed with arrogance. They have long felt uncomfortable (to put it mildly) at having their security assured by what's seen as a bumbling if not incompetent nation an ocean away. The Old World was a lot wiser, perhaps, but unfortunately the New World was a lot stronger.

Reykjavik was not an unmitigated disaster. Over the longer run, it proved something of a mitigated disaster. Europe's post-Reykjavik metamorphosis constitutes one of the startling and satisfying developments in arms control of late.

Where once there was only pressure for progress, there became only pressure for prudence. Where once there were only cries of "Faster!" there became mostly echoes of that great American philosopher, Gene Autry: "Whoa, big boy!" The same European leaders who sat on my couch to advocate getting an agreement—nearly any agreement would do—now crossed the ocean to caution us from proceeding too quickly down this "dangerous disarmament road." We have to take it easy, they'd warn, especially on this INF business, as if we had done more than watch the Soviets approach the position we proposed in 1981.

THE FALLOUT

Within the administration, opinions varied about Reykjavik. A week after returning, we gathered again in the Situation Room to decide whether to present in Geneva what we had proposed in Reykjavik. Do we reoffer to eliminate ballistic missiles within ten years in exchange for Soviet concessions on SDI?

Present was the usual cast of characters. But absent were the hordes of White House staff and department advisors who often lined the walls, striking terror in the hearts of those gathered around the table. When the President held a meeting of "principals only," everyone became more conciliatory. When he held a meeting with staff galore, everyone became more contentious. Neither the State nor the Defense Secretary wanted word spreading through his department that he had given ground, agreed with the opponent, or done anything other than to read and cling fast to those carefully crafted "talking points" the staff had devised.

This meeting began as many then began, with the Secretaries of State and Defense squaring off on SDI and the ABM Treaty. They carried on in this vein for more than half an hour before I motioned to John Poindexter that I wished to join the fray.

Actually I wished to change the subject. Looking at the President, I said that I'd recommend we set aside the Reykjavik proposal to eliminate all ballistic missiles; the notion was neither feasible nor wise. Indeed, it was downright dangerous. Just as I got on a roll to present my reasons, Poindexter (sitting next to me) broke in. I was bringing up something the President had already decided, he said. There was no sense in my continuing.

Yes, there was, I replied with some agitation. Even if you decided once, Mr. President, you should reconsider now. At least you should hear the arguments against it and know the resistance that proposal has engendered. Europeans felt that nuclear weapons, especially on ballistic missiles, had spared them a rerun of the first half of this century when they suffered two "conventional" wars. They didn't like either one much. Since U.S. nuclear protection began over Europe, at the midpoint in this century, there haven't been any such conflicts. They like that a lot.

Besides, we were going down a dead-end path. By extolling such grandiose schemes as the total elimination of this or that, we were setting ourselves up for a fall. If we ever achieved a 50 percent strategic cut, it would be a letdown compared with the expectations we had built up.

Shultz rebutted me, but on substance rather than procedure. He asserted that the American people would gladly pay what it took in order to eliminate nuclear weapons—my argument had been over the zero–ballistic missile proposal, which as always he mistakenly equated with zero nuclear weapons—since the bomb caused people considerable consternation. The administration was now spending around $300 billion on defense—Cap jumped in: "$288 billion, George"—and we could have a conventional deterrent, he reckoned, at somewhere around $400 or $450 billion a year. (Where these figures came from, I could not imagine.)

I started to respond, but the President motioned to speak. "The people are with us" on SDI and on our defense program.

"That's just not the case, Mr. President," I suddenly heard myself saying in a tone I had never before used in his presence, let alone to him. "The people will *not* be with us if we say that the most massive arms control agreement ever must be accompanied by the most massive increase ever in peacetime military spending. The two just don't go together in most people's minds."

The Chairman of the Joint Chiefs, Admiral Crowe, then motioned to speak. Like me, he had not been called upon by Poindexter. But he wished to report on the Chiefs' study, initiated after (not before) Reykjavik. His point was clear: "Mr. President, we've concluded that the proposal to eliminate all ballistic missiles in ten years' time would pose high risks to the security of the nation."

To me, this was an astonishing statement. The President's top military advisor calling his own arms control proposal highly dangerous to the country! I was floored.

Others, strangely, were not. Don Regan kept peeking into his blue three-ring notebook with the presidential seal on the cover and the latest stock price quotations inside. Shultz looked at Crowe stone-faced. Weinberger, holding two or three pens of various colors, scribbled something down. Poindexter looked bothered; this was not how he had scripted the meeting. And Crowe continued in his pleasant, professional manner.

He explained the value of the strategic triad, the staggering problems the Joint Chiefs had already identified going to an all bomber and cruise missile nuclear deterrent, particularly in light of the massive Soviet air defense system (we have next to none). He gently reminded the President of extended deterrence, how our protection of Western Europe and Japan necessitated a robust U.S. nuclear posture.

He went on to say that NATO's twenty-five-year strategy of "flexible response" demanded that we have a counterforce capability, which did not seem possible without ballistic missiles. Besides, the Joint Chiefs could not envision a safe transition from where we are today to an American deterrent without ballistic missiles in ten years' time.

Even if that could be safely done, we might be broke in the meanwhile. This type of transition would be exceedingly costly, as we'd need an extensive air defense system, new bombers, and God knew what else. He roughly estimated at least a 12 percent real increase each year over the ten-year period—the Congress was then allocating zero real growth for defense—if the scheme was to be implemented. It might cost more.

These results were tentative, Crowe continued, as they needed to work on the study some more. But it seemed clear that the elimination of ballistic missiles in ten years would necessitate a massive arms buildup. Even then it would leave our country less secure than before such a transition began.

So went the guts of the Chairman's report. I looked around the Situation Room, again feeling I was the only surprised one there.

Don Regan peered up from his notebook and was grouchy as he began to say how difficult it was to get a word in edgewise in this meeting. (More people jolted with these words of Regan's than with those of Crowe.) The Chief of Staff had something important to say, he informed us. The President's budget requests were being finalized over the next month. If we decided to go with this conventional defense that Secretary Shultz was talking about, we would have to change the budget figures fairly soon.

This was too much for me. I spoke up again. "Mr. President, there are two questions on the elimination of ballistics: Is it wise? And is it feasible? I already said why I don't think it's wise, and I believe the Chairman said something similar. But in any case, it certainly is not feasible. The Soviets will *never* go along with it. So to boost the administration's requests for the defense budget by 50 percent, going from $288 billion to $400 or $450 billion, does not seem wise, either."

Upon returning to my office afterward, I called one of the participants on the secure line. He began by asking whether anyone in that room, besides Admiral Crowe and me, had any sense of reality. That had to be the wildest, most unrealistic discussion he had ever witnessed. The only sensible suggestion was that we concentrate on the 50 percent cuts and shove the other stuff (about eliminating this and abolishing that) aside.

Soon the White House publicly announced that the administration had coalesced around a "unified position" in support of zero ballistic missiles. The military, it was said, supported the "broad principles" of this approach.

The day after the NSC meeting, I was asked over to the "tank" at the end of that week to meet with the Joint Chiefs. They allegedly wanted to hear where arms control was heading; they actually wanted to hear where this administration was heading. Naturally I accepted. I asked my staff to study how we could verify and manage an elimination of all ballistic missiles without endangering the nation.

The next day I received several urgent calls from Poindexter's deputy. The National Security Advisor wanted word relayed to me in the clearest manner possible. He "insisted" that I "stand down." I was not to go into the tank with the Chiefs. I was not to proceed with the study on zero ballistic missiles. If I would not go along, Admiral Poindexter would be calling me from Air Force One, where he was then traveling with the President on the campaign trail.

I resisted. I argued. I objected. But after a long and bitter conversation, I consented. The 1986 election was just days away. The President did not need any further complications or any more flaps over Reykjavik. I did what I was told, apologized to the Chairman of the Joint Chiefs, and made some excuse to my staff to spike the study.

I was aggravated, thinking of that great line from Shakespeare, "What tangled webs we do weave when first we practice to deceive." Soon thereafter I met with Secretary Shultz and Chief of Staff Regan separately to say that I wanted to leave my position as director of the arms control agency. Each seemed genuinely thunderstruck. You want to leave now, just when arms control is progressing so nicely?

They asked me why.

CHAPTER 2

REOPENING THE ARMS TALKS

REYKJAVIK DID NOT bolt out of the blue (though it seemed like that afterward). Nor did any of the other summits of the Reagan years. The substance of them all—negotiating the levels and types of nuclear weapons and especially the fate of SDI—had its origins in the talks between Secretary of State George Shultz and Foreign Minister Andrei Gromyko on January 8 and 9 of 1985.

To be there was to be "present at the creation" of serious work on strategic arms and SDI in the 1980s. This session was to prove path-breaking on INF, too; the Soviets indicated some serious-ness in this previously abandoned area of arms control merely by agreeing to reconstitute separate INF talks. Before this January 1985 session, all the arms control dealings in the Reagan admin-istration were vapid. Afterward, there was more to them.

That Shultz and Gromyko allocated nearly all their time trying to settle an issue that was not settled, could not be settled, and need not have been settled—this too is both interesting and re-vealing.

Along with substance, the procedures established during these two days were those used over the next three years of the admin-istration. Secretary Shultz assembled his team and set out to accomplish something in an area he often felt uncomfortable handling. Contrary to my expectations, these procedures some-how worked.

And surely the atmosphere, not only in Geneva but around the world watching Geneva, was something special, something un-precedented—for our team, anyway. This sense of being where the whole world was watching had not occurred for us before but was to occur several times afterward.

All the hype, all the wonder, all the mystery that surrounds nuclear talks—it came in abundance during those two days in Geneva.

·   ·   ·

The scene at the Inter-Continental Hotel was bedlam as we arrived in Geneva on that cold January day in 1985. All three network anchormen broadcast their nightly news programs from this international gathering place, unkindly dubbed "the city of lost causes." It was as close to a summit as one could have without the American President or Soviet General Secretary being there.

The air was alive with speculation and trepidation. Would the Soviets return to the arms talks? Would they deal seriously with the Reagan administration? Would the chill in Soviet-American relations, at long last, pass?

All of us wondered, and none of us knew. We did know that the quasi-comatose General Secretary, Konstantin Chernenko, and his band of octogenarians were looking for a way to hobble back to the table, which they had left in a huff when we began deploying our Euromissiles in 1983. Our first signal came during the summer of 1984 when Moscow offered to open talks to "stop the arms race in outer space" (read SDI), only to renege when we replied that we wished to deal with reducing nuclear weapons, too.

It was a typical Soviet foul-up of the time, engineered by "Dr. No" of Soviet foreign policy, then Foreign Minister Andrei Gromyko. That was a time when, according to Gromyko's successor Shevardnadze subsequently, the Soviets were busy "slamming doors." They thereby gave up a golden opportunity to establish arms talks, which on their side, anyway, would have highlighted the dangers of SDI.

Then, just before Thanksgiving, Chernenko tried again. He wrote Reagan to propose that Shultz and Gromyko meet to talk about INF and strategic nuclear arms as well as SDI. It was a triumph of American patience, *their* returning to the talks on *our* terms. And it came unexpectedly—to me, anyway; I had written the President a year before (on February 3, 1984), "The Soviets will almost certainly *not* return to separate INF negotiations unless we are willing to roll back our INF deployments." So much for my expert counsel then.

Later, all of us saw it as a triumph as we met in the Situation

Room after being called hurriedly by then NSC Advisor Bud
McFarlane. Strange as it seems now, we were fairly excited about
resuming the talks.

We didn't fully appreciate the advantages of *not* having them.
Each time someone pressured the administration to "make a gesture" to improve U.S.-Soviet relations (read: make a concession
or give something away), we could respond handily that Moscow
must first send its negotiators back to Geneva. When Canadian
Prime Minister Pierre Trudeau delivered a lengthy exhortation to
this effect at a mostly vapid "economic summit" of the industrialized nations, Ronald Reagan could, as he did, shake his head,
lay down his eyeglasses purposefully, and then flatten him with
a restrained, "Pierre, what am I supposed to do? They're not even
at the table!" as he glared across the table.

During the year of the Soviet boycott, hours of the President's
time went to more productive activities. Public expectations of
what arms control could deliver were lowered; defense planning
became somewhat more realistic; and Congress was a tad more
accepting of how Western security was based on arms and not
arms control, as would be the case forevermore.

But that sweet period was to end, with none of us having the
wit to realize how sweet it was. President Reagan, Secretary
Shultz, and indeed the populace at large viewed the Soviet shift
as opening "great opportunities" for real arms control (which
never has "modest opportunities"), rather than the shuffling and
blathering that came during Reagan's first term. All of us saw it
as yet another vindication of the President's tough-guy approach;
"just say no" to unreasonable Soviet demands.

This was our mood as we ginned up for the gala Shultz-Gromyko meeting. The usual papers were written, the usual debates
ensued, and the usual meetings were conducted.

In the Situation Room, the President found rare consensus
among his oft squabbling advisors. We agreed on resuming the
talks. We agreed on seeking three sets of talks—one each on INF,
START, and SDI—with the first two picking up where they'd left
off before the walk-out. And we agreed to try to expunge the
Soviet rubbish about "preventing an arms race in outer space"
from the task of the third forum on SDI.

So on substance, everything worked out tidily. On procedure
was more activity, generated by Shultz, who watched such matters closely. The Secretary wanted NSC Advisor McFarlane and

his entire SACPG ("sack-pig") to accompany him. This was a rather novel move, but an ingenious one. With Bud along, the Secretary would be protected from second guesses at the White House. With Richard Perle and the Joint Chief representative along, ditto from the Pentagon. With the rest of us along, he could feign a united front even if he lacked one. The entourage would show we were ready to tackle the serious work seriously, should the Soviets be willing.

Yet I felt uncomfortable about it. Not that I minded being part of the big event, to which the world would turn its gaze at that particular moment in history. It was just that I deemed it unbecoming for a U.S. Secretary of State to lead a traveling road show of arms controllers. This, I told Shultz frankly, would merely play into the hands of our critics, who had long and loudly bellowed that we couldn't get our act together on arms control. Still Shultz insisted, saying that he might actually need such expertise (something that frankly had never occurred to me). Regardless, our presence would be a sign of serious purpose. And traveling together might bring us together. On these points, he was right. I grudgingly accepted and was glad later that I had defied my instincts.

The Secretary's large party assembled at Andrews Air Force Base for the flight to Geneva. Our plane was dubbed *Ship of Feuds* in tribute to the fights magnified by the press, particularly those between Perle and State Department's Richard Burt and involving our one-time INF negotiator Paul Nitze. A small contingent of press people joined us, with the bulk going on the backup plane.

In Geneva, we were mobbed by the media, who sought some fresh tidbit to report before the main talks opened. The two delegations alternated sessions between the American and Soviet missions, with most of us waiting in an adjoining room while Shultz, McFarlane, and a few others met with Gromyko and a few of his top staff. After each session in our mission, Shultz would walk next door and relate, almost word for word, what had transpired. When meeting in the Soviet mission, we would retire to our secure quarters for the debrief.

Soon the dialogue took shape. Gromyko stressed how the three areas—INF, START, and SDI—were interrelated. There was a natural connection, he maintained, between the types and numbers of nuclear weapons and the types and effectiveness of defenses against such weapons. Thus we had to consider everything together; the grammar school ditty, "All things related are, such that when one touches a flower, one disturbs the farthest star," sprang to my mind.

Shultz agreed such a relationship existed—who could deny it? —but maintained that we should strive to make progress wherever possible. If in INF, fine, let's move there. If on START, so much the better. And if, which didn't seem likely, on SDI, okay, too. What we *couldn't* do, Shultz insisted, was to hold up progress in one area until all three were resolved. That, he told Gromyko, was an action plan for inaction.

Gromyko lived up to his stolid reputation. Endowed with a nearly singular ability to repeat the same thing endlessly without shame, he proceeded to display this rare skill. Decades before, Nikita Khrushchev had quipped that ol' Gromyko, who had negotiated with President Franklin Delano Roosevelt in the White House, could stay put on a block of ice until it melted. Here Khrushchev was wrong; no block of ice would melt with that man perched on it.

Round and round the discussion went thus. Drawing on my college major of theology, I told Shultz that this situation was akin to the Trinity: we should just think of these three new arms talks like a good Christian thinks of God—the Father; God—the Son; and God—the Holy Ghost. Three entities, yet of one entity. Either because others had not been so schooled or because Gromyko would not be inclined to grasp the Trinity analogy, my counsel was left suspended.

Most of the others, but primarily Shultz, considered this "interrelationship" matter between the three topics a real problem. I found it unreal and abstruse. Why not just let it be and don't discuss it? I argued, this time to more receptive listeners. Look, Moscow holds the Soviet negotiators in Geneva on a short leash. If those in the Kremlin later decide to move ahead in one area, they will. If they want to tie the three and not move in one without progress in the other two, they'll do that, too. They'll take either course regardless of what we say or do here. Their future moves will depend on factors we can't foresee and they probably can't foresee, either, at this time. Our task is merely to tell them that *we*, at least, will not hold one negotiation hostage to the other two. And if they *do*, we'll criticize them for thereby blocking arms control progress. Shultz and the others found that too indefinite an approach.

So round and round we went, both within the U.S. delegation

and between the U.S. and USSR delegations. It seemed an increasingly tough nut to crack.

Yet, as things go in this bizarre business, it was not a nut that needed to be cracked, then or ever. For none of this abstract talk had much if anything to do with resuming the talks.

Why not propose a "joint communiqué," someone suggested, after some hours of such mind-numbing talk about all these interrelationships, that simply set the date for the talks' resumption in Geneva? That would call their bluff. That would show us if they were serious or not.

It seemed like a clever suggestion, and one that meshed with the diplomats' propensity to commit thoughts (such as they be) to paper. A communiqué could offer guidance to the negotiators, outline their work plan, give the opening date, and leave it at that, someone else chimed in. Everyone concurred and set about the chore, unaware for the moment that this approach raised its own set of problems.

WEDGING IN HUMAN RIGHTS

Relating such discussions years later makes them seem more coherent and contemplative than they actually were. Sure, we sat around a table discussing these points, but not in a quiet, deliberate manner.

Someone was always entering or leaving the room; others were scribbling notes or revising talking points; aides would ask Shultz or McFarlane if a *New York Times* photographer could take "just a few" photos; other staff members would ask them about logistics or timing; McFarlane worried about when to call the President; and *entre nous* was the usual dose of posturing, repeating, and question-posing that proves to be the bane of all meetings.

Things were always happening; stimuli was constantly coming our way. During a break the second day, just as Shultz *et al* returned to our waiting room to relate the latest Gromyko pearl, a staff fellow announced (breathing heavily to lend his words greater import) that he had just heard on the radio that Jim Baker was moving to Treasury and Don Regan to the White House. This instantly intrigued McFarlane and Shultz, the latter surprised since Regan had labored hard on the tax reform bill just then before the Congress. Bud wondered what that would mean to

White House operations and his own room for maneuver. (Little did he know!) Only after all this got hashed out did we return to the subject at hand.

During our early morning huddle that tension-packed second day, Shultz asked what other subjects he should raise with Gromyko. Naturally some suggested human rights, which had not been standard fare on the U.S.-Soviet agenda during this administration (then again, nothing much was standard, as the agenda had been so scant). Others objected; most eloquent and effective was the State Department's Director of Political-Military Affairs, General Jack Chain, who asked rather fiercely, "Why poke 'em in the eye just when we're trying to conduct serious business with them?"

The rebuttal came back. Human rights *was* "serious business." Still Shultz demurred. Pleas were made. We just *had* to raise this topic; it was right and politically essential. After some to-ing and fro-ing, Richard Perle made the cutting case: Why expect the Soviets to mind if we did raise it? They may not pay the least attention to our concerns; they haven't in the past, anyway. Surely they wouldn't scrap whatever they came to do just because we brought up human rights.

Much to his credit, Shultz bucked his own State Department advisors and sent word that he wished to meet with Gromyko alone before the morning session. From that time forth, Shultz was a vigorous proponent of hitting Soviet officials hard for inhuman treatment of their own citizens. He said at dozens of our meetings that he put human rights at the top of his concerns. His personal sessions with just released Soviet refuseniks in Israel and in America reinforced his feelings. After all, these were real people leaving real oppression for real freedom. It had a human dimension to it that all this arms control stuff lacked.

Without question the human rights high point—for me, anyway—came a couple years later in Moscow. A few of us broke from our incessant arms control meetings to attend a dinner at the American Ambassador's residence, the Spaso House. This was not just any dinner, but a Passover Seder, commemorating the passage of a people from bondage into freedom. And these were not just any guests, but the main Soviet dissidents and refuseniks from around that country.

The occasion took on special meaning for me, not just because I am Jewish, but also because I moved around the room with

Shultz to meet people I had mentioned in my human rights speeches when an Ambassador to the United Nations. Associating real people with the usually unpronounceable names I had read in the General Assembly was thrilling. These people, scorned in their homeland, would be held up as exemplary citizens in almost any other country.

The most poignant moment of all came when Shultz and I approached a young Russian mathematician. He quietly introduced his wife, then seven-plus months pregnant, and pointed out his two young children, who were running around the room. He desperately wanted to make that passage from bondage to freedom but was denied by the modern-day pharaohs in the Kremlin a few blocks away. He was also shaking, as he had been on a twenty-day hunger strike before the Seder to dramatize his plight.

He then reached in his coat pocket and took out a letter addressed to President Ronald Reagan. Handing it to Shultz, he said simply, "Keep it up. Just keep it up. You're the only thing going for us in the world."

Shultz, the seemingly immovable Buddha, looked down misty-eyed while the rest of us were reduced to tears. The Secretary then took the podium to tell the dinner guests, who regarded him with everything from appreciation to adoration, that they in turn should "keep it up." Deliverance would come, if only they kept the faith and their determination; freedom was, after all, an inalienable right for people everywhere. Later I came across the words of Lord Bryce, who wrote a century ago in his classic *The American Commonwealth* that American democracy had "the type of institutions towards which, as by a law of fate, the rest of civilized mankind are forced to move, some with swifter, others with slower, but all with unresting feet."

That was a beautiful moment in Moscow, one of the highlights of my time in government, if not of my life. To me, this was one of the splendid moments of George Shultz's years of service.

But back in Geneva that January of 1985, human rights lacked such glory. Indeed, as Perle foresaw, it lacked much of anything. Shultz duly escorted Gromyko into a side room, which he thereafter called the Gromyko Room, of the U.S. mission, and the Foreign Minister duly listened to our pleas for greater human rights. At least he must have heard some sounds while staring at the wall as Shultz spoke. After the Secretary stopped his plea,

Gromyko asked if there was more. Yes, Shultz said, and proceeded to make the human rights case again, this time more forcefully. Again a blank stare by this blank face at a blank wall. After a few more soliloquies like this, Shultz gave up. Yes, he was finished, but Gromyko had better remember what he had said. Without a word or gesture, Gromyko rose and proceeded into the next room.

Since then, Shultz's persistence has paid off. Not only has human rights become a permanent part of the U.S.-Soviet agenda, but it became *the* dominant feature of President Reagan's last summit, held in Moscow. Slowly have the Soviets accepted human rights as a topic of serious discussion; no more wall staring occurred after Gromyko departed. They have agreed to separate working groups on human rights and seem more responsive to the lists we routinely hand them with names they should release. And as the Soviets have responded, partly due to our pressure and probably due more to Gorbachev's *glasnost,* we have urged them to change their laws and practices, focusing less on individuals and more on the levers and systems of repression within the USSR.

THE WORK PROGRAM

Meanwhile, we heard the initial Soviet response to our draft "joint communiqué." As expected, they wished to stuff in that rhetoric about the dire dangers of SDI, as if speculative U.S. research programs on defensive systems (similar to what they have been doing for years) were somehow more dangerous than *existing* offensive nuclear weapons, which could obliterate the world.

It was a tough case to make, but the Soviets are adept at making outlandish arguments. So reflexive was their opposition to any American military decision that they called President Carter's 1977 cancellation of the B-1 bomber an "escalation of the arms race" and a complication to the ongoing SALT II negotiations.

We strived to knock out such anti-SDI rhetoric and came up against a fundamental problem: whether the communiqué should delineate a "work program" for the new talks. Most advisors, including those supposedly feuding over everything, felt strongly that it should. Having a work plan is an efficient, productive way to proceed. Moreover, delineating what each set of talks—INF, START, SDI—should accomplish would keep them

distinct. This would further our objective of three separate negotiations, rather than the Soviets' objective of one.

I was on the wimp side. Sure it would be nice to devise such
a work program, but we can't get one. And we don't need one.
I was comfortable with a come-as-you-are type negotiation—
either side raising any issue it wished—partly because that's the
only kind possible with Soviets.

People have to learn in this business. Each time a new arms
talk opens, we go through the same ritual, with the same result
after much agony. Our side seeks to set a title and approach to
the talks—as practical-minded Americans are wont to do for any
negotiations—while the Soviets demur. After some weeks,
months, or years, our envoys conclude that this exercise is hope-
less. They give up, and everyone then proceeds on an ad hoc basis.

After nearly fourteen years of meeting in Vienna on conventional arms, we abandoned the talks before agreeing on a title for
them (MBFR or MFR) with the Soviets. Similarly in INF, we even
concluded a treaty after seven years before agreeing on a work
plan or title; we said these negotiations were over Intermediate
Nuclear Forces while the Soviets said they were over "medium-
range missiles."

Still, most of our delegation sought to propose three separate
work plans for the three sets of talks. I pleaded for settling on
some vapid words that conveyed a vague sense about the overall
negotiations and leaving it at that. Papers flew back and forth
that day while Shultz and Gromyko continued their mental gymnastics over "interrelationships." Gromyko explained, in every
way, how there could be no progress in one area, like INF, without commensurate progress in the others, especially SDI. He was
adamant.

It was all words. None of it had anything to do with ensuing
Soviet foreign policy (whether it would have, had Gromyko
stayed in his job, will forever remain unknown). As things happened, over the next five years amazing progress was made in one
area, INF; some in another, on START; and none whatsoever on
the third, SDI.

Of more concrete concern, we found that the Shultz-Gromyko
round-and-round discussions had little bearing on anything, including the results of this meeting. But we could not have known
this then.

We did know that time was running out by midafternoon that

second day, January 9. Meeting as a delegation, we gulped hard and decided to accept the pernicious Soviet phrase that the "objective of the negotiations will be to work out effective agreements aimed at preventing an arms race in space," provided that they accepted our language, which followed: "and terminating it on Earth, at limiting and reducing nuclear arms and at strengthening strategic stability." (The capital "E" somehow crept into this document; who put it there?)

By then, most of the specific "work plans" for each of the three talks had dissipated if not disappeared. Any lingering substance was exorcised. Its vestige remained in one sentence, which helped show that the ministers' palaver was not all for naught: "The sides agreed that the subject of the negotiations will be a complex of questions concerning space and nuclear arms, both strategic and intermediate-range, with all the questions considered and resolved in their interrelationships."

Stringing together a strange succession of words to convey no clear thought is normal in diplomacy, even though it strikes any outsider as remarkable. When becoming Secretary of State, George Marshall commented on how he could understand heads of government but had trouble with any Foreign Ministry types, even "our own State Department" people, who "use mysterious language."

Violating Confucius' first principle, that words be used to convey meaning, does allow diplomats to bridge or paper over differences, as we intended here. This practice allows momentary agreement even though it opens the way to disagreements down the road. No better case exists than with the ABM Treaty, whose "reinterpretation" set off a firestorm during the Reagan years. Much of that controversy was due to yesteryear's paper-overs and inattentiveness to the precise meaning of words.

For instance, a Soviet interpreter told me during a long luncheon in Moscow in October 1987 that the very same Russian word in the ABM Treaty was translated into the English verbs "to provide" in Article I; "to create" in Agreed Statement D; "to construct" in Article III; and "to develop" in Article V. In the same treaty, we used the single term "development" in places where the Soviets used ten different words to convey the same concept.

HOLDING OUR BREATH

By that final afternoon, we on the U.S. side had gone as far as we could go. Any further and the Soviets would have a bigger hammer to hit us on SDI.

Yet Secretary Shultz wanted to succeed. He knew his boss, our boss, wanted to succeed; and so did the rest of us, to varying degrees. To leave Geneva without resuming the talks would lead to more accusations of Reagan's undying hostility toward the "evil empire." Worse yet, as Assistant Secretary of State Rick Burt never stopped emphasizing, were this meeting to break up without even setting the date for another such meeting, the Allies would have conniptions. It would be seen as a real setback.

Shultz kept reiterating that the President sought not *any* agreement, but a good agreement; he did not want *any* communiqué, only a good one. This was it, he and McFarlane had agreed, our final offer. If Gromyko bought it, fine. If not, so be it.

Partially for dramatic effect, though mostly out of frustration —dealing with Gromyko could do that to the most patient of souls—the Secretary bitterly remarked that we were dealing with the enemy here, a bunch practicing "genocide" in Afghanistan. Opening the talks would, lest we forget, lend them a legitimacy they did not deserve. So if they couldn't buy this version, to hell with them. Working himself up, Shultz said that he didn't feel like setting another meeting with Gromyko; he'd have nothing more to say later than he had now, Shultz reasoned. While Rick Burt made a last plea to set up another session if this did not work out, Shultz stalked out.

As the core group left, I turned to Rick and offered to bet him one dollar. Sure it would work; I exuded supreme confidence. As he grabbed the bet, I made the same offer to any comers. Interestingly, each of the State Department aides (including our Ambassador to Moscow) took the wager, save one—Shultz's executive assistant Charlie Hill. All the representatives from *other* agencies —the Pentagon, CIA, and White House—agreed with me that the Russians would accede to the communiqué. After shaking hands all around, we headed to the coffee table to bide our time. I was not as sure as I sounded.

Part of the world's hopes at this moment sprang from the assumption that relaunching the arms talks would "break the deadlock" in superpower relations. This in turn would enable us to make more progress on other diplomatic problems around the globe. This is how arms control has long been billed, even by the *realpolitik* Richard Nixon. The Soviets' willingness even to *enter* arms talks, he explained as President in a 1972 report to the Congress, "indicates constructive intentions in political as well as strategic areas" and such "progress in controlling arms can reinforce progress in a much wider area of international relations."

Nixon wrote this, but it was not to be; it is another common assumption which is actually another myth. This line of reasoning is a brand of linkage which is more a figment of human imagination than a reality of international affairs.

To me, the incessant debates over linkage—whether arms control is, should be, or can be linked to Soviet behavior elsewhere —is little more than words soaring into the stratosphere, never touching earth. There is no evidence that Soviet behavior—or ours, for that matter—has been much affected by linkage. And there's plenty of evidence in this area.

The Soviets certainly did not slacken their support of North Vietnam in order to "improve the climate" for SALT I. Nor did we forgo the bombing of the Haiphong harbor in the spring of 1972, on the very eve of the planned Nixon-Brezhnev summit to conclude and sign the ABM and SALT I accords.

Nor is there evidence that arms control helps the overall U.S.-Soviet relationship in any concrete way. Sure it helps in a sentimental way, by warming the atmosphere. But that may or may not be a good thing, depending on whether the reality is as improved as the perception.

Summits and other high-level meetings—which have become inexorably tied to arms control—have warmed the overall relationship without improving concrete matters much over the years. The year after the U.S., Soviet, British, and French Foreign Ministers met in 1955 to sign the Austrian State Treaty, Moscow cruelly put down the Hungarian uprising. Not long after the U.S.-Soviet summits to sign SALT I and the ABM Treaty, and later the U.S.-Soviet understanding on superpower conduct, we went on strategic nuclear alert to keep Soviet troops from entering the 1973 Middle East conflict.

Soon after the Glassboro summit between Soviet Prime Minister Kosygin and President Lyndon Johnson, the Soviets came crashing into Czechoslovakia. A few months after President Carter gently bussed President Brezhnev on the cheek upon signing SALT II, more than one hundred thousand Soviet troops stormed into Afghanistan.

Such a sobering chronicle does not mean that summits or arms agreements—the ratified SALT I and ABM Treaty or the signed SALT II—lead to worsened U.S.-Soviet relations. It only means that they do not necessarily lead to improved relations. There is no apparent connection between the graciousness and gala of summitry and the peace and calm of the world.

The same can be said for holding arms talks. Many people believe that increasing dialogue decreases differences, but there is no evidence for it. The period when no U.S.-Soviet arms talks were held—November 1983 to March 1985—was quite a calm one on the world stage.

In contrast, in precisely those years when we conducted the most arms talks with the Soviets, the Russians were most aggressive around the world. From 1975 to 1979, there was an expansion of both arms negotiations and Soviet power abroad. The United States and the USSR then conducted talks on strategic arms, conventional arms, chemical weapons, arms transfers, antisatellite weapons, Indian Ocean naval deployments, limited nuclear tests, and a comprehensive test ban. You name it and we then negotiated over it.

Yet the Soviets then engaged in the planning, manning, and funding of assaults against a pro-Western nation by a communist group each and every year: in 1975, South Vietnam; in 1976, Angola; in 1977, Ethiopia; in 1978, Cambodia; and in 1979, the two big ones, Afghanistan and Nicaragua. Add on, though with less aid from Moscow, Laos and Mozambique.

Whatever reality lies in linkage rests in American politics. It rests in our own handling of Soviet relations, rather than in the U.S.-Soviet relationship itself or in Soviet behavior abroad.

In our democracy, there is no way to separate Soviet behavior around the globe from arms control. This linkage affects our behavior rather than theirs, as it has since the dawn of strategic talks. After Glassboro, Johnson and Kosygin agreed to announce the opening of SALT talks at noon on August 20, 1968; Johnson scrapped that announcement when learning, only a few hours before noon, that Soviet tanks then began invading Czechoslovakia. President Carter, who regularly renounced linkage, asked the Senate to shelve SALT II and canceled other ongoing arms negotiations after the Soviets invaded Afghanistan. And President Reagan delayed the opening of START talks in December 1981 because of the imposition of martial law in Poland.

DIFFERENT NEGOTIATING STYLES

Though he could get worked up, as in Geneva when going into his last session with Gromyko, Secretary Shultz generally proved a calm bargainer. While the President prided himself on his abilities as a negotiator, the Secretary had prided himself on his prowess as an arbitrator.

The two are distinct. A negotiator bargains with clear ideas about his or his clients' interests, which he strives to maximize. An arbitrator goes into such sessions attempting to find a middle ground between two competing positions. With Reagan delineating the boundaries for concessions and not generally pressing hard for a deal, Shultz could work his magic. In many ways he was an ideal Secretary for a boss who had strong ideological leanings but was content to leave the details to others.

Although generally true, this distinction was never that crisp. Shultz could become angry about Soviet behavior, especially about Soviet repression. And at times the President could lose his ideological bearings, as when he compared Russian leaders with Hollywood film magnates.

During that Roosevelt Room meeting before Reykjavik, Reagan denounced Moscow's push for world domination. Within a couple of minutes, though, he was talking about his days as a negotiator for the Screen Actors Guild. He told how he longed to negotiate with Gorbachev as he had with the film representatives then. During one session, Reagan related, he found himself at the urinal standing next to a management leader. They began talking and concocted a solution to some knotty issue. If Reagan would propose it at the table as his own idea, then the other side could buy it. This they agreed to do, there in the men's room. And this they indeed did, back in the negotiating room. Everyone was delighted with the outcome of this "urinal diplomacy." If only he could get into a situation like that at Reykjavik, he shared with us, then he and Gorbachev could make a real settlement.

This is a fine approach, as I told the President at various times, if the two sides really wanted to agree and if they shared basic values. They can divvy up the same pie in an equitable manner, if they are negotiating over the same pie. With the Soviets, however, we have shared few if any basic values, and neither side has felt much compulsion about reaching agreement on fundamental issues.

Bargaining with the Soviets, I found, involves a constant struggle to reach common ground between sides sharing almost no basic values. It is like the old quip about the marriage between a wealthy Hollywood producer and a young starlet: he's in it for the matrimony and she's in it for the alimony. Reykjavik came asunder when Reagan made a stab at "urinal diplomacy," with Gorbachev's full complicity.

While Shultz and Gromyko could go back and forth over this business of interrelatedness, they left the communiqué drafting to others. Later Shultz and Shevardnadze adopted a similar style: they remained on the grand plane and left the specifics to others. Each feared deep involvement in the substance of arms control, both recognizing their technical limitations.

At times this led to peculiar role-playing. Before each meeting of the Foreign Ministers, the two Geneva delegations would work hard to specify the areas of agreement and disagreement. The Americans and Russians would tell each other that the disagreements would be left "for the ministers to resolve." When the great event arrived, when the Foreign Ministers met, they would immediately refer these very issues back to their teams of experts, from whence they came. For this group included the negotiators who had been unable to resolve the issues in the first place.

During those sessions, we "experts" would work on the unresolved topics as best we could. When hitting a roadblock, Akhromeyev, their head of delegation, would threaten to send the matter "up" to his minister, knowing full well that Shevardnadze did not want it back and that he, Akhromeyev, did not in fact want Shevardnadze to solve it.

At times this procedure took on imbecilic dimensions. During the September 1987 meeting in Washington, for instance, Shevardnadze suggested that we experts (again, mostly the negotiators) draft a directive for the two ministers to send to the negotiators, mandating that their work be accelerated. This tail-chasing was duly done and taken by the press at the time as a sign of genuine progress.

Sometimes Shultz could be wonderfully frank when finding

himself in the midst of arms control minutia. Right before the December 1986 Washington summit, Soviet Ambassador Yuriy V. Dubinin urgently sought to call on the Secretary. A time was arranged, and he entered Shultz's inner sanctum to read an important demarche from Moscow concerning INF verification. After he finished reading, Shultz asked if the Ambassador could hand him the paper so he could read it himself.

When this was done, Shultz looked up to say that he had no idea what all these words were about. Did Dubinin? The Ambassador took the paper back, read it silently this time, and attempted to paraphrase it. Shultz stared blankly. No, Dubinin finally admitted, he had no idea, either. Maybe one of us experts would know. Or maybe he should go back to the embassy and find someone there who would know. Or someone in Moscow who would know.

Shultz deemed that a capital idea. None of us heard about the issue, whatever it was, ever again.

GENIUS OF DIPLOMACY

While the actual work of diplomats is narrow and frustrating, the anticipation of diplomatic success is grand and inspiring. As the Marquess of Salisbury, British Secretary of State for thirteen of the last twenty-two years last century, wrote:

> There is nothing dramatic in the success of a diplomatist. His victories are made up of a series of microscopic advantages: of a judicious suggestion here, of an opportune civility there, of a wise concession at one moment and a farsighted persistence at another; of sleepless tact, immovable calmness and patience. . . .

Shultz and, even more so, Max Kampelman taught me that the genius of diplomacy is anticipation—not only anticipation that problems will be solved before they become unmanageable, but anticipation of changed conditions that could improve the overall situation. In the diplomacy of arms control, for instance, we can anticipate how an agreement could help reduce the risks of war, save money, lower arms, or warm relations. In the diplomacy of regional issues, we can anticipate changes in Moscow that might help stop the conflict.

Hence do diplomats point to the future—to the next party Congress or Politburo meeting or round of talks or summit. As Dostoevsky knew so poignantly, humans need hope.

So the world, as always, was longing for hope in January of 1985. After a year of no talks, the Kremlin at last seemed ready to reopen the dialogue. There appeared a chance for the superpowers to work out differences on arms control. After that, who knew where this could lead?

And I did expect the Soviets to reopen the talks. Gromyko was the sole cause of my doubts—this guy seemed so totally indifferent. Still, I figured the Marxist emphasis on "objective reality" would triumph over his personal inclinations. The Soviets were objectively on a losing course. Slamming doors has been tried and found wanting. The Soviets could not lay claim to the mantle of being a peace-loving nation if they refused to return to Geneva. Surely they would concede to our final communiqué offer. Or would they?

Even if they would, our finely crafted, if somewhat incoherent, document would have little lasting effect. It did not say much and would not matter much even if it did. With the Soviets, even an agreement painstakingly reached can be soon forgotten.

Like the old Russian tale of a farmer selling the same cow twice, Russian negotiators try to sell the same proposal (at least) twice. The prime example was alluded to before—their long and strong insistence upon including the U.S. "forward-based systems" (FBS), such as nuclear-capable aircraft or other U.S. systems based in or around Europe. They included these since they defined a "strategic system" as one capable of reaching the other's territory.

This may sound logical but is blatantly one-sided. Such an approach restricts our forces in Western Europe able to hit Russian territory but excludes their systems able to hit West European territory. Successive U.S. administrations saw it as part of the classic Soviet wedge-driving, to divide us from our fellow NATO members. So successive administrations dismissed such a definition out of hand.

This issue preoccupied SALT I like none other. The Soviets knew they had hit upon a good line of attack, as the Allies fretted that we would shortchange their security. After much pulling and hauling, the issue was resolved in SALT I. The Soviets could have more nuclear launchers if they dropped their demand to include our FBS.

After SALT I came SALT II, where, lo and behold, they again insisted on including FBS. We objected, but they explained that they had dropped their demand only temporarily.

Round the horn we went again. The November 1974 Vladivostok Accords were hailed as the end of this issue since the Soviets therein agreed to equal strategic levels *without* FBS. Little did we suspect that, two months after Vladivostok, the Soviets would begin the next round of Geneva talks by slapping down a proposal that included—guess what?—forward-based systems once again.

Late in SALT II, the Soviets again dropped this demand but again received compensation for such generosity. Moscow could keep 308 heavy missiles, while we were permitted none in exchange.

Into START the American and Soviet negotiators went where again the Soviets demanded—now for the fourth time—that we include FBS. Rather than feel a tinge of guilt over having been compensated twice for something that deserved no compensation in the first place, they feigned resentment. This was unfair! They had now signed three accords without including FBS and would not be wronged again! They had "gone the extra mile" enough.

So, nothing ever seems to get settled with the Russians. Even those issues that *are* settled, even on the highest level, get unsettled.

The clearest example happened after the 1985 Geneva summit, where President Reagan and General Secretary Gorbachev agreed that the Geneva negotiators would tackle verification early on. This was a triumph for us. Verification is "our" issue. It's one usually relegated to the end game and not handled too carefully during the mad rush then. And despite the best of intentions, there always *is* a mad rush at the end. Soviet negotiators say that the first third of any negotiations takes a few months; the second third a few years; and the last third a few hours.

Yet when I next visited the negotiators in Geneva a few months after the 1985 summit, their head INF negotiator, Ambassador Alexei A. Obukhov, said verification would come last. He was not about to deal with it until all the "substantive" issues had been resolved.

I was puzzled. Had we misinterpreted what Gorbachev had agreed to? Had Gorbachev changed his mind? Was Obukhov not reading Gorbachev right? Or was Obukhov not caring what Gorbachev said?

Hard to say; at least I never found out. What was easy to say was that Obukhov would leave verification until last. And that was that.

At other times, the Soviets keep their word but little else. They follow the letter and break the spirit of an agreement. The classic example happened with the 1975 Helsinki Accords, which allowed Western observers to inspect Warsaw Pact field troop movements. We and the Allies deemed this a breakthrough, at least we did until we first tried it. In February of 1978, Western observers went to the *Berezhina* military exercise in the USSR western military district. Our fellows were not allowed to bring their own cameras or binoculars, as such was to be furnished by the host country. Yet when they arrived in Byelorussia, our inspectors were given binoculars that could not be focused. They were blurrier than the naked eye. The Warsaw-bloc military officers had done nothing illegal; they had, after all, handed out binoculars.

TIMES OF ANGER, TIMES OF LAUGHTER

The Soviets can be just as aggravating for no apparent reason as they can for some reason. This I learned early on—in fact, during my first trip to Geneva as Arms Control Director.

It was in October 1983, soon after the Soviets had shot down the Korean Airliner KAL 007 and concocted one excuse after another, only to end up viciously accusing us of engaging in a spy mission. Still, there was a glimmer of hope then that they would get serious about arms control, especially since our Allies were standing firm against the European antimissile protests and we were standing firm against the American freeze movement.

Brimming with the confidence characteristic of someone new on the job, I entered a magnificent chalet turned into a fine Geneva restaurant. I greeted Ambassador Victor Karpov, the chief Soviet negotiator, cordially on the doorstep, having known him for some time. Each of us brought two others—I, Ambassador Ed Rowny and a note taker, and he, a note taker and a deputy. We needed no interpreter since Karpov's years in this business had sharpened his command of English.

"You look more prosperous than ever," I told him jocularly, noting that the sumptuous Geneva dining was adding to his already ample physique. We were placed in a private room and seated at a round table. To chat a bit before diving into the substance, I remarked upon that morning's news, how South Korean Cabinet members had been blown up in Burma by a North Korean hit squad. It was terribly shocking, Karpov concurred, though careful not to assign blame to the North Koreans. I then innocently asked Karpov if he had ever visited South Korea.

Something seemed to snap, as he turned red in the face and began sputtering his words. The good Ambassador launched into a vitriolic diatribe about the KAL incident. "You brought this whole crisis on," he began, arms soon waving. "You must stop spying, or else we'll take more forceful action."

"Like shooting down another innocent passenger plane, Victor?" I asked in a calm manner before mentioning the discrepancy between what Soviet officials said about the incident in Moscow and what the Soviet pilot said on the tape played before the UN Security Council.

This ignited the fiery Karpov once again. After a few heated exchanges, I was ready to surrender. We had covered the subject and already sunk too low for my taste. I began to sip my soup, waiting for the storm to pass.

"Are you finished?" I asked a few minutes later. "I suggest we move on to arms control. It's bound to be more productive." I casually mentioned how I regretted that Karpov had raised the KAL incident in the first place.

This was a big mistake, as it triggered another invective. "No, Kenneth, it was *you* who first raised this unfortunate incident!" Karpov said seemingly sincerely. "And you did so to ruin the atmosphere," as if there had been any appealing atmosphere there to ruin.

Now we had something new to argue about—who had first raised the KAL incident. That discussion also went nowhere. After another flare-up and another wind-down, I wedged in a question on the arms talks. No, Karpov retorted, he was not able to make progress on arms control after, well, after all this. We finished lunch somberly.

As we left the chalet, though, Karpov wrapped his arm around me. "Kenneth, it's a shame what happened," he said. "I was ready to make progress on arms control if only *you* had not raised this KAL business." He broke into a broad smile, maybe realizing how aggravating he was at that moment. Or maybe not.

There are also moments when it is pleasurable to deal with the Soviets. Not many, but some.

Hearing about Akhromeyev's World War II experiences over

dinner in Geneva was one such pleasurable occasion. Ribbing my Soviet counterpart at the United Nations in 1982, and being bettered in turn, was another.

This episode happened during the Spanish Ambassador's luncheon for fifteen or so UN Ambassadors to honor Christopher Columbus's birthday (or some such). Feeling a bit ornery, I looked across the table to the deputy in the Soviet delegation, Richard Ovinokov. "Richard, what about the news this morning?"

Whenever American and Soviet envoys talk, as at E. F. Hutton, other diplomats listen. A silence descended over the rest of the normally chatty crowd.

"What news is that, Ken?"

"Why, the Israelis shot down some ninety MIG-21s and -23s today, without losing a single Israeli plane. I have written a lot on the awesome Soviet military power, but here goes little Israel picking off these top-of-the-line Soviet fighters bing, bing, bing, without suffering any casualties at all. Maybe there's not much to fear from you guys after all."

Richard retorted: "No, Ken, you've got it wrong. The Israelis did *not* shoot down ninety Soviet planes. The Israelis shot down ninety Syrian pilots."

"Touché," I said while everyone chuckled.

Formal Talks

But that much levity is rare in this profession. Spontaneity too is rare when dealing with the Russians. Repetition and vitriol are the names of that game.

The world was watching Geneva on that late afternoon of the second day to see if the arms talks would resume. The press didn't know, in part because we didn't know and in part because we had clamped on a press blackout during these meetings, which only added to their drama.

And it drove the press nuts. There were the key anchormen and thousands of journalists from everywhere with nothing to say. Gromyko had agreed to the blackout, but during the evening of the first day the Soviets spread the word around town that things were not going well.

So the mood became gloomy, as the bewitching hour of closing time approached. All the tension was centered on whether formal talks would begin again.

Over the years a mystique has grown about these arms talks. Since they are shrouded in secrecy, outsiders assume that they are witty and wonderful, something akin to what transpired during the Congress of Vienna.

Actually they are stiff and deadly dull, a forum where symbolism triumphs over substance. Details can be handled in them, but there is no heavy lifting of the big obstacles.

Not that the talks suffer from any lack of staff. They suffer from an excess—officials from various agencies in Washington watching each other as carefully as they watch representatives from Soviet agencies. The paucity of progress is matched by a plethora of participants; at times some forty-two delegates are assembled around the table—twenty Soviets and twenty-two Americans, including, on our side alone, seven full Ambassadors. This approximates the number the United States had stationed everywhere around the world in the 1930s.

When it's our turn to host a session in Geneva, the U.S. representatives line up by protocol rank at the door of our boxshaped Mission. Soviet diplomats arrive on the dot of the appointed hour and enter, likewise in order of rank, each Soviet shaking each American's hand down the row. In hockey, this lineup occurs after the game; in the big game with the Soviets, it happens before and after each session.

Delegates gather around a long wooden table, translators in the middle and loads of staff aides lining the walls. The visiting delegation always faces the door—a relic from medieval times when diplomacy was not the gentle profession it has become, when a "stab in the back" from one's host could rightly be feared.

The home Ambassador courteously invites his counterpart to deliver the opening statement. The Russian then drones on, translations after each paragraph breaking the monotony but not alleviating the boredom. A comment or a formal statement may then be offered by our leader, again needing translation. After this ritual, the statements are traded so that each side's experts can scrutinize them for nuances that might have been missed during the oral presentation. Usually there aren't any, but the officials lining the wall still try to find some.

Some discussion may then ensue, but often not. The hosting Ambassador will thereafter rise and invite his counterpart to recess for a more private deliberation. The American number two likewise strolls off with the Soviet deputy, the U.S. military representative with his counterpart, and so on down the line in a Noah's Ark–like procession. The two intelligence officers may even confer with one another, each pretending to be a diplomat but everyone knowing better.

In June of 1982 this led to an odd situation wherein the KGB fellow said he had heard on the radio that morning that his counterpart's boss had just been fired. Our man started to dash off, thinking Bill Casey had left, when the wry Russian said that Secretary of State Haig had been dismissed. He reminded our man that they were both diplomats, lest he had forgotten.

Something more may happen in these gatherings—all of which end when the number ones finish in their corner—but normally it's slim pickin's. After the visiting team departs, the delegation scurries to the "bubble" to dissect what happened. Afterward reams of words are sent out by secure telegram to the waiting hordes back in the capitals. Whoever reads all such cables cannot do much more during a normal workday.

Sterility at the table makes for constipation in the process. President Dwight Eisenhower foresaw this when, during a 1955 press conference, he said, "As everybody has always known, any move for disarmament is going to be slow, tortuous, and certainly gradual, even at best." Little did he know to what extent: the Limited Test Ban Treaty of 1963 came after eight years of effort, SALT II after seven years, and INF after more than six.

Although I found the whole scene in these formal Geneva talks at variance with my tempo, our representatives seemed to like it. After a while they even developed something of a Stockholm syndrome and began praising their counterparts. Sir Harold Nicholson wrote: "There is always a tendency among diplomats who have resided for long in foreign countries . . . to find that their loyalties become a trifle blurred"—but I had not expected it from our experienced negotiators in Geneva.

During my first official visit there, our START negotiator Ed Rowny extolled Karpov's virtues, though staying quite sober about the difficulties of any dealing with Soviets. Ambassador Karpov was actually a fine negotiator, tough but reasonable when the time came to wheel and deal, whereas the INF negotiator, Yuli A. Kvitskinskiy, was a phony sophisticate, Rowny related. Paul Nitze, our top man on INF, made it a point to tell me that Kvitskinskiy was erudite, wise, sophisticated, and had imagination, while Karpov lacked any of these traits.

It was remarkable how both hardheaded Americans, with years of experience negotiating with the Soviets even before the Reagan administration, considered his counterpart an able foe but saw the other's counterpart as woefully inadequate. Actually, I found Ambassador Nitze's appraisal right on the mark, especially after having a marvelous dinner among the three of us during which Kvitskinskiy brilliantly analyzed the Free Democratic party in West Germany (the country he specialized in and later became Ambassador to). Karpov turned out to be somewhat brutish, especially to the wife of a United States Senator a year later. He had trouble keeping his hands off her legs during a dinner in the spring of 1986, causing her to walk out.

Later, when Nitze gave up the mantle to State Department's Mike Glitman, the modified Stockholm syndrome persisted. Ambassador Glitman found his counterpart, Obukhov, a real intellectual—smart, abstract, thoughtful. I found him a bit insufferable. My first encounter with his infamous "numbalogues" came during my first encounter with him, at a reception when he lectured (or hectored) me for thirty minutes nonstop, seemingly without taking a breath. His barrage came straight out of the Soviet news agency Tass, so it meant little to me. With that furrowed brow and those piercing eyes, he emanated unpleasantness. Perhaps he'd been insufferable before attending the University of Chicago for a time years ago; he most definitely was afterward. Obukhov seemed to delight in being abusive to Glitman, which, true to his profession, Glitman seemed not to mind.

TIGHT-LIPPED AND MADDENING

Generally, however, our negotiators do a fine job, given the amount of sheer nonsense they must endure in their work. Most maddening has been the Soviets' traditional refusal to furnish data on the subject of the negotiation. Throughout SALT I, they refused to reveal information about the size or composition of their forces. We had to supply numbers on *our* forces and estimates on *theirs*, while their delegates just nodded, grunted, objected, or gazed afar à la Gromyko.

So tight with information have Soviet negotiators been that they deemed it a concession to reveal even their own proposals. After Gorbachev's January 15, 1986, "megaproposal" to eliminate all nuclear weapons within fifteen years, our negotiators probed for days about how this would work. Was Gorbachev talking about missiles? Launchers? Warheads? Would he include battle-field systems? What type of aircraft? Allied systems? The Soviets had no answers to these, the obvious questions that had to be addressed if this was a serious proposal.

Similarly, they can play games on the most mundane of issues. They can make us expend inordinate time and energy working out when to adjourn one round of talks and begin the next. At times their top negotiator will quietly offer dates and ask our man to propose them formally at the table. When he does so, the Soviet then says that those dates may not work out; he'll have to check with Moscow. Later, "on instruction," he reports that he cannot agree to "the American dates" but can agree to a counter-proposal. The "Soviet dates," which differ by a day or two, are then accepted. Somehow, everyone feels a sense of accomplishment at the end of this two-step.

No wonder an American negotiator once quipped that dealing with the Russians is like dealing with a defective vending machine—you can kick it or jar it, but talking to it does no good at all. And no wonder that when something important *has* to be accomplished, both sides resort to Foreign Minister meetings. Of the eight such meetings from our initial Shultz-Gromyko talks to the Washington summit, five were held in the nine months leading to the completion of the INF Treaty. That's when something important *needed* to be done.

Serious Soviet officials too can see that the emperor of the arms talks has scant clothing on. That is why they have often probed for a "more direct channel" into the White House. During SALT I days, they had their direct channel via Henry Kissinger, an ap-proach that got things done all right, but sometimes got the wrong things done. Missing on our side was the technical exper-tise needed in this technical field and knowledge about what the Soviets were up to and why. This arrangement resulted in the unconscionable situation where the head of the U.S. delegation, Ambassador Gerard Smith, knew less about the American offer than his counterpart sitting across the table from him. Dobrynin shared information of what Kissinger was up to with his col-leagues, while Kissinger shared little or nothing with our delega-tion.

In 1985 and 1986 Moscow again probed for some new avenue

into top U.S. decision-makers. They then contacted, of all people, a California physician who had long worked for liberal Democratic Senator Edward Kennedy. Through him—or Senator Kennedy, this was never clear—they wanted to open a "separate channel" to Reagan. Word of this swiftly reached the President, who was intrigued enough to call a meeting about it. He liked this kind of thing; perhaps it reminded him of a novel by Tom Clancy, whom he adored.

We told the President that this was crazy. Shultz especially wished to get a hammerlock on the arms control process. The Soviets should not choose who deals with them from our side; the President should. Going through this liberal Kennedy staffer to get to Reagan did not seem too adept an approach. I made the point, as kindly as I could, that such back-channeling placed enormous demands on top administration officials to keep things straight—what to tell their colleagues and what to hold; what to share with the Congress and allies and what not; and likewise with the Geneva negotiators. Implied in my point (no doubt lost in its subtlety) was that we would trip all over ourselves. This administration was not the most tightly controlled organization in the best of conditions. We had a tough enough time managing the front channel.

WINNING MY BET

But the reality of the Geneva talks was overshadowed by the hopes their reestablishment portended to us, and to all the world, that first week of January 1985, as we awaited word from Shultz in the adjoining room. While he went over our final offer on the communiqué with Gromyko, the rest of us sauntered around. No one then, or seemingly ever, uses that precious time to good effect—sitting down and working out what the Secretary should say if it does or does not work; jotting down points for him to tell the President; whatever—but somehow that never gets done.

In any case, we were not held in suspense long. Within a few minutes someone bounded into our room to say that Shultz and Gromyko were heading out the door. As at Reykjavik later, their faces told the story—at least Shultz's did; Gromyko's face never told anything.

They walked from the U.S. mission conference room to announce to the press outside that an agreement had been reached to start up the arms talks once more. This too began a precedent; from then on, any time the ministers would agree on something big—a summit date, the resolution of the Pershing I issue, or some such—they would announce it swiftly, before it leaked out with a perverse spin.

To help Shultz prepare for the inevitable press conference, we fled back to the Inter-Continental Hotel in a mad-rush motorcade. Once there, we walked through a sea of eager reporters trying to buttonhole each of us for some tidbit. The "press blackout" was still in effect (on our side, at least), so we plunged through the crowd until we reached the safety of the elevators.

We proceeded up to the Secretary's suite, where he and Bud McFarlane were telephoning the President, who was delighted with the news.

We then gathered to help guide Shultz. True to his academic background, the Secretary silenced everyone in order to read the final joint communiqué. He read this concoction of words over which we had struggled so hard. They were nearly unintelligible, particularly the meat of the document, which declared that the negotiations would handle "a complex of questions concerning space and nuclear arms, both strategic and intermediate-range, with all the questions considered and resolved in their interrelationships."

Having read the communiqué and remembering all the interrelationship gibberish—the Trinity issue—Shultz looked quizzical. He asked us how he could possibly explain these words. I suggested that he could resort to the press secretary trick of saying simply that the document spoke for itself. Others, more dedicated to diplomacy, gave long, elaborate explanations of what we had accomplished, none of which seemed to sink in—to me, at least.

So late that night, before the thousand or so media types from around the world, Secretary Shultz opened his press conference by reading the entire communiqué—this soaked up time—and then uttered these immortal words: "While the statement speaks for itself, I would like to give you my own views on what has been accomplished." He put the events in his own way, which was understandable though scarcely illuminating.

While standing around with the other U.S. officials in the grand ballroom of the press conference, I humbly collected my winnings. We then fanned out to brief members of the press in detail.

Shultz wanted us to tell our story around the world, meeting with Allied and other leaders as much as possible. Again this was a smart move. Consultations have enormous value, almost regardless of what is said. Process counts for much in diplomacy; personal attention to key friends around the world helps here, as in every field of human endeavor.

In yet another innovative step, I was asked to make rounds in Eastern Europe. The idea, I believe it was Shultz's, was neat: to inform key, non-Soviet communist leaders of our stance in arms control and security issues. We could inform them more than the Soviets ever bothered (or wanted) to do. So with a delegation from the National Security Council, Arms Control Agency, and State Department, I set out for Yugoslavia, Hungary, and Romania.

First stop was the first breakaway communist state, Yugoslavia, where news of the celebrated reopening of the arms talks was met with more trepidation than salutation. Those in Belgrade, whether in the government or think tanks, feared "another Yalta." Wasn't the United States cutting another deal with the Soviets? Wasn't this stuff about interrelationships in the talks, including the focus on SDI, really a way to make a "Yalta over outer space"? Strange thoughts from people who were only indirectly though still significantly affected by the postwar settlement of Eastern Europe.

In Budapest, Hungary, I found the opposite: rather ordinary discussions with rather extraordinary people. There still exists a vivaciousness in the Hungarian national character that even forty years of communism has not snuffed out. Perhaps I was awed by Hungarian humor and good-naturedness because of my ancestral past. Or perhaps I was impressed after learning some years ago that an overwhelming majority of the top scientists on the Manhattan Project came from that little country.

No such brilliance was apparent during our discussions there, nor did the subject matter warrant this. But in order to conduct some serious business there, I tried some mischief. During my "private" discussions with the U.S. Ambassador in his bugged Budapest residence, I spoke at length about how poorly Gromyko had done in the two-day talks with Shultz. He looked old; he acted feeble; he became confused at times; he gave ground needlessly; above all, he did not realize that our instructions from the President provided Shultz with far more leeway than we ended up needing to take. Gromyko could have driven and reached a far better deal. I made these arguments in all "confidentiality" and repeated them once or twice in Budapest for good effect.

Later I mentioned my ploy to Bill Casey, who loved all ploys, and explained that my objective was simply to provide some ammunition to Gromyko's critics. I hoped it helped, but who knows?

The best part of my Eastern European tour though was yet to come. I would not have suspected it on the slow train from Budapest to Bucharest—I again won a wager, this time choosing the latest arrival time for the train, which turned out to average under forty miles per hour.

Romania was then in the throes of yet another energy/economic crisis caused by the Stalinist economics and politics of dictator Nicolae Ceausescu. For one month before we arrived, it had been illegal for anyone to drive a private car anywhere in the country. Schools had been closed. Factory workers were let off for two weeks' unpaid "vacations." Streetlights were turned off. Public transportation was scant or shut down.

The place was freezing, not only outside (which is expected there in January), but also inside, for most of the heat had been shut off. Apartments, nearly all office buildings, most hospitals, and old people's homes were all without heat. Embassy personnel were being evacuated because of the cold. From the moment we arrived until the moment we departed, we shivered.

The morning our "consultations" began, I was wearing my suit and a sweater and kept on my deerstalker hat, overcoat, and gloves while sitting in the Foreign Minister's once elaborate but now shoddy conference room. The Foreign Minister himself was not so drab; a Francophone (speaking beautiful French, the language of most of our talk), he was quite intelligent—with a large cranium and wavy flaxen hair, he looked like an intellectual—and he liked to debate. He seemed more inquisitive than most I met there, especially after spending some time with Ceausescu's brother, leader of the Romanian army, who is an insufferable bore and braggart.

The Foreign Minister graciously hosted a luncheon in our honor, held in one of the only two restaurants still operating in the capital city. It was located in a dreadful Russian-style hotel with mammoth square rooms. The room seemed, if anything, starker and colder because it was so dimly lit. A fifty-watt bulb beamed from the three-story-high ceiling. We groped our way to the long formal table decorated with several candelabras, which were more appreciated for their heat than for their light or beauty.

After some chatter, we sat down for the usual toasts. Then, as the heavy meal was brought out, the Foreign Minister resumed our discussion from that morning. I had, he recalled correctly, stressed the fundamental differences between open and closed societies, between democracies and communist countries. He was struck, again rightly so, by what appeared to be my condescending tone toward communism and my feeling of confidence, even superiority, regarding our way of life.

He could not let this stand, he proclaimed (I assumed he was told to do this after our meeting), for I was either ill informed or malicious. Didn't I realize that the Romanian people were happy with their form of government and life? They had chosen Ceausescu as their supreme leader. Before, they had suffered cruel Nazi occupation. They were now united behind his inspiring leadership and that of his marvelous family (Ceausescu's wife had been exalted during the just ended party conference, and his brother headed the army). Didn't I know the people's love for their leader? Hadn't I learned of his accomplishments?

His questions begged a response, but probably not one as extreme as I gave. "Mr. Minister, both of us were trained in political science and studied Marxism. Both of us know that Karl Marx continually harped on 'objective reality.' "

"Yes, of course."

"Then let us too talk about 'objective reality.' Here we sit, at your kindly invitation, in our coats and hats, trying desperately to keep warm in one of the only restaurants operating in this once-proud capital of a country that was among the most prosperous in central Europe between the wars. Here you sit extolling the glories of your communist system, speaking while I can see your breath!

"Who would choose a life like this? Who would welcome a system that deprived people not only of any vestige of human rights, but also of such basic human needs as heat? The 'objective reality' of this situation is dreadful, as much as I appreciate your kindness."

With that, the discussion too turned chilly, and I counted the hours until I could be out of that place. Not long thereafter, this Foreign Minister was dismissed.

Likewise for the Soviet Foreign Minister. We would be done with that sour face of Gromyko and contend with the coldly smiling face of Shevardnadze.

We would also contend with something even tougher—the new three-ringed arms talks we had worked so hard to reestablish.

CHAPTER 3

THE GENEVA
SUMMIT

EACH SUMMIT DEVELOPS a personality of its own. Surely Ronald Reagan shaped the personality of our first summit, held in Geneva in November of 1985, much as Mikhail Gorbachev shaped the second, at Reykjavik a year later.

And each summit develops a significance of its own. For the public, it was the image of those fireside chats in that small lakeside villa where the leaders of the world's two main adversaries talked out—rather than fought out or yelled out—their differences. For us in the delegations, it came from seeing this new phenomenon on the world scene, Mikhail Gorbachev, up close and personal. It constituted quite a contrast, a delightful contrast, to our impression of how a top Soviet leader usually acts.

Not that we really *knew* how a very top Soviet leader usually acted. Among us, only George Shultz had ever met Gorbachev, when he accompanied Vice President Bush to Chernenko's funeral. Shultz swiftly spotted something special about the living leader, which he described to a few of us upon his return from Moscow in March 1985.

Recently, I happened across misplaced notes with the scrawled label "Shultz's Views after Chernenko Funeral on Gorbachev." The rare notes I took read as follows:

> G. comfortable with self. Confident but not overbearing. Can decide things. Businesslike and bright. Sense of humor. Can be provoked but keeps control.

Apparently the new fifty-four-year-old leader gave a statement for three quarters of an hour, after which Shultz gave our pitch. Human rights brought up and he was provoked. Seemed in control without making a point of it.

The Secretary then reflected presciently:

> Gorbachev will be good at atmospherics. Not just an empty guy but full of content. Very different kind of person from others . . . Potential for very strong person. Effortlessly in charge. Acted like a man who had been running things for long while.

But confirmation of all this lay ahead. None of us, besides Shultz, had any experience with Gorbachev. And none of us on the U.S. delegation had any direct experience with summits then.

Indeed, the Geneva summit was most special because everything was so novel. Among our group, only the President seemed confident and surefooted, but then again he always did.

And, strangely, each summit develops an emphasis of its own from among the agenda items of the U.S.-Soviet relationship. At Reykjavik, it was arms control, arms control, and more arms control. Later at Moscow (May–June 1988), the President punctuated human rights. Here in Geneva, the President hammered on regional issues, especially Afghanistan.

In this, he especially excelled. And in this, he most disregarded the advice offered by his advisors. At Geneva, anyway, the two were related, as we can see throughout this tale of our initial summit.

· · ·

The first person to greet the President at the door of his Geneva chalet, after he had met Mikhail Gorbachev for the very first time, was the correspondent for *Playboy* magazine. Ron Reagan, Jr. had been milling around with us, waiting impatiently while the scheduled noontime arrival of his father came and passed. Dressed in a red balloonlike smock and khaki bell-bottom pants, he stood out from the rest of us, who wore dark pin-striped suits that day, November 19, 1985.

"What took you so long, Dad?" he asked as the President bounded into the regal hallway. "It's those interpreters," Reagan said with less surprise at seeing his son among our group than we felt at having him there. The translations that morning reminded the ex-actor of foreign films wherein someone on screen talks

endlessly while a one-sentence subtitle—like "That's fine"—
flashes on the bottom of the screen.

The President was even more buoyant than usual as he explained his delay. Don Regan soon shooed us all upstairs to the
Maison De Saussure for lunch. We were already running a half
hour late, he pointed out.

Once we gathered around the long oval table, the President
began talking about how Prime Minister Margaret Thatcher and
Queen Elizabeth II differed over America's actions in Grenada
three years back. What brought this subject to his mind just then
I cannot conceive now, even if I could then. It was interesting,
however. After the President elaborated at length to a group dying
of curiosity, though not about this, I piped up, "Well, what did
you think of Gorbachev, Mr. President?"

Reagan took a few bites of the scrumptious fish caught in Lake
Geneva and prepared by the White House chef—a dramatic pause
if ever there was one—and then recounted what had happened.

He began his first session alone with Gorbachev by being
quintessentially himself. Rather than regurgitate his State
Department–furnished "talking points," he was Reagan; he was
personal. The President opened by remarking how odd life can
be. There they were—he and Gorbachev—each of humble
origins, born in small towns in the middle of nowhere, now leaders of the two greatest powers on earth. There they were, sitting
next to each other, bearing so much responsibility!

Reagan excelled at such a human approach, which made him a
natural diplomat. He took the opposite tack from his advisors, or
from predecessors like Woodrow Wilson, who, as historian Walter Wyle wrote about him at the big summit at Versailles, "seems
to see the world in abstractions. To him railroad cars are not
railroad cars, but a gray, generalized thing called 'transportation.' "

Gorbachev obviously warmed to Reagan's warm touch and told
the President how they must try to overcome the big problems
facing the world and their relationship. Gorbachev, too, poured
on the charm, which worked well. He avoided the main contentious issue of SDI, which only Reagan mentioned that first morning. Gorbachev spoke of his desire for more trade and economic
cooperation—long hyped by them as the pathway to peace—and
then moved on to a topic sure to captivate Reagan's heart.

The United States and the Soviet Union could begin to improve their relationship through scientific cooperation on such things as, say, earthquake research. Gorbachev's scientists advised him to warn the President that California would have an earthquake within a few years. In fact, as the President recalled for us, the Russian experts gauged a two-thirds chance of an earthquake hitting 7.0 to 7.5 on the Richter scale, and a three-fourths chance of 6.0 to 6.5, within the next three years. (It has not happened yet.) Gorbachev offered to send Soviet scientists over to explain all this.

Gorbachev hit a button. Reagan is a man filled with certain set pieces—all politicians are, but Reagan much more so than most —and here was a doozy. The President repeated for us what he told Gorbachev, his routine on the 750-mile long San Andreas Fault in southern California. He reiterated its history, starting with A.D. 500 or so, what past earthquakes had done to California, and so on. He delivered this monologue, as he no doubt had perfected when Governor, with an actor's verve that made it seem fresh.

My colleagues proceeded to eat while I watched this captivating performance, quipping at one point how he should have told Gorbachev that he was not moving back to California, fortunately, within the next three years. I tried to estimate how much time was consumed by Reagan's delivery and the interpreter's translation of his San Andreas Fault gig while the world wondered what momentous issues the two most important people on earth were wrestling over during their initial encounter. With the *Playboy* correspondent first to greet the President, and most of the morning spent on this rather unexpected topic, I found the summit quite intriguing thus far.

Gorbachev used the sparse time left to get in some mild licks. He told how U.S. policy was driven by a military-industrial complex and directed by right-wing groups. He singled out a Heritage Foundation "summit briefing paper" and threw in some publication from the Hoover Institution—which pleased Secretary Shultz, who had been associated with Stanford University—but the President just shrugged that off.

Gorbachev had been good, that was clear to Reagan, and he liked him just fine. Yet I was skeptical, recalling Andrei Gromyko's words when "nominating" Gorbachev before the party faithful as General Secretary: "Comrades, this is a man with a nice smile but iron teeth." Everyone in that hall then related this description to the Russian fairy tales about a tyrant with a nice smile and iron teeth who gobbles up little children, as in the Hansel and Gretel story.

I warned how Gorbachev might show those "iron teeth" by becoming harsh later on. He could threaten to walk out of the summit or refuse to send his negotiators back to Geneva, or some such stunt. One or two others around the table made similar warnings.

The President listened, ate a bite, and said he knew exactly what he would do in that case. Another dramatic pause. "What's that?" someone asked.

Reagan pushed his chair back. "I'll ask him," he said, putting his hands on his hips and tilting his head slightly, "Mike, what about all those nice things you whispered to me this morning? You're not going to take them back, are you?" playing the role of the dashed lover to the hilt.

It was a wonderful moment. And an important moment. The President knew how to handle his personal relationship with Gorbachev, as he knew how to handle personal relationships with anyone.

We could not have suspected it then, but this was a pivotal summit, one which began the gradual yet momentous transformation of the Reagan administration. In Geneva then and there, the administration began to come full circle on key aspects of our relations with the Soviet Union.

Taking office fixed in the belief that Soviet leaders are inherently dangerous and expansionist, capable of lying, cheating, and stealing to achieve their nefarious objectives, as Reagan said during his first presidential press conference, he came to see Gorbachev as strikingly different. The President saw him as an appealing character; as the first Soviet leader to accede to real reductions in nuclear arms and the first not to be expansionist. Gorbachev played on this theme repeatedly during that summit; for instance, he told Reagan that he first learned of Soviet troops heading into Afghanistan over the radio (dubious at best, given his position on the Politburo even then).

But it worked. And it took hold—so much so that three years later, after the December 1988 Washington summit, the President said:

Possibly the fundamental change is that in the past, Soviet leaders have openly expressed their acceptance of the Marxian theory of the one-world communist state. . . . Their obligation was to expand and make the whole world [communist]. I no longer feel that way.

Taking office considering Soviet behavior the world's prime problem, Reagan came to consider nuclear weapons its main problem. The administration assumed office practically brandishing nuclear weapons; Secretaries Haig and Weinberger and NSC Advisor Dick Allen proclaimed nuclear weapons as the final arbitrator of geostrategic competiton with the Soviets, which was why the strategic account skyrocketed most in the early Reagan years. Haig spoke glibly of a nuclear "demonstration blast" above Europe; Reagan mused about confining any nuclear war to Europe; and Weinberger advocated that we "prevail" in any nuclear exchange. Such a nuclear-centered policy in Reagan's first term metamorphosed in his second into extreme antinuclear talk that resembled the nuclear bashers of SANE more than the nuclear planners of SAC.

Taking office distrustful of any decent dealings with the Soviet Union, the President came around to proposing an unparalleled, even mind-bending, degree of cooperation in moving to a world of fewer offensive weapons and greater defensive capabilities.

Taking office leading a *jihad* against technology transfers to the Soviets, the President came to offer the most massive technology transfer in history by sharing SDI.

And taking office believing that Western security rested on an arms buildup, President Reagan came to believe that it rested largely or significantly on arms control. With this transformation came the gradual change in top National Security Council advisors from the likes of Cap Weinberger, Bill Clark, Jeane Kirkpatrick, and Bill Casey to individuals like George Shultz, Frank Carlucci, Colin Powell, and Bill Webster.

GENEVA ISSUES

After the laughter around the Maison De Saussure table died down, the conversation turned heavier. The President was wondering again about the Soviet argument, which seemed sensible to him, that the French and British missiles be counted in the INF negotiations. After all, these were Western missiles, part of the blue arsenal. Wasn't the Soviet Union, the red team, justified in worrying about these forces? Especially since the Soviets are paranoid, having suffered so many invasions from the West?

The arms control mafia gathered around the luncheon table displayed our wares. We had to exclude British and French systems since the United States had no right to negotiate over their weapons. They could negotiate with Moscow if they wished (which they definitely did not). Besides, the U.K. and French missiles together constituted a tiny fraction of the Soviet nuclear arsenal, only 4 percent then, and a declining fraction, since a decade earlier that figure was 7 percent. But such points did not grab the President.

Again he mentioned Russian paranoia, so I used the opening for my favorite discourse. No political entity goes from being a small duchy around Moscow a few centuries ago to a massive empire spanning eleven time zones today—as the Soviet Union has—by constantly being invaded. Sure, Napoleon and Hitler marched to Moscow, and sure, the Soviets stress such invasions incessantly.

Nonetheless, Russia has been more often the perpetrator than the victim of invasions. Indeed, as Harvard professor and Russian scholar Richard Pipes has written, czarist military specialists in 1898 completed a history of Russian warfare; they concluded, with some pride, that in the thirty-eight wars it had waged since 1700, Russia had fought only two defensive campaigns. The other thirty-six were offensive.

Hence one reason why, even during czarist days, it fielded a military force far beyond what was needed for homeland defense. Russia's—and later the Soviet Union's—search for supreme security meant supreme *in*security for its neighbors. As former Chancellor Helmut Schmidt once quipped, Moscow's idea of a "secure border" is one with Russian soldiers on both sides of it.

That history lesson completed, I resorted to a quip, having by then learned that this, not evidence from czarist military specialists, was the way to reach Reagan. How could the Soviets *not* be paranoid, I said, smiling, since the USSR is the only nation in the world surrounded by hostile communist states? The President warmed to that. "No wonder they feel so nervous! With all those commies around them, who wouldn't feel bad?"

With that, the lunch ended.

Sessions like this constitute the joy of summits, and they were a joy to be part of. The grunt work comes earlier, when deciding what will make it into the President's briefing books. The contents of those big books is important; once something makes it in, it makes it as official U.S. policy. And the contents reveal the views of the permanent bureaucracy that staffs and shapes every administration.

I tried conscientiously to keep abreast of the flash paper flood that preceded this summit, or any summit. This time it was especially important as Reagan's first. So I waded through the material, albeit with a sneaking suspicion that the President was not, like me, scrutinizing every word. Yet I felt it a high calling to stop faulty or biased information from going in to the President. Having been in government for a decade by then, I had learned that, if nothing else, occupying high office allows one to stop bad things from going forward.

In this I mostly failed, but it mattered less than I initially suspected. Sitting in my brown rocking chair a night or two before leaving for Geneva, I waded through the reams of paper and made guttural noises when coming across particularly grating sentences.

The President was told that we then stood at an important juncture in U.S.-Soviet relations—how many State Department briefing papers told how many presidents the same thing before how many summits?—and after long years of "misunderstandings" had come opportunities. Maybe the President should seize the "opportunities" by proposing to Gorbachev that we draw up "new guidelines" for our negotiators. To say what? To do what? To lead to what? None of this was explained.

Instead I found bureaucratic words on process. The substance was confined to this: The President should tell Gorbachev how he must feel burdened by Soviet military expenditures and that he undoubtedly must wish to reduce such spending.

Even if this were true, why should Reagan say what he suspected Gorbachev to feel, instead of what he, Reagan, felt? Besides, what the briefing paper stated was not clearly true. While Soviet military spending would be crushing for us—approaching three times the percentage of our gross national product—it evidently has not seemed so to a whole line of Soviet leaders. The rubles they chose to spend on arms were probably, to them, their most productive expenditures. This money was seldom wasted—the Soviet defense complex is the most competently managed in that society—and obviously bought Soviet rulers real benefits. Superpower status, for starters. Without its hefty military, the USSR would be relegated to Third World status, known as a veritable failure in agriculture, technology, industry, and big exporter only of raw materials and its most culturally and artistically gifted citizens. Its military is the Soviets' strong suit. Why should they give up most of what they do best and what makes them what they want most to be—what every nation would like to be—a big-league player?

Besides, the implication here was that a U.S.-Soviet arms control agreement could enable Gorbachev to alleviate that heavy defense burden. But this is almost assuredly false. Arms control has never saved money and showed scant prospect of doing so. Gorbachev likely knows this, even if Reagan was told otherwise.

But the State Department briefing materials on human rights were worse. What a president should say here could not be simpler: Freedom is what America is all about. Our people want liberty for all people—for Russians, Czechs, Poles, Afghans, whomever. Full stop.

What the President was told to say here was something different and something convoluted: This human rights business was hurting prospects for "the relationship"—some separate entity suspended out yonder—to improve. Reagan should tell how the "atmospherics of the relationship" would get better if we could only point to results on human rights. That would make it easier for us to move forward in other areas. Abstract words and an apologetic tone, made worse by further advising the President to highlight the concerns of the Congress and Jewish groups, rather than his own or those of the whole country.

My reading became more painful with each new page. The section on "regional issues"—the euphemism for Soviet or Soviet-sponsored aggression in Afghanistan, Nicaragua, Angola, Cambodia, Ethiopia, and so forth—began incongruously. The President was to impress Gorbachev with his scrupulous reading of the Soviet constitution (a document Gorbachev probably never read and which, regardless, is regularly disregarded by Soviet leaders). "I understand your constitution calls for you to support national liberation movements," he was told to begin, then to add that we should nevertheless find political, not military, solutions to these problems. More antiseptic language; more of an apologetic tone. All too typical of the State Department style; all different from what President Reagan believed and what he eventually said.

But I didn't know this then. I did know that this material was heading into the President on the eve of his first summit. That was distressing. I put down the big black notebook in disgust, feeling depressed at how some things never changed, even in a conservative administration. Secretary Shultz had signed the briefing book's cover memo to the President; either he'd read it and agreed or had neglected to read it at all. Neither was a tribute.

For some reason, I then turned to the back of the book, that section containing the First Lady's schedule and "talking points." These were to prove even more memorable.

During her first coffee with Raisa (whom she would grow to dislike intensely), our First Lady was instructed to recall her September 1984 encounter with then Foreign Minister Gromyko when he'd urged her to whisper, "Peace. Peace. Peace," in her husband's ear each night. Nancy had not come up with a witty reply when Gromyko said that, but she could try one now, a delayed instance of what the French call *pensée d'escalier*. Gromyko need not worry, the briefing papers guided her to say, since her husband had lived through two world wars (she needn't mention that he was very young during the first and spent the second in Hollywood making wartime movies), so he knew firsthand the importance of "Peace. Peace. Peace."

Having thus responded to Gromyko, the First Lady could turn to terrorism and tell Raisa how it was a scourge against civilization and so forth. The briefing paper did not tell her, since she need not mention it, that the Soviets funded terrorist groups or that its bloc nations trained and armed terrorists. Her approach was to be distinctly positive—"We all have an interest in combatting terrorism"—even personal—"as you know, my husband was shot and almost killed."

The First Lady then had to do a reversal; of course "his assailant was not a terrorist," but a deranged and lovesick individual. No matter. "Americans must live with the problem daily," which, though dramatic, was not evident. "Your country has also been victimized by terrorism," she was guided to add. This flash of "talking points" substance might have surprised Raisa, who might not have known that the United States has been remarkably free of terrorism but surely would know that the Soviet Union had been.

All of this seemed to me ludicrous though harmless. Ladies' chatter, as imagined by some callow Foreign Service officer.

Of more import were the words for the First Lady's first conversation with the First Adversary himself. Over dinner the first night, she would be seated next to Gorbachev. She could break the ice by talking about, what else? "Our experts describe you as an activist. . . . Your predecessors started their careers in the 1930s. You are a man of the postwar era. How do you see yourself?"

Once that est-like opening played out, Nancy could get to the heavy part. "Americans have always liked the Soviet people. I remember how we admired your courage during the Second World War," she was to say, skirting how the war began with the Nazi-Soviet Pact or ended with Yalta.

Then came the zinger of the First Lady's "talking points" for this evening, or any evening:

> Our peoples have some basic things in common. We were shaped by our open Western frontier of opportunity. The great expanse of California—the symbol of the golden American dream—is my home. Russians had the great free spaces of Siberia. Our people think and dream on a grand scale.

Good briefing papers not only remind a First Lady where her home is, but also lead one to say the darnedest things. I had visions of Gorbachev later assembling some of his buddies (if a Soviet General Secretary has buddies) for a nightcap to tell them how "you fellows should have heard what Nancy gibbered about tonight, comparing California with Siberia as great open frontiers of opportunity!" They wouldn't have believed him.

THE REGIONAL INITIATIVE

Presummit meetings proceeded somewhat better than the presummit papers. One of my proudest moments occurred during such a meeting in the Situation Room, held two days before the President's address to the UN General Assembly in September.

NSC staffer Don Fortier, a most promising individual who was to become John Poindexter's deputy before being stricken down by cancer, had devised a "regional initiative." It was a stroke of genius and shows what one person in government with initiative and creativity can pull off. The initiative highlighted Soviet aggression in the five biggies—Afghanistan, Nicaragua, Ethiopia, Angola, and Cambodia—and helped move public focus from where the Soviets wanted it, riveted on arms control.

The scheme itself was no great shakes: the warring factions would negotiate among themselves, the United States and Soviet Union supporting such talks and trying to keep out foreign military aid, and an international effort would then help the healed country economically. The prospect of warring factions settling their disputes with the communist regimes seemed less likely than Abraham Lincoln settling our Civil War differences with Jefferson Davis, before some "world body" gave the reunited nation money. But no matter. The point was to change the subject and not to settle then-unsettleable disputes.

While we sat in the Situation Room discussing all this, the silver coffee urn with a lively Presto flame popped loudly in the corner. Hearing the sharp cracking sounds made everyone in the room even more jumpy than normal. It was so shattering to the nerves (to say nothing of being disruptive to the discussion) that during such sessions I rose from my chair, walked over, and snuffed the darned thing out. The coffee got cold, but at least we were spared the thought that the President was being shot.

Amid the *pop! pop! pop!* Secretary Shultz summarized the summit preparations. He was justifiably proud of having established a four-part agenda—regional issues, human rights, arms control, and bilateral issues—though nothing much was happening then on any of them.

As always in such conversations—no matter what the administration or the times—the conversation soon turned to arms control. It seemed the most promising area for progress, just as it always seems, and the most important to preserving humanity.

Then, as often over the years, I made a pitch to avoid making arms control the fulcrum of U.S.-Soviet relations. "Your Secretary of Housing may tell you, Mr. President, that housing is the most important issue in the world. The Transportation Secretary likewise on transportation, and so on. But I can tell you arms control is *not* the key issue between the United States and the USSR."

No arms control deal can prevent nuclear devastation, reduce the risk of war much if at all, save money, or increase U.S. security, again much if at all. U.S.-Soviet arms control could easily hurt but cannot easily help the nation; it is something to view more often with trepidation than anticipation. The opportunities for a bad bilateral agreement seem infinite, those for a good agreement quite limited. So we, the President and all of us, had to resist the relentless push to have arms control overpower issues that bear more directly on war and peace.

The Soviets push arms control hard in public, even though their Founding Father despised the subject. Lenin deemed disarmament nothing more than a squishy bourgeois sentiment. "Advocacy of 'disarmament' is the most vulgar opportunism; it is bourgeois pacifism. . . . Arming the proletariat in order to defeat, expropriate, and disarm the bourgeois [is] the only possible tactic of the revolutionary class."

Despite personal disgust, Lenin knew to use disarmament to confuse and divide the enemy. Soon after the revolution. Lenin hand-wrote his Commissar of Foreign Affairs, G. V. Chicherin, to accept his government's first invitation to an international meeting, a disarmament conference at Genoa. Lenin instructed Chicherin to unveil a "comprehensive pacifist program," which the old-fashioned communist intellectual resisted. Pacifism, Chicherin wrote Lenin, and reflecting Lenin's true sentiment, was a "petty-bourgeois illusion." Lenin wrote back:

> Comrade Chicherin: You are nervous. . . . You and I have fought pacifism as a program of the revolutionary proletarian party. This is clear. But who, where, when, has ever denied this party [the right to] utilize the pacifists for the purpose of disintegrating the enemy, the bourgeoisie?

Since Lenin, the Soviets have often used arms control for this purpose. They score easy propaganda points by initiating proposals which portray them as a peace-loving country. Announcing a new arms control proposal—no matter how visionary, no matter how impractical or unprepared, no matter that nothing comes of it—puts Moscow in a favorable light. One arms control press release can remove some stigma of Soviet marauding in myriad parts of the world.

Pushing arms control plays into their singular strength, military might. Pushing arms control also pushes moral equivalence; it makes them equal to us morally. And arms control accents nuclear weapons and thereby puts the USSR and the United States apart from all other nations. Finally, pushing arms control pressures us to make concessions (in scrapping various weapons systems or stopping SDI); in other realms, such as regional disputes and human rights, no one expects us to make concessions.

This I said or summarized that day, as I did many times in many ways over the Reagan years. Heads would nod; listeners would wonder why it needed repeating; and then the conversation would turn to how we might take a new initiative in arms control.

This occasion was no different. Soon after my piece was presented and seconded, Secretary Shultz proposed that the President insert into his UN speech some new squiggle on arms control. When reminded that the speech would feature Fortier's regional initiative, he recommended keeping that and merely adding in a new arms control bit. What it would say or do was neither mentioned nor asked. Some new move, though, would help set the summit stage.

Each meeting develops a certain rhythm and at times takes a tricky bounce. This one did. The President was taken by Shultz's position. It would jazz up his speech. Ed Meese agreed and swung into his standard operating mode, developed over twenty years at Reagan's side, of crafting some nice phrases for Reagan speeches. We could "plant some seeds to be nurtured" in future arms control, he mused, or some such.

With the posse galloping off in this direction—people flipping through the draft text to find the right spot to insert some still undefined new notion—I spoke up. This would be a big mistake. It would reinforce the summit focus on arms control. Whether the first Reagan-Gorbachev meeting was a success or failure would then depend upon how much of SDI we would concede to make progress. Are we going to allow an "SDI summit" even though they would never allow a "Sakharov summit" or an "Afghanistan summit"? I asked.

The President stopped shuffling through the speech, sat back, and, in a rare instance, reversed himself. I had a point; this arms control business had become too prominent. Anything new in arms control would only steal the focus from the regional initiative. So let's not do that.

I felt wonderful. But in government, the funny bounces continue. Even after the President's decision that meeting, we did devise a new arms control initiative for the Geneva summit (though not for the UN speech). It came not from the State Department, but, of all people, from Bill Casey and me.

NSC Advisor Bud McFarlane had been racking his brain for some way to propose making SDI a matter of cooperation rather than antagonism with the Soviets. It was not easy to do, but Bud was thinking along the right lines.

Bud knew his President, who had been unstoppable ever since the 1984 debate with Walter Mondale when he'd popped the notion of sharing SDI with the Soviets. No one else liked this idea, but Bud knew that in government, as in politics, you cannot beat something with nothing. So he was looking for a way to make lemonade out of a lemon.

Wasn't there something Reagan could offer Gorbachev here? Something to pour into our hitherto empty talk about a "cooperative transition" to greater defenses and fewer offensive missiles? Something less preposterous than wholesale "sharing SDI"? Something less harmful?

Bill Casey had been thinking along the same lines after hearing the President harp on this idea. Casey thought of the President building on Dwight Eisenhower's "open skies" proposal made thirty years before and presented at the UN General Assembly. Maybe Reagan could propose "open labs" for SDI research.

After Casey made his pitch, I asked in the Situation Room meeting if he would *really* want Russians running around his top-secret facilities and those of the most sensitive, high-tech laboratories in the United States. Not really. So why not make the idea reciprocal? I suggested. "Our labs would be open to them if theirs were open to us." Casey grinned, no doubt realizing he could thereby have the sizzle but remove the steak.

The birth of a proposal. Open labs it would be, but only on a reciprocal basis. And we would take the "first step for peace" by offering to have SDI Director General James Abrahamson brief the Soviet arms delegation in Geneva. This was later done with some fanfare, though with little import. The Soviet delegation sat through the same slide show routinely given on Capitol Hill and in Veterans of Foreign Wars halls around the country—a briefing some Soviet officials had seen loads of times and were no doubt bored by seeing again.

As things happen, we spent less time developing the open labs idea then than Reagan and Gorbachev spent arguing about it later on. They each weaved open labs throughout their ongoing dispute over SDI, the President failing to understand why Gorbachev would not want to start these reciprocal visits pronto and Gorbachev incredulous that the President would ever share the least bit of SDI.

Usually the arms controllers would staff out proposals over months and take hours of top-level time on ideas that would go nowhere. In this case, Casey and I spent a couple of minutes on a proposal that then consumed a hefty chunk of prime summit time.

REAGAN FEELING FINE

All the preparations behind us, we headed for Geneva. Anticipation ran high, as did fears—especially on the summit's eve.

The President did not look well that Sunday in Geneva and apparently did not feel well. He said he had not slept well. He seemed dead tired that day. His eyes took on a glazed look, and during a briefing on missile facts and figures, his whole body seemed to wilt. His warning for us not to forget that here was the enemy and to hang tough seemed more forced than genuine.

But after the Reagan-Gorbachev bonding over the San Andreas Fault, the summit mood was set. One could then relax a bit and watch Gorbachev and Reagan at their best, which was very good indeed.

Gorbachev was a born charmer. He began by telling the President how he agreed that defense was better than offense "on the human level," which was why SDI captivated Reagan's imagination. Yet reason had to prevail.

Gorbachev was a born boxer, too. He started swinging by saying that, as a political leader, he could not agree to SDI. A defensive system like that would lead to a new spiral of the arms race, would bankrupt both societies, and so on. He delivered the points repeated endlessly in *Pravda*, but they seemed more pungent coming from The Man himself.

The Soviets, he warned, could and would counter SDI with more offensive weapons. SDI might work against a weakened retaliatory force, for a second strike, but would fail against a full first strike. Hence, he explained, SDI showed that the United States sought strategic superiority and a first strike capability. Besides, Gorbachev said, the President must be influenced by the knowledge that SDI would pour $600 million to $1 trillion of new money into the military-industrial complex.

So if the right decisions were not taken in the next year to eighteen months, the consequences would be grave. In summary, Gorbachev said that the President wanted to catch a "firebird" with this program.

When Reagan replied with his points, those from his head (or heart) rather than his State Department briefing memos, Gorbachev hit back quickly and aggressively. In this, he resembled the best of courtroom lawyers. I wondered how a onetime party hack who had carefully climbed his way to the top of a rigid society not known for its use of adversary proceedings could have mastered debating techniques so well. Imagine how adept he would have been had he honed those skills in an open society, where in law or politics or business debate is the norm.

Not that Gorbachev was (or is) technically masterful. The nits and nats of arms control or much else, for that matter, are hardly Reagan's strong suit; yet they are hardly Gorbachev's, either. Someone like Gromyko or Karpov or Akhromeyev could muster arms control arguments, but Gorbachev stayed on the grand plane. He knew enough to rebut Reagan's points, just as Reagan knew enough to rebut his points. Both remained on such a high level of abstraction that it was hard to relate their dialogue to actual arms negotiations.

Later that same summit, Gorbachev tried pleading once again. He said he understood that Reagan was committed to test, develop, and deploy space weapons. Still, he hoped that this face-to-face meeting would change the President's mind. Some people had said that the United States would lose face if it were to agree to ban SDI, Gorbachev continued, but "believe me, Mr. President, you would not." Reagan refused and argued some more until Gorbachev, piqued once again, claimed that the President was not showing him any respect. SDI would torpedo the whole arms control effort, he said, so we needed to "close, lock, bolt, and lock again" space weapons.

Gorbachev, like Reagan, is a people person. As longtime House Speaker Sam Rayburn once said about politicians, "A man who can't size up another person when he walks in the room had better be in another profession." Gorbachev could size up another person, especially this person. Using a nice blend of hostility, humor, and flattery, he would hold his substantive positions while winning Reagan emotionally. Best of all, he mentioned how much he enjoyed watching one of Reagan's movies. This triggered a Reagan set piece about how and when he had made that film, the mishaps surrounding it, the reviews following it, all the standard Hollywood talk Reagan adored repeating and Gorbachev, the Communist party *apparatchik*, no doubt enjoyed hearing. Gorbachev brought Reagan back to the world he adored, the world before the presidency, the world he felt comfortable in.

And he joked with the President. During their first dinner together—the one where Nancy was supposed to grease the way by comparing California with Siberia—Gorbachev told how the President's hopes to improve the U.S.-Soviet relationship reminded him of a cartoon. It pictured the President on one mountaintop and Gorbachev on another peak with a deep valley between them. Reagan, with his arm outstretched, said, "Let's be friends. You take the first step!"

Next day he told the President about a caller to a talk-radio show in the Ukraine who posed a riddle: "What's an infallible solution to an unsolvable problem?" The radio announcer replied, "I'm sorry, but we don't discuss Soviet agriculture on the air!" That joke becomes better when known that it was told by a man who took over the agriculture portfolio for the Central Committee in 1978, when the Soviet grain harvest yielded 230 million tons, and gave it up in 1981, when it hit a calamitous 155 million tons.

Reagan loved the humor, as he loved the whole affair. He ignored the advice of Soviet experts like George Kennan, who once wrote, "Don't act chummy with them. This only embarrasses them individually, and deepens their suspicions. Russian officials abhor the thought of appearing before their own people as one who has become buddies with a foreigner. This is not their idea of good relations."

But then again, Gorbachev ignored this, too. He relished the chumminess, not only with the President, but with the whole U.S. delegation. Only hours after Bud McFarlane mentioned during dinner how he loved chocolates, a beautiful box of Godiva's finest was delivered to his room in Geneva, compliments of the Gorbachevs.

The new General Secretary brought something to the Soviet leadership it had lacked since Nikita Khrushchev, namely personality. Although this would not have mattered to a President like Richard Nixon or Jimmy Carter, it made all the difference in the world to Ronald Reagan.

I was not sure then that these "good vibes" were all to the good. I kind of liked the old-fogy Soviet leaders, those averse to risk-taking at home and therefore abroad. Those without pizzazz or the energy to do much made me feel safer.

Indeed, Konstantin Chernenko struck me at the time as an ideal Soviet leader, a stodgy Party man from beginning to long after he became a comatose General Secretary. Unable to walk in a room by himself, incapable of reading a prepared text without inverting pages and wheezing so badly that no one could understand the words anyway, too infirm to greet visiting dignitaries with more than a programmed nod, Chernenko personified Soviet stagnation. Someone unkindly joked that each morning his staff held a mirror to his nose to see evidence of moisture. In essence, Chernenko could not conceive, let alone initiate, a bold Soviet move anywhere in the world. I slept better at night knowing Chernenko breathed and "ruled" the massive Soviet empire.

Ironically, it was during the reign of this quasi-mannequin that the Russians veered onto a new path for U.S.-Soviet relations. It was when Chernenko was on top, in June 1984, that Moscow offered to open arms talks on space. That same fall Gromyko visited the Oval Office for the meeting with the President, thereby undercutting Walter Mondale's campaign charge that Reagan couldn't deal with the Russians. In November Moscow suggested reopening the talks, with even a separate INF forum. In January 1985 the Shultz-Gromyko talks reopened the arms negotiations; and in March 1985 Moscow sent a new negotiating team to Geneva. All this, which we now associate with Gorbachev's foreign policy, happened before he became number one, when Chernenko was yet General Secretary.

But Gorbachev was Reagan's kind of guy, and the President loved it all. Here in the opening moments of the summit show, the press riveted on him, Reagan took charge. Without a topcoat, he looked like a million dollars on the steps of Villa Fleu d'Eau greeting Gorbachev (actually twenty years younger), who looked much older in his heavy overcoat, scarf, and gray fedora. Then the jaunty Reagan guided the General Secretary gently up the stairs as if welcoming him into his home. It was everything Reagan did best, everything Reagan could ask for.

With a personable Russian, Reagan made the occasion even more personal by staking out a summer house on the shores of Lake Leman and staging their private chats in front of the roaring fireplace there. An ideal photo op—for two men who take to photo ops—highlighted by Larry Speakes's brilliant stroke of dubbing this the "fireside summit."

Unfortunately, the ladies did not hit it off as well as the men.

Nancy Reagan and Raisa Gorbachev first began their spat while their husbands indulged in their personal lovefest. Each woman is tough, both are used to being center stage, each likes to talk a lot, and, worst of all for Nancy, Raisa is far more substantive and knowledgeable. She surely adds to Gorbachev's appeal, as someone who appears like a stylish Western woman. And, as has been quipped, she is the first Soviet First Lady who weighs less than her husband.

While flashy in the West, Raisa knows her place in the East. She may be on Mikhail's arm strutting down the airplane steps when arriving in Europe or America, but she departs from the rear door of the Aeroflot plane relatively unnoticed when they arrive back in Moscow. Only Mikhail pumps hands and smiles cheerfully through a Soviet receiving line.

Not everything during that summit was for show, as was almost the case in the Washington summit a year later. After our lunch the President and Gorbachev met again, this time turning their conversation to regional issues. Again the bulging briefing books were pushed aside, mentally as well as physically (if they had ever been present mentally to Reagan). The President put on a splendid performance. The UN initiative, which had done little to shift public attention away from arms control, surely succeeded in capturing the President's personal focus. The centerpiece of "regional issues" moved from the Middle East, where the superpowers most readily tangle, to areas of the world where communist regimes seized and hold power by force.

The President was best where he should have been best, on Afghanistan. He became worked up over that issue the way he became worked up over anything, through direct contact. Afghan freedom fighters ushered into the Oval Office regularly had an effect, but more powerful was Reagan's searing experience with Afghan children. He told us one time in the Cabinet Room how the Soviet helicopters dropped pens and other attractive things that detonated when the Afghan children tried to play with them. Seeing small Afghan children with their limbs missing got to him.

So when Gorbachev scoffed at Afghanistan, saying he had first learned about it over the radio, the President laid into him. Shaking his head slowly, speaking softly in that golden raspy voice, Reagan let loose with words he had uttered in DAR halls, Young Americans for Freedom meetings, and American Legion conventions over the years.

There you are, he began, practicing, well, genocide in Afghanistan. It's a poor country; nonaligned, Third World. It's not any
threat to you. And the poor oppressed people in Nicaragua, Angola, and the other places—the Fortier litany came out here—the
communists in power are fighting national groups that just want
freedom. Why do you have to act like this? What makes the
Soviet Union an aggressive country? Are you still trying to take
over the world?

The sound was so kindly, the words so biting, that Gorbachev
must have been jarred by the disparity. He heard nice sounds at
first and then received the Russian translation of the most direct
or even harsh indictment of Soviet behavior ever delivered to the
top Soviet man. The only person present more flabbergasted than
Gorbachev must have been the State Department note-taker.

To his credit, Secretary Shultz never tried to tame Reagan at
such times. Even when the President was not present, as during
a Moscow Foreign Ministers meeting a few years later, Shultz
was tough when Gorbachev was ornery. The Secretary let him
have it on the KAL 007 airline shootdown, Afghanistan, regional
issues, and especially human rights. On these subjects Shultz
could be as direct and forceful as Reagan.

Briefing us after this regional discussion—or mugging, as it
happened at the Geneva summit—Shultz told us that he detected
a slight change in the way Gorbachev talked about Afghanistan.
He mused that they may be reevaluating their stance there. No
one else had picked this up, so he let it pass and we all dismissed
it. Within two years, though, it was clear the Russians *had* reconsidered their Afghan debacle and wanted out. Whether they had
decided by then, or were deciding then, and Shultz's ear was keen
enough to pick that up, or whether his observation was mere
coincidence, will remain a mystery, at least until the Kremlin
opens its archives. But in retrospect, it was remarkable that
Shultz made this comment.

Dinner that night was a cozy affair, with just a dozen or so
present. Maybe Nancy asked Gorbachev how he saw himself and
whether he saw Siberia as she saw California (her home). In any
case, Gorbachev interested Reagan by quoting the Bible during
his toast. He must have been in a religious mood that night, since
he mentioned meeting Russian scientists who wanted him and
the President to stay in Geneva until they had resolved the
world's problems, right up to Christmas if need be.

One dinner guest told me afterward of his disappointment with all the stories, jokes, and amiable chatter. None of them wanted to talk about the serious business at hand, he said.

Why such an experienced American diplomat was so disillusioned by this startled me. Rarely on such occasions do top officials choose to grapple with the most pressing issues. Contrary to public perceptions, high officials are reluctant to engage in too much serious discussion; they know that most of the real, pressing issues cannot be settled by talk. A former Ambassador to Germany once told me that *never* during all his years at that post had the President and the Chancellor held even one decision-making meeting. Each "brought up" issues their staffs shoved before them, responded as prescribed, and then indicated that the Foreign Minister and Secretary of State should recommend something to them. The two heads of government would discuss what their spokesmen would say to the press afterward and mostly share stories and experiences with one another. Even when leaders must grapple with big issues, the outcome may be unfavorable, as at Versailles or Yalta, or the matter may remain unresolved. Some things simply won't resolve.

Diplomacy is often relegated as last resort to solve major problems. Marcus Aurelius once told of a ruler who wanted to eliminate his opponent. "Can we poison him?" he asked. "No, his guards are too adept." "Can we defeat him?" "No, his army is too strong." "Well, then let's try diplomacy."

Diplomacy is usually powerless itself to settle big conflicts, an impression reinforced by a quick look at recent summits. The 1955 Khrushchev-Eisenhower summit rendered the "spirit of Geneva," which faded even before Soviet tanks stormed into Hungary the following year. The 1961 Khrushchev-Kennedy summit, itself a near disaster, came the year before the Cuban missile crisis. The 1967 Johnson-Kosygin summit at Glassboro, though eminently forgettable, was followed a year later by the Soviets' invasion of Czechoslovakia. And the 1979 summertime Carter-Brezhnev summit came only months before 110,000 Soviet troops poured into Afghanistan.

Not that summits provoke Soviet invasions—that is clearly farfetched—but neither do they prevent them. Summits may not contribute to global instability, but, contrary to popular belief, they don't contribute much to global stability. Rather, they leave problem areas pretty much unchanged.

The Geneva summit was no different. Following their morning

session the second day, Reagan returned for a jocular lunch at the Maison. After he ducked into the washroom, he bounded to his place at the oval table. There he stood for a moment, looking naughtily around until others started realizing something was amiss. The President stood with one sleeve of his suit coat hanging down without an arm in it. When everyone spotted this, he looked aghast at the empty sleeve, felt it up and down with the hand of his other arm, and exclaimed in shock, "My God, where did it go? It was here this morning!"

The President was doing well and feeling well, and, with him, the two were always related. At one point during those two summit days, I took Don Regan aside to congratulate him for getting the President in the right mood and especially for keeping his head straight.

There were more meetings that second afternon and more spats over SDI. This was only natural as Reagan and Gorbachev came at this issue from opposite poles. Reagan considered SDI "the answer" to nuclear blackmail which inflicts the world, while Gorbachev deemed it a new blight on mankind. When the President touted our "open labs" proposal as someday leading to total sharing of SDI, Gorbachev gagged. He couldn't believe any President would share such high technology with the Soviet Union, as he told Reagan. Anyway, he didn't need American help on SDI. He just wanted America to stop developing SDI, that was all. However engaging the conversation was, productive it was not.

The President eventually realized that they were merely going around the circle again. So during one coffee break, he proposed that they again stroll down the hill to that small summerhouse with the roaring fireplace. Remembering his previous walk there in freezing weather without an overcoat, Gorbachev replied cleverly, "Mr. President, if you want to take a walk down there again in this freezing weather, go right ahead. If you'd like to speak to me alone, then let's go next door. It's warmer." They went next door.

RETURN TO HUMAN RIGHTS

Unlike his approach on nearly everything else during that summit, Ronald Reagan followed the script on human rights. As a result, he was less forceful and less successful.

It was odd for a man who so clearly considered America a

"shining city on the hill," the beacon of freedom in the dark world of oppression, to pull punches on such a straight attack. Odd for a man who knew and felt deeply about the glories of freedom to use diplomat-speak when discussing them. His tone was not what one would expect from a man who later, at Moscow State University, stood under a huge marble bust of Lenin and in front of a mural commemorating the Russian Revolution, sermonizing on the glories of liberty.

When in the communist capital of the world, Reagan roared about freedom. When in the capitalist capital of Geneva, Switzerland, Reagan tiptoed around the topic.

Reagan was not being Reagan; he was being messenger. Shortly before his first summit, Richard Nixon had convinced him that the only way to help Soviet dissidents was through "quiet diplomacy." He should take Gorbachev aside, tell what a problem this thing was back home, and hope for the best. To go public, to raise this issue with the press, would only embarrass the Soviets and look like we were trying to take credit. This would hurt the refuseniks and dissidents, the last thing a sensitive fellow like Reagan would ever wish to do. Better to be a workhorse than a showhorse here.

So he followed Nixon in tone and technique. So he mouthed the briefing material—all this stuff about hurting "the relationship" if human rights weren't improved, and so on. This was the President's worst hour in Geneva; it was to become his best in Moscow.

The President did that routine on Wednesday, the second day, before an evening reception at a Swiss château hosted by the Swiss government. We aides piled into our assigned cars at the Inter-Continental Hotel and drove onto the château grounds near the lake. Even then I was struck by the relative lack of security; Swiss guards waved us through in our specially marked cars after a cursory glance through the windshield. No individual checks and no metal detectors were used for a fairly small affair that included the leaders of the Soviet Union and the United States. Armies of newsmen and camera crews positioned themselves across the entrance.

The two delegations mingled until their leaders appeared; then all eyes fixed on them, the Americans generally gawking at Gorbachev, the Russians at Reagan.

Before they came, though, White House Communications Director Pat Buchanan and I had a glorious time with the Russian arms control squad. Pat started the fun by asking Velikhov, the Soviet two-timer who manages *their* SDI program and castigates *our* SDI program on the U.S. lecture circuit, "Why do you fellows object to SDI so much?"

"Because it wouldn't work," he replied. Well, we continued, what's your problem with that? If we ever knew of a Soviet military program that wouldn't work, we'd support it. In fact, it would be our favorite Soviet program. Do you *really* mind our wasting defense funds?

"SDI would start a new round of the 'arms race,'" they countered. What "arms race"? There hadn't been any "arms race" in recent times; in the 1970s, you fellows increased your defense spending by 3 or 4 percent each year while we reduced ours steadily nearly each year. And how can our SDI trigger a new "arms race" when you have not only researched, but also built part of such a system around Moscow? You have been spending some fifteen times more on strategic defense than the United States since signing the ABM Treaty in 1972. Who has followed who, even if there were an "arms race"?

"As our leader, Mikhail Gorbachev, told President Reagan, SDI is really an offensive system. It could wipe out Soviet facilities, even cities." So SDI *will* work—we pointed out politely—if it would be able to do such nefarious things. But it won't. Velikhov, as a scientist, surely knew that the devices we were exploring in SDI could not pass through the atmosphere; they work only when traveling in resistance-free space. Hence they will not be able to strike targets on the ground, or Soviet cities.

And if SDI really was an offensive system, meant to wipe out Soviet cities, why were you blaming us for violating the ABM Treaty? we asked. That treaty deals only with *defensive* systems; it does not restrict offensive weapons at all. Finally—Buchanan and I drilled them, having warmed to the combat by then (it didn't take long)—why would we build SDI for offensive use? If we wanted more offensive power, SDI would be a waste. Nothing could be more devastating, accurate, or reliable an offensive weapon than a ballistic missile, and we already have loads of those. So why dole out more cash for new offensive weapons that wouldn't work as well as the ones we have?

No, Pat and I concluded while looking interested, you fellows have to have better grounds for opposing SDI. What are they?

The Soviet team was becoming quite defensive by then. "We don't like SDI since it would force our scientists to devise countermeasures, which they can do." So again SDI *would* work, at least before your guys built countermeasures. Supposing these countermeasures didn't work. A lot of your technology doesn't work, you know.

The Soviets were becoming more confused and aggravated. Velikhov then quoted Gorbachev, who, at length, earlier that day, had warned Reagan that if we built SDI, they would build one cheaper and better to boot.

"Why would you do that?" we asked. "If SDI wouldn't work, would trigger a new 'arms race,' be offensive, costs loads of rubles, and be easily countered, you'd still build one? Why?"

No matter, we told the Soviets, who were stumbling around by then. Forget the contradictions and welcome aboard. We are now doing what you have been doing for years—researching how to protect our people. If you do more of this research, that's fine. It's better for both of us to pour money into protecting our own people than into obliterating each other.

Velikhov and his crew were rescued at this moment of ultimate reconciliation by the arrival of the Reagans and Gorbachevs. So we stopped the tag-team match and began to mill around, mostly watching every move the First Couples made.

While Reagan and Gorbachev chatted briefly, I spotted a U.S. naval officer with his wrist chained to the renowned "football," the briefcase that contains codes for the release of nuclear weapons. Standing a few feet from him was a stout and solemn Red Army officer who likewise clutched a briefcase and stared steadily at Gorbachev. It flashed through my mind how the two officers had better not mix up their briefcases or who-knew-what would happen in a crisis.

I wondered if they would meet, or at least greet one another. Acknowledge the other's presence. But they did not.

Still, they carried the most important packages in the world, packages that could decide the fate of the world. For how nuclear weapons would ever be used—if God forbid, it ever came to that —is far more critical than how many of them exist. What is contained in those briefcases counts far more than anything conceivably contained in an arms treaty.

The strategic justification for arms control—not the political or economic justifications, which are easier to dispel—hinges on whether an agreement would help prevent a crisis from escalating. This it could achieve by forcing the United States or the USSR to reduce and redirect their strategic forces away from a hair-trigger deployment.

Either side can, of course, reduce or redesign its forces without arms control. Regardless, even at lower levels with safer nuclear weapons—those less vulnerable to attack—they can be used responsibly or irresponsibly in a crisis. Herein lies the Achilles' heel of strategic affairs.

Despite all the time and attention top officials heap upon arms control, they all but ignore strategic crisis management. New presidents are routinely given elaborate Air Force briefings, so technical and stilted as to be nigh unto incomprehensible. They and top presidential assistants may practice a drill once or twice but soon turn to other issues and fear a press leak if they rehearse more.

The ignorance of those who must be prepared for such a moment—for no matter how unlikely, the future of humanity may well depend upon it—became clear the day President Reagan was shot in March 1981. At that tense moment, Secretary of Defense Cap Weinberger told his new colleagues that he had already changed the status of our strategic forces. What for? How? Weinberger didn't seem sure whether the new status was a higher level of alert. No one was sure how we were expected to follow through on the change or how Moscow was likely to react. The only thing clear that came out of this murky episode was that the top Reagan officials did not have the foggiest notion of what to do with the U.S. strategic arsenal in a crisis.

Yet there will be real crises, as there have been. Not only postwar crises such as those over the Berlin airlift, missiles in Cuba, the Yom Kippur war, and so forth. There are also false-alarm crises, in which a president might need to make some weighty decisions fast and in the midst of utter confusion.

In November 1979, this type of situation seemed to be coming. Apparently a low-level military officer in the North American Command post in Cheyenne Mountain (NORAD) wished to play a computer war game using a World War III scenario. He did not know (or remember) that any time the main computer was blocked, the backup system would automatically come on line. The fellow stopped the main computer from sending messages to other U.S. military commands around the world—as he should have—but he did not think to cut off the possibility of such outside transmissions from the backup system.

It happened. The main computer playing the World War III scenario became blocked. This threw the information onto the backup system, which instantly fed it to commands around the globe. SAC officers dashed for their strategic bombers—the boys "kissed Mom good-bye," according to a commanding officer I spoke with later—revved up their engines, and proceeded to begin executing their wartime plans. While this was happening around the world, the people in NORAD figured out what went wrong and contacted other commands. Still, it took more than ten minutes to stand down the operation.

That same year, a computer malfunctioned somewhere in the strategic warning system. Instead of sending out a series of zeros on incoming ballistic missiles or warheads, it sent out a series of twos. National Security Advisor Zbigniew Brzezinski was notified in the middle of the night that 222 weapons were heading toward CONUS, the continental United States. A moment or so later he was told 2,222 were on their way. When word came of 22,222, he knew it was a malfunction rather than a nuclear alert.

The experts reassure me that such kinks are now out of the system, but something can always go wrong. A president and his advisors can, if they know what they are doing, prevent a technical error from becoming a calamity. This they can manage better if they thoroughly understand and routinely practice the drill for releasing nuclear weapons. After all, this *is* their highest obligation.

Leaving technical and human error aside for a moment, I had qualms about U.S. targeting plans. The fewest options exist for the most likely scenarios, the use of a very small number of nuclear weapons—ones-zies and two-zies, as they're called in the trade—to cause the Kremlin to halt a conventional attack without believing we had launched an all-out nuclear barrage.

And I never understood why the United States placed top priority on targeting Soviet leadership facilities. The simple explanation was that we should threaten to hit them hardest where they care most; and the leaders naturally care most about protecting themselves. Still, if successful, this approach would eliminate the possibility of halting a nuclear engagement before it blew up the world. While no one knows if there could indeed be a "limited" nuclear war, it is a good guess—and essential for planning

—that there could be. If deterrence generally works *before* any nuclear explosion, it may work in spades *during* an initial nuclear exchange, when both leaderships would reel in shock and take stock. For this, someone in authority must still be alive.

Unfortunately, I never detected any evidence that President Reagan spent much time on this topic, and worse yet, I had loads of evidence that he approached the issue in the worst possible way. He would occasionally and rather casually say that we had to release our missiles if we knew theirs were coming in. I piped up on more than one occasion that this approach, dubbed "launch on warning," is dangerous, thoughtless and immoral. (I used nicer words with the President but said them quite forcefully.) To proceed toward the destruction of the Soviet Union, and most probably the world, on the basis of information spewed out of a computer is neither responsible nor wise.

The U.S. and Soviet officers with ghastly wares in their briefcases followed Reagan and Gorbachev into separate rooms, where they formed receiving lines. We proceeded, in no special order, to chat with Raisa and Mikhail Gorbachev, while members of the Soviet delegation were greeted by the President and First Lady.

Gorbachev was well briefed and quite adept. He had something personal to say to members of the U.S. delegation and tried his best to impress as well as to charm. The General Secretary greeted me with an inquisitive look. Then he said, "So you're Ken Adelman. I've read much about you in our press. Now I can place the name with the person." Yes, the Soviet press did write a lot about me, I replied, though kindly refrained from adding that none of it was kind. Their accusations were outrageous, when they were fathomable. One *Izvestia* piece claimed I was a "zoological anticommunist," of all things; I would have taken offense at that, had I understood it. Maybe the Russians were confused by all this American talk about hawks and doves.

After that reception, we had to buckle down to business. U.S. and Soviet officials had to craft the summit document. Why we needed one, I never understood. Communiqués are to me the bane of diplomacy, an inhibitor of frank talk between officials, and the most time-absorbing and time-wasting endeavor yet conceived. Even treaties can be overprized, as longtime British Foreign Secretary Lord Salisbury wrote in 1891:

I do not think we must rate too high the effects of the bonds constituted by signatures on pieces of paper. If nations in a great crisis act rightly, they will act so because they are in unison and cordiality with each other, and not because they have bound themselves to each other by protocols.

And communiqués are far less important than protocols. Yet our State Department officers and especially their diplomats absolutely adore them. So they devise them, albeit at times slyly.

Evidently elated by the prospect of a summit after such a long dry spell, mid-level State Department officials began to craft a lengthy "draft communiqué" with their colleagues in the Soviet embassy in Washington. This began two or three weeks before the summit but was not known around town until the week before Geneva began.

Defense Secretary Weinberger went ballistic upon hearing the news and especially after reading the text. He launched an attack on how the draft communiqué contradicted what he and the President believed, pointing to key phrases. "Serious differences" between the United States and USSR, the document intoned, "can only be overcome through sustained dialogue"—not, it seems, by Moscow changing its actions to stop its repression within and aggression abroad. We would both affirm "the importance of adhering to international commitments and agreements"—not letting on that President Reagan reported clear evidence of the Soviets violating nearly all such agreements: SALT I, SALT II, the ABM Treaty, the Helsinki Accords, the Geneva Protocol of 1925, and the 1972 Biological and Toxin Weapons Convention.

When the President was let in on this communiqué cavort, he put a stop to it. But typical of his style, the matter was then dropped. Neither he nor Shultz, nor anyone on their staffs, asked who had started this minuet. Or why. On whose authority? Or, most critical, who on our side had agreed to this "draft" language as something Ronald Reagan should sign?

Ours was an accountability-free administration; individuals were not held responsible for their actions. During my nearly seven years in the administration, I never saw or heard of anyone being disciplined for wrongdoing, no one called in and chewed out for any misdeed. The closest the President came was when he was supposed to dress down David Stockman for his true confessions in the *Atlantic*. Reagan invited him for the only private lunch Stockman ever had with the President—a novel form of punishment—and showed him at the end of this congenial affair press guidance telling how Stockman was taken "to the woodshed."

On that Wednesday night in Geneva, the final night, the Soviets wrangled over the communiqué in their usual way. The good tidings between Gorbachev and Reagan did not trickle down to the Soviet delegation, which began of course by reintroducing the Washington-crafted "draft communiqué." Being suspicious, they no doubt concocted some diabolical explanation for why State Department officials halted their collaboration a few weeks earlier.

Once that draft was canned, the bargaining became interesting. To give one typical example, we wanted our bilateral student exchange programs to involve *real* students—not the mid-fortyish, rotund, and balding types the Soviets commonly sent to study metallurgy at the University of Utah in "exchange" for a twenty-three-year-old coed studying Pushkin's early life.

This may seem like a distraction—how important is a student exchange compared with a nuclear exchange?—but it is not. Properly done, exchange programs can be extremely valuable. Sending Americans to live in Moscow is traditionally a harrowing and eye-opening experience, especially for those who go over as liberals (no one comes back as a liberal). The American exchange students I've met over the years, including Fulbright scholars I dined with in Moscow in November 1971, uniformly become sobered about the place and thus the system.

Less beneficial have been the Soviet "students" coming here. Some have picked up high-technology information, but probably not many. Others were impressed with our nation and society, but so what? They cannot do much about it. Besides, their impressions may not be so favorable. The only former Soviet exchange student I knew well was arms control Ambassador Obukhov, who had studied under the great international relations professor Hans Morgenthau for a spin. And he was quite insufferable to Americans afterward.

However, Third World exchange programs with the Soviets nearly always help us more than them (the students *or* the Soviets). African, Asian, and Latin American students attending Patrice Lumumba University outside Moscow—the school designed and built for them, which I visited years ago—come away former Marxists. It is those attending the London School of Economics or the Sorbonne or Berkeley who have come away as newly committed Marxists. When I met with them, students at Lumumba complained bitterly of racism; they described in gory detail how Muscovites would never allow African or dark-skinned Latin American or Asian students near their daughters. And the PLU grads I met during my two and a half years in Africa ranged from being critical of to being hostile toward the Russians.

In any case, the Soviet communiqué drafters diddled in Geneva when we pressed for a program clearly confined to young students. At one point they suggested that each government "guide" their cultural agencies toward this type of program. We needed more and said that certainly the mighty Kremlin could do more than "guide" one of its government agencies. It could "instruct" it on what to do.

This took hours of wrangling; such is the nature of summit statements or any negotiations with the Russians. We fight like mad over individual words, and then usually watch them descend into the historical memory hole. The amount of time spent crafting such statements is around three times the length of time anyone else remembers them. These documents are carefully negotiated, dramatically released, hurriedly grabbed by the press, quickly perused, and then summarily forgotten.

They oft have a half-life measured in hours, which is true even of their sliver of substance. A few years after the Geneva summit, I was standing near U.S. Information Agency Director Charlie Wick one day with nothing much to say, so I asked him what became of that summit-started student exchange program. He looked puzzled for a moment, then mumbled something about his staff still working with the Soviets to launch the program. Details remained to be solved. They may still remain so.

Nonetheless in the summit-time frenzy, people feel themselves engaged in a life-or-death struggle. And we found life. "We really took them to the cleaners," a top member of the U.S. team bubbled at 3 A.M. when the negotiations ended. It may seem paltry to everyone in retrospect, but it seemed golden to us then.

There had been snags along the way, with Secretary Shultz telling Gorbachev himself late Wednesday night—after the Swiss reception—that people like Ambassador Karpov needed a good kick in the ass for blocking progress. Such blunt language, rare for Shultz, seemed terribly dramatic at the time. It seems less so now; what was there to get so agitated about? In any case, Gorbachev chuckled nicely and let things be.

We were particularly delighted that the joint statement read like real English, rather than Russian-sounding English. We marveled at how the bulk of the words came from us, not thinking then of the downside—that our working exclusively in English left the Soviets open to "translate" the communiqué phrases to their liking later. We had, for instance, agreed to limit "intermediate-range missiles," which they translated as "medium-range systems." This was no great sin, until, that is, they added "within range of Europe" in the Russian version. This sleight of hand changed the negotiations from global in scope (our position) to applying only to Europe (their position).

In addition to such language changes came the inevitable problems with implementation. The sentence we most cherished, and fought hardest for, committed the President and General Secretary to have their delegations negotiate verification up front, at the same time they negotiate missile numbers. We wanted this since verification, so critical to us, is usually part of the stampede at the end. As mentioned, unfortunately, it was not to stick as Ambassador Obukhov simply refused to negotiate verification provisions after Gorbachev had pledged that he would do so.

WORDSMITHING

On our final summit night I was in a small group drafting presidential remarks, which seemed the most substantive thing I could do.

The President's remarks before the joint session of Congress the next night were of utmost concern to the White House staff; his remarks in a joint appearance with Gorbachev the next morning were relegated to secondary importance. Seeing a clear field, I ran there.

Not that I lacked any thought about what Reagan should say at such a moment. I knew it had to be upbeat; Gorbachev and Reagan were determined to make the summit a success, and thus we had to declare it so. But I felt there should be more to it than that, something grander about U.S.-Soviet relations.

I took China's relations with the Soviet Union as a model of our relations with Moscow. The Chinese knew how to treat the bear. Rather than being blinded by klieg lights, they stayed riveted on results. They developed a clear, concise, and consistent policy of improving relations only if the Russians removed "the three obstacles" by 1) withdrawing their troops from Afghanistan; 2) reducing their forces along the Soviet-China border; and 3) getting Vietnam's troops out of Cambodia.

Establishing the "three obstacles" constituted shrewd *private* diplomacy, since the Soviets then knew what was expected of them, and shrewd *public* diplomacy, since each time a Soviet diplomat approached a Chinese, out popped the "three obstacles." This exercise in Chinese water torture kept the relationship on China's agenda, not Russia's, and provided a yardstick by which to measure "improvements."

If poor, backward China could pull off ingenious diplomacy, why not rich, mighty America? By most measures of power, China stands weaker than the Soviet Union and yet has made itself the demander in that relationship. By any measure of power except military might, we stand taller than the Soviet Union and yet have often assumed the posture of supplicant.

During the summit buildup in Washington, I devised our own "obstacles." We could repeat three or four issues in presidential speeches, congressional testimony, and public appearances to focus attention on our concerns.

So ran the theory. It stayed as theory. I could not sell the idea in Washington. Everyone deemed it brilliant for the Chinese but somehow not right for Americans. I never understood why; I did, though, understand a turndown.

Until, that is, I was there in Geneva, sitting in the temporary White House offices in the dead of night drafting remarks for the President to deliver the next morning. Now is the time to strike, I reckoned, since success in government takes persistence more than any other single virtue.

Bud McFarlane, utterly exhausted and utterly dejected by then because of his unending fights with Don Regan, peered into the hotel room office at 3:30 A.M. as I was scribbling away. Pale and woebegone, he most resembled the ghost of Hamlet's father stalking the earth from the vasty deep for a few hours until the cock crowed.

I asked Bud, who wasn't even staying in the hotel but in the quarters aside the President's château, what I should draft. He gave some abstract response, the best he could muster then, and soon vanished just as mysteriously as he had first appeared. I knew I had clear running room.

The next morning, November 22, 1985, I sat in the front row of Geneva's International Conference Center and watched the

President, with Gorbachev seated next to the podium, deliver the American version of the "obstacles." It was Americanized by his speaking of a "report card" for the summit. The President said he could not fill it out yet but knew how the summit should be judged. There were four key questions:

1. Will we join together in sharply reducing offensive nuclear arms and moving to nonnuclear defensive systems to make this a safer world?
2. Will we join together to help bring about a peaceful resolution of conflicts in Asia, Africa, and Central America so that the peoples there can freely determine their own destiny without outside interference?
3. Will the cause of liberty be advanced?
4. Will the treaties and agreements signed, past and future, be fulfilled?

My summit-time success, like so many others, was short-lived. Not only are summit statements commonly ignored by others; they can be ignored by the speakers themselves. Certainly the President never expressed the least interest in these questions either then or subsequently. For a year or two afterward, I tried to induce members of the administration to repeat these four questions and to evaluate Soviet performance accordingly. I failed in Washington after the summit, just as I failed there before it.

I then asked a group of like-minded Senators to sponsor a "sense of the Senate" resolution requesting the President give grades on Soviet performance, as the President said he would do. This too never got off the ground. My stealing a page from Chinese statecraft had a half-life of a half day.

After Reagan and Gorbachev made their separate remarks at their joint appearance that morning, we all felt summit overdose. I was uplifted to hear my words in the President's melodic tones but still felt enough was enough.

Reagan felt similarly as we stood around in a small second-floor room in the Conference Center for the final reception and farewell. After the glasses were filled with champagne and some halfhearted but sparingly brief toasts were muttered, after more milling around and stilted talk, Gorbachev again sprang to life. He suddenly asked if he could speak to Reagan alone. They sprinted off with one interpreter to the next room, some pantry or part of the kitchen, I assumed; I envisioned how stunned the Swiss cooks and waiters would be to see the world's two most important people enter their private domain.

I wondered what that little chat could be about, when, before we could get our glasses refilled, the two of them reappeared. Another awkward moment. More shuffling, before Gorbachev told the President that this—pointing to the pantry—marked the fifth time they had met. Reagan replied, "No, this was the eleventh time American and Soviet leaders have met. The eleventh summit." Gorbachev said it somewhat louder and more emphatically; this was their fifth time together. Reagan said no, it was the *first* time he and Gorbachev had met, their first summit. "No, our fifth." Gorbachev stuck by his guns, causing the stumped President to become more miffed. He looked at us rather plaintively, and I offered help: "Maybe he means that this"—motioning to the pantry—"was the fifth time the two of you have met alone."

"Is that what he meant?" Reagan replied with a pained look, first at me and then at Gorbachev, who was getting all this through interpreters. He smiled and nodded, which piqued Reagan even more. "It doesn't matter how many times we meet," Reagan said, suppressing his agitation, "but what we accomplish when we do meet."

By then, Reagan had had quite enough of Gorbachev, enough of Geneva, enough of summit shows. And it showed. He thrust out his hand to Gorbachev and said good-bye.

It took me months to decipher Gorbachev's pantry ploy. Why would anyone do or say something so asinine, especially someone as sharp as Gorbachev? It puzzled me.

Then it hit me. This two-step could only be explained as something a Western-style politician would have done to build up the number of private meetings with the President of the United States. Normal mortals would not think of such a thing, but senators or congressmen or governors or mayors would do just what Gorbachev did if they had his brass. It is better to have five private sessions with the President than four. Odd but acceptable behavior by our politicians becomes odder and unexpected behavior by the General Secretary of the Soviet Union. But, then again, Gorbachev is cut from a different cloth than his predecessors.

After Reagan's short shrift to Gorbachev's shenanigans, the General Secretary began his round of good-byes. All eyes were fixed on him, leaving the President momentarily alone, unscheduled, and nearly unwatched, a rare moment in the life of a president. On his own for that split moment, Reagan did what comes naturally; he walked over to the waiters to introduce himself, hardly necessary, and to thank them for the champagne. While he moseyed over there, I told him what a splendid job he had done over the past two days, especially on SDI and the regional issues, and how proud I was to work for him, especially on occasions like this. He beamed—everyone likes flattery, even a president—and then became the shy, "aw, shucks" guy of the movies.

At Least They're Talking

Communiqués finalized and issued, good-byes said, speeches written, the sole chore left was to help shape the news. The summit was to be a success, despite the lack of anything specific to point out. We only had the prospect of another summit, but happily this happened to suffice.

We unanimously urged the President not to raise this matter, not to become the *demandeur* by asking Gorbachev for another summit. We all felt very strongly about this then, though why escapes me now. Regardless, Reagan popped the question while he and Gorbachev were crossing a parking lot. Gorbachev said something about how Reagan had never been to Moscow. Reagan replied that Gorbachev had never been to Washington. Why didn't he come? Then he, Reagan, would go to Moscow. Gorbachev accepted on the spot. How 'bout next year? That too was fine with Gorbachev. He'd be delighted.

That set, we were set. The President was tickled; he had taken this as the measure of success and had done it all by himself, without the staff paving the way or getting in the way. Besides, he was determined to get Gorbachev to America; he repeatedly spoke of getting him up in a helicopter in southern California, en route to or from his ranch, and pointing out the backyard swimming pools that, he would tell Gorbachev, were actually owned by the workers. This, Reagan figured, would impress Gorbachev, even amaze him no end.

"At least they're talking." The press and world commentators, relieved by this summit, would be doubly reassured by the scheduled next two summits. Unaware of the steadily disappointing record of postwar summits, most people consider such a dialogue inherently reassuring. "At least they're talking" assumes that they cannot then also be fighting, forgetting that Hitler and Mussolini excelled at being exceedingly talkative and exceedingly aggressive at the same time.

This also assumes that without the two leaders talking, no one is talking. Yet American and Soviet officials talk daily, many times daily in fact, not only in the embassies of Moscow and Washington, but also in the United Nations, in embassies around the world, and at sundry conferences. Moreover, if either has anything particularly novel or critical to say, they can write or call, as diplomats did for centuries before summits became such an international fixture.

And this assumes that the more "they're talking," the more they're agreeing. America's high divorce rate should dispel that notion; ex-husbands and -wives may have had difficulty communicating, but they had to understand each other better (coming from a common culture, speaking a common language, and having enough in common to be married in the first place) than a president of the United States and general secretary of the Soviet Union.

The prevailing myth that more talk leads to more agreement, so fetching and enduring, ended for me during my two years at the United Nations. I had daily dialogue with my Soviet counterpart, Ambassador Richard Ovinokov, somewhat more than I wished and far more, judging from his pained look and generally grumpy demeanor, than he wished. We discussed every regional or human rights or arms control issue; they all arose in one form and forum or another at the UN. Yet the more we spoke, the less we found we had in common. We disagreed on virtually everything.

Or nearly everything. We *could* agree on restricting both the UN's power and its voracious appetite for more funds. And on the urgency of stopping the spread of nuclear weapons around the world. One day, in fact, he and I cooperated on a nonproliferation resolution. Richard, normally taciturn at best, became a bit effusive. He complimented me: "Ken, I'm going into the General Assembly to say that you deserve credit for doing a great job on this resolution."

"Oh, no, you don't, Richard," I warned him. "You're not going to ruin my reputation so easily. If you do that, I'll take a right of reply"; I would use the UN device of following a speaker to rebut his views. Richard chuckled, but our chumminess vanished by the next day when we were back on opposing sides. This was not due to any lack of communication, just to a lack of shared values and interests. The more we communicated, the more we realized the differences between us.

PACKAGING THE PRODUCT

During Bud McFarlane's ghostly appearance the night before, I had asked him if there was anything more I could do to help him. As a matter of fact, he said, there was. Would I mind riding back on the White House press plane to "do backgrounders"? I'd be delighted, I replied.

Dead tired, I found myself engulfed for eight hours by scribbling, inquisitive reporters as I told every tidbit I could recall. They were starved for news after the press blackout, which mostly worked—the Soviets violated it some, but so what?—though it kept an embarrassing leak alive for days longer than otherwise would have been the case. Defense Secretary Weinberger's sobering summit eve memo to the President had leaked out. It contained little more than a patronizing warning not to give away the store, though it played into the press's favorite pastime of highlighting splits in the administration.

In any case, my job was kind of fun—who wouldn't relish being surrounded by media dynamos hanging on your every word?—though somewhat raucous.

I first knew this was no ordinary ride when the Pan Am 747 pulled out of the gate and taxied down the runway. The other passengers were heading for the bar or greeting one another chummily. I stopped a stewardess who was scrambling to take her seat when the captain announced the takeoff and asked why few others were sitting down. "This is the White House press plane," she replied simply. Forevermore, that scene has symbolized to me the arrogance of some members of the press. Those there, anyway, seemed incapable of obeying the most common and sensible rule of proper behavior.

Meanwhile the President flew to Brussels to be heaped with kudos and bathed in glory by other Western leaders. He then took off for Washington, where his presidential helicopter whisked him from Andrews Air Force Base right to Capitol Hill.

Reagan understood, better than any modern president, Napoleon's wise admonition that "one cannot govern without romanticism." The seventy-four-year-old President completed his twenty-hour working day with a peppy address about his first summit to the Congress, which roared its approval.

CHAPTER 4

MYTHS OF ARMS CONTROL

QUICKIE HISTORIANS are now calling the INF Treaty one of the high points of the Reagan administration. Perhaps future historians will prize it just as highly.

If so, this treaty will be unique in the annals of history. For despite all the hoopla accompanying arms control over the years, little has been accomplished by it. And little can be accomplished by it, for a whole host of reasons.

Those reasons are presented briefly in this chapter, which serves as both an introduction and a backdrop to the INF drama. For without glancing back for a moment and looking around at the myths pervading the formal arms control process, little of the INF uproar makes sense. And little of the years of disappointments makes sense.

The Europeans hold these myths most fervently, the Germans most particularly. So it is fitting that we begin this tale sitting with a German leader discussing this very subject.

· · ·

Early in 1984, with the television cameras whirring, Dr. Hans-Jochen Vogel, the genteel leader of the German opposition Social Democratic party, entered my august office. As fate would have it, the office had been the Secretary of State's abode during World War II and for more than a decade afterward. Many of the decisions on how to defeat and then reconstruct Germany were made in this very room.

Dr. Vogel, whose brother incongruously is the head of Germany's Conservative party, came with a message. Ever since the Soviets walked out of the arms talks in December of 1983 because of our INF missile deployments, he had worried. Now he had come to Washington not to pressure, mind you, but merely to "think out loud" about how to entice the Soviets back.

Maybe, he suggested, we could offer to count British and French missiles in the INF talks. We both knew that Paris and London wouldn't like that—actually, they would fight it tooth and nail—but at least that concession might entice the Soviets back (presumably we could worry about France and Britain later). Or maybe we could slow down the INF deployment schedule; that might interest them. Or dangle new economic loans; that was always possible. Well, what ideas did I have?

None. Instead I wanted to know from Vogel what was so important about getting them back. Granted, we wanted arms control, some of us did somewhat anyway. But if the Soviets weren't interested enough to come to the table, they clearly weren't interested enough to cut a deal. And we could wait them out without much damage. Our missiles would be deployed on time and in numbers that would maintain Western security nicely without any arms deal. So we were in fine shape.

Dr. Vogel disagreed. "We just can't have a situation where the United States and the USSR aren't negotiating over arms."

"Why not?"

"Well, you know what would happen if the two superpowers weren't talking for long."

"What?"

He looked at me with horror. "You know," he said, frowning as he waved his arms around in what I took to be the shape of a mushroom cloud. "You know what would happen."

"No, that's not right," I tried to explain.

"What then?"

"What would happen is just what *has* happened today. The sun would rise. People would wake up. They'd eat breakfast. Get dressed. Go to work. Kids would go to school. You know, life would just go on. Today, we had no arms control talks, and life went on, just as it had for centuries before the world ever knew of arms control. Life went on. Arms control is not an essential element in the planet's existence," I explained, though with scant success.

Herr Vogel felt otherwise, as many people throughout the West have come to feel. Ironically, his attitude would have precluded the singular arms control success of the Reagan administration, the INF Accord. In any negotiations, if you want a deal badly enough, you get a bad deal. Only the President's relatively blasé attitude about having an arms accord—for the first five years in the Oval Office, anyway—and our ambivalence over concluding an INF accord, made the bargain possible.

Besides being poor tactics, hyping arms control constitutes poor judgment. As President Carter's Secretary of Defense Harold Brown said truthfully, "Measured against these glittering possibilities, the achievements of arms negotiations to date have been modest indeed. . . . In all, not much to show for thirty-five years of negotiations and twenty years of treaties."

Perhaps nowhere in life is the disparity greater between exalted public expectations and a dismal track record than in arms control. No area of science, medicine, or even public policy would continue to elicit so much hope after so many years of unsuccessful effort. Arms control must be approached as one of the intangibles of life, a rite seemingly needed to satisfy some deep longing in our collective soul.

Maybe the hopes we associate with arms control arise from the dread of annihilation that lies deep in what Carl Jung called our "collective unconscious." The Armageddon motif—that the earth will perish and mankind will end—interestingly predates the advent of nuclear weapons. It even predates the Christian notion of the Last Judgment and Armageddon itself.

As Richard Pipes explained in *Commentary* (August 1984), ancient religions in Babylon, India, Iran, and classical Greece tell tales of a cosmic holocaust consuming the world by fire. The Indo-Germanic peoples and the Nordics include a similar motif, as of course does the Bible. Zephaniah 1:18 tells "in the fire of His jealous wrath, all the earth shall be consumed; for a full, yea, sudden end He will make of all the inhabitants of the earth." The New Testament adds II Peter 3:10 about the day "the Heavens will pass away with a loud noise, and the elements will be dissolved with fire, and the earth and the works that are upon us will be burned up." Even secular writings offer the same concept; Montesquieu wrote presciently of someone "discovering some secret" that might "exterminate whole countries and nations."

So it seems that fears of Armageddon come from something deep in the human psyche. In Judeo-Christian tradition, God did the destroying but at least allowed a Day of Judgment. Now it could be man without any final judgment. As Professor Pipes states, "Thus, agnosticism intensifies an anxiety that has its origins in religious beliefs, leaving the horror, but robbing it of hope."

This archetype played out in the 1930s when annihilation literature focused on chemical weapons, especially combined with aerial warfare. British Prime Minister Neville Chamberlain was typical in portraying "people burrowing underground, trying to escape from poison gas, knowing that at any hour of the day or night death or mutilation was ready to come upon them." Total war would come about if any war erupted. "Whichever side may call itself the victor, there are no winners, but all are losers."

The ultimate irony was that, when the war in Europe came, the only weapon *not* used was chemical arms. This interwar fearmongering turned out wrong, not because of any kindness by Hitler—he used gas to exterminate Jews—or of any international legal treaties—he gave them all short shrift—but simply because of deterrence. German intelligence estimated that the British and French had much larger stockpiles of chemical weapons than they actually had. The German High Command dreaded retaliation in kind if they initiated a chemical attack, and Hitler, who had been gassed as a young corporal in World War I, agreed.

After the war, the Armageddon motif of course fixed on nuclear weapons. This fostered a vast literature and veritable film festival on nuclear apocalypse. And it brought a wave of dire predictions, such as, in 1960 during relatively tranquil times, C. P. Snow prophesying that if events proceeded on their current path, nuclear war was "a certainty" within ten years.

When nuclear war became portrayed as our world's prime problem, nuclear arms control became its main solution. This perspective persists even though nuclear weapons have long been recognized as primarily political instruments rather than military weapons. They constitute what the great Chinese strategist Sun Tzu deemed the most effective of all instruments of war: "To subdue the enemy without fighting is the acme of skill."

Nuclear weapons cast a shadow over political settlements. Their effect began at the very dawn of the nuclear age. At Potsdam in July of 1945, after President Truman received news from General Groves that the Los Alamos test had proven successful, Truman apparently became more confident of America's role in the world. Henry Stimson wrote in his diary then that when Winston Churchill learned of this development a few days later, he remarked that he knew something was up since Truman suddenly seemed bolder in challenging Stalin.

Proof of the point that nuclear weapons help shape international affairs is admittedly hard to come by. But it seems more than mere coincidence that we came out rather well from the Berlin crisis and the Cuban missile crisis when we enjoyed awesome nuclear superiority, and fared less well in the 1970s after the Soviets reached nuclear parity. Granted, this is surely not due solely to the changed nuclear equation—nothing in international affairs has a single cause—but to dismiss any relevance of the nuclear balance is similarly off-base.

Herr Vogel's dread of annihilation and resulting desire for arms control was restricted to U.S.-Soviet nuclear arms control. This is understandable, since herein lies the danger of total obliteration.

But it is also convenient. As Canadian Ambassador Alan Gottlieb once told me, arms control is the attempt to control *others'* arms, never one's own. For Britain, France, and China, what matters is controlling American and Soviet nuclear arms, not their own. They resist talks on their nuclear systems like the plague. And for the Soviets, arms control is naturally an attempt to control American arms. For West Germany and most other states, it is the effort to control the type of arms they lack, nuclear arms.

This is especially true of Third World countries, which have increased their military spending much faster than industrialized nations or Communist countries. Their ability to pay for arms is, however, far lower. Countries like Libya, Syria, Tanzania, and South Yemen spend more of their meager GNPs on arms than the average NATO nation.

While nuclear arms catch the world's eyes, conventional arms cost the world's treasures in gold and blood. Today, upward of 95 percent of all military spending goes for conventional arms. And it is with these, not nuclear bombs, that lives are lost. During this century, around 150,000 people perished by nuclear weapons while one thousand *times* that number, or 150 million, have been killed by conventional weapons. In one recent year, 1982, some thirty-six conventional wars raged, killing some four million people and wounding countless more.

So this century's Armageddon has been conventional, not nuclear. Even if fears of a nuclear Armageddon are legitimate, given the awesome power of nuclear weapons, then the presumed solution of arms control is misplaced. For as long as nuclear weapons exist, which they will forevermore, the potential for total annihilation will likewise exist. Arms control on short- or medium-range nuclear weapons, as in the INF Treaty, does not change that equation one iota. These systems constitute small change compared with the big strategic stuff.

But neither would strategic arms control have much of an impact on preventing what folks fear most—total destruction. The strategic reductions envisioned in START would still leave both sides with many times more strategic weapons than they had during the Cuban missile crisis, to say nothing of the thousands of tactical and battlefield systems and air- and sea-launched nuclear cruise missiles. In a nutshell, the nuclear numbers have become so astronomical that no arms control effort could ever preclude the possibility of Armageddon.

Even if arms control could reduce these numbers, having fewer nuclear weapons does not necessarily mean less risk of nuclear war. Indeed, having fewer nuclear weapons might actually raise the likelihood of war by prompting either side to "use 'em or lose 'em" for fear that its smaller nuclear force was at greater risk than before. Today's high numbers allow for a redundancy that helps preclude this type of panic in a crisis.

The proper goal of strategic arms control is not across-the-board reductions but selective reductions in those systems most vulnerable and those with a "first strike capacity." This is fine in theory but tough in practice. For instance, a 50 percent cut in strategic arms would naturally prompt each side to cut its oldest weapons while retaining its newest ones. But it is generally the newest systems that have the most warheads packed on the fewest missiles. Our MX and the Soviets' new SS-24 both have up to ten warheads apiece, while our Trident submarines have some 180 or so warheads.

Rather than enter this strange and specialized realm of nuclear accountancy, we should stay on the grand plane: nuclear weapons per se are not the main problem. U.S.-Soviet competition in regional conflicts, stemming from Moscow's acts of or support for aggression, *is* the main problem. These grabs can always escalate and lead to large-scale, and then nuclear, conflict.

Thank goodness both Moscow and Washington are keenly aware of this. Hence the remarkable record, rather unique in the annals of history, of two major powers assiduously avoiding instances where their military forces rub up against the other. And hence the growing taboo against "nuclear gunboat diplomacy" in the postwar years.

While President Truman may have tinkered with brandishing the bomb to help ease Soviet troops out of northern Iran in 1949, and President Eisenhower may have done likewise to help promote an armistice in Korea in 1953, and while Presidents Kennedy and Nixon brought nuclear weapons slightly into play in 1962 and 1973, this dwindling practice has now been all but discarded. In all my government years, I never heard anyone broach the topic of using nuclear weapons. Ever. In any setting, in any way.

As President Reagan never tired of saying, nations do not develop mistrust because of arms. Rather, they develop arms because of mistrust. Western mistrust has been based on the Soviets' seventy-year record of repression within and aggression beyond its borders. With Gorbachev's reforms, this may be changing; a less aggressive and repressive Soviet Union would do more to preclude Herr Vogel's type of nuclear nightmare than a hundred START treaties or a thousand INF accords.

No Reductions

The more sober argument for arms control centers around its use in reducing nuclear weapons, not in precluding a disaster. The INF Treaty reinforced the popular notion that arms accords cut arms, though INF was the exception rather than the rule.

For masked behind the rhetoric of arms control drastically reducing weapons is the reality of arms control actually pushing a buildup of weapons. This is rather perverse, violating the raison d'être of arms control. As Florence Nightingale said, "Whatever else they do, hospitals should not spread disease."

I have come to believe that we have more nuclear weapons today because of the arms control process than we would have without it—not enormously more, especially given the astronomical numbers today, but more nonetheless. For arms control seems ideally tailored to boost military programs and with them defense spending.

This stems from the way government works, not just our government but any government, and not just now but at any time. Winston Churchill wrote about this phenomenon in the 1930s:

The elaborate process of measuring swords around the table at Geneva . . . stirs all the deepest suspicions and anxieties of the various powers, and forces all the statesmen to consider many hypothetical contingencies which, but for this prolonged process, perhaps would not have crossed their minds.

While Churchill wrote, Japan began initiating the only known use of biological weapons, during its occupation of Manchuria. Apparently this was fostered by the very negotiations Churchill was denouncing, the Geneva disarmament talks, which resulted in the 1925 accord banning chemical weapons use. These negotiations were a natural reaction against the horror of chemical weapons used in World War I, weapons that caused up to a million casualties and some ninety thousand deaths.

Before these talks, Japan lacked any knowledge of such dastardly weapons. But during the talks, a young Japanese officer asked probing questions about the technology involved—how the weapons were made, stored, delivered, whatever. Being Japanese, he took copious notes. The other negotiators, being European diplomats, spelled out in detail precisely what they were banning. The young officer took such critical information back with him, where it was, like most technologies that go to Japan, first copied and then improved upon.

Right after the Geneva Convention, according to recent sources, Japan built a chemical weapons factory on Okino-shima, a tiny island off Shikoku on the east side of Bungo Strait. Chinese army records conclude that 2,000 Chinese were killed and 35,000 injured by chemical weapons manufactured in this plant during Japan's brutal occupation of "Manchukuo." The young officer who attended the Geneva talks apparently became the director of Japan's chemical and biological weapons program.

The push to arm that ironically arises from arms talks can similarly be demonstrated in recent years. Up to 1987, the Soviets retained more INF nuclear weapons during and because of the INF talks than they would have had there been no talks. They felt the natural desire of any negotiating team to attain the maximum leverage; in this realm, that means having the maximum number of missiles, even if they are not needed.

To put this case in a nutshell: The Soviets' SS-20 missile was their follow-on for the older Soviet INF missiles (SS-4s and SS-5s) deployed in the early 1960s to the tune of six hundred or so. The older models were the missiles Khrushchev tried to sneak into Cuba in 1962, so they would scare the daylights out of anyone within range.

As the new SS-20s came on stream, the older missiles were retired at a robust rate of some eighty per year. When arms talks heated up, Moscow's missile retirements slowed down. In 1979 and 1980 destruction of the SS-4s and SS-5s virtually stopped while Moscow assessed NATO's decision to deploy our missiles and to negotiate at the same time. From mid-1980 to early 1982, when these negotiations languished, destruction of the SS-4s and SS-5s resumed at their eighty-per-year clip. Then, as the INF talks came to life, their retirement slowed and again nearly stopped. At the end of 1983 the Soviets walked out of the INF negotiations and increased the destruction of their older INF missiles. The dismantlements reached an unprecedented peak in 1984, when there were no negotiations at all. Almost half the existing SS-4 force and the last of the SS-5s were then destroyed. When INF negotiations resumed in spring of 1985, the Soviets again slowed such missile reductions.

There is nothing especially nefarious or mysterious about this. It is only natural for a Kremlin arms controller, if such a thing exists, to urge his Defense Minister *not* to give up unilaterally what is being negotiated bilaterally. Whether such memos flowed back and forth in Moscow remains unknown.

They did in Washington, however, where I was the guilty party. Early in my term of office, staffers in the Arms Control and Disarmament Agency drafted a letter for my signature—in government, no one writes what he signs or signs what he writes—to Defense Secretary Weinberger. I asked him to retain several "boneyard" B-52 bombers on active status so that the number of our strategic bombers, and thus of our overall strategic systems, could be as high as possible. We needed them for leverage in the talks, I argued.

Secretary Weinberger wrote back that the Pentagon would much prefer cutting up these B-52s. The bombers could never get off the ground if the balloon ever went up; they were useless militarily. To dismantle them outright would save money. Keeping them on "active" status meant they had to be minimally maintained, which cost money.

I replied to Weinberger's reasonable letter by reiterating our need for higher numbers of strategic forces to give us more negotiating leverage. Eventually I triumphed. Unfortunately Weinberger reversed his previous decision. He said it was a temporary measure, but knowing the way the Pentagon works, that directive is probably still in force.

So in the mid-1980s the number of strategic weapons increased because of ongoing arms control talks. In the mid-1970s I witnessed an increase in the number of strategic weapons because of completed arms control accords. When serving as assistant to the Secretary of Defense in 1976 and 1977, I watched civilian authorities urge a reluctant officer corps to build up our nuclear arsenal to the levels permitted under the 1974 Vladivostok Agreement. Though widely heralded—Secretary of State Henry Kissinger announced after the signing that the accord would "mean a cap has been put on the arms race for a period of ten years"—even *The New York Times* editorial deemed this a bit much: "If this is 'putting a cap on the arms race,' then a shrimp can whistle, as a former Soviet leader, Nikita Khrushchev, was fond of saying."

And indeed the push was made in the Pentagon to build up our nuclear arms in order to reach the limits permitted. Otherwise, it was said, the Soviets would gain advantage in a weapons category highlighted by the accord. And given the Jackson Amendment of 1972 requiring all arms agreements to be equal as to U.S. and Soviet force levels, filling up the categories was deemed politically essential whether or not it was militarily essential, or even wise.

Similar pressures from a pending or concluded arms accord influences administrations in other deleterious ways as well. For instance, the United States retained its fifty-four jumbo Titan missiles long after they became a threat to American farmers as well as to Soviet military planners. The order to retire this long obsolete force finally came midpoint during the Reagan administration, and even then after a most astonishing incident.

In the early 1980s a Titan missile repairman dropped his wrench down a silo in Arkansas. The wrench punctured the missile's fuel container. No one suspected any damage but eight hours later the missile exploded, killing two men. Scarier yet, the huge nuclear warhead—the biggest in our arsenal, with the potential for an unbelievable blast—blew off the five-foot-thick, reinforced-concrete steel hatch (weighing some 750,000 pounds) and flew some 150 yards from the silo. The image of a Titan warhead tumbling down the Arkansas country road is not terribly comforting.

Similarly, two weapons systems that most bedeviled the Reagan administration were systems initiated or warped by the arms control process. The short, sad tale of the antisatellite system

(ASAT) and the MX missile tells how arms control can drive up rather than hold down the number of modern weapons.

ASAT exists in large part because of arms control. It was effectively introduced early in the Carter administration primarily because the President sought leverage in the newly initiated ASAT arms talks. At that time, the halcyon days of negotiations, the United States and Soviets launched talks over strategic arms, conventional weapons in Europe, arms transfers, nuclear testing, Indian Ocean naval deployments, and chemical weapons. ASAT was added after President Carter learned that the Soviets had an operational ASAT system while we had abandoned ours years before. Having opened the talks, he then searched for leverage to make them successful. He ordered research on the F-15 ASAT program and subsequently approved some tests.

The Air Force really did not want the program. It had higher priorities and fewer funds for its top programs. Thus ASAT was accorded a low priority. This lack of institutional support led to endless research and testing problems, one highly publicized failure after another—delays on the date of initial operations, lowering the numbers of tests, whatever. Knowledgeable hands on Capitol Hill came to call ASAT a "dog of a system," which it became.

On the eve of Reykjavik, the House Armed Services Committee finally succeeded in squashing the ASAT program. Congress prohibited any ASAT tests against objects in space, precisely the type of test the program then needed. In early 1988 the Air Force recommended that the F-15 ASAT program be scuttled altogether —this after $4 billion of increasingly scarce defense dollars went down that hole, after umpteen efforts by President Reagan, Secretaries Shultz and Weinberger, and everyone else high in office to save it, and after the Russians suddenly became keen on negotiating over it.

Whether an ASAT *should* have been built is a close call. It makes sense for us to gain the ability to shoot down Soviet satellites, if they already have the ability to shoot down ours; our ASAT would deter them from using their ASAT in a crisis. Ideally, of course, it makes more sense for neither of us to have that capability. Satellites are useful things, best not threatened. For they enable either side to obtain reliable and timely intelligence on the other's forces, which is needed for military warning and for arms control verification. And they enable the President and presumably the General Secretary to retain command and control over their nuclear and conventional forces.

But whether an ASAT *would* have been built is less debatable. It would probably not have been, were it not tossed into the curious world of arms control.

The story of the MX missile differs in its particulars but leads to the same destination. It was twisted and somewhat ruined by arms control. The massive missile, the center of so much controversy for so long, originated in the Ford administration. The Soviets had just deployed a slew of new land-based missiles, which prompted Presidents Ford, Carter, and Reagan to push the MX despite repeated public and congressional resistance.

Part of that resistance came from the MX's design, which was shaped mightily by arms control considerations. SALT I and SALT II, casting a shadow over strategic planning for some fifteen years, limited primarily the number of missile launchers rather than the number of warheads on any missile. Hence the cost-minded Air Force naturally sought to pack the greatest number of warheads onto each missile. Though initially designed to be mobile, the MX grew so large in order to carry a whopping ten warheads that it could no longer travel on the highway.

Arms control, having encouraged more warheads and thereby precluding the missile's mobility, then fouled up its mode of deployment. Air Force designers were told, in short, to design an invulnerable yet verifiable way of deploying the beast—one capable of being counted by Soviet arms controllers, yet incapable of being targeted by Soviet missileers.

As anyone might imagine, this proved to be a tough assignment. So the Air Force wandered from basing mode to basing mode with admirable agility but increasing implausibility. After more than thirty stabs, the general public joined congressional experts in concluding that the Pentagon didn't know what it was doing. MX was plagued by the snicker factor.

Murphy's law worked here, as it does so often in government, and the Reagan administration's penultimate solution to the MX problem was the worst of all possible solutions. MX became a highly capable, highly vulnerable missile that lacked both rationality and strategic logic. As a weapons system, the MX was highly proficient, with good reliability and amazing accuracy. But because it was housed in fixed silos, MX became quite vulnerable. It was a most inviting target.

Hence the arms control process helped push the MX toward becoming precisely the kind of system that arms controllers (or anyone concerned with strategic stability) most heartily condemn: a system that would impel a president into a use-it-or-lose-it posture during a crisis.

The MX too became a "dog," the strategic albatross of the Reagan administration, unable to be salvaged politically in any way that made much military or economic sense. This was true even after the prestigious Scowcroft Commission recommended the President go for half the number of MXs the Carter administration had sought. So a high political price was paid for a low strategic prize—a mere fifty MXs deployed after more than a decade of debate, at a cost of $5 billion, and after unbelievable political torment. The House of Representatives alone voted on the MX more than twenty-five separate times, with the President and Secretaries of State and Defense dolling out staggering political capital each time merely to keep this dubious program alive.

Peering Ahead

The INF Treaty that Herr Vogel and other Europeans longed for, much more so when it seemed nearly impossible than when it came within sight, did reduce the INF nuclear arms. But it did not reduce the *overall* number of nuclear weapons.

Indeed, the number of Soviet nuclear arms built during the INF negotiations far exceeds the number destroyed because of these negotiations. Moreover, Europe will not necessarily be less under the nuclear gun; Soviet nuclear weapons capable of hitting our NATO Allies will grow threefold from the time the INF talks began until the time all the INF missiles are eliminated.

Unfortunately, a strategic accord holds little more prospect than INF to really reduce the total nuclear numbers.

How can this be, with all the talk about a 50 percent cut? For starters, no arms accord encompasses all nuclear weapons; START is confined to strategic arms, leaving out thousands of other nukes. With all the hullabaloo about INF's "eliminating an entire class of nuclear weapons," we are removing weapons with only 364 of the 4,600 or more nuclear warheads deployed in Europe. Those remaining are mostly impossible to encompass in a nuclear arms treaty because they are "triple-capable" systems—in layman's terms, capable of delivering conventional or chemical or nuclear munitions. Since it is impossible to verify this distinction, and since NATO increasingly will rely upon such systems to deliver highly accurate conventional arms, these should not be tossed into the arms control pot.

Even within the category of strategic arms, a START accord billed as a 50 percent reduction may not make 50 percent reductions in all strategic arms. Despite being called a "comprehensive" strategic arms agreement, no such thing exists. No agreement can be "comprehensive" enough to limit the number of bomber weapons or air-launched cruise missiles, of which there are thousands. A treaty can only limit the number of bombers able to carry such weapons, as nothing more is verifiable. We are unable to peer inside Soviet bombers to count the weapons loaded. Ditto with sea-launched cruise missiles; this category of nuclear weapons cannot be arms-controlled, either. Again verification is the rub. These cruise missiles (basically pilotless airplanes) can be carried on nearly every type of ship— from a submarine, they can be fired out of a normal torpedo tube; from surface ships, they can be launched in any number of ways —so there's no real way to count them.

The Soviets have adamantly insisted that these systems, sea-launched cruise missiles (or SLCMs), be included in a START Treaty. Marshal Akhromeyev brought up the issue during the all-night session at Reykjavik and harped on it during each succeeding session. Without including these systems in an agreement, he said, there would be no agreement, something he reiterated in even stronger words to me during a ninety-minute private meeting in his Kremlin office, just down the hall from Gorbachev's, in March 1989.

Throughout the last evening of the Washington summit, on December 8, 1987, the American and Soviet delegations wrestled over this issue with great intensity, though to no effect. Marshal Akhromeyev and his colleagues then described a device to detect a nuclear presence on naval vessels. The device could be operated from a specially equipped helicopter or low-flying airplane, they claimed, though we doubted it. Despite our repeated questions, the Soviets came up dry on the details. In his press conference the following day, Gorbachev covered the same ground. He claimed that such remote monitoring of nuclear weapons aboard ship was possible.

American scientists claim no such device exists, and even if it did, it could not work as Gorbachev claimed. For no device could possibly detect nuclear weapons on submarines at sea, since the water would block such detection. On *any* ship, such a device could tell only whether nuclear material was on board. On a nuclear-powered ship, nuclear weapons could be stacked near the nuclear reactor and thereby shrouded. Besides, all this could be shielded by a simple metal plate, which could preclude detection of anything nuclear. Even a Geiger counter-like mechanism held up to a nuclear-armed cruise missile does not register if the missile's covering is thick enough.

Even if all these technical problems were miraculously solved, an awesome political problem would remain. Because of it, we'd be foolish to agree to such a verification scheme. For to allow the Soviets to monitor the presence of nuclear weapons aboard a U.S. Navy ship would effectively end our postwar policy of "neither confirming nor denying" the existence of such weapons at sea. And without that policy, U.S. ships might well be barred from port calls in Japan, the Philippines, Greece, and probably in other spots throughout the world. The United States could not allow the Soviets to know that certain ships carried nuclear weapons without officially informing our Western Allies first. If we did that, the Allies' veil of innocent ignorance would vanish, and with it would go most of our worldwide Navy deployments.

Thus any future strategic agreement must necessarily be a limited one. It will exclude nuclear armed bombs and cruise missiles and other systems, just as it will not limit such key elements of strategic strength as accuracy, reliability, and command-and-control capabilities. This matters, for in arms control—as in wage and price controls, or pollution controls, or any type of controls—to limit only some things is to let others run free. Actually it is to encourage the others to increase, which can thwart if not nullify the entire enterprise. As with a balloon, when some parts are pressed down, others parts inevitably bulge out.

This too is borne out by experience. SALT I limited the number of land-based missiles with a range of 5,500 kilometers or more. So after signing SALT I in 1972, the Soviets began building a land-based missile with slightly less range—some 4,000 to 5,000 kilometers—to sneak under the limit. This new missile was none other than the SS-20 which wreaked such havoc across the alliance from 1977 to 1987.

Furthermore, the Soviets can thwart specific arms limits even without explicitly violating the agreement. For instance, the United States and the Soviets agreed to count Yankee-class missile-carrying submarines in SALT I. The Soviets dutifully "retired" a Yankee submarine, as the treaty prescribed and in the manner it prescribed: removing the ballistic missiles and slicing the boat in half before our very (satellite) eyes. This Yankee sub was taken off the accounting books as a strategic nuclear system.

But then, instead of retiring the two halves of the submarine hull, they inserted a new midsection to carry scores of nuclear-armed cruise missiles, and welded the three parts together. Back to sea this Yankee went, thereby increasing the threat the submarine posed to the United States—but still scrupulously conforming to the SALT I provisions.

Some of us broached this "dirty little secret"—that the number of nuclear weapons may well *increase* under a strategic arms reduction accord—during National Security Council meetings. At the session following Reykjavik, the Chairman of the Joint Chiefs, after some prompting on my part, made this point in general terms. He sketched out some new programs to accompany these "50 percent reductions" in order to assure "military sufficiency" during and after the specified reductions. But he never spoke of the real budget-crusher from a START accord, namely the refashioning of U.S. strategic forces.

As previously mentioned, our newest systems (the MX missile and Trident submarine) pack the most warheads on the fewest platforms. This is fine for an agreement limiting platforms but not fine for one limiting warheads. In that case, stability dictates that we build more missiles and submarines with fewer warheads on each. Yet to build a new land-based missile with one warhead, like the Midgetman, is horrendously expensive, more than $25 billion for a mere 500 warheads. To build new submarines capable of carrying fewer warheads is even more costly and slow in coming. The Trident program took nearly twenty years from its initial funding to its initial deployment.

The President seemed not to take this point on board. He seemed surprised when first learning the "dirty little secret," especially after the Director of the Office of Management and Budget said that the defense budget would actually *rise* as a result of the strategic agreement.

Likewise, the message never made a dent in the mind of Don

Regan. A few weeks before that NSC meeting, while lounging upstairs at the Hofti House in Reykjavik, Regan and I had a lengthy debate on the savings or costs of an arms agreement. But in his book, *For the Record*, he reiterates prevailing but misguided views. He asserts that Gorbachev "had compelling reasons for reducing the ruinously expensive Soviet nuclear arsenal," not having understood (or believed) that this is the cheapest part of the Soviet arsenal. Showing rare modesty by admitting that he lacks expertise on international affairs and Soviet studies, Regan continues unabated: "But I do know something about economics and finance . . . believing that these were the keys to an agreement on nuclear arms, I spoke my mind to the President." He explains what he said:

> Gorbachev's motives in seeking a reduction in nuclear arms seemed to me to be almost entirely economic. When the possibility of a summit on arms reduction arose, I looked at the Soviet budget. . . . The bottom line was that in the Soviet Union, as in every other nation state in history, money talked.

Such a neo-Marxist belief—that economics controls, rather than politics or defense—may be more convincing to a White House advisor and ex-chairman of Merrill Lynch than to Kremlin leaders. For them, security talks. Power talks. Money pales.

For the Soviets to believe that money talks more than security and power would constitute an enormous change from the Soviet Union's seventy-year history. It would amount to their cashiering their singular ticket to superpower status, military might.

It has become a cliché—though clichés are sometimes true—that the Soviet Union is unmistakably a political, cultural, economic, and social failure among major powers. It has been a success only as a military power. For the Soviet Union to reduce its military might would be for it to reduce its importance, to give up its strong suit and compete in areas where it lacks any competitive advantage. If Gorbachev leads the USSR far down this road, it may mean his demise or may mean that the Kremlin has run out of all possible alternatives. Such a move would be a suretale sign of utter desperation.

Yet to Regan the Soviets *need* arms control to save them from economic ruin. Regan's own words are a caricature in themselves: "Faced with the choice between bankruptcy and a fall from power that would deliver the USSR back into the hands of the faction that had all but ruined her economically, he [Gorbachev] would have no choice" but to come around to accepting our position in the arms negotiations.

Such clarity may distinguish Regan, but his message is common. The Soviets' longing for the "peace dividend" in arms control was presumed long before the world heard of Donald T. Regan. It has been promulgated more by conservative Republicans than by liberal Democrats (probably because Republicans devote themselves more to amassing money while Democrats devote themselves more to politics).

In any case, the argument showed up some thirty-four years ago. During a June 30, 1955, NSC meeting (to quote a memorandum in the Eisenhower Library):

> Secretary Dulles said he believed that the Soviets genuinely wanted some reduction in the armament burdens in order to be able to deal more effectively with their severe internal problems. Accordingly, the Soviet Union may be prepared to make concessions.

Since then, the case has been made with increasing vigor, though with decreasing evidence. No arms agreement has saved much money; most have cost one or both sides more than they were spending before the treaty.

Even the INF Treaty may not save money, despite its being the first to eliminate a whole category of nuclear weapons. For starters, the big money has already been spent. The Soviets have already developed and built their impressive SS-20 force. The cost of deploying such forces, once built, is minimal. The manpower cost is also minimal; the Soviets keep these troops in uniform anyway. If they were not caring for the SS-20s, they would be doing something else. The cost of operating the missile force itself is relatively piddly since, unlike planes and boats and tanks, missiles do not do anything. They have slight wear and tear and no hefty maintenance costs.

On our side, too, these factors apply. The INF systems we are eliminating were built and paid for. Indeed, the price of our fielding the Pershing II and GLCMs in Western Europe—some $7 or $8 billion—was considerable. We could have handed the Europeans some twelve thousand main battle tanks as a gift for the same amount and perhaps far more deterrent effect. Besides, this $7 or $8 billion represents merely the price of the missiles, not our ten nuclear missile facilities built in Europe for the INF deployments; one base, that in Comiso, Italy, for instance, cost a cool $100 million by itself.

And there are the costs of dismantling our missiles and verifying their compliance. Our On-Site-Inspection Agency, recently established to handle INF verification, came in with a first-year budget request of $82.7 million. Eventually INF verification will end up costing around $300 million in direct expenditures and involve hordes of people for years. Ambassador Ed Rowny quipped, "Some people say that the reason we've got 4.9 percent [low] unemployment is that so many people are getting jobs in verification." These are merely the direct costs; hidden costs come as the CIA boosts its expensive satellites and backup personnel to help verify the treaty.

The fourth, as yet unknown, added expense is the follow-on system that almost invariably comes on the heels of an arms treaty. After SALT I the Soviets continued their massive strategic buildup and added on the new SS-20, while we accelerated funding on a host of strategic programs. Likewise after SALT II. Following the INF Accord, NATO has been debating a new short-range nuclear system, the upgraded Lance, to slip under INF's range limitations. Thus to believe the old line that arms control can save gobs of money is akin to Dr. Samuel Johnson's calling second marriages a triumph of hope over experience.

Still, why couldn't a strategic arms accord—not a peripheral agreement like INF or a questionable one like SALT I, but a *real* one like START—save each side considerable funds? Even if it would not be comprehensive, couldn't it be economical? Theoretically, it could be. Practically, though, not so.

To begin with, the entire strategic force accounts for less than 15 percent of our defense budget (and theirs), which equals around 3 or 4 percent of our federal budget. This translates to a minuscule portion of our gross national product and only around 1.5 percent of their GNP. Hence strategic forces constitute a small part of their economy and an even smaller part of ours. More than 80 percent of either side's defense spending goes for manpower and equipment outside the strategic realm.

Even within this financially peripheral category of strategic arms, not all or even most of the funds would be saved in an arms accord. Surely some—most likely more and surely newer—strategic forces would be allowed, as well as the whole strategic infrastructure. At lower overall levels, we may well need a newly fashioned strategic force, one with fewer warheads on more platforms, to retain the same level of strategic stability at lower levels. Scrapping the huge Trident submarine force, which has been in development since the early Nixon administration, to build smaller missile-carrying submarines or scrapping the MX (in development since the Ford administration) for the Midgetman would be staggeringly expensive.

Add on the high costs of dismantling strategic systems, improving our elaborate command-and-control system, which again rises in importance as the number of weapons declines, and building even more powerful intelligence facilities to monitor the new treaty. The respected Chairman of the Select Committee on Intelligence, Senator David Boren, announced during the INF debate that we would have to vastly improve our coverage of the Soviet Union with more, and more sophisticated, spy satellites to monitor any START treaty. According to press reports, he seeks a whopping $15 billion allocation for several all-weather satellites to help monitor START.

Indeed, this technology costs billions and billions of dollars; I know because I argued with Bill Casey year after year for such a system, but he showed me the staggering costs and mumbled how there was no way to fund "all this." Furthermore, Casey's successor, William Webster, has said publicly that the United States would need intelligence gathering at more than 2,500 weapons locations around the Soviet Union to verify missile dismantlement under START. This too would be exceedingly expensive.

As if these factors were not enough to discredit the idea of a sizable "peace dividend," along comes the Joint Chiefs' mandate to maintain "military sufficiency" under any agreement. If a president would not allow them to build new strategic weapons under an accord lauded as reducing strategic weapons, then the United States may have to move to bolster conventional arms. And, as everyone knows, this is the really big price tag. Since the Soviets enjoy advantages in conventional arms, we would need to build heartily or else be recognized as an inferior military power. Since World War II, the United States and NATO have relied first upon nuclear superiority and then nuclear sufficiency to keep deterrence strong without spending too much on defense.

As early as 1949, David Lilienthal, the first head of the Atomic Energy Commission, spoke about the "widely held notion that an atomic weapon stockpile affords this country a relatively cheap and easy solution of our problems of military security." That notion still persists and prevails.

We have needed nuclear weapons to deter the Russians in Europe; they have not needed nuclear weapons to threaten conquest of Europe. The less we have of that cheaper deterrence, the more we need of the costlier deterrence.

Ironically this problem might be worsened, not eased, in the unlikely event that the Soviets would save significant sums from a strategic accord. Although they might shove these savings into the civilian sector, again they might not. Whatever resources were saved from strategic arms might go into augmenting its conventional superiority. They could thereby build weapons more usable and, in many ways, more dangerous. Given a choice between the Soviets' fielding another fifty SS-18s or another five aircraft carriers or tank divisions, I'd readily choose the former. Obviously, if the overall Soviet military effort were to shrink under a strategic accord or during the time of such a pact, this would benefit Western security. Such a Kremlin decision, however, would be made because of factors other than arms control, as will be treated in the concluding chapter.

Before leaving this topic, I must mention the irony of all this focus upon arms control saving money in a government that habitually wastes money, even on arms control projects. Upon entering the Arms Control and Disarmament Agency, I found to my horror that for years it had spent millions of dollars to support doctoral students writing "arms control" dissertations. Two intriguing projects the agency funded were entitled "The Hypothalamus of the Rat: A Study in Aggression Control" and "Order in the Underworld—A Study of the Cosa Nostra." The latter thesis turned out to be four inches thick. It began:

> This study seeks to illuminate the nature of war and peace in multi-actor systems, such as in international politics, by examining the relative peace and order which has existed in a certain historical period in the American underworld of organized crime.

This examination of "gangland multi-actor politics" ended with twenty-six single-spaced pages of scholarly bibliography that included 366 entries.

THE POLITICS

The substance of arms control shows that it is unlikely to yield cost savings. The politics of arms control, both within and beyond an administration, mightily reinforces this conclusion.

Any administration has to "buy" support from the Joint Chiefs of Staff, and perhaps the Pentagon civilians, to finalize an accord. Presidents know that without JCS approval, a treaty could never gain Senate ratification. In a recently released recording of his telephone conversations, President Kennedy worried about the Joint Chiefs' support for the Limited Test Ban Treaty in 1963: "If we don't get the Chiefs just right, we can blow, get blown. . . . The Chiefs have always been our problem."

President Carter's stab at a comprehensive test ban was doomed from the start since the Joint Chiefs stood foursquare against it. The JCS supported the INF Treaty in large part because the military were never eager for INF deployments in the first place. Civilians in the Carter administration initiated this effort —partly as a ricochet of the "neutron weapon" fiasco, partly to help reassure the Allies while SALT II was up for Senate consideration, partly in response to the SS-20s, and for sundry other reasons—with the military merely acquiescing.

Having appreciated their power over the fate of arms accords, the Joint Chiefs have become masters at leveraging their support. They have learned to attach conditions, supporting an agreement only if such and such a program is assured. They sign no blank checks.

Such leveraging has never been terribly subtle. During the Senate hearings on the 1963 Limited Test Ban Treaty, the Chief of Naval Operations laid down a list of tough "safeguards." The Admiral said he expected that "this treaty, together with the safeguards we have laid down, will perhaps stimulate our test programs." Senator Scoop Jackson responded, "I would hope that would be the case, too." And indeed it proved to be the case; after this test ban treaty was ratified, our nuclear testing program flourished as never before.

With SALT I nearly a decade later, the Joint Chiefs realized that President Nixon, NSC Advisor Kissinger, and Secretary of Defense Melvin Laird were all wheeler-dealers. So that administration sent up SALT I to the Senate along with a hefty package, euphemistically entitled "SALT Related Adjustments to Strategic Programs." The Trident submarine budget skyrocketed from

$140 million to a whopping $942 million the year after SALT I was signed. In addition, the Pentagon would proceed apace on placing many warheads on its missiles, building a new fleet of manned strategic bombers, and developing a new type of strategic arms—cruise missiles.

No wonder Senator Stuart Symington, a member of both the Foreign Relations Committee and the Armed Services Committee, said at the time, "It seems to me that these SALT talks are being used in an effort to sandbag the Congress into heavy additional arms expenditures when the hope of all of us . . . was that agreements . . . would make it possible for us to reduce armaments." Congress was hardly "sandbagged," since it went along most willingly. Even a certified hawk such as Senator Harry Byrd caught the irony: "I am trying to understand how it [SALT I] curbs the arms race. . . . It certainly doesn't do it in regard to military expenditures."

Accompanying SALT II was an even more robust buildup. To gain any chance for ratification, the Carter administration felt compelled to pledge two hundred MX missiles, upgrade the warheads on the Minuteman III missiles, develop the new Stealth bomber, and build an array of cruise missiles. A whopping boost in overall defense spending, 5 percent real annual growth, was also tossed in. But even all this didn't suffice; the Senate Armed Services Committee voted 10–0 that SALT II was "not in the security interests of the United States" even before the Soviets invaded Afghanistan. After that, all chances were gone, and President Carter knowingly withdrew the treaty from Senate consideration.

The Carter administration had to accompany an arms control treaty with an arms buildup ironically because of the arms control process. The message emanating from the Senate deliberation of SALT II was clear: the United States was falling behind in strategic power. Even the liberal Senate Foreign Relations Committee, in its report on SALT II, found: "The SALT debate in the Senate has increased the awareness of the Congress that certain steps must be taken to modernize and strengthen our strategic, theater, and conventional forces." Hence Senator George McGovern lamented that SALT II would lead not to arms control but to arms increases, and liberal writers like Fred Kaplan wrote, "SALT, far from limiting strategic arms, has, in fact, spurred the arms race to a new level of intensity."

And in recent times—contrary to the fears of conservatives and hopes of liberals—public support for defense spending has been related to neither the negotiating nor the consummating of an arms control agreement. Harris polling found that more people worried about the Soviet threat after SALT I was signed than before. Likewise, support for a defense buildup was highest soon after SALT II was signed (also during the twin crises of Afghanistan and the Iranian hostages). Finally, a nosedive in support for defense came when nothing was happening in arms control, between February 1981 and November 1982, when, according to Gallup, the percentage of those who said the United States was spending too little on defense went from 51 percent to 16 percent. The bottom line: the American people are not lulled by arms control. Rather, they base their support for defense on their perception of the threat.

One final argument on arms control economics. There's the more sophisticated argument that arms control may not provide a cash rebate, but it can avoid defense expenditures that otherwise would be needed. The classic example here is the jewel in the crown of arms control, the ABM Treaty of 1972. This accord, it is claimed, saved the United States and USSR millions of dollars that each would have spent for an ABM system to provide strategic defense. This is technically correct. Anticipated costs of a full-scale ABM system ran into the tens of millions of dollars, and this expenditure was precluded by the treaty.

Yet this argument is hasty and untrue. The costs "avoided" by the treaty would have helped our ICBM (or land-based missile) survivability. To accomplish this same goal, we are ending up spending so much more, especially if we proceed with the mobile Midgetman missile. This would mean a penny saved and a whole wad of dollars spent (for the same purpose) later on.

Related but distinct from the economic arguments for arms control is the shopworn contention that it saves us from "unlimited competition." No less a light than former National Security Advisor and nuclear analyst McGeorge Bundy put this argument in a nutshell:

> Arms control is a field in which it is quite easy to look good and get nowhere, but the truth—for both sides—is that reliable and stabilizing agreements are vastly better than unlimited competition.

Overlooking the tautology that "reliable and stabilizing agreements" are good ones, we can still ponder whether the choice really is between arms control and "unlimited competition." It seems not to be.

Competition is always limited—by the expenditures each side chooses to make on strategic weapons, by scientific and engineering resources, by manpower, by military needs relative to the threat, and so on. It is an easily forgotten fact that 80 or 90 percent of either side's military arsenal is, in Bundy's phrase, "unlimited" now, as it has always been. There are no treaty limits on tanks, ships, most planes, guns, soldiers; yet these costly military capabilities are not subject to rapid buildups, as is regularly feared in the strategic realm absent a treaty. The number of Soviet tanks does not triple every few years, as is anticipated in strategic categories without an accord.

Even under a strategic agreement, the competition may be effectively "unlimited." The Soviets entered SALT I with some 1,400 strategic weapons; it ended SALT I, after fairly faithful compliance, with around 10,000 weapons, a sevenfold increase. Under SALT II they more than doubled the number of such weapons, besides adding two new or modified land-based missiles, two new or modified submarine-based missiles, and two new bombers. If this constitutes what Mr. Bundy means by limited competition, it is hard to imagine "unlimited competition."

Thus far in the strategic realm, the Soviets wanted no limits that would significantly alter their five-year military plans. So they have taken their strategic programs and left some headroom above their anticipated force levels when devising previous strategic arms proposals. Such became crystal clear during last-minute SALT I negotiations in Moscow, May 1972. General Secretary Leonid Brezhnev, after agreeing with President Nixon on the silo size permitted for some missiles, spoke on an "open" (unclassified) telephone line to a defense official, who told the boss that this deal was fine; a missile then in development would fit within such specifications.

In SALT II the Soviets rather rudely rejected the Carter administration's initial March 1977 offer of "deep reductions" in strategic arms. They wanted high limits, as was recognized later by the Senate Foreign Relations Committee. Its pre-Afghanistan November 1979 report stated, "A vast increase in the quantity and destructiveness of each side's strategic power will occur during the period of a treaty that seeks to limit strategic offensive arms."

Granted, the Kremlin is not unique in this regard. The Pentagon also seeks to leave our modernization plans as unaffected by a treaty as possible. But over the years their military has been more successful at this than ours.

Likewise the Soviets' attempts to stop our military deployments have been more determined than our attempts to stop their programs. During the early Reagan years, they tried doggedly to stop our INF deployment in Europe. During the late Reagan years, they tried desperately to stop our SDI research.

In both instances the Soviets had a clear strategy but used flawed tactics. On INF they blustered and threatened the European governments rather than coo and woo the European publics. On SDI they likewise blew cold rather than hot; they harangued the program heatedly rather than ignoring it coolly.

Arms control, it is often said, helps bring "predictability," which the Soviets prize above all and which we need for prudent defense planning. But this too is a myth pervading the field.

I admit to being mystified over the notion of a "Soviet strategic breakout"—either under an arms control agreement, as feared by conservatives, or without one, as feared by liberals. Reliable U.S. intelligence on Soviet programs and Soviet sluggishness in building and then fielding new strategic systems relegates "breakout scenarios" to thriller novels. It takes around a decade to design, test, and deploy most new strategic arms; if radically new in design, it takes longer.

We have always received sufficient notice to respond, if need be, to their new weapons. Indeed I know of no strategic "surprises" over the past twenty or thirty years. In fact, the briefings I received in the Pentagon in the mid-1970s on future Soviet systems conformed to those I received in the Arms Control Agency nearly ten years later on current Soviet capabilities. Some previous estimates even gave them too much credit; their cruise missiles, new strategic bombers, and advances in air or missile defenses took longer to develop than we had previously anticipated.

Soviet surprises have not come from strategic weapons breakthroughs. They have come from their regional moves—the Cuban missile crisis in 1962, the Middle East war in 1973, dispatching Cuban troops to Angola in 1975, the invasion of Afghanistan in 1979, the shootdown of the KAL airliner in 1983.

Granted, Moscow too has been surprised by our reactions to their actions. Our indignation over their Angola gambit must have startled them, and our rage over their storming into Afghanistan may have shocked them, especially after our apparent indifference to the previous Marxist takeover of the government there. Surely Kremlin leaders did not expect to hear the President of the United States call their invasion the gravest crisis since World War II.

What about the familiar claim that arms control helps U.S. intelligence gathering? Another myth.

The argument goes that the arms control process gives us information about Soviet programs, information augmented by the exchange of data and now on-site inspection. Equipped with such knowledge, we can then tailor our forces to the threat as it exists, rather than as we conjure it while spinning "worst case" scenarios.

Yet arms agreements can actually *hurt* our intelligence-gathering efforts. The first nuclear agreement, the Limited Test Ban Treaty of 1963, which banned nuclear explosions in the atmosphere, deprived us of information about Soviet nuclear weapons. Underground tests are tougher to detect or decipher than atmospheric tests.

Fortunately for our intelligence, however, the Soviets have consistently violated this agreement by "venting"—that is, allowing radioactive material from such tests to cross international boundaries. We have protested this in diplomatic channels on more than forty occasions over the past twenty-five years, to no avail. So ironically the damage to our intelligence has been mitigated by their treaty violations.

Arms control can hurt intelligence also by blinding us to what we might otherwise see. Our much vaunted satellite capabilities —enabling us to read the license plates of cars in the Kremlin parking lot—work wonderfully well if the cars are parked outside with the license plates clearly shown. We cannot detect military systems that are stored indoors or camouflaged or moved about the great outdoors of the Soviet Union. And these, more than license plates, are what we need to see.

Even big and unimportant items outdoors and stationary can be missed. Incredible as it now seems, U.S. intelligence did not find the now infamous Krasnoyarsk radar for three or four years after its construction began, even though it is several football fields large with a structure twenty-seven stories high; even though it is neither mobile nor shrouded; even though it is located on the only railroad line within a huge distance; and even though it is adjacent to a sizable Soviet ICBM missile field.

Shortly after the radar was "discovered" in August 1983, NSC Advisor William Clark called a snap meeting in the White House to assess its meaning and importance. I asked the CIA analysts why they had missed this huge structure for all these years, despite what was reported as constant satellite coverage of the area. After going through a number of good explanations—unusually cloudy weather, the top priority given to nearby missile fields, some budget-mandated cutbacks in large area coverage—the analysts said they did not expect Moscow to build this type of phased-array radar at that spot. I asked why. After all, locating it there filled in the only area of the country lacking such radar coverge then. The analysts did not expect it there, they replied, since the spot was not "on the periphery facing outward," as the ABM Treaty permitted.

We all were taken aback. U.S. intelligence analysts performed their search presuming the Soviets would not violate the ABM Treaty, rather than looking everywhere in order to detect any violations.

Treaty provisions have warped U.S. intelligence estimates in another instance as well. For years the fact that SALT II limited any missile to no more than ten warheads inclined the intelligence community to attribute ten warheads to Soviet SS-18 missiles. They did so knowing the SS-18s were capable of holding twelve or fourteen and still fulfilling their military mission, knowing there was no way to tell what the missiles did in fact contain, and knowing that estimates should be made on the basis of capabilities and not treaty provisions. Only recently did the community change these estimates.

More damaging still is the diversion of U.S. intelligence resources from serious tasks bearing on our national security to arms control tasks bearing on Soviet adherence to some arcane treaty provisions. For instance, the intelligence community poured men and machines into learning whether the Soviets used buildings constructed for SS-7 missiles to house people or parts associated with their SS-25 missiles. SALT II did not permit this. So the CIA had to analyze which activities were done in which buildings, a silly exercise if there ever was one.

Why do it, then? Because the President must report to the Congress yearly on any and all Soviet violations. He needs the facts.

Thus the CIA must examine every possible violation, no matter how recondite or immaterial to our national security.

Thus did it have to dive into the distinction between SS-25 and SS-13 missiles. Since SALT II limited each side to one "new type" of ballistic missile, and since it defined a "new type" as more than x, y, and z different from an already built missile, the CIA had to scour its files for information on SS-13 flight tests conducted in the 1960s by this missile that was retired years ago. U.S. security was obviously unaffected by the performance of a missile already dismantled, and U.S. intelligence had better things to do. Yet this was done in order to detect and report on violations of SALT II, an unratified agreement the President had denounced as "fatally flawed" and one that would have expired (had it ever gone into effect) by then anyway.

Ditto for Backfire bomber production rates. This constraint was not even included in the SALT II treaty; it was handled in a side letter. Regardless, whether the Soviets produced thirty-two Backfires yearly or twenty-eight makes no difference to our national security, yet it made every difference to arms control compliance. So it too was analyzed. How the Soviets dismantle an aged strategic system is of no concern to anyone but arms controllers, yet the intelligence community pours precious resources in this area too in order to check compliance.

The arms negotiations could have harmed our security also by our giving out more information than we take in, but we'll never know this balance sheet. A professional group that strives mightily to be cautious with their Soviet "colleagues" in Geneva, our negotiators are still Americans. They are still friendly, chatty, and innately trusting. God only knows how much has been said over the years that should not have been said in talks around the table, around the town, and during endless rounds of social gatherings.

ON-SITE INSPECTION

Hope springs eternal, especially in arms control. Maybe in this new age we can help rather than hurt our intelligence gathering, especially with the advent of on-site inspection in the INF Treaty.

Yet this too is oft oversold. The "site" is restricted to that acknowledged as a facility associated with a weapon limited by the treaty, which are not necessarily the Soviets' most important military sites. And the "on" is narrow; U.S. inspectors only go to sites at particular times. Knowing when we will come to call, the Soviets have time to hide whatever they can or wish. It is safe to say that no U.S. inspector will *ever* be shown a Soviet violation. If any Soviet official allows such, his career will not exactly prosper.

From the people who brought the world Potemkin villages can come rather deceptive on-site inspections. A century ago the Marquis de Custine wrote, "Russians conspire with miraculous harmony to make duplicity prevail in their country. They have dexterity in lying, a naturalness in falsehood." Many a visitor, like himself, "is fed on illusion" and needs to distinguish "Russia as it is and Russia as it would like to show itself to Europe."

Some visitors have not made this distinction. Vice President Henry Wallace, for instance, visited a Stalinist labor camp at Kolyma in 1944. He was never shown one prisoner. He knew nothing of their measly food allotments or their light clothing to weather the frigid 60 below Siberian temperatures. Thousands of Stalin's enemies and other victims were starved, frozen, or worked to death at this site between 1932 and 1954. When Wallace visited, however, the watch towers were removed and the hearty guards dressed as workers. Wallace later wrote about the "big, husky" laborers he met who shared a pioneering spirit like our settlers out West. The food served was so delectable that, as he wrote, it "led me to inquire about the presiding chef of this mining camp."

This may be excused due to the times (during our "wartime alliance") or the man. But the phenomenon has been widespread, as described by Malcolm Muggeridge, who lived in Moscow during Stalin's terror. He witnessed

the extraordinary performance of the liberal intelligentsia, who in those days flocked to Moscow like pilgrims to Mecca. And they were one and all utterly delighted and excited by what they saw there. Clergymen walked serenely and happily through the anti-god museums, politicians claimed that no system of society could possibly be more equitable and just, lawyers admired Soviet justice, and economists praised the Soviet economy.

Surely the times have changed and even the Soviets themselves have turned bitingly critical of such hypocrisy. Still, some things change slowly: American officials got paint on their hands when inspecting a Soviet military installation at Gomel, the site of a previous violation, at Christmastime 1987.

On balance, thus far arms control has not contributed to our overall knowledge of Soviet military programs. Indeed, U.S. intelligence knows less today about Soviet strategic programs than it did at the start of the arms control process.

THE LONG SWEEP

So where does all this lead? Surely not to adoration of arms control, but to seeing it in its proper light—warts and all. Not much to show for an enormous effort.

When I first arrived at the Arms Control and Disarmament Agency, I commissioned a study to compare what arms agreements delivered with what was expected of them. The words of those championing the accords before they took effect was compared with what happened afterward. The study was conducted by a group at Harvard University, hardly a hotbed of right-wing fervor, and was headed by Al Carnesale, who later advised Democratic candidate Michael Dukakis. It concluded:

> What is most striking about the arms control experience surveyed here is what it did not do. Those who hoped arms control would bring about major reductions in existing or planned inventories or slow the introduction of new and more capable technologies have little grounds for satisfaction. Nor do those who looked to arms control as a means for constraining the emergence of a large, modern Soviet arsenal. . . .

Despite all the attention and commotion accorded arms control, the study noted, "The stridency of the debate, however, provides little clue to this modest reality; proponents and critics, liberals and conservatives, hawks and doves—all seem to exaggerate the potential and actual impact of arms control."

The Harvard group examined recent agreements concluded in the nuclear age. The same dismal record dogs prenuclear arms deals, though the quantity is tiny. Besides the Geneva Protocols, there were but two arms treaties concluded by the United States before World War II. Both dealt with ships; neither was a success, though each holds its own charm.

The Rush-Bagot Agreement of 1817 was an act of reconciliation, after the War of 1812, between the United States and Britain, which then ruled Canada. This treaty stands as a model of diplomatic expediency; it was negotiated in just two days.

Designed and sold as a measure to "demilitarize the Great Lakes" by preventing a "naval arms race" there, it did no such thing. Both sides worked around the treaty provisions by stashing warships in nearby dockyards and by constructing "commercial" vessels easily convertible to military use. And each built more arsenals on land, the Americans erecting forts along the border—even building one fort on Canadian territory until this error was uncovered.

The second accord, the Naval Treaty of 1922, limited capital ships but not submarines or cruisers, the systems then coming on stream and which proved most critical in World War II. Historian Samuel Eliot Morrison described this stab at disarmament:

> The U.S. Navy scrapped 15 new capital ships . . . [but] at the end of 1934 Japan denounced the . . . treaties and started a frenzied building program which, by the time war broke out in the Pacific, rendered the Japanese navy more powerful in every type of ship than the U.S. and British Pacific and Asiatic fleets combined.

As for cost savings, these were fleeting and soon offset. Again Morrison: "[The] naval limitation saved the American taxpayer of 1922–1937 millions of dollars, but the taxpayer after 1941 paid a hundredfold for this futile gesture."

These accords should have been better. For one thing, they were not negotiated between political adversaries, as the modern accords have been. The nineteenth-century deal was struck by two former enemies, the United States and Britain, each seeking reconciliation. The twentieth-century endeavor was restricted to World War I winners; it excluded defeated Germany and then-ostracized Soviet Union. But they weren't better, and commentators turned somewhat bitter from the experience.

In the past quarter century, arms control has made a spectacular comeback, despite its previous unimpressive record. Positive news has been squeezed out of the sorriest situation, which brings to mind the Russian folktale of the doctor, arriving too late at the bedside of a man who died of a fever, asking the dead man's family if he had been sweating. Upon learning that he had, the doctor breaks into a smile. "That, in any event, is certainly a good sign."

REDUCTIONS ARE NEEDED

Despite its woeful record, the goals of arms control—fewer nuclear weapons and greater safety—should be vigorously pursued. There in my office with Herr Vogel in 1984, I tried to explain how prudent Western defense planning could lead to a safer world with or without an arms accord. Should there be one, I said, fine. If not, that should be fine, too. I quoted Dean Acheson as saying that we can never get a good agreement unless we are fully prepared to live without one. Vogel listened politely, not believing a word of what I was saying.

Nonetheless, it is true. It is not essential to have an agreement in order to have a more secure world. There can be arms control without reductions or greater safety—the pattern from the Rush-Bagot Agreement through SALT I and SALT II—and some achievement of these goals without arms control—the pattern now unfolding.

Given the huge, even ludicrous, nuclear arsenals on each side, some types of additional strategic systems provide a smaller amount (if any at all) of additional security. While the United States cannot accept clear Soviet strategic superiority, anything around parity is good enough. This is particularly true given the total mystery of what would actually happen, humanly and technically, during an actual nuclear engagement.

Given this perspective, we can safely forgo any new land-based missile deployments, whether MX or Midgetman, whose $25-plus billion price tag is a bit steep.

While in office, I advocated building no new ICBMs. Doing even worse than David Livingston, whose lifetime as a missionary in Africa produced but one convert, I gained none at all during my years in government. My colleagues remained unconvinced that, in this category anyway, enough was enough. Further, I persuaded no one that the once unique features of land-based missiles were no longer as unique.

ICBMs have long been extolled for their "prompt hard target kill" capacity; Bud McFarlane, for one, never tired of harping on this. It sounds good and seems technically sophisticated. Still, it's too convoluted. When would we ever need this capability? To be "prompt" means the missiles can be fired quickly, something that seems to be needed to respond to a surprise Soviet attack.

But this in turn raises quandaries and dangers. If our response were based on mere computer-spewed information, the President should certainly *not* launch these "prompt" missiles, or any missiles. He should order our strategic bombers aloft and put our nuclear force on high alert. But he should *never* fire anything unrecallable—and thereby risk blowing up parts of Russia and possibly the world—on the basis of computer information. This stance of "launch on warning" or "launch under attack" without absolute, incontrovertible evidence that weapons have detonated on our soil is immoral, foolish, and possibly suicidal.

Yet if our response follows such detonations, the missiles need not be so "prompt." They need only to still exist and work. Likewise, they need not have a "hard target capacity" since many Soviet "hard targets"—its missile silos—would no longer be "targets" at all; they would be empty. Besides, the new Soviet land-based missiles are mobile; a "hard target" kill capacity is not needed to target them.

Whatever residual need exists for a "hard target kill capacity" can be carried by today's fleet of Minuteman missiles and tomorrow's fleet of strategic submarines. For the first time ever, they too could take out hard targets, and promptly at that, if cruising near Soviet land.

ICBMs have also been promoted for having retargeting features, yet our existing missiles have this capability, so we need not build new ICBMs for this reason. And the new missiles on submarines too will have this feature.

Granted, the President's command and control over submarines is less sure or secure than over land-based missiles. But sound improvements have been made here with redundant systems to communicate with commanders at sea.

Granted, too, there may be a time when our submarine force becomes vulnerable. Count me as a skeptic, though. Despite all the scary Navy briefings on this score over the years, the trends have been going the other way. The oceans are becoming more opaque and less translucent. Should there be a breakthrough in antisubmarine warfare; however, we would have sufficient warning time. And given the state of relative technological sophistication, in all probability we would achieve such a breakthrough before the Soviets. Hence we would then have time to regroup and rethink.

Finally, land-based missiles are appreciated for their high reliability. Yet missiles on submarines have also become quite reliable recently. And one can question the ICBM's grand reputation in this regard. The only recent time these missiles were test-fired from operational silos, the test failed. Since then, and this was years ago, no tests from actual silos have been ventured. We do know, however, that during most of 1986, part of our land-based missile force would not have worked since its computers were loaded with the wrong launch codes. "You could have pushed the button and nothing would have happened," said a SAC official at the Montana base where this occurred. "They would have sat in their silos."

The approach advanced here, building no new ICBMs, should not be equated with advocating a new "strategic diad" of planes and boats while altogether eliminating the land-based leg of the triad. We should keep the Minuteman missiles operational—change the batteries when necessary and improve the guidance system when possible. We should either keep them in hardened silos—which recent research shows makes them less vulnerable than previously believed—or fit them with a "carry-hard" protection whereby we would move the existing number of missiles around into many more holes so the Soviets would not then know which hole lodged a missile. And we should proceed with the first stages of SDI to assure greater protection of *all* critical strategic sites, not just missile silos but also command-and-control facilities and the like.

Lest all this become too technical for the reader, suffice it to say that the land-based missiles we have are good enough. They will last long enough. They have no wear and tear since, thank goodness, they are never used. Changing parts can make them last forever. Our future strategic programs can accent SDI and strategic cruise missiles. Those deployed in the air would be stabilizing as they are carried on slow, easily detectable, and recallable bombers. Those at sea would be stabilizing for similar reasons.

All in all, this strategic posture would, over time, usher in a less dangerous world of fewer nuclear weapons, given the normal attrition rate in various systems. The more that cheap, accurate, and reliable weapons (like cruise missiles) are placed on relatively cheap and invulnerable platforms, the greater the stability. The more that defenses can be built to discourage any rational Soviet or Third World military planner from being able to knock out prime targets in the United States—and to protect us against accidental or unauthorized attack—again, the greater our security.

Couple these moves with the grand trend away from nuclear weapons altogether. For modern technology now allows the use of conventional arms for missions once allocated solely to nuclear arms. The accuracy of conventional weapons is becoming incredible, down to around one meter (or three feet) for a cruise missile after flying thousands of miles.

By relying more on satellites, remotely piloted vehicles, electronics, and thermal imaging, our forces can better aim at targets deep behind enemy lines. New precision-guided missiles, target-seeking warheads, and air-delivered mines and explosives can attack these targets, be they tanks or permanent command posts, far in the distance. This technological revolution enables conventional arms to substitute for nuclear weapons, just as NATO has replaced the nuclear Nike-Hercules air defense with the non-nuclear Patriot system.

Such moves raise the nuclear threshold and make the early use of nuclear weapons less likely. Such provide the President with more options in crises. Rather than today's set-piece escalation from conventional arms to nuclear weapons, for instance, NATO could respond to a Warsaw Pact attack by geographical escalation, by targeting the invading forces *and* prime targets in Soviet territory itself, all the while staying on a conventional plane. Such technological advances would also help with messy Third World contingencies. Instead of pilots flying off to bomb parts of Libya, for example, we could fire cruise missiles offshore or from far-off aircraft and be sure they'd hit the right tent.

The traditional arms control process, and its product, can complicate, stall, or even prevent this long march backward toward a less nuclear world. It would do so in part because no way exists to verify whether a weapons system is conventionally or nuclear-armed. Any serious verification scheme has to count any dual-capable system as "nuclear-armed" which in turn prompts the military to make those weapons "nuclear-armed" in order to maximize their firepower.

Absent such an encumbrance, the military could move toward greater conventional use of its now deemed "strategic" weapons —cruise missiles and manned bombers like B-52s. The Air Force, especially the Strategic Air Command, is eager to equip more than half its B-52s with conventional arms, as was done during the Vietnam War. These bombers could be used in Europe or in the Third World against supply depots, headquarter bunkers, and communication centers.

Such technological moves, allowed to run their natural course toward greater stability, both reflect and reinforce the reduced saliency of nuclear weapons in our world. Nuclear arms remain important, but the shadow they cast is becoming shorter and dimmer. Gone is the day when anyone could say, as did Senator Edwin Johnson of Colorado, that with "vision and guts and plenty of A-bombs," the United States could "compel mankind to adopt the policy of peace . . . or be burned to a crisp."

"Nothing Else in Life Really Matters"

Whether such sensible steps can be taken, given the enormous pull of formal arms control, is questionable. I was once hopeful that progress would come in the Reagan administration—led by a man whose skepticism of arms control was pronounced before entering office and whose knowledge of the field was largely confined to Dr. Bellison's anti–arms control treatise, *The Treaty Trap.*

But such hope was not long sustained. The deepest disagreement I had with Secretary of State George Shultz over the years stemmed from my presenting the thrust of this approach in a winter 1984 *Foreign Affairs* article entitled "Arms Control with and Without Agreements." Secretary Shultz kindly read every page and went over the article meticulously with me in his private office. And even though NSC Advisor Robert McFarlane wrote me a laudatory memo after making suggestions for slight revisions, Shultz was angry upon the article's publication. He told me so himself, just as he told others.

Perhaps this was a matter of timing; the Soviets signaled willingness to return to the table between the time he read the piece and the time of its publication. Mostly, though, I attribute his reaction to the unconventional nature of the thesis itself.* It is always tough to go against what John Stuart Mill called "the tyranny of prevailing opinion" within an administration or any group.

---

*For a full explanation, see Chapter 7, page 291 and following.

Not only do secretaries of state look to an arms control agreement to furnish part of their historical legacy, but presidents and members of Congress, and indeed the public at large, have come to *expect* an arms control agreement during a president's term in office. Certainly President Reagan would have been disappointed had the INF Treaty not panned out.

I did not grasp the full extent of arms control's lure until mingling one night in 1983 or 1984 at the British embassy. During a gala dinner in honor of opposition leader Neil Kinnock, I was assailed by Kinnock's wife, an antinuclear activist of most fervent conviction. After telling me of her singular dedication to stopping the installation of our INF missiles in Britain, she implored me to help conclude some agreement with the Soviets, the sooner the better.

In a heartfelt manner, Mrs. Kinnock then looked into my eyes and said, "Nothing else in life really matters, does it?"

"Nothing else than what?" I asked.

"Than arms control!" she suddenly replied.

When I retorted, "Sure. Family. Peace. Country. Freedom. All these things matter," she added pedantically, "But all these things are impossible without arms control! I'm sure when you think about it, you'll agree that nothing else in life really matters."

Since then, I *have* thought about it. Quite a bit. I remain to be convinced, however.

CHAPTER 5

THE WASHINGTON
SUMMIT

THERE WAS HARDLY any "behind the scenes" during the Washington summit, my last summit in office. What was interesting was vaunted in public, namely the captivating personality of one Mikhail Gorbachev and the warm reception Washington extended him. What happened in private, especially between the President and the General Secretary, was either jumbled or disappointing.

The real "behind the scenes" action comes in the lead-up to and aftermath of the Washington summit, action which helped shape the INF Treaty and limit the damage that came in its wake. These were tricky issues to handle, critical to handle right.

For regardless of how good a job we might have done—and admittedly, opinions differ here—the treaty's effect will last long beyond the Reagan administration. All the returns aren't in yet on its overall value, for reasons made clear as we walk through the Washington summit. We will take several diversions to tell the strange twists and turns in the actual making of an arms control treaty.

• • •

Gorbachev did the town when he came to Washington in December 1987. This third Reagan-Gorbachev summit was to be my last. I left government as Gorbachev left town and, like him, with more mirth than melancholy.

If the essence of the first summit, Geneva 1985, was "getting to know you"; and the second, Reykjavik 1986, was "let's go for broke"; the core of the third, Washington 1987, was "hey, look him over." From the moment Mikhail Gorbachev pulled up to the White House South Lawn entrance in his armored Zil limousine, to the blaring trumpets and twenty-one-gun salute at its close, everyone gawked. The Washington scene resembled a college fraternity house during rush week, but there was only one pledge.

Gorbachev leaped into Washington almost in a single bound. He stopped briefly in London for a rehearsal with Prime Minister Margaret Thatcher. I would have liked to witness that session, since Mrs. Thatcher is the only world leader I have heard argue as intensely and interminably as Gorbachev. He's at least a better listener.

When Gorbachev and Raisa arrived at Andrews Air Force Base, they were on a high. The steely though somewhat moody Soviet leader seemed like an excited kid coming for the first time to the Big Top to watch the circus parade. His first visit to America was chockablock: meetings with the President were crammed between sessions with intellectuals, members of Congress, the Vice President, publishers and business leaders, and of course the Washington elite who attended breakfasts, lunches, and dinners for Gorbachev. The State Department luncheon (with a Russian-singing glee club from Yale, of all things) lasted until nearly four o'clock on Wednesday, a few hours before Gorbachev's reciprocal dinner for the President in the Soviet embassy. Gorbachev's arrival in Washington, like Reagan's visit to Moscow six months hence, made the summit less a business affair than a social affair or public spectacle.

As Gorbachev scurried from event to event, Washington elites who had become casual in the presence of power gawked shamelessly. Washingtonians were snarled up in traffic that became gridlock. Wave after wave of police vehicles with screeching sirens accompanied the sleek Russian limousines. In a city whose inhabitants scarcely glance up when presidential motorcades zoom by, something unique was happening. And when the General Secretary bounded from his limo in the heart of downtown D.C. to "press the flesh" à la Lyndon Baines Johnson—as a hapless Vice President George Bush looked on, amazed—something special had happened. A woman on Connecticut Avenue squealed after meeting Gorbachev that it was like meeting the Messiah on earth! "If Gorbachev were an American, he'd be as American as apple pie," House Speaker James Wright said inanely after his breakfast with the Man.

Not that everything was so scripted that it came off with boring precision. We had some unboring cliff-hangers on both ends, the night of Gorbachev's arrival and the very hour of his departure. The first raised doubts about the summit centerpiece, the signing of the INF Treaty, the second about what was anticipated as the next summit's centerpiece, the strategic arms accord.

As always, the Washington summit began for us long before it began for them, for Gorbachev and Reagan. Secretary Shultz and Foreign Minister Shevardnadze held a record number of meetings, five over an eight-month period, to shape things up for this summit. Soviet diplomats told us quietly, "No more Reykjaviks. Let's have things planned and structured." We sought the same.

The most critical of these sessions occurred in Moscow in August 1987, just when the Reagan administration most needed CPR as it was rocked by that summer's Iran-contra revelations.

To prepare for this preparatory meeting for the summit, American and Soviet delegations in Geneva worked painstakingly day after day, night after night, to hammer out "joint working documents." They highlighted substantive areas of agreement and disagreement for "the ministers" to resolve. All their dedicated work came to naught as their arduously negotiated tomes were left untouched by the ministers. Secretary Shultz's caution led him to have us "experts" handle the intricacies, which naturally pleased us no end. Foreign Minister Shevardnadze was, if anything, more skittish yet, especially since Marshal Akhromeyev commanded both Gorbachev's respect and mastery of the subject. Shevardnadze preferred that Akhromeyev and his "expert" team work out meddlesome issues, as did Akhromeyev himself. So when the U.S. and Soviet "experts" threatened to refer troubling issues "to the ministers," both sides knew it was a bluff; the ministers did not want the referral. They would send it back to us.

In Washington, meanwhile, most of the same players disputed most of the same issues with the President. The new National Security Advisor, Frank Carlucci, tried to cobble together a U.S. position with saintlike patience but without godlike results. Lengthy sessions were held in the White House with Carlucci, Shultz, Weinberger, Crowe, Acting CIA Director Robert Gates, the new Chief of Staff Howard Baker, Budget Director Jim Miller, the negotiators, and, more often than not, the President himself.

Though the participants tried to work through the issues, the discussions wandered far afield. Our Washington battles had all too little to do with the huge differences between American and Soviet positions in Geneva. Instead, they reflected the favorite hobby horses of Cabinet officers or their staffs.

The Situation Room sessions began with the military's effort to rectify—what else?—Reykjavik. There, among other sins, we had somewhat inadvertently squeezed into five years the strategic arms reductions anticipated in the START Treaty. The Joint Chiefs deemed this downright dangerous. They needed more time to build up compensating forces for those they had to dismantle. Such a time frame may have been impossible anyway, since the destruction of so many systems took more than five years. Could we walk the Reykjavik offer back to seven years?

This was one of hundreds of issues yet to be resolved with the Soviets, by no means the most important or contentious. I suggested the Soviets would welcome such a stretch-out. This pleased the Joint Chiefs but prompted others to insist we "get something in exchange for it," if the Soviets would like it. Tough bargaining is always advisable with those fellows, but to expect something in return for rectifying our own mistake struck even me as a tad excessive.

Adding to our woes on this matter was the President. He seemed confused, probably presuming that our much-heralded 50 percent cuts in strategic arms actually meant 50 percent cuts, not increases in various parts of our (and their) strategic arsenals.

After some thrashing about, we all agreed that Shultz should mention this slight altercation to Shevardnadze and try to "get something for it." When he did so, the Russians were nonplussed. Sure, a seven-year reduction schedule could be managed. In fact, they asked if we could stretch out the INF reduction period from three to four years. At least they did not ask for something in return.

This was not the only issue we wrangled over before the Washington summit. At Reykjavik Reagan had offered Gorbachev ten years of no SDI deployment in exchange for various Soviet concessions. The Pentagon subsequently sought to shorten this time frame from ten years to seven. Secretary Weinberger claimed SDI research had made such stunning progress that it might be ready before 1996, in fact by 1993. When Howard Baker asked about nudging up the revised date to 1994 and Cap grudgingly agreed, Baker quipped, "Generous to a fault."

Such high-level gatherings around the Situation Room Table

invariably favor an Arms Control Director, who has the enormous advantage of spending full time on this one topic. So while Shultz and Weinberger might devote fifteen minutes on an arms control issue—wedged between time on the Persian Gulf or Central America or whatever—I could spend fifteen hours. With a small but technically proficient staff, I did not have to craft advice to the President to please many fiefdoms within the agency, as Cabinet officers are oft wont to do.

Having a solid working relationship with both Shultz and Weinberger—though I was usually closer to Weinberger on the issues—I tried to help dampen their differences.

Now and then it worked, as on the hottest issue in this pre-Moscow debate. The topic concerned whether or not Shultz should *discuss* the ABM Treaty in Moscow with Shevardnadze. This was battered about for more than half an hour when I jumped in to call it a "phony issue." Shultz was right to say that we had to be ready to discuss it with the Russians, yet Cap was right that we should not alter our position when doing so. Why not reiterate in Moscow what we had reiterated about the ABM Treaty regularly over the years in Geneva, Washington, or wherever?

Both men laid down their markers. Cap never wanted to reinterpret or reemphasize the ABM Treaty; Shultz never wanted to freeze our position if we found sound reason to change it. And this matter was left at that.

Substance seemingly settled, in a fashion, for this Moscow meeting, Weinberger raised one final matter: whether to have the Moscow meeting at all. If there was to be a meeting, he didn't want it to be in Moscow where every U.S. facility could be compromised. KGB fellows had penetrated the most inviolate parts of our embassy, it was then thought, and this raised security concerns about all of our Moscow facilities.

Shultz retorted with two arguments—no place was perfectly secure, and Moscow would be made secure enough by the time we arrived. He did not reveal his real reason for keeping the meeting there, that he wanted to meet with Gorbachev, which was simply impossible elsewhere. Howard Baker chimed in that he did not like the notion of "being run out of town" by the Moscow embassy scandal. The phrase evidently caught the President's fancy, as he used it the following day to explain why he was sending Shultz to Moscow regardless of the Marine caper then unfolding. It was a nice phrase, even though its meaning was a bit murky. We were not "in town" to be run out of it. Rather, we were debating whether or not to *go* to the town. Moreover, as Cap put it, "the town" was Moscow, and what is so bad about "being run out" of that place?

Having reached at least momentary consensus, we were ready for our departure. The Secretary of State amassed his usual gaggle of arms control advisors, taken more for bureaucratic solace than their professional contributions, but it made us appear to be gunning for bear. And perhaps the press would interpret our large numbers as a sign of our great sincerity.

Our problems went beyond appearance. Shultz lacked clear guidance on what he could do, though he was laden with guidance on what he could *not* do. After long and arduous machinations, he was given less leeway than his office entitled him, scarcely more, in fact, than our Geneva negotiators were given. And what was new in his guidance would be distinctly unappealing to the Soviets, nothing to bridge the differences with them over strategic arms or SDI. Because of some low-level braggarts in the Pentagon and whiners in the State Department, his teeny leeway in authority and his orders to deliver the bad news to the Soviets became magnified in the press. Shultz took such public humiliation in admirably good stride.

Once in Moscow, the team worked hard and fairly well. None of the three issues that consumed us so passionately during the preparatory sessions in Washington—stretch-outs for reductions under START; stretch-ins for deployment of SDI; and whether to discuss the ABM Treaty—concerned us at all in Moscow. We divvied up the work on the whole nine yards of arms control issues as well as the human rights and regional matters.

The meetings' pivotal moment came late, during the last session between Shevardnadze and Shultz. It involved an issue that had never been so much as mentioned in our Washington sessions. And it rose in a most peculiar way.

For some reason, Shevardnadze asked whether or not we would agree to "begin" negotiations on short-range INF missiles, those able to travel less distance than SS-20s or Pershing IIs but farther than battlefield weapons. After receiving several scribbled notes, Shultz said that since 1981 we had in fact insisted upon including such systems in any INF deal. It was the Soviets who sought to exclude them.

Shevardnadze plunged on, undeterred. Were we willing to *begin* negotiations on these weapons, or were we not? Gorbachev said publicly that these were critical systems. In fact, he wanted to eliminate them altogether. So would we open negotiations on them?

Shultz sensed that Shevardnadze was trying to put him in a "gotcha" posture. If we concurred, they could take credit for proposing yet another negotiation on a nuclear weapon important to the Europeans. If we declined, better still; they could claim to have proposed a move toward peace only to find that we had refused.

Shevardnadze kept pushing and Shultz kept dodging. Around and around they went. At certain times the Soviet delegation seemed thrown into confusion, which might have been due to genuine misinformation, but I doubt it.

Behind such verbal playfulness lay hard security concerns. The Moscow meeting culminated when Gorbachev, in its closing moments, flipped out the offer to eliminate all such short-range INF systems. This was then dubbed the "second zero" of the INF zero option, the first being the elimination of longer-range INF systems like the SS-20s, Pershing IIs, and ground cruise missiles.

The proverbial Martian would have regarded this as good news for the West. The Soviets had loads of them—somewhere around one thousand—and stationed some of them in East Germany and Czechoslovakia. We had none; West Germany had around one hundred equipped to carry U.S. warheads aboard, but they were headed for the scrap heap anyway. Gorbachev's offer to jettison up to a thousand Soviet nuclear arms facing Western Europe while asking us to eliminate next to nothing had to be good news for us.

But it wasn't taken that way. Logic and politics do not always mesh, and the Martian does not live in Western Europe.

The leaders there recognized the advantage of Gorbachev's destroying those one thousand missiles staring at them (actually at the West Germans). They certainly did not want a new round of American deployments of missiles (which would in turn trigger a new round of rowdy protests across Europe). Yet, they viewed Gorbachev's offer as adding fuel to the fire of a denuclearized Western Europe. This they feared, especially since Reykjavik, as they did not want a nonnuclear world or a nonnuclear Europe. Nuclear weapons, especially those with an American flag on them, helped compensate for Soviet conventional and chemical weapon superiority. This they all knew, though only Thatcher would say so often and out loud.

Gorbachev's "second zero" would only reinforce everything bad about the first zero, the elimination of the Pershings, cruise missiles and SS-20s. Such concerns were manageable in normal times, but when the two superpower leaders began chanting hymns of a nonnuclear world, the times are no longer normal. The Allied dimension of this issue was to play out, in all its drama, after we left Moscow and landed at NATO headquarters in Brussels.

Meanwhile, Secretary Shultz trudged through his four-part agenda in Moscow. As usual, though, nothing much happened on the other three items, even though we spent from eight to past midnight one night on regional issues.

Back in the secure part of our embassy afterward—was anything really "secure" anymore, especially in Moscow?—Shultz asked if any of us had found anything more interesting in that discussion than he had. I noted how impressed I was with Shevardnadze's knowledge of the Reagan doctrine. He had it down cold. He had explained it more clearly than I had ever heard anyone do in Washington. "America reserves the right to give military, economic, political, and moral assistance to all these groups fighting communist governments, doesn't it?" he asked Shultz at one point. "You're doing the same thing in Nicaragua as in Afghanistan and Cambodia, aren't you?"

On the plane ride back home the next day, I told Shultz that an idea had popped into my head when listening to how he and Shevardnadze roamed from Central America to Asia to Africa to the Persian Gulf, each repeating their well-known and well-worn positions. Why not raise Eastern Europe next time? Why not, when covering the various regions during the evening, say, "Mr. Minister, I now wish to give you our views and receive your views on central Europe. To us, it seems that in Hungary, or in Poland, or in East Germany, thus and thus is happening." Initially, Shevardnadze would be aghast. Since Yalta, the fate of Warsaw Pact countries has not been a matter of serious dialogue between Washington and Moscow. But why not make it so? If hours of discussion focus on Central America, our backyard, why not spend hours on central Europe, their backyard? Why not reiterate that American goals now remain as they were at Yalta—

"free and unfettered elections" and state sovereignty, which can come with the symbolic removal of that gash across central Europe, the Berlin Wall, and then the emerging of a civil society? Shultz listened, thinking, I presume, that the time had not come for such a discussion. It will, though, before too long. At least, it should, and the sooner, the better.

CHALLENGING OUR ALLIES ON THE WAY HOME

Talk of Eastern Europe was not uppermost in our minds when we left "the workers' paradise" after these ministerial meetings. Instead fears of the Western Europeans dominated our thoughts.

As was customary after each Shultz-Shevardnadze or Reagan-Gorbachev meeting, the Secretary of State stopped in Brussels. This was another stroke of Shultz genius; many times Old World diplomats care as much that you speak to them as what you say to them.

This was the exception, however. We spent most of the night after leaving Moscow crafting a "gotcha" proposal of our own. Shultz would tell the NATO Foreign Ministers the next morning that we would wait to respond to Gorbachev's "second zero" offer until they decided upon what they wanted us to do. Secretary Shultz presented two clear options: we could a) accept, thereby eliminating Soviet systems and precluding our own; b) reject, allowing the Soviets to retain a certain number which we would then match. What we could *not* do, he made plain fourteen ways, was any third option: to reject Gorbachev and yet not build up to match the Soviet numbers.

Yet this third option was precisely the German government's favorite, as it would seem to douse the fires of European denuclearization by keeping alternatives open for future short-range INF deployments. The third option, though, was essentially an empty one: Options do not deter; only weapons deter. If the Soviets had these nuclear weapons deployed, it seemed to us, NATO should either deploy some number or both sides should go down to zero. We should not accept a thousand warheads on their side and zero on ours if we did not need to. Even if we gained the legal right to build up, the probability of the German government mustering the political will to deploy new systems in the aftermath of an INF treaty was nil.

The Foreign Ministers gathered around the North Atlantic

Council table at NATO headquarters in Brussels understood the arguments, but again they felt trapped.

Each had his own particular reasons for not wanting Gorbachev's "second zero," the elimination of the shorter-range INF missiles in Europe. The French relished their nuclear weapons; even under the Socialists, they were in the process of increasing their nuclear arms budget more rapidly than their conventional arms account. And the French mostly abhorred arms control deals; they had refused to join the previous European conventional arms talks, to sign the nearly universal Non-Proliferation Treaty, or to restrict their controversial nuclear testing program.

Likewise, the British valued their nuclear forces. Prime Minister Thatcher often expounded on the glories of nuclear deterrence. And at that moment she was on the verge of a political campaign against the antinuclear Labour party. She did not welcome the idea of Reagan and Gorbachev seeming to support the position of her opponent Neil Kinnock.

The Germans, as always, were the big problem. As Winston Churchill once said, the Germans are either at your knees or at your throat. This time, they should have been on a couch, as their behavior showed signs of psychological distress. Not that they should have been traumatized; I had personally explained to the German Ambassador in Washington a month beforehand that the Soviet negotiators had been murmuring about the possibility of a second zero. So Bonn had had sufficient warning to get its act together.

But it didn't. When the Gorbachev offer came, the Germans were all over the lot. Chancellor Helmut Kohl despised distancing himself from his mate Ronald Reagan on anything. Yet he also despised having his geographically small country (the size of Oregon) singled out as Europe's prime nuclear battlefield. To accept the second zero and thus to eliminate all the short-range INF missiles from Europe would leave only the tactical or battlefield nukes. Thus the only land-based nuclear weapons left in Europe would be those able to detonate on German territory—conceivably used against Warsaw Pact forces on West German territory or, with greater luck, on East German land.

Chancellor Kohl told visitors with some passion how his own son worried that arms control was turning Germany into the sole locale of a nuclear conflict. And Kohl's top advisor later came tearing around Washington to denounce Gorbachev's second zero proposal by quipping that the shorter the range of nuclear systems, the more Germans potentially die.

"German singularity," as it was dubbed, tugged at German heartstrings. It fed their traditional feelings of victimization, of being the victims of foreign wrongdoing. Hitler was, of course, the master at playing upon this deep German sentiment, but he was not the first or last to arouse it. The left has fostered such feelings in the postwar period by portraying Germany as a mere pawn between the superpowers. Now the right would exploit it by harping upon being abandoned in U.S. security concerns.

All told, the INF episode rocked the postwar German approach to security. Their unspoken, and unspeakable, policy has been to export German vulnerability as far and wide as possible to other NATO countries. German security has been based on the *inse*curity of its guarantors. Having INF systems on the continent meant that the Russians could target all of Western Europe with their land-based nuclear forces, as American INF systems could target Soviet territory. Removing all INF systems, both short- and long-range, placed the brunt of the nuclear focus upon the one NATO country least able to carry it, West Germany, the sole country unable ever to rely upon its own nuclear deterrence. Germany was indeed the victim.

To add salt to these gaping wounds, Gorbachev's kindly offer wreaked havoc within the already divided German polity. It reinforced the antinuclear sentiment Kohl was bravely attempting to squash. It thus hurt Reagan and Kohl's friends and pleased their foes. Foreign Minister Hans Dietrich Genscher was delighted; the stalwart Defense Minister Hans Woerner was dejected.

Indeed, by then the INF negotiations had cracked West Germany's postwar security consensus, no small liability in itself. The "second zero" set the conservatives in Kohl's party on the path of anti-Americanism. Unlike those in France and Britain, German conservatives had long been heartily pro-American. After the Moscow meeting and quickie NATO session to discuss Gorbachev's gift, the German right joined the German left in grumbling about American indifference to their security concerns.

ONE MORE TIME

None of this German thrashing about terribly troubled official Washington. The President was delighted that Gorbachev had seen his opening bid of one zero and raised him a zero of his own. So Gorbachev *had* been serious at Reykjavik about wanting to get rid of all these nuclear weapons! I'd known he was!

Best of all, the President felt he would achieve his long-awaited arms treaty. Despite all the nay sayers outside the administration and all the doubters within, he *would* be proven right. Never again to be tormented by the likes of Walter Mondale calling him the first president since Chester Arthur (or whomever) not to reach an arms agreement with the Russians.

Secretary Weinberger steadily supported the zero option as well and thought the Shultz alternatives to the Europeans—put up or go along—just dandy. Shultz, for his part, welcomed working on a foreign policy issue, especially one in arms control, that actually produced some results, no matter how painful the results came out to some of his European colleagues. So the Germans were left to thrash about largely by themselves.

For we still had a summit to capture, and all signs were go on that front. Gorbachev had shown his bona fides by offering a way to resolve the main outstanding issue for an INF accord.

More meetings in Washington. More time spent on the issues of Washington—SDI, the ABM Treaty, START, the usual mix. Shevardnadze reciprocated our visit to Moscow with his visit to Washington that September of 1987. The most contentious issue then was the fate of the German-owned short-range missile, the Pershing I, which was reaching its life expectancy in any case. Kohl had previously offered to dismantle these missiles at the same time the United States and the Soviets dismantled their INF systems. After a delicate diplomatic dance, Shultz and National Security Advisor Frank Carlucci worked out a solution acceptable to the German government.

This issue came on like a summer thunderstorm—it had not been a matter of discussion, let alone contention with the Soviets before then—but it passed quickly. I can only surmise that this was Moscow's way of again swiping the Germans, an impression reinforced during that Washington meeting's only dramatic moment: Shevardnadze told Shultz that this was a critical issue for them, "especially since these missiles are in German hands."

Looking up from his papers, he said pointedly and gravely, "We had a bitter experience with the Germans."

The President held his normal Oval Office meetings with Shevardnadze. On one such occasion, the two of them swiftly ran out of things to say. Rather than break up ahead of time and risk the press dubbing this trumpeted meeting a failure, Reagan ingeniously showed Shevardnadze around the office, taking particular pride in his Remington cowboy sculptures. The two of them lingered over each and every one, which burned up loads of time. And then they had lunch.

Right after the cameramen stampeded in to capture the lunch scene, Shevardnadze brought up the Krasnoyarsk radar, saying that he also had suspected that it was a violation before the Soviet military explained to him why it was legal. When we asked for such evidence, recalling how Soviet and American officials had discussed this one issue for more than 225 hours in Geneva by then, the conversation turned to more mundane matters.

"I'm a farmer," the President said to Shevardnadze (prompting me to ask Frank Carlucci, sitting to my left at the table, what crops he raised), "so I'm interested in your agricultural reforms." Shevardnadze threw a lot of words at this answer even though there were no agricultural reforms under way then. Vice President Bush chimed in on his experiences in Iowa; he was spending loads of time there preparing for the upcoming Republican primary. And so it went.

Shortly after Shevardnadze departed, plans began for one last ministerial meeting, back in Moscow, to set up the summit at long last. Even by the extraordinary standards of summitry, enough was becoming quite enough already, which the Soviets surmised as well. They assured us Gorbachev would set the summit date with Shultz during the final preparatory meeting. They assured us wrong.

Moscow Once Again

In late October of 1987 it was Moscow or bust. Coming as it did on the heels of the October 19 stock market crash, the by then inevitable failure of the Bork Supreme Court nomination, persisting embarrassment over Iran-contra, and rising tensions in the Persian Gulf, the trip received much more attention than it deserved. For it was the administration's only good news.

Moscow became suddenly fogged in while we rested in Helsinki, so we had the treat of taking the overnight train from there to Moscow, passing endless miles of dilapidated wooden shacks along the way. Over breakfast one reporter told of his attempt years before to photograph one of these shacks. When he stopped his car and climbed out, the KGB agent following him rushed up, waving his arms. "No photo. No photo. Is not typical."

After our arrival and a heavy luncheon at the luxurious Foreign Ministry château in town, we buckled down to work. We were set to wrangle over the remaining INF issues with the head of the Soviet Geneva delegation, First Deputy Foreign Minister Yuli Voronsov. But we soon ran into the standard Soviet stonewall—their refusal to reveal essential information.

This was long the Achilles' heel of arms control, as the Soviets refused to reveal the size or composition of their own forces. The worst instance of this arose during SALT I when the Soviet military representative interrupted our diplomat while he was presenting our estimates of their forces. The two men adjourned to the next room, where the Soviet officer asked that we stop furnishing data on Russian military might. "Members of my delegation are not cleared to receive such information," he said with a straight face.

This is not incongruous in a society that, before *glasnost*, shrouded in secrecy the most mundane information—telephone listings, maps of Moscow, even the names and existence of Soviet villages and towns. In late 1988 chief Soviet mapmaker Victor Yashchenko told how, for half a century, the Soviet secret police had ordered his staff to locate cities first on one side of the river, then on the other, and then omit them from the map altogether. Peninsulas wandered around successive Soviet maps, as did nearly everything else. "Rivers and roads were moved," said Yashchenko. "City districts were tilted. Streets and houses were incorrectly indicated," while the "correct maps were classified, practically without exception."

This is as bizarre as having Soviet negotiators extend such secretiveness to their own negotiating positions, which is precisely what happened again in Moscow. We began by delineating some thirty unresolved INF issues, presenting and explaining our position on each. Minister Voronsov raised objections and left it at that. For instance, we proposed the number and location of on-site inspections, to which he demurred. We understood their objections, we said, and wanted to learn about what they sought instead. Each time we did so, however, the Soviet delegation huddled in hushed tones for several minutes before resuming. It depended on many factors, they finally replied. What factors? Another huddle. It was hard to say.

After around an hour of this runaround, I grew impatient: "Suppose we agreed to *your* proposals. How many inspections, for example, do you want?" Another huddle yielded another dodge. It depended on many factors. "Minister Voronsov," I said as calmly as I could, "we are trying to learn *your* position. You are making it impossible for us to know what you propose, let alone try to bridge the gap between our two positions."

Finally they blurted out that they had to consult with "higher authorities" and would tell us at noon the next (and final) day of the meetings. We arrived at the appointed hour at the appointed meeting house, not far from the Kremlin, only to find no Russian diplomats were present. They had stood us up.

A few hours later Shevardnadze told us some of their positions. We felt relieved—why? I wondered later—and referred these knotty issues back to the Geneva delegations, from whence they had come.

But the true drama in Moscow that fall of 1987 happened at a higher level, during Secretary Shultz and National Security Advisor Carlucci's strange meeting with Gorbachev.

In a word, Gorbachev lunged. Perhaps sensing Reagan's weakness back home with his cascade of woes, the General Secretary lunged for some assurance that we would give on SDI in order to have a productive summit. Did that mean "in order to have *any* summit"? Hard to say, since this session then took a tricky bounce.

One man can, as I say, make an enormous difference, even in government. While Shultz pondered, Frank Carlucci jumped in. Gorbachev needed to understand that SDI was the President's program. Any concessions on it *had* to be made by him, not by them. But lest Gorbachev get his hopes up, he should know that the President simply would not renegotiate the ABM Treaty. Nor would he abandon the broad interpretation of the ABM Treaty. In that case, Gorbachev said, seeming stunned, they would just be wasting their time at a summit, wouldn't they?

The Carlucci truth telling caused the session to take a sharp turn. Gorbachev wanted to mention something else that was bothering him—bothering him quite a bit, in fact. He then picked up a State Department report describing how Radio Moscow and other Soviet propaganda outlets had accused the United States of being accomplices in the murder of Swedish Prime Minister Olof Palme, of intentionally spreading AIDS around the world, and the usual slanders. Gorbachev denounced the report roundly. How could you people issue such a report? Shultz and Carlucci were caught by surprise; neither had ever heard of it, let alone read it. After being issued some months before, like most government reports, it had vanished from view—until, that is, it was seen in Gorbachev's waving hand.

When Gorbachev asked why Americans always said such nasty things about the Soviets, Shultz fired back. It was because the Soviets were always *doing* nasty things. Like invading Afghanistan. Like meddling in Central America. Like shooting down the KAL airliner. This verbal spat escalated when Gorbachev asked Shultz how much we had paid the KAL 007 pilot's family for the intelligence work he had conducted for us.

Needless to say, conditions were not ripe for setting the summit date. So it was not set. The press wrote this off as another Reagan calamity. Shultz and Carlucci were proud, knowing that the President would heartily approve. Conservatives were reassured that the administration was not groveling or growing as soft as it seemed. And the American people took it in stride, showing their desire for American officials to sit down with the Soviets but to stand up to them when necessary. Only the diplomats, our State Department and their Foreign Ministry souls, took it hard.

What really happened? During their next swing through town, I asked this question of a Soviet Deputy Foreign Minister who was in a position to know and who tells the truth more often than not. He led me to believe that former Ambassador to the United States, Anatoly Dobrynin, fouled up the ministry's carefully choreographed script. Dobrynin did an end run, showed Gorbachev the disinformation report, and then got him worked up over SDI. Gorbachev responded.

Maybe so. Maybe bureaucratic politics explains everything in government. Or maybe the true explanation lies elsewhere, like with Gorbachev himself.

Maybe the man hoped to score some SDI gains in exchange for conceding to a summit, which he reckoned the faltering administration needed badly. Sure, it would be a risk, but the downside was marginal; he could always reverse himself afterward.

Or Gorbachev may just have gotten emotionally carried away. For a seemingly controlled and appealing person, Gorbachev can be brutish. I noticed a pattern in his behavior: in most meetings, Gorbachev picks out some point on which to badger his interlocutors. He can be churlish in a way not seen in any Soviet leader since Nikita Khrushchev—with Reagan in Geneva on several issues, with Reagan at Reykjavik on SDI testing, with Council of Foreign Relations celebrities in the fall of 1986 on human rights, and then in Moscow with the blowup over the State Department report.

To hell with it, he just may have felt then. First Reagan turns him down at Reykjavik, and then Reagan's minions nix his hopes of ever getting at SDI. What *would* be the point of another summit?

Apparently there was a point to it. For within days after we returned, word came into the White House that Shevardnadze would be winging to Washington the very next week to "continue the discussions." Surely he and Gorbachev knew that there was nothing more to discuss, except the summit date.

By then they realized that even though a summit would help Reagan, it would also help Gorbachev. He might have seemed ten feet tall while making the rounds in Washington, but his actual position may have been shaky just then. With his country in palpable economic decline and coming into political turmoil with *glasnost* and *perestroika,* the main thing going for Gorbachev then was his positive image abroad. Besides, taming a resolute anticommunist like Ronald Reagan before he rode off into the sunset would constitute a coup for any Soviet leader.

Gorbachev needed a summit, wanted a summit, and had his summit. The Shevardnadze rectification trek set the date, causing mild discomfort when it came on Pearl Harbor Day, but Reagan spun that mishap around by telling how fitting it was to usher in peace on a day long associated with war.

Summit Eve

Arrangements were finalized, though there were jolts all along the way. Gorbachev was furious at his treatment by the United States Congress (he is not alone), which initially invited him to

address a joint session and then, with surprising bipartisan support, unceremoniously uninvited him. Word from the General
Secretary was that he did not care whether he addressed a joint
session or not; he cared plenty, though, that it had been set and
then canceled.

The White House moved in and out of this waltz, acting all too
passive, even mellow, about the arrangements. Secretary Shultz
finally negotiated a compromise with Shevardnadze on how Gorbachev would handle the congressional side of his visit; during
one Foreign Minister's meeting the two men spent more time on
this than on all the outstanding issues of INF. The Soviets agreed
to have the Secretary of State host a lunch for Gorbachev at the
State Department. I had seldom seen Shultz cheerier than when
he received this good news.

At last, after all that work, the summit arrived. The Shultzes
welcomed the Gorbachevs at Andrews and joined them for a
drink that evening. Afterward, when he was telling us about Gorbachev's jubilant mood, we received some not so jubilant news
that threw us into a quandary.

Scheduled the next day was the summit centerpiece, the INF
signing ceremony. Suddenly there was a problem. The Soviets
had not handed over a photograph of their SS-20 missile, as they
were explicitly required to do before treaty signature. "There is
no such photo," Dobrynin, who flew in with Gorbachev, told a
State Department official on the way into town. "We only have a
photo of the missile canister." The box it comes in does not
count for much.

We sat around Shultz's conference room pondering what to
recommend to the President. He had his heart set on the signing
ceremony, which justified his tough negotiating style and was
the culmination of everything he had hoped for. Yet for him to
sign before the Soviets had done what they explicitly agreed to
do would be risky diplomatically (they might then never give us
the photo) and embarrassing politically. At the same time, for the
President to take some middle course, to presume the Soviets
would comply later or to sign but not send the treaty up to the
Senate before receiving the photo, would seem too namby-
pamby.

None of us had any good ideas—there was more posturing than
thinking around that table—so we broke up late, determined to
sleep on it. The sleep did not help me; by morning I still had

nothing to recommend. Fortunately I needed nothing. By seven-thirty that morning, when I arrived in the office, the Soviets had somehow produced the photo, the one that had not existed the night before. We breathed a sigh of relief.

VERIFICATION MANIA

The summit-eve session was merely the opening salvo in a six-month debate over INF verification. The United States Senate would never agree to ratify the treaty until convinced that it could effectively be verified. This is only normal; verification is one of the few areas of arms control on which there is wide consensus.

I once believed this conventional wisdom and gave who-knows-how-many speeches extolling its importance. But I have changed my mind. Verification is interesting and can be informative, but it is far less important than assumed.

To begin with the big picture, compliance simply does not mean much in a country like the Soviet Union, which is based on the rule of men and not of laws. Even under *glasnost,* that society lacks the hallmarks of legal protection: a constitution to establish and circumscribe institutions of government, an independent judiciary, and general adherence to the laws of the land.

From its first lawyer-in-command, V. I. Lenin, to its present one, Mikhail Gorbachev, Soviet authorities have respected power and privilege more than process and law. Although laws against violent crime and the like apply to most people (though not to top KGB brass), all laws do not apply to all people, and many laws do not apply to *any* people. In essence, laws in that society are worked around or ignored as often as they are observed. A Russian legal authority at the Soviet Institute of State and Law, Vladimir A. Tumanov, wrote that changes in Soviet law do not lead to changes in Soviet behavior. Disrespect for the law is "a problem, if not a disaster," and he furnished a nice example. "A railway boss announced at a party conference at a locomotive depot that the first fifteen articles of the law were not valid in respect to that depot." So they were not enforced.

Soviet authorities, customarily impervious to their own constitution and domestic laws, cannot be expected to be meticulous about agreements reached with their principal adversary. As the Marquis de Custine wrote after a journey to Russia last century,

"I do not blame the Russians for being what they are. I blame them for pretending to be what we are."

Secretary Shultz seemed miffed that summit eve because the Soviets were already playing loose with the INF procedures, even though he surely realized that they break deals or cut corners on the deals they make. During one of our trips to Moscow, the Soviets agreed to broadcast a full interview with Shultz—no restrictions and no cutting. They stuck by the deal, at least until he began harping on Afghanistan. The translator trailed off as the Secretary told of the Soviets deploying 120,000 troops there and he stopped altogether when Shultz continued, "We cannot understand that. Afghanistan is no threat. It has been a devastating war. They don't want you there. They want peace with you, but they don't want you occupying their country." Within the expansive Soviet Union, the only individuals to hear those words outside the television studio were English speakers with acute hearing tuned to that station in the afternoon on a weekday. Not a large audience for such an important statement.

Most vitally, verification is empty without enforcement. We pay for police detection in order to lead to police apprehension and then criminal incarceration. If our local crime rate climbed, we would not expend more efforts on detection if no arrests were allowed.

In treaties with the Soviet Union, no arrests are allowed. We can and have detected Soviet violations, indeed a clear pattern of them over a long period of time. We have detected plenty and done precious little about any of them. Verification without compliance becomes posturing, and enforcing compliance is impossible between nations.

Moving from the big picture to more particular considerations, I conclude that verification simply cannot be done with much confidence these days. INF seemed ideal: the treaty involved very few systems, eliminated them all, contained on-site inspection, and so on. Yet it was not. The INF provisions furnished "low" to "low-moderate" confidence of verification. For the first five years or so, we would have around two or three chances out of ten of detecting a Soviet violation of that treaty.

During a briefing in the Situation Room in March 1987, I so informed the President, Vice President, Chief of Staff, National Security Advisor, Secretary of State, and others. I opened the briefing, I must say, with a bang. Pointing to a poster-size satellite photograph on an easel, I said, "Here, Mr. President, is the best photo we have of Soviet SS-20 missiles on patrol. We could get such a *good* photo since we knew this group of missiles was going out of their garrison just then and could snap the missiles here, a few miles from their base."

As I spoke, the President squinted. "I don't see any SS-20s. Where are they?" he asked about what seemed like nothing more than an aerial photo of a forest.

"Well, I don't see any either," I admitted. "But the experts tell me that these things here"—pointing to something dark, like a tree stump or a mound of dirt, if it looked like anything at all— "are SS-20s."

In the Soviet Union, which encompasses one-sixth of the earth's landmass, U.S. intelligence just cannot see and count mobile missiles. Since we never knew how many INF missiles the Soviets produced—we knew they had some 441 deployed and estimated they had up to 400 in storage or for training—we could never know whether they had destroyed them all, as the treaty required.

But I presented a model of equipment that could help us verify the treaty. There on the Situation Room table was a model befitting a president—complete with a little train, little trucks, little photo-taking equipment, tiny fences, model housing, and a few figures representing the poor Americans who would be stationed around Soviet production plants, final assembly areas, or storage facilities to count the number of missiles leaving these places. Though it would be costly, difficult to negotiate with the Soviets, and hard for us to take (the Joint Chiefs, CIA, and FBI dreaded having Soviets living near our sensitive defense plants), this scheme would help verification. Yet even with this Cecil B. De Mille production, we could not have high-confidence verification.

The President grasped the point quickly. He grimaced and then asked if the real problem wasn't that the Soviets could take any plant, like "a washing machine factory," and turn it into an SS-20 factory. I told him yes. They might have a tough time converting a washing machine factory into a SS-20 plant, but they could possibly build and hide a new SS-20 plant. Easier still, they could keep some SS-20s stashed away, and we would never find them. Someone else at that meeting inanely suggested having a third party, like the Swedes or the Danes, conduct the monitoring for us. I opined that this was a lousy idea. We agreed with the Soviets on monitoring our own treaties, without allowing others to butt in. Besides, the Europeans were not dependable; not one government there found the Krasnoyarsk radar a Soviet violation, even though such a finding was nearly unanimously accepted as such within the United States.

Though initially bleak, our verification would improve substantially over time as any Soviet missiles not destroyed would age. Since they were prohibited from testing any SS-20s, the reliability and thus military utility of any hidden force would decline.

The scheme I showed the President depended critically upon continuous on-site presence around Soviet facilities that built SS-20 missiles. This took some doing to achieve but was accomplished during my second favorite Foreign Ministers' meeting (after the Shultz-Gromyko session in Geneva in January 1985). This was the final Shultz-Shevardnadze meeting I attended, likewise in Geneva, in November 1987.

The Washington summit, date set by then, loomed just two weeks ahead. Its centerpiece was to be the INF Treaty signing, but we had no treaty to sign. Above all, we had this whole on-site inspection procedure remaining to work out. We needed, in particular, a continuous presence at the Votkinsk Machine plant in the USSR, near the Ural Mountains six hundred miles east of Moscow. This was where the Soviets put SS-20 missiles together from their various stages. If we were to surround that installation with our inspectors for a number of years with the ability to check (at least spot-check) what came out, we could rest assured they were not assembling the banned missile there, at least. While outside this facility, which also turns out washing machines, dairy equipment, underwater drilling rigs, auto parts, and other stuff, we could sort through these items and look for the missiles. And although they could make SS-20s elsewhere, our monitoring would at least drive up the costs and risks of their cheating.

So we asked for a continuous presence of Americans around that facility, to which the Soviets surprisingly acceded without much fuss. Fine, they told us, you station a team continuously around a Soviet missile facility. We then can station a team continuously around an American missile facility. Reciprocal rights are the name of the game.

Fair enough in theory, but there *was* no reciprocal site in America. We had no single spot, à la Votkinsk, where we assembled Pershing IIs. We did so in loads of facilities; more accurately, we *had* done so, since we no longer even built Pershing IIs. So for a considerable time we asserted that we need not offer a reciprocal site since we had no reciprocal process. This line eventually wore a bit thin—Americans are not as adept at endless repetition as the Soviets—so the Joint Chiefs scrambled to turn up something to offer the Soviets. They found several facilities that had been used for Pershing missile production, either the Pershing I or II. This, they asserted, was the complete list of Pershing production facilities, which we passed along to the Soviets.

Ambassador Obukhov pointedly asked one day, "How about such-and-such place?" which was not on the list. No, Ambassador Glitman assured his counterpart, we never built Pershings there. He sounded sure; the Joint Chiefs' list was complete. Back in Washington we were less sure, so we asked the Pentagon to recheck it. After a day or two word sheepishly came forth: Yep, they should have listed that place. Somehow it got left off. Any others the Kremlin might know about?

After getting through that one, we offered a way to solve this problem. The Soviets should consider all the facilities we had listed (plus the one they found) and tell us which ones would, to them, constitute a "reciprocal facility." Then we'd decide on one facility. So they would come up with a list of acceptable choices, and we would choose one for them to continually monitor.

Max Kampelman worked this out in his careful and skillful way with Voronsov. This played out, and Minister Voronsov agreed on any of five American facilities, one called Longhorn, which was 150 miles east of Dallas near the dusty town of Marshall, Texas.

Once Voronsov included Longhorn on his acceptable list, the Joint Chiefs became nervous. Not because it was especially sensitive; rather because Pentagon brass considered it singularly insensitive. Long ago, it had built some Pershing parts but had since degenerated into a test site for flares and small arms. The more I heard about it, the more I envisioned a skeet-shooting range on the outskirts of the town portrayed in the movie *The Summer of '42*. It took a week of careful checking, and a lot of high-level head scratching in the Pentagon, to finally (though grudgingly) tell our negotiators that, okay, the Russians could camp out

around Longhorn. From their list, that was the site we had chosen
for them to monitor.

Thus things stood that November 1987—summit day minus
two weeks—when Shultz and his caravan arrived in Geneva.
Jumping out of the official cars into the Inter-Continental Hotel,
I felt a flush of emotion as I recalled the first Foreign Ministers'
meeting there nearly three years before. This time no anchormen
were present; there was no great hoopla and no carnival atmosphere. Only serious issues stood before us, more serious than
those discussed then.

Before long Shultz and Shevardnadze turned their minds to this
problem. The Secretary of State, meticulous as ever, reviewed the
bidding: There was no real need for a reciprocal site since we had
no reciprocal process; you insisted on one and we gave in; we
asked for a list of possible sites; you gave us a list of those acceptable. "Right?"

"Right."

"Okay. We choose Longhorn."

Shevardnadze demurred. "Why Longhorn?" He was agitated.
An American told how we assumed it was acceptable, since it
was on *your* list. "But why Longhorn? What's there?" Shevardnadze persisted during one of the rare plenary sessions where the
top delegation sits around the table before breaking into the more
productive "working groups."

As always, Shultz referred this substantive issue to one of his
experts, this time turning to the Joint Chiefs' representative, Admiral Jonathan Howe (who had worked for Shultz as Director of
the Political-Military Directorate). Admiral Howe is a wonderfully competent and honest individual, all too honest at that
particular moment.

"Nothing much," Howe replied. "Nothing much happens at
Longhorn. Years ago, it used to make parts for the Pershing, but
that equipment has been destroyed. Now it stores some army
flares and small arms; hence its name, the 'Longhorn Army Ammunition Depot.' No, nothing happens there."

I could not believe my ears, but Jon was at least being straight.
Shevardnadze probably could not believe his either, but he used
the point to good effect. For the reasons Admiral Howe presented,
we can no longer accept Longhorn, Shevardnadze asserted. Shultz
called time out. We would have to return to the issue after lunch.

During that lunch, held at the Russian mission and hosted by

Shevardnadze, Max Kampelman and I were seated with Ambassadors Karpov and Obukhov. We chatted amicably about my impending departure, scheduled immediately after the summit. The two Russian negotiators were clearly worried, but not by this, to be sure. Never, in fact, had I seen them so uptight. They constantly harped back to the morning's discussion and kept pressing.

"Why couldn't you accept the facility in San Diego? Or the Hercules facility in Magna, Utah?"

"Come on," I retorted. "We played by the agreed rules and chose a facility on *your* list."

"There's nothing to inspect there, in Longhorn. You heard Howe," they both said seriously.

"That's why we chose it," I exclaimed. "Do you think we're dumb? We checked it out carefully; yeah, nothing happens there, which is why you can go ahead and monitor it. If there was something sensitive, we wouldn't want you there."

Back and forth we went. I joked that I had purchased the only motel in Marshall, Texas, as I knew that business there would boom once it became known that the Russians were coming. They did not find my remark funny (maybe it wasn't).

Anyway, after lunch we met in the secure bubble of our mission, bigger, thank goodness, than that in Reykjavik. Counsel was divided, but many of us agreed that we could accept another site. Due to skillful lobbying by Martin Marietta's chief Norm Augustine, whose time in the Pentagon as Under Secretary of the Army had served him well, that company's facilities were eliminated from the list of possibilities.

That morning, the new NSC Advisor, General Colin Powell, had called his old boss, now Defense Secretary Carlucci, to ask about other possibilities. After some scrambling around—why must all such decisions be made at the last minute, even when people can see them coming weeks ahead of time?—Carlucci gave the green light to some alternatives. There were sensitive facilities at the Hercules, Inc., plant in Magna, Utah—a large producer of ballistic missile stages for the MX, Trident, and Minuteman—but we were told not to worry. We could move the most sensitive equipment away before the Soviets arrived for inspection. (On the plane going home, I told Shultz that at both Votkinsk and at Magna, Utah, huge moving vans would soon be backing in to take out anything significant.)

So it was no longer to be Longhorn. It was to be Hercules. The managers there shared none of our sense of triumph at solving the last big INF issue. Instead they feared the prospect of having up to thirty Soviets living in their midst for some thirteen years. "The Russians knew exactly what they wanted," Hercules president Edward J. Sheehy said later. "We got nailed." As a slight consolation, the National Security Agency pledged to make the company's internal communications system immune to electronic eavesdropping (another invisible cost of the INF Accord, but welcome nonetheless).

Before leaving Geneva that November, Shultz had a private chat with Shevardnadze to find out what had happened. "Longhorn was on *your* list."

Shevardnadze was his most disarming self. With that wavy gray hair, wry sense of humor, and affable nature found commonly in Georgians (though rarely in Russians), the Foreign Minister could occasionally be appealing. "You're right. It was on our list. Yuli [Voronsov] was wrong to mention it. Our negotiators were wrong to reiterate it. We were wrong."

What can a fellow do with an explanation like that? Nothing but accept it.

As a footnote to history, it should be added that, alas, Longhorn *did* retain some connection to INF, unbeknownst to us, them, and everyone then. A year or two later the U.S. Army found a dozen Pershing I missile parts still there. The Army's explanation was marvelous: "The parts were rejected as defective by the Defense Department when they were built ten years ago, and they've been in storage since then. They were simply overlooked in the initial inventory."

So be it. May this episode rest in peace.

The Ceremony and the Dialogue

President Reagan may well have been blissfully unaware of the INF glitch—not having the photo, having the photo—as was the public. They knew only of the long-scheduled INF signing ceremony in the large and elaborate East Room of the White House, where Dolly Madison once hung her laundry to dry.

It was thrilling to sit just behind Nancy and Raisa and watch something conclude that had consumed much of my life for five years. Who would have suspected, during the confirmation ordeal that preceded my entering the office, that I would be witnessing a signing ceremony during my last two days in office? That the Russians would finally accept a proposal President Reagan had made in 1981? That I could actually support a U.S.-Soviet nuclear arms accord? That this would be the first agreement to be approved by the Senate for ratification since 1972?

I sat there filled with the spirit of Tertullian, a third century theologian who said about miracles, *"Certum est quia impossible est"* ("It is certain because it is impossible,") while Gorbachev and Reagan signed and made gushy statements about the accord. History too takes funny bounces.

After the hoopla, Reagan and Gorbachev met for their private discussions, which became their least interesting summit talks. Much of their time was spent congratulating one another; the rest was spent misunderstanding each other.

On SDI, Gorbachev was uncommonly calm. His sense of determination, if not desperation, on SDI had dissipated if not disappeared. Gorbachev adopted a Californian (or Siberian) laid-back posture about it all. He told American officials that his prior virulent opposition had only raised U.S. support for SDI.

He was right, even if late. Gorbachev, renowned for his quick grasp, was an appallingly slow learner on this. Years before he should have shrugged off SDI as a visionary mission bound to fail. But this stance first emerged here, during the December 1987 Washington summit. Just a month before, as we have seen, he still went gangbusters against SDI during his Moscow meeting with Shultz and Carlucci. Now he began to change his approach, and with it his style (calmer, cooler) and substance (praise for the ABM Treaty rather than scorn for the SDI program). He could head toward the same destination on a different road.

Gorbachev's change in attitude may have come from adopting shrewder tactics or from realizing that reality was moving his way. Any successor to Ronald Reagan would not emulate his fatherly love for SDI, and surely George Bush does not. Any Democrat President would oppose it—Michael Dukakis had dubbed it a "magic gizmo" that neither would nor should work—and any new Republican President would verbally support it and probably leave it at that.

Congress too was going Gorbachev's way. Funding for SDI was nearly leveling off at considerably less than what we estimated the Soviets as spending. Besides, Congress had knocked nearly one-third out of the President's request in 1987, while also re-stricting the SDI program technically. For instance, Congress took the wind out of research for space-based interceptors, those able to hit a Soviet missile in its initial boost phase. Theoreti-cally, at least, this is the easier phase to zap a missile, which is a big and "soft" target with little possible protection; further, a missile flies a perfectly predictable course without zigging or zag-ging, is easily identified, and carries all the warheads. Practically, though, this phase constitutes a tough hit since the boost phase lasts less than two minutes.

So Gorbachev had every reason to play it cool. Unfortunately, we would play it clumsy. This led to a classic Reagan-Gorbachev misunderstanding.

ENDLESS DEBATES OVER SDI

The presummit Washington slugfest over SDI assumed new dimensions after Cap Weinberger left the administration in No-vember 1987 and Carlucci moved into that post. No more high-level debates were held on something so vapid as whether or not to discuss the ABM Treaty with the Soviets.

Instead, we found new issues to wrangle over, though strangely the Secretaries of State and Defense got on the same (wrong) side. They wanted explicit Soviet concurrence for our robust SDI test-ing program. Otherwise, they asserted, Congress would never allow such testing.

Good logic, but a slight problem arose over gaining such con-currence. President Reagan had repeatedly nixed negotiations with the Soviets over the type of testing the ABM Treaty permit-ted and what it prohibited. So during these Situation Room ses-sions, these two argued strenuously, and in unison, that we acquire Soviet concurrence on something about which we refused to negotiate with them. Further, they demanded a green light "for vigorous SDI research since otherwise Congress wouldn't allow it."

I thought this strange. "The Soviets are never going to be more generous with SDI than the U.S. Congress. Unlike all the Soviets, at least *some* members of Congress have American interests at heart." When I said that, the Situation Room erupted in hoops and hollers. The President asked whom I might have in mind. Others cracked that they hadn't met many, and so on. The words were ridiculed and the logic dismissed. Besides, my position seemed soft. Why not try to sign up the Soviets to the type of vigorous testing SDI needed to prove its worth?

Unfortunately SDI's program managers never specified what this might entail. They never managed to define precisely what tests they needed, or to justify all possible needed tests as within our interpretation of the ABM Treaty. So even if Gorbachev and his delegation had, by some miracle, agreed with this unified State-Defense approach, we would not have been ready.

In fact, we didn't need to be ready, since no miracle came or could come. The Russians are never going to solve a president's problems with the Congress, especially on such a hot issue as SDI testing. Nor would Moscow grant approval now for our SDI deployment later, as we were asking the Soviets to do.

Undeterred, the President tried. Hence the misunderstanding. In the Oval Office after the INF signing ceremony, he told Gorbachev that after the agreed no-SDI-deployment period, the United States wanted to deploy SDI. The now mellow and no doubt fatigued and gorged Gorbachev said simply, "Go ahead." Reagan left it at that, silently delighted that he had finally snared the "green light" we had tried to capture at Reykjavik. Gorbachev presumably meant there was nothing he could do about a future administration proceeding in this manner; of course it would have to be justified by the ABM Treaty or the United States would have to withdraw from that treaty. Either constituted a potent political obstacle for any future president.

All this came out during the summit's last day. Gorbachev met the press to reiterate his points on SDI and everything else. Though a telegenic man, he still had not mastered a Western press conference. His opening remarks put everyone in a stupor before they ended forty-five minutes later. Meanwhile the National Security Advisor Colin Powell briefed the press on the President's views. For days the media was filled with stories on whether Gorbachev had in fact accepted SDI deployment, as Reagan maintained and Gorbachev adamantly denied. This led to confusion galore. As was becoming eerily more common, the Soviet side got the story straighter: "We postponed our quarrels" was the way the Soviet spokesman Gennadi Gerasimov explained the issue when queried.

The Reagan-Gorbachev dialogue on other issues proved no more satisfying. The President was more pointed on human rights than he had been in Geneva, though less so than he would be in Moscow. Gorbachev was if anything more resistant. Unlike the President, he spoke quasi-spontaneously from handwritten scribbles of key points that he, not his bureaucracy, wanted to address, and in his own way.

"You are not the prosecutor and I am not the accused," Gorbachev blasted back when Reagan broached the human rights topic. "We have to strike a balance here. Otherwise you will get nothing out of us." No balance was struck, and nothing much came out of this.

On another U.S.-Soviet agenda item, regional matters, the fizzle was gone from the Reagan-Gorbachev talks since they had announced their departure from Afghanistan. The Fortier "regional initiative" still framed the litany of Soviet-manned or -planned or -funded aggression around the world, but both the allegations and responses had, by then, become routine. More remarkable, though rather unwelcome, was Reagan's quasi-apologetic tone. Here was the man who built a career on commie-bashing excusing the head commie for genocidal practices: "Well, you must remember that there were other leaders under which this [the Afghanistan invasion] happened. He [Gorbachev] inherited that. And those leaders are the ones who had created the puppet government. Now, whether he knows that—to what extent they did that, I don't know."

Reagan said this even though Gorbachev presided over Soviet forces in Afghanistan longer than Brezhnev and when they killed most of the one *million* or more Afghan civilians. It was during Gorbachev's first year in power that a chilling half of all Afghan peasants had their villages bombed and a quarter had their livestock killed and water systems destroyed. Also under Gorbachev, the communist forces increasingly violated Pakistani air space and perpetuated numerous terrorist acts in Pakistan, perhaps even the 1988 plane crash which killed its president, Zia ul-Haq, and the American ambassador, our colleague Arnold Raphel.

The only other interesting tidbit on regional issues came during a quickie Reagan-Gorbachev talk while strolling around the White House South Lawn for a classic "photo op." Something prompted Gorbachev to bring up Central America then. With interpreters panting to keep pace with these two robust walkers, catching intermittent words as best they could, the General Secretary may have called for mutual restraint in the area. He might have muttered something about stopping arms shipments there if the United States would do likewise. Who, besides Gorbachev, knows what the hell he said?

Again, Reagan was pleased with what he thought he heard from the interpreter of what he thought he heard Gorbachev say. Again, less was there than met the ear. When later probed as to what Gorbachev really said or meant, Soviet officials, too, scrambled. Then they said Moscow would stop military assistance to Nicaragua if the United States halted such aid to the contras and also to all nearby countries like Honduras, Guatemala, and Panama. Before inquiring whether this included all of Latin America, American officials lost interest. This too took a number of days to sort out.

MERRYMAKING

Such sour aftertaste followed a wonderful summit feast and merriment in Washington. The summit was to be Gorbachev's summit, and he dazzled one and all.

People fix on personalities, not on INF verification or SDI testing requirements. Gorbachev, however short on substantive give, was long on personal charm. He and Raisa did it all and did it right.

Showing talents as a Western-style politician, Gorbachev had a personal tidbit to dole out to the celebrities and personalities he met. He worked a receiving line better than anyone I have seen since watching Jimmy Carter meet each of the hostages in Wiesbaden on the day of their release (January 21, 1981). There Carter commented about a son's latest Little League game or passed along a wife's words; here Gorbachev mentioned, among many other things, books. He complimented author Stephen Cohen on his biography of the soon-to-be-rehabilitated Bukharin, took exception with Richard Pipes over his Soviet writings, commented on the novels of sundry New York authors, and loved hearing raves about his own book, aptly entitled *Perestroika*.

Gorbachev came to conquer, rather than to see, and did just that. "Gorby fever" raged in Washington and indeed around the nation. In a wonderful twist, some California doll maker switched heads so that no-longer-selling Ollie North dolls became fast-selling Mikhail Gorbachev models.

Gorbachev also wanted to nourish his personal relationship

with Ronald Reagan, primarily to assure the President's visit to Moscow that spring. As one Russian put it, "The main job of Moscow is to ensure that Reagan is engaged in the arms control process until the end of his presidency." For better or worse, that was what Reagan wanted as well—and looked to us, his arms experts, to ensure.

As always, the American and Soviet arms control teams met to address the substantive issues unsettled in Geneva. This summit, more than that in Geneva or Reykjavik, had a split-level quality to it. The President and General Secretary conducted their general and oft confusing discussions and attended their whirling engagements, while we plodded along catching only flickers of what transpired in that upper stratosphere.

Though at times disjointed, this is how arms control must work, being so intricate and even esoteric—often resembling what Prime Minister Palmerston said about the Schleswig-Holstein dispute last century: Only three people had ever really grasped the issue; one is dead; another has forgotten it; and the third is in an asylum. The use of radiological detection apparatus for SLCM verification, a device we discussed for hours that night during the Washington summit, is hardly the stuff of common knowledge (or of much fascination, to tell the truth).

So we went about our separate tasks, the President and General Secretary at their level, the arms experts at ours, each curious about what the other was up to. The tempo quickened, as always, as the summit ending time approached. After some preliminary chats, we met formally and seriously that Wednesday, the last night. It never ceased to amaze me how the most serious business always seems to be left for the last minute. We sat in the small and by then crowded Secretary of State's conference room for some hours before and past midnight, dispassionately bartering over nuclear arsenals with the military leader of our main adversary.

"Well, you see, we have many of our bombers stationed deep inside our country, which can come over here in not too many hours," one Soviet representative asserted antiseptically that evening. At rare times some emotion entered, as when the mild-mannered Marshal Akhromeyev flared when one of our negotiators began his set piece on SDI, which Akhromeyev (like all of us) had heard innumerable times before.

After the positions had once again been laid out, our real work began. Members of the delegation took pen in hand and started to haggle. Along with others on our team, I worked on SDI with Ambassador Obukhov, famous for his "numbalogues," and his aides. Each of us, as always, tried to tilt the language Reagan and Gorbachev would issue the next day so as to advance, but at least not compromise, our own position. We spent the better part of an hour tangling over inserting the word *new* in one paragraph—about what eludes me now—before I headed over to the refreshment table.

Obukhov strolled over as well. "Look, we're not making great progress here, are we?" I said insightfully. "So let's agree to proceed along faster. I know your positions. You know ours. Let's work on language that doesn't cause either of us any grief. Then we'll get done." Obukhov readily agreed, so we proceeded to craft anodyne language.

Still, there remained some brackets—the tool of our trade which signifies unresolved language—that our side kept in the draft. That left something for either Shultz and Shevardnadze or Reagan and Gorbachev to resolve as they saw fit.

In this case, the brackets enclosed nothing too momentous, just some language on the ABM Treaty and SDI that required a Talmudic scholar to analyze. The issue stayed unresolved, simply because it could not get resolved without one side or the other making a substantive change in policy.

Shultz met with Shevardnadze over breakfast the next morning in an attempt to remove these brackets. The Secretary of State mustered up the best case he could, and they debated the language. Then Shevardnadze raised a new issue or two that had not been thrashed out the night before.

Gorbachev kept his breakfast schedule at the Soviet embassy and was due to arrive at the White House for his final working session at nine or so. By nine-thirty or ten the President was getting antsy, feeling that he too had been stood up.

There were some rocky times ahead, some during the waning hours of the summit but more during the waning months of the administration, after the summit's close but in part because of it.

THE LEGACY

Modern summitry consists largely of television images, which, unlike articles or books, make a deep and immediate impact and then vanish, leaving only a general, even subliminal, impression. The Washington summit was like this, with one exception.

The signing of the INF Treaty was the first U.S.-Soviet nuclear arms agreement signed and to be ratified in fifteen years, and in my opinion probably the last for another ten or fifteen years, if ever. It is likely to become a prime historical legacy of the Reagan administration and thus deserves delving into.

That is precisely what the Senate proceeded to do and what commentators and historians will do for years to come. The signing of the document did not end our work on that treaty, for it triggered a chain of events beyond the year remaining of the Reagan administration, some good and some not so good.

As evident by now, I came to the INF Accord as a card-carrying skeptic on arms control. Before and during my tenure as Arms Control Director, I believed that arms control was vastly overvalued in public discussions, even by the Reagan administration. The average American has been led to believe that someday, somehow, arms control can or even will deliver us from danger. It has often been equated with "peace" by officials who know better and assumed by American citizens who should be told better.

Arms control can never substitute for Western security. At best it can contribute something marginally helpful and at worst do damage. This is its clear historical record. When all is said and done, much more has been said about arms control than has ever been done by it. Even the august Walter Lippmann came to realize that arms control, at least as practiced in the 1920s, did not live up to its billing. Indeed, it might have contributed to the ensuing horrors. He wrote in 1943:

> I was too weak-minded to take a stand against the exorbitant folly of the Washington Disarmament Conference. In fact, I followed the fashion, and . . . celebrated the disaster as a triumph and denounced the admirals who dared to protest. Of that episode in my life I am ashamed, all the more so because I had no reason for not knowing better.

Lippmann grasped the main point: "The disarmament movement was, as the events have shown, tragically successful in disarming the nations that believed in disarmament"—but not those nations bent on aggression, which are those which cause security threats in the first place.

What arms control cannot do is what it is most widely expected to do—bring lasting peace to a usually turbulent world. To equate an "arms control agreement" with a "peace agreement" is the most damaging perversity. Parchment cannot bring peace, so arms control cannot bring peace. At times it can help improve the political climate, but historically even that has not been true.

And even if true, improving the climate is not always beneficial. The U.S.-Soviet relationship should rest upon whether Soviet behavior allows the relationship to improve. It would be detrimental for "the climate" to improve while the Soviets continue fuelling and fostering revolutionary movements around the world. That would be akin to a physician pumping a sick patient full of cortisone, which, though it eases pain momentarily, endangers the body by closing down nature's warning system.

Moreover, arms control has a false ring of finality about it, at least in public discourse. This too overpromises. "When is it going to end?" people ask about the "arms race." "When will we do without the nuclear weaponry, soldiers, and the big arsenals accumulated all these years?" The true answer is, just about when we can dismiss the local police force or the national FBI because there are no more problems of domestic safety. In other words, never.

Still, I felt pride for having contributed something to the INF Accord President Reagan and General Secretary Gorbachev signed on December 8, 1987. While appreciating its liabilities, which led to problems during the Senate ratification process and anxieties in Europe, I still believe it to be, on balance, beneficial.

After all, the treaty did solve the one problem it set out to solve, which is not bad in any endeavor in life, let alone in arms control.

It solved the problem we conservatives and every European government identified in the mid-1970s as grave: the advent of the SS-20—a triple warheaded, mobile, accurate, top-of-the-line missile aimed at our primary Allies around the world. It did so by mandating the elimination of all these missiles and precluded any missiles in this range by the U.S. or USSR for all time.

Moreover, the accord set five positive precedents for whatever arms control agreement happens to emerge in the future.

First, INF led to real reductions in nuclear weapons, even to removal of this category of nuclear arms. Those of us in the security fraternity know that reductions per se can be destabilizing if done wrong, but these reductions were done right. And reductions were made on these systems in contrast with previous arms accords, which were touted as limiting nuclear arms but actually accompanied arms buildups. Since SALT I was signed, for example, the Soviets have added some seven thousand strategic ballistic warheads. Since SALT II, the Soviets have doubled the number of their ballistic missile warheads, a prime measure of strategic might.

Second, INF resulted in "unequal reductions to equal limits." In layman's terms, the Soviets have to reduce missiles that carry four to five times more warheads than the missiles we have to eliminate. Since the Soviets have achieved superiority in critical areas of strategic weapons, conventional arms, and chemical weapons—all areas of active negotiations today—this principle of "unequal reductions to equal limits" is critical to establish and perpetuate.

Third, the INF accord broke new ground on verification techniques. We insisted upon on-site inspection, exchange of data, continuous monitoring around production facilities, and more to determine if the Soviets were cheating, or at least if they were cheating easily and cheaply. Although the treaty's degree of verifiability ended up not particularly high, it was as high as we could have made it. And though the importance of verification is overrated, it is better to know if the Soviets do cheat than to live in blissful ignorance.

Fourth, INF dealt exclusively with U.S. and Soviet arms. The Soviets tried twice to tie an INF agreement to SDI, but we twice succeeded in nixing that. And no restrictions were placed on British or French nuclear systems, even though Moscow insisted on that too during the first five or six years of these talks.

Fifth, and most important to me, INF stands as a model of how to negotiate with the Soviets. It's relatively simple: Conceive a good proposal, one that solves the problem the negotiations are supposed to solve, and basically stick to it. If deployments are the alternative, as they always should be, go ahead and build up while talking about going down.

We should not, as some in the State Department are always prone to do, begin with a proposal that puts top priority on being "negotiable," one that thus sits midfield between our security interests and theirs. Count on the Soviets to propose something starkly in their own interest, as they always do. In a word, they play to win, and we have often played to tie. If we first propose something good for both of us, we then are left negotiating between midfield and their ideal outcome.

After fashioning proposals in our clear interest, we should wait them out. We should "just say no" to unreasonable Soviet demands, no matter how vigorously or often they are propounded.

Had we listened to the Soviets, and often the accompanying chorus from the traditional "arms control community," we would have ended up with no INF agreement at best and a bad INF agreement at worst. Time and again they told us things that turned out to be just plain wrong:

- When the Soviets threatened to walk out of the negotiations in 1983, they said that arms control would be dead if NATO's deployments proceeded.
- When the Soviets did walk out, they said Soviet negotiators would not return to the table unless we took our missiles out or at least halted our deployments.
- When the Soviets demanded inclusion of the British and French systems, they said that somehow we had to compensate the Soviets for our Allies' systems.
- When the Soviets tied progress in INF to SDI, they told us that somehow we had to restrict our defense research to have an arms agreement.
- When the Soviets said that they could make a deal on systems in Europe but not in Asia, they deemed this good enough, at least for a start.
- When the Soviets wished to restrict our defense of Europe by including aircraft, they pushed us to accede.
- And all the while, the chorus at home and in Europe asserted that the Soviets would never agree to give up their enormous number of SS-20s for our modest number of INF weapons.

This approach of hanging tough in the face of Soviet intransigence may sound unexceptionable, but it is. Contrast it, for instance, with the approach taken by President Franklin Delano Roosevelt. He explained his stance toward Stalin at Yalta: "I think that if I give him everything I possibly can without demanding anything in return, then noblesse oblige, he will not attempt to annex anything and will work to build a peaceful and democratic world." FDR should not have bet on it, surely not from Stalin.

QUALMS ARISE

Nevertheless, immediately after the glow of the East Room signing ceremony faded, the INF Treaty became stalled in the Senate and set off apprehensions in Europe. Having at last concluded a beneficial arms control agreement, the administration heard more wailing than welcoming. Instead of saying, "We've won!" many began grumbling that we may have been better off losing or not having played at all.

This may be only natural. Arms control, like many things in life, seems afflicted by the "approach-avoidance" syndrome. While off in the horizon, it is universally championed; but the closer it approaches, the greater becomes the urge to avoid it.

Thus does arms control resemble medieval love—enchanting to adore "pure and chaste from afar," but disappointing to view close up. The abstract notion of cutting nuclear arms—even "eliminating a whole class of nuclear weapons completely," as in INF—is more alluring than the specific treaty provisions and their political effect turn out to be. Dulcinea loses her luster upon close scrutiny.

Each pro-treaty argument has a dark side to it. For instance, although the treaty *does* eliminate an entire class of nuclear missiles, each side nonetheless has built more nuclear warheads since the talks began than they will destroy as a result of them. And, to take another example, while the treaty *does* eliminate the SS-20 threat poised at Europe and Asia, the Soviets nonetheless continue to build newer SS-24 and -25 missiles, which pose an equal or even greater threat to the Europeans and Asians.

These are the rational arguments and, ironically, not the critical ones. For the "rational fallacy"—that what is intellectually right is right—happens to be the most frequent error committed by government policymakers and most commentators. Big issues raise big emotions, however, whether rational or not. "At the constitutional level where we work," Supreme Court Chief Justice Charles Evans Hughes told the newly appointed Justice William O. Douglas, in 1939, "ninety percent of any decision is emotional. The rational part of us supplies the reasons for supporting our predilections." So it is on the international level, only more so.

One of my worst blunders in government was to give the President bum advice based on rationality. In February 1986, when Gorbachev made his sweeping yet fatuous "megaproposal" to eliminate all nuclear weapons by the turn of the century, we met to fashion a U.S. response. Trying once again to make lemonade out of a lemon, we read into Gorbachev's plan his acceptance of the zero option for INF missiles in Europe. Our response had to set some limit on their INF missiles in Asia.

During the mini-NSC meeting then, I recommended that the President propose the Soviets cut their Asian systems by 50 percent. Secretary Weinberger took strong exception to this. We should stick to the total zero, in Europe *and* Asia, and permit them no missiles in Asia or anywhere else. This, he argued justifiably, was best for our verification, for European security (since the SS-20 could be moved rapidly into Europe from Asia in a crisis), and for Asian security. Besides, the Japanese would never accept my scheme.

I shot back: Sure, the Japanese would prefer zero—we all would —but they would like the 50 percent cut just fine. Why wouldn't they? Initially Japan did not feel as threatened as Europe by the SS-20; it never even contemplated U.S. deployments in Asia (deployments in Japan would violate their "no nuclear" policies), and consequently Japan endured no uproar over our deployments, as had nearly every European deployment country. My approach was a good deal for Japan; something, namely removal of half the Soviet SS-20 threat facing it, for nothing in return on their part.

While the presidential decision remained in limbo, the word came reeling back from Tokyo. I was woefully wrong, and Weinberger was more right than he ever suspected. The Japanese had hit the roof in a most uninscrutable manner. They felt stronger on this issue, our Tokyo embassy reported, than on *any* other security issue in the postwar era.

Why this virulent reaction? Not because of the reality, which they understood to be favorable, but because of the perception, which they took to be insulting. For President Reagan to make such a proposal would relegate them to second-class status, something Asians abhor above all else. To eliminate SS-20s from Europe but not from Asia would signal greater U.S. concern for Europe's security than for theirs. Moreover, such a scheme would set off a grand debate on nuclear weapons in Japan, something that government wished to avoid like the plague.

I quickly recovered from being proven so wrong (Napoleon said, "I have so often in my life been mistaken that I no longer blush for it") and then set back to work on the problem. We eventually managed to square the circle when a creative analyst in the Arms Control and Disarmament Agency, Lou Nosenzo, concocted a proposal that would leave the numbers the same— Soviet 50 percent cuts in Asia—but confine those missiles remaining to two Soviet bases straddling Europe and Asia. That suited the Japanese just fine.

The bulk of opposition to the INF Accord, whether rational or not, stemmed mostly from its origins in 1979. With the hand dealt the Reagan administration in 1981, we played the game about as well as it could have been played.

For a variety of reasons—primarily backlash from the neutron weapon fiasco and from SALT II, and the advent of the threatening SS-20 missiles—NATO then landed on a "dual track" approach. We would open negotiations on these missiles immediately and deploy corresponding U.S. missiles four years hence if the talks did not succeed. And we would continue deploying until they succeeded or until 572 of our missiles had been deployed in Europe.

At first I wondered whether the coming Reagan administration *should* play out this hand. In 1980 I participated in a phalanx of Reagan transition groups, including that for the State Department. On a relatively quiet Saturday afternoon, I talked with then Secretary of State–designate Alexander Haig about the dual track decision. I did not think it particularly wise since it made Moscow, in effect, an unseated member of NATO's inner council. The Soviets could influence our missile deployments with their own positions on arms control. Furthermore, the public rationale was at odds with the military justification; if U.S. missiles were needed to couple our security with Europe's, they should be deployed regardless of what happened to the Soviet SS-20 force. If, alternatively, our missiles were intended merely to counter theirs, Western leaders should stop talking about their "coupling effect."

Haig listened attentively as I proposed that the incoming team "reexamine" the issue and maybe negate the 1979 NATO decision. Then he demurred.

Haig knew the issue inside and out, having been Supreme Commander in Europe during the dual track deliberations. He expressed his own reservations about the way politicians had handled the matter but wished to proceed anyway. To walk the decision back would send the wrong signal—that the new administration was reversing not only its predecessor, but also the other fifteen NATO member nations. That would shatter our credibility, dismay our Allies, and weaken our power around the world. Not a way to enter office.

Haig made a compelling case. He was quite right to see the instant damage that would come from reversing the 1979 decision, while I was correct in envisioning the eventual damage that would come from implementing it. As things turned out in this peculiar business of ours, Alexander Haig became one of the most vociferous and effective opponents of the INF Accord, while I heralded it.

In any case, we both recognized then that there was no good course open to us. This too is typical of government. As Machiavelli wrote some five hundred years ago, "No government should ever imagine that it can always adopt a safe course; rather, it should regard all possible courses of action as risky." The die was cast. And the Reagan administration never seriously reconsidered whether it should proceed with INF negotiations and deployments. Only how.

THE ZERO OPTION IS BORN

Within his first year, the President held a National Security Council meeting in the elegant Cabinet Room with a full complement of Cabinet officers and an army of aides lining the wall. At this meeting, Secretary of Defense Caspar Weinberger promoted the zero option—if they would eliminate all their INF missiles, we would deploy none of ours. Though the zero option was implicit in the 1979 NATO policy statement, Secretary Haig took strong exception to it. He wanted our INF deployments regardless of the fate of their SS-20s. Arms control could serve as the cover for the European governments to get our missiles deployed, but they must be deployed. Haig presented his case forcefully and, characteristic of his style, ominously. Sitting beside him as a stand-in for Jeane Kirkpatrick, I supported the zero option as most desirable, while Haig glowered.

The President was instantly and visibly taken with Weinberger's idea. It was easy to understand and appealing to describe. If successful, it would preclude our deployments before they were scheduled to begin in December of 1983. And it would make verification better. None of us suspected it then, but Reagan must also have been moved by his inner secret, that this might lead down his enchanting road of a nuclear-free world. The President's instincts were reinforced by Weinberger, who knew his boss well. The President might well win the Nobel Prize if the zero option came about, Cap suggested. That did it.

After speedy consultations with European leaders, the President gave one of his smashing public performances to unveil the zero option. Rather than delivering it on prime time in the United States, he wisely chose prime time in Europe. The speech was so well received that European leaders soon found themselves trapped. Whatever doubts they then harbored were buried under overwhelming European public support.

But they, like others, doubted whether the zero option would work. Many of them deemed the Reagan proposal a modern-day variant of the Berchtold Proposal, named for the Foreign Minister of Austria-Hungary who, after the assassination of Archduke Francis Ferdinand, spent one night rephrasing his country's ultimatum to Serbia to make sure it could never be accepted. Reagan turned out to be right; many others turned out to be wrong.

Haig's reasons for opposing this approach were sound, though to me insufficient. They were to become the key factors causing consternation in Europe and adding to the lengthy deliberation in the Senate. They deserve their due, especially since the effects of the INF Accord will last long beyond the Reagan administration.

First and foremost was the fear of decoupling Europe's security from ours. This concern goes to the very heart of the alliance, indeed of any alliance. Will the protector come to the aid of the protected when needed? Europeans feel a natural unease, having twice seen their continent ravaged before being rescued by a reluctant and late-coming United States. This concern prompted Charles de Gaulle to doubt America's security guarantee in the nuclear age, when such a rescue might result in America's own demise. "No one in the world—in particular, no one in America —can say if, where, when, how, or to what extent America's nuclear forces would be used to defend Europe!" he pontificated in the early 1960s.

Europeans had some reason to doubt American credibility during the hottest days of the INF debate. Amid other startling revelations on the Iran-contra escapade, former National Security Advisor Robert McFarlane was asked whether he would trust the United States as an ally "knowing all you know about U.S. foreign policy." Without hesitation he replied, "No," and the matter was then dropped. As the Italian paper *Corrière della Sera* commented, "The fact that the U.S. foreign policy . . . has seriously lost its credibility is now accepted without discussion even by the U.S. Congress." It is not actually that bad, but doubts remain strong.

Thus the physical symbol of U.S. commitment that Secretary Haig and like-minded souls sought by our INF missile deployments. With U.S. systems able to hit Soviet territory based in Europe, Moscow would be even more reluctant to attack. Moreover, our deployments would help reassure Europeans; regardless of our will, we might be forced to enter a major war there at the outset.

These factors assure "coupling," that America's security is made indivisible from Europe's security. But what Haig et al neglected to say is that arguments over coupling and decoupling can, in almost every instance, go both ways. To wit: some Europeans argued that putting our missiles into Europe was decoupling since we could thereby have a nuclear exchange with the Soviets confined to Europe. U.S. territory may not be directly (or at least initially) involved. Others, like Haig, argued the opposite: taking our missiles out of Europe would be decoupling by signaling less desire to defend Europe.

This back-and-forth mirrors a similar—and similarly confusing and inconclusive—debate in the 1950s and now. Then, the initial Soviet deployment of intercontinental ballistic missiles (ICBMs) was deemed decoupling. Their new ability to strike America directly, it was said, would mean that America no longer had to regard Europe's defense as our front line of defense. Said simply, America would never trade Chicago for Hamburg. Yet after President Reagan launched SDI, the opposite argument was made around Europe: SDI, by enabling the United States to regain our *in*vulnerability, would be decoupling; with SDI, we could sit back, safe and satisfied, when Europe was put at risk. So in the 1950s U.S. vulnerability was deemed decoupling; in the 1980s any U.S. *in*vulnerability was deemed decoupling.

More examples can be offered, but the point is clear: weapons systems are neither coupling nor decoupling in themselves. Interests and values are. Besides, Haig's argument flies in the face of his own statements, made when Supreme Commander in Europe, that deterrence worked and the alliance was strong. We then had no U.S. INF missiles deployed there. When had they become essential to bind the alliance? Hence the big message: coupling did not begin when our INF missiles came in at the end of 1983, and coupling will not end when they are removed over the coming years. The United States will still have some 4,500 nuclear weapons in Europe to complement and supplement our 300,000 troops long stationed there.

What was clearly decoupling, however, was all this talk about decoupling. Prominent Americans constantly warning Europeans that the INF Accord signaled less U.S. commitment to them made this more of a worry. It reinforced the worst fears of Europeans themselves, and it prompted such outlandish appraisals of the INF Treaty as this one from the Paris daily *Figaro:* "There can be some doubt as to who, the U.S. or the Soviet Union, comes out the winner. But the identity of the loser appears evident: Europe."

Joining Haig both in initially opposing the INF Accord and constantly reiterating its decoupling effect was Henry Kissinger. The irony of the deservedly-esteemed Kissinger making this pitch was too much. For it was Kissinger who, in 1979 after leaving office, made one of the most decoupling speeches ever made by such an eminent personage when he suggested in Brussels that no U.S. president was likely to use our strategic nuclear forces to rescue them, as this would mean suicide for us.

There is a double irony here: in that same stunning speech, Kissinger added, "It is also necessary that either the Soviet nuclear threat in theater nuclear forces against Europe be eliminated (which I do not see possible) *or* that an immediate effort be made to build up our theater nuclear forces." In plain words, he was claiming that if somehow the Soviets would eliminate their INF missiles, we would not have to install ours. Alas, the zero option was in fact suggested by Kissinger a few months before NATO enshrined it, two and a half years before Reagan proposed it, seven years before Gorbachev accepted it, and eight years before Kissinger opposed it.

While weapons systems are neither coupling nor decoupling in themselves, insensitivity to an ally's security *is* decoupling. This works both ways. All too often for my taste, Europeans are insensitive to American security interests, as with their public criticism of our actions in Grenada and Nicaragua. They expect us to help fend off communism on their continent but feel little compulsion to help us, even verbally, fend off communism on our continent. If they cannot bring themselves to support us, they can at least keep silent. Yet the one-way street of security concerns has become standard. As Karsten Voight of the left Social Democratic party in Germany told me once, "We like coupling with the U.S. on risks to us, but don't like coupling on risks to you."

Related to this decoupling argument was the military case against the INF Treaty. Haig, his successor General Bernard Rogers, and other retired officers unfurled their standard numbers-crunching case. Removing our INF missiles would, they claimed, preclude NATO's military arm from "covering" certain Soviet targets. But this argument was easily countered: The treaty reduced many more Soviet missiles—in their lexicon "targets"—than it removed the number of our systems able to hit those targets. As Winston Churchill once said, "However absorbed a commander may be in the elaboration of his own thoughts, it is necessary sometimes to take the enemy into consideration."

This case countered, a new military argument arose. The NATO military needed our INF systems to provide rungs on the "ladder of deterrence," extending from tactical and battlefield nuclear weapons to short-range INF to longer-range INF to the strategic nuclear forces. This ladder enabled NATO to adopt "flexible response" as its doctrine since the 1960s. Moreover, NATO military planners had long tried to move away from such heavy reliance on strategic forces at one extreme and on battlefield nuclear weapons on the other. The INF Accord contradicted that move.

The military's logic was impeccable, but the realities were implacable. Europeans' discomfort with nuclear protection was on the rise; as European strategist Christopher Bertram wrote, "Deterrence is only credible if it frightens the adversary more than it does one's own population." And Europeans' fear of the Soviet threat was on the decline. This has been true ever since NATO adopted flexible response, which ironically was just about the time the weapons filling out that strategy were removed. The first American INF systems—the Thor and Jupiter missiles located in Britain, Turkey, and Italy—were eliminated in the 1960s because of their vulnerability and limited utility and as an unspoken outcome of the Cuban missile crisis.

As was the situation then, the INF missiles' utility was questionable. Unlike their forefathers (Thor and Jupiter), the 1980 systems of Pershing IIs and ground-based cruise missiles were mobile. This helped diminish their vulnerability, but not by much.

Indeed, the "dirty little secret" through the INF debate was that our INF missiles were of limited utility. The best argument for the treaty was the one that could never be used, namely that our systems were no great shakes. Granted, they were mobile, but on practice drills they were accompanied by a siren-shrieking police escort in a caravan of up to forty vehicles. This made them hardly undetectable to the Soviets. Meanwhile they rested in locations in full sight (to say nothing of range) of high-rise apartments. It would not take a snappy Soviet *spitznats* squad to knock them out in the first moments of any aggression.

Worse yet, only a handful, if any, of the Pershings were normally armed with nuclear explosives. In wartime they had to be married (some by using easily-shot-at helicopters) with the warheads. In a time of crisis the same procedure would be taken, if a German government ever consented to such an awkward and vulnerable procedure. This is most doubtful; many Germans would fear provoking the Soviets or repeating the disastrous 1914 mobilization process.

On top of all this, our Pershing missiles could not even hit Moscow. They could reach Soviet territory all right, but not the capital or the extensive military assets around it.

I could only smile during the untold hours I spent listening to Soviet negotiators, spokesmen, and military experts describe the fearsome threat the Pershing IIs posed to their country. Their fevered pitch reached near hysteria as the December 1983 deployment date approached. Previously, they claimed the Pershings could wipe out Moscow in twenty minutes, then seventeen, then fifteen, and late in the game it became seven. The Soviets would not believe these missiles were unable to hit Moscow—perhaps they were never told, but I doubt it—and with good reason.

I could not believe it, either. When new on the job, I had the Pershing missile engineers come in to explain how this could be. The missile had been specifically designed, they said, with a range long enough to hit Soviet territory but short enough to preclude hitting Moscow. How and why could such a decision come out of the U.S. government? It can only be explained as a product of some interagency task force.

Most biting were the political arguments against the INF Accord. Here, though, Haig, Kissinger, Richard Nixon, and the others had a point. Indeed, the whole INF escapade had damaged our relations generally with Europeans, especially with Germans, and most particularly with German conservatives. And indeed, all the returns are not yet in. If the damage so vividly anticipated comes, if European (in particular German) jitters increase along with yearnings to be neutral and non-nuclear—and if this is somehow due to the treaty, rather than Gorbachev or the natural progression of things—then INF would not have been worth it.

Despite the ruckus over the short-range missiles, which seemed to tear at NATO in the spring and summer of 1989, I do not believe the INF Accord was primarily or even largely responsible for the damage. Critics point to the double zeros as leading to eventual disaster, but the Germans displayed signs of ambivalence or ambiguity or, least kindly, schizophrenia before INF came along, during it, and will no doubt long afterward. The short-range missile issue is merely an outward symbol of Germanic soul-searching in Wagnerian grandeur.

Besides, the slippery-slope argument, that a seemingly harmless step can lead to eventual disaster, permeates all arms control disputes. It is the last refuge of those opposing a move. However, it assumes a determinism that does not need to be. When Justice Oliver Wendell Holmes was told that "the power to tax is the power to destroy," he responded, "Not while this court sits." If INF is condemned as leading toward an onrush of denuclearization or neutralization, then Western actions *beyond* INF will be more foolish than the actions taken that led to the treaty.

Fears run rampant, and Chicken Littles have long perched in NATO. "Alliance in crisis" has been its tag line since NATO came into being, through the 1956 Suez crisis, the early 1960s uproar over the multilateral force, the Vietnam War disputes, the clash over refusing to help U.S. strategic airlifts to Israel during the 1973 Yom Kippur war, the Carter era debacle over the neutron bomb and disputes over SALT II, the pipeline spat, Grenada, the bombing of Libya, and Nicaragua. All these put the alliance "in crisis." All were endured and eventually overcome.

And European complaints are to be expected, whether over INF or most anything. "When the Americans and the Russians quarrel, the Europeans are afraid. When they agree, the Europeans panic," goes the old adage. Europeans can complain when Americans and Soviets are *not* talking, for fear we will then blow up the world, and when we *are* talking, for fear that we will carve up the world. It is either Armageddon or Yalta.

Until Reykjavik, they generally complained about Reagan not pushing hard enough on arms control. After Reykjavik, they fiercely complained about Reagan not being prudent enough on arms control. They can complain when the dollar is too strong and when it is too weak, when U.S. interest rates are too high or too low. In short, Europeans can complain.

While seemingly indiscriminate, there is a pattern to their griping. Europeans most often complain about change. They usually wish to maintain the status quo, no matter what that happens to be at any moment. If there are no U.S. missiles in Europe, they prefer no missiles there. If there are missiles in Europe, they prefer keeping them there.

Ditto on major arms control issues. When the Carter administration was finishing SALT II, the chief European leaders recoiled. President Carter practically had to chase the leaders of France, Britain, and West Germany around Guadeloupe in their bathing suits to wring out a statement of mild support for SALT II. When the Reagan administration was finishing SALT II—ending our adherence to it after five years—leaders of these same countries balked.

Such behavior is due partially to their amazement and bewilderment at how we handle government, especially our seemingly chaotic way of foreign affairs decision-making.

It is also due partially to cultural differences. Europe's resigned and even skeptical outlook does not mesh easily with America's energy and inventiveness. Europeans often consider problems as things to be avoided or tolerated; we believe they exist to be solved. When we know something, we feel compelled to do something about it; they don't. We relish something new; they resist much new. We lurch; they cringe.

Compare the words of that quintessential European diplomat, Lord Acton, describing a statesman's job—"to watch with hopefulness the process of incalculable change"—with those of the quintessential American, Theodore Roosevelt: "Far better it is to dare mighty things, to win glorious triumphs, even though checkered by failure, than to take rank with those poor spirits who neither enjoy much nor suffer much, because they live in the gray twilight that knows not victory nor defeat."

Given these temperamental differences, the best way for us to proceed is to propose change and expect the Europeans to hesitate, cogitate, and even complain before finally coming around. We need to realize that they cope best with only one problem at a time; even then they need ample time to work the issue through their labyrinth, to cut their political deals, to manage their ever-anxious publics, and to arrange themselves to accommodate any new situation.

Lastly, European behavior is also due partially to their awkward, even humiliating predicament—proud peoples with a rich culture and history depending upon a distant and dubious protector. Though they lack esteem for the way we handle mutual security matters, they are stuck with it. They have become the modern Peter who, when asked by Christ if he would desert, replied, "Lord, to whom else shall I turn?"

After the war, Europe turned to America. And there seems no turning back. Coming upon a half century hence, the contours of European security remain strikingly as they were then. Europe's defender and greatest friend, Dwight D. Eisenhower, predicted this with some regret during an NSC meeting soon after he became President in 1953:

> Properly speaking, the stationing of U.S. divisions in Europe had been at the outset an emergency measure not intended to last indefinitely. Unhappily, however, the European nations have been slow in building up their military forces and have now come to expect our forces to remain in Europe indefinitely.

In fact the Europeans did *not* need to build up their own forces. They looked over and saw our overwhelming nuclear superiority in those early years. Thereafter, all our talk about making them cough up more money for defense was a bluff, as they increasingly grasped. Our tough rhetoric would never be matched with any tough response. Why should they have done more?

Thus have they remained dependent on America, and with a crippling effect. No proud peoples can be proud of such dependency, especially when possessing sufficient resources. Today,

NATO countries *absent* America have a larger population and a much higher GNP than all the Warsaw Pact countries, *including* the Soviet Union. Since they spend so much less on defense, they are clearly outgunned and outmanned by Pact forces.

Understanding such factors does not rectify them. Probably nothing could. The Reagan administration, and the U.S. Senate afterward, had to deal with European qualms over the INF Accord. We consulted extensively during the negotiations, listened carefully, and then proceeded along. Our trump card was always that the zero option was *our* proposal, NATO's proposal. All of our elected leaders had been touting it for six years. All of our Foreign Ministers and Defense Ministers had issued communiqués twice yearly during those six years. We had to take yes for an answer.

THE DEBATE ENDS

That argument finally carried the day. The Europeans put on a faint smile and went along.

Most Americans put on a broad smile when thinking about the INF Treaty. They trusted Ronald Reagan, especially on security matters. Firebrand conservatives mustered a campaign against the administration, which reminded me of the Siamese fighting fish—those colorful, scrappy creatures who put their best efforts to killing or maiming each other rather than enemy species. The Conservative Caucus ran newspaper ads pairing Ronald Reagan to Neville Chamberlain and Mikhail Gorbachev to Adolf Hitler under the incendiary banner "Appeasement is as unwise in 1988 as it was in 1938." Like-minded groups flooded the mails with an anti-INF barrage. But it never took hold. Americans simply felt that Ronald Reagan would not sell our security down the river.

On the eve of the Moscow summit in May and June of 1988, the Senate finally decided that the INF debate must end. The vote must be taken. It was overwhelming. The Senate just could not turn down the most conservative president in the postwar era on an accord he had proposed six years before. Otherwise the Senate would signal that it would never again ratify a U.S.-Soviet arms accord. Even some who doubted its worth were persuaded by this argument.

And partisan politics played a role. Republicans could not turn down their leader, nor could they diminish the Office of the Presidency, which they traditionally support, especially in foreign affairs. Democrats have raised arms control to the top of their international wish list, so they had to cheer.

The self-styled Europeanists—Haig, Kissinger, and the like—recognized that however much the Allies would quake over our ratification of this treaty, they would quake even more if the Senate refused to ratify it. The effect then would be the worst possible one. European sentiment might demand the removal of our missiles while Soviet SS-20s remained. Even if nothing this dire happened, American steadiness and coherence in foreign affairs would again come under severe doubt. Realizing such factors, Henry Kissinger ended up arguing that INF was a damaging treaty that had best be ratified rapidly. There was something quintessentially Kissingerian about it all.

IT COMES TO A CLOSE

These problems lay before us that day, December 9, 1987. Our immediate problem was in finding Gorbachev and having him show up for his final meeting with the President.

At last he arrived at the White House, nearly two hours late. The President approached his car to greet him and said ever so graciously, "I thought you'd gone home!" Soviet diplomats told me later that he had spent the time not just pressing the flesh on Connecticut Avenue, but also checking back with Politburo members in Moscow. If true, it may have indicated that Gorbachev lacked sufficient power to decide on summit language by himself, but I doubt it since the language was convoluted and ephemeral. He might just have been an adept politician checking in with key players back home to make them feel a part of it all.

After the final luncheon, there remained a bit more language to work out. The press later portrayed this final session as a cliffhanger, but it lacked suspense (to me, anyway) at the time. Shultz and his team, and Shevardnadze and his squad, were still meeting in the Cabinet Room when the U.S. Marine Band struck up songs on the White House South Lawn for the farewell ceremony.

"I hope the band knows a lot of tunes," one colleague quipped to me. It didn't need to, since the two delegations finished our business in good order and in relatively good shape. We heaved a sigh of relief and met among ourselves for one last time. Some members of our team predicted gloom and doom for SDI because of the final agreed summit language.

I thought otherwise. No one outside the ten or so of us would understand the language in question—how both sides pledged to "observe the ABM Treaty, as signed in 1972, while conducting their research, development, and testing as required, which are permitted by the ABM Treaty, and not to withdraw from the ABM Treaty, for a specified period of time." President Reagan and Secretaries Shultz and Carlucci thought the "as required" meant as required by the fulsome test program we needed to advance SDI. Gorbachev interpreted the same phrase to mean "as required" by the ABM Treaty.

More agreed language covering more contradictory views leading to more post-summit disputes over what the document really said, or meant. This was the stuff of specialists, though, since the world at large cared nothing for what the document said or meant. They were right; it too has been lost in the annals of history.

While some worrywarts still fumed in the White House, Max Kampelman and I ducked out to the South Lawn to catch the farewell ceremonies. We stood in the rain, some nice Secret Service agent bringing us an umbrella to share, during these, my last hours as Director of the U.S. Arms Control and Disarmament Agency. Dean Acheson once said that to leave government is to die a little. Maybe so, but to be in government is surely to live a lot.

A few feet away, the President was bidding the General Secretary adieu with flourishing farewell remarks, to which Gorbachev responded in kind. While listening, it occurred to me that the two leaders' words were nearly identical. "Imagine if Gorbachev had taken up Reagan's text and Reagan had accidentally picked up his, Max. No one would tell the difference!"

He chuckled, even though I said this with some regret. Presidents, indeed all U.S. officials, should be able to pass the "switched texts" criteria for remarks with nondemocratic leaders, especially Soviet leaders. Anyone listening should be able to tell if the texts were mistakenly switched. Later in Moscow, the President would pass this test with flying colors, but not here.

We followed the President, First Lady, and others into the White House, where Secretary Shultz kindly complimented the President, who hugged Nancy with joy during a warm and wonderful moment. The ever-diligent staff then guided Reagan back into the Oval Office to help him prepare his Address to the Nation for that evening.

CHAPTER 6

THE ANNUAL
SALT DEBATE

RETREAT IS COMMONLY KNOWN to be the most difficult of all military maneuvers. That it should be so in arms control is less known, though just as true.

Last chapter, we witnessed the troubles that arise from negotiating and entering an arms accord. This chapter, we will see the staggering problems that result from leaving one.

SALT II should have been scuttled at the outset of the Reagan administration. That's what the voters must have expected when voting for the candidate who opposed SALT in 1980. That's what the press must have expected from a man so intent on implementing his clear program. That's what the Soviets may have expected from such a viscerally anticommunist conservative.

For sure that's what *we* expected upon joining Reagan's administration. For many of us later entering arms control posts, our first experience with Ronald Reagan came under the auspices of the Committee on the Present Danger, which led the anti-SALT II charge and where Reagan served as our most prominent member and I, for one, served on the executive board.

But, as happens in government, what could have been assumed had to be examined. And delayed. And examined again. And pondered. And fought. Nothing happens easily in government or comes cleanly.

Why this should be so is not so clear. That it is so becomes very clear when reliving the tortuous path toward the demise of SALT II.

• • •

Most of my appearances before congressional committees over the years were, happily, uneventful. This one, in February 1985, proved otherwise.

I was appearing before the Senate Armed Services Committee to discuss Soviet treaty violations. After the formal testimony and some scattered questions, I glanced over to see Senator Edward Kennedy's face turning red, his mouth twitching, and his whole body fidgeting. Obviously agitated, Senator Kennedy began blurting out his problems with the state of play in arms control.

"It seems to me that we are getting the worst of all worlds," he said, working himself into a bit of a lather. "The administration is complaining about the violations . . . [but] we are not getting any corresponding actions by the Soviets in terms of compliance. . . . What the administration is doing is showing these allegations and not getting any action." Still, we wanted the Soviets to come back to the bargaining table. So what gives?

Rather than fire back (in part because Kennedy was on to something), I decided to respond calmly by explaining that the yearly reports the administration issued on Soviet violations were mandated by law. Besides, we informed the Soviets in private before levying any public allegations.

Before making these points, I had been guilty of what in the UN would be deemed an "unfriendly act." I, the witness, had asked Senator Kennedy, the inquisitor, a question. This mortifies a Congressman or Senator and enrages his staff, who do not prepare him to answer for himself. My question was this: "Do you doubt the administration's claim that the Soviets cheat on arms control? In particular, do you suspect that they may not have cheated on the ABM Treaty by building that radar at Krasnoyarsk?"

No, Kennedy said, the Russians made a mistake there. That was a clear violation. Everyone was certain of that.

"Was the administration wrong, then, in publicly saying this? And in reporting other Soviet violations, as required by law?" I went on to reason that the Soviets surely knew about their actions. The U.S. government knew about them. The American people would be the only ones left uninformed, unless their leaders came clean. Besides, we had to obey the law, which, incidentally, passed the Senate unanimously.

No, the American people had a right to know, the Senator agreed. And the administration had to follow the law.

But still, Kennedy was baffled: "Going into the negotiations, [the Soviets] are going to say, My God, if we have been violating there, the U.S. publishes these and then really doesn't do very much about it, so let us get on with the next negotiation. Maybe we can go ahead and continue to violate."

Later, in private, I asked the Senator if that led him to believe that President Reagan should refuse to send our negotiators back to the bargaining table, if the Soviets wished to return.

He looked at me silently.

If that was his reasoning, I suggested that he write the President or make a public statement to that effect. People would find that view interesting, especially coming from him.

Senator Kennedy, splendid at delivering a set speech, faltered. He looked confused, perhaps because he was confused.

And he was right to be confused. Soviet violations do confuse people. They confuse administrations. Once the subject of the debate became what to do about Soviet violations, the administration faced problems galore. This issue was to plague us throughout most of our tenure. The fate of SALT II became an annual, quintessentially symbolic issue.

Deeming it such in no way minimizes its importance. Symbols *are* important; they can arouse more fury than disputes over mundane matters. The passions unleashed by national, ethnic, or religious symbols were aroused here by SALT II, a symbol of arms control, which in turn has become a symbol of hope in a world threatened by nuclear annihilation.

Though arms control symbolizes peace on the grand level, it becomes exceedingly technical on the practical level. Between them resides a world of hard politics—domestic politics involving the sundry bureaucracies, Congress, outside interest groups, and the press—and international politics involving the Allies and Soviets.

Despite decision-making theories or models used in graduate schools of government, the best way to picture how arms control works is to envision bumper cars at an amusement park. The various participants and groups bump into one another incessantly as issues come along. Progress can come only if a participant is determined to plunge ahead despite the detours, diversions, dents, and bruises. Persistence is essential—the sheer will to leap over hurdles and around obstacles to get anything done. If this gives the impression of chaos in U.S. decision-making, it is not far off the mark.

Arms control also requires a mind able to work in a world of abstractions. This first struck me over a luncheon in Munich,

West Germany, during the annual Wehrkunde meeting one year. Sitting with arms control experts from around Allied capitals, I mentioned that I had been a theology major in college. Fred Ruth, then the German government's arms control honcho, remarked that he too had been a theology major. Karsten Voight, the liberal Social Democrat's arms control expert, chimed in that he too had studied theology, as did a Britisher and some others seated with us. We all had turned from the scholarly study of theology to the quasi-practical profession of arms control.

Even before the modern field of arms control rose in the 1960s, previous efforts at disarmament were played by abstract, mostly wishful thinking. Andrew White, chief delegate to the Hague Convention of 1899 and American Ambassador to Germany at the time, remarked that the "queer letters and crankish proposals which come in every day are amazing." No more amazing than the proposals adorning the op-ed pages of today's leading newspapers, which often have scant bearing to Soviet strategic thinking or behavior. Mental gymnastics, exercises in abstract thinking, many reflecting a mathematical bent (interestingly, much of modern arms control, as a field, sprang from mathematics). The Soviet Union becomes akin to the ghost at Banquo's banquet, a force that may haunt the affair yet strangely is not present.

Abstractness and hard politics came together in the battle over SALT II. Neither the treaty's opponents nor its advocates could ever demonstrate that its results would significantly affect real U.S. security interests; such makes this an ideal case study of how arms control works, indeed how Washington works on emotionally laden issues.

An Enduring Issue

More than ten years after I entered the Pentagon to serve as assistant to the Secretary of Defense, Donald H. Rumsfeld, I dined with my former boss in Washington, D.C. During the course of the evening, in the spring of 1986, Rumsfeld asked me what were the big issues in arms control then.

I told him that *the* major issue was the same one we wrestled with during his tenure in the Pentagon—namely SALT II. President Ford wanted to finish the treaty fast, before the 1976 elections. He was dissuaded by the prime factors affecting most big decisions on arms control: substance and politics. Substance came from Rumsfeld, who argued knowledgeably that SALT II would not stem the Soviet strategic buildup, and the political punch came from everyone: Ronald Reagan was running hard against both detente and Ford, so concluding SALT II would put the nail in the President's coffin for that close nomination.

Hence was President Ford's SALT II shelved, to be quickly, even hastily, picked up by President Jimmy Carter, who finally concluded the accord in the summer of 1979. His National Security Advisor, Zbigniew Brzezinski, wrote in his memoirs that Secretary of State Cyrus Vance "hoped that a new SALT agreement would pave the way for a wider U.S.-Soviet accommodation, while I saw in it an opportunity to halt or reduce the momentum of the Soviet military buildup." Good goals, but neither was accomplished.

Since the treaty ended up unequal in some politically embarrassing ways—the Soviets were allowed "heavy missiles" while we were allowed none; they did not have to include their newest Backfire bomber while we had to include our aged bomber, the B-52, and so forth—a national debate ensued. The opposition charge was led by the Committee on the Present Danger, which included Ronald Reagan and many of his future advisors—Richard Allen, Paul Nitze, Max Kampelman, Gene Rostow, Ed Rowny, and myself. Our case was echoed in the unanimous Senate Armed Services Committee report. All our expertise and devotion proved unnecessary, however, as the matter became moot after the Soviets invaded Afghanistan. Reagan blasted SALT II during his 1980 presidential campaign, calling it "fatally flawed" for sundry reasons, among them that it was unverifiable.

Actually SALT II was more verifiable than past accords and future ones devised by Reagan's own administration. The treaty to ban all biological and toxic weapons, concluded in 1972, was conceded as being basically unverifiable when the tough-minded Nixon signed it and the Senate approved it for ratification, as it lacked *any* verification provisions at all. (Ironically, our administration did find Soviet violations of this accord, so it must have been more verifiable than anticipated then.)

President Reagan made loads of speeches extolling verification, speaking in absolutes about how a treaty had to be watertight or totally verifiable or the like. But INF, the one treaty he concluded, was harder to verify than key provisions of SALT II.

START, the treaty that preoccupied his administration, was of much lower verifiability than SALT II. His draft treaty to ban chemical weapons was even tougher to verify, if not altogether impossible. Finally, the first arms control treaty concluded by Reagan's administration, that on confidence-building concluded in Stockholm, was completed when we agreed to worse verification provisions than even Europe's neutral nations sought.

Many of these lie in the past, and we need not rehash past mistakes or difficulties. In the future may be a START accord, built on the foundation of the Reagan administration, though one destined to be far less verifiable than SALT II or INF. Why?

First, START limits factors such as warheads and throw weight, which, though indisputably of greater strategic importance, are indisputably tougher to verify. SALT I and II merely counted deployed missiles and planes and missile-carrying submarines, which are easier for us to count and much tougher for them to hide. U.S. intelligence cannot, however, count the number of warheads on Soviet missiles; it can only detect a missile's carrying capability or the number tested. And given modern technology, neither side has to test its full complement of warheads; hence they can test a missile with six warheads and load it confidently with ten.

Second, strategic systems coming along are smaller and more mobile, thus much harder to detect or count. Cruise missiles and land-based mobile missiles cause the most headaches yet stand at the forefront of new Soviet strategic power; over the next decade, half of the Soviet land-based missiles will become mobile, carrying some three-quarters of their total warheads.

Our satellites have sparse ability to detect these relatively small and mobile systems in that vast Soviet empire; they even missed the massive Krasnoyarsk radar. Our human intelligence is spotty and limited, too. Though *glasnost* may help in the future, traditional Soviet secretiveness has plagued us in the past. For example, Western intelligence did not know that Yuri Andropov, the number-one man in the USSR then, had been married until Soviet television showed the weeping widow at his graveside. By then, this information was not any longer useful to us. This was a huge information gap about the second most important man in the world, one who had been head of the KGB for the previous twelve years and was thus of keen interest to our intelligence community.

Third, Soviet concealment and deception have grown over

time. They are now capable of scrambling most of their telemetry (data from missile tests) and have other ways to deny us this information, even if such scrambling (called encryption) were to be banned. The Soviets now know when and where our satellites pass overhead and can hence hide critical items or practices during such times.

Fourth, arms control is now aimed at deep reductions. Obviously, at lower levels verification assumes higher importance. For the Soviets slyly to cheat by 100 on their strategic missiles and planes, limited to 2,250 in SALT II, is of negligible relevance. For them to cheat by 100 on their intermediate mobile missiles, limited to zero in INF, is of enormous significance.

Fifth and finally, previous Soviet cheating raises the need for better verification. A sharp security guard keeps keener tabs on a convicted shoplifter than on a regular customer.

To peer ahead at another arms control effort, concluding a worldwide ban on chemical weapons will be essentially impossible to verify. This may dash a dream of President Bush's, who during the 1988 campaign proclaimed this as a top priority of his presidency.

Why, one may ask, would the Reagan administration, publicly committed to a celestial standard of verification, propose a draft chemical weapons accord that could not be verified? For good reasons, as it turns out.

A worldwide ban on chemical weapons *is* a noble goal. Chemical weapons, which cost one million casualties in World War I, have returned on the world scene, and with a vengeance. The Soviets helped the Vietnamese pour "yellow rain" on innocent H'mong people of Cambodia. Iraq then used poison gas against the foreign foe of Iran and its foe within, the Kurds. Libya has been busy constructing the largest chemical warfare plant in the Third World at Rabta, one capable of producing tens of tons of nerve agents each *day*.

Even before chemical weapons became so ominous, the State Department wished to find some new arms control initiative in that dry year of 1984, when the Soviets were boycotting the talks. So the Secretary of State publicly announced that we would introduce a draft treaty to ban chemical weapons.

Having pledged this, Shultz had to work hard to make it true. We in ACDA began busily drafting treaty provisions while the Defense Department fought the treaty (and us) tooth and nail.

The showdown came, as always, before the President at a NSC

meeting. Secretary Shultz touted the treaty as a noble effort, besides having his credibility on the line to deliver what he had pledged. Shultz had delivered his speech in Europe, where our Allies pined for such negotiations.

Secretary Weinberger countered that the treaty was ill conceived and ill advised. Shultz, according to Weinberger, should not have spoken as he did. The United States needed chemical weapons, not a chemical weapons ban. The Soviets had built up a huge quantity of the stuff, while for some nineteen years we had produced none at all. Deterrence in this realm was quickly ebbing.

I pointed out to the President that the treaty was essentially unverifiable. Seconding me, after some prompting, was CIA Director William Casey. Weinberger concurred heartily. If we *had* to offer a draft treaty in Geneva, he advised, it should at least provide for inspections anytime and anywhere, to search for clandestine chemical stockpiles in all countries. This seemingly nifty approach had one slight problem—*we* could not live with it. The intelligence community did not want Russians running around its most sacrosanct facilities. Nor did other sensitive agencies relish this prospect.

Even with all this, I supported offering the draft treaty as the only real way of enticing Congress to fund the chemical weapons program we needed. The administration's argument was that the best way to deter a chemicals attack was to have a chemicals stockpile; that was what the World War II experience had taught us. But in the existing political climate, that argument simply would not work.

Opponents could smear congressional members with "voting for poison gas." But our offering the treaty in Geneva would give our congressional supporters and those wavering in the middle the cover they needed. No, they were *not* voting for poison gas. Yes, they *were* voting for the negotiations to ban chemical weapons altogether, everywhere, by everyone around the world. This could come from the incentive of renewed U.S. production.

The President's decision seemed up in the air until Vice President George Bush, prepped ahead of time, indicated his willingness to present the treaty himself in Geneva. That struck Reagan as a worthwhile activity for his Vice President, so the treaty moved forward and was unveiled by Bush in April 1984.

After that, it moved forward too quickly, a rare problem in the annals of arms control. By the time the Reagan administration was winding down in 1987 and 1988, the Soviets were winding up. They seemed willing to buy on to our "anytime, anywhere" inspection provision and urged speedier negotiations. They had called our bluff—quite insincerely, I believe—but they called it nonetheless, prompting us to search for other grounds for stalling. Here was an instance where we should *not* take yes for an answer.

For the moment, however, our treaty tabling ploy proved a stellar success. Congress has approved the new binary chemical weapons program, and deterrence here is being reinforced.

Arms Control to Build Up

The notion of offering a treaty that allegedly reduces weaponry in order to increase weapons did not originate with chemical weapons. It has a grand tradition; President Nixon launched conventional arms talks in 1972 in order to stop Congress from passing the Mansfield Amendment, which would have forced withdrawal of U.S. troops from Europe. His tactic worked marvelously well.

This genre of arms control, though, is a dangerous one for democracies. It plays too loose with the truth and proves successful only if everyone knows and sticks to the rules—keeping the treaties unconsummated. This becomes a tricky business, given the diplomats' penchant for paper accomplishments and the public's esteem for an arms pact.

Nondemocracies perform this type of nonsincere diplomacy all the time. They avoid the trap of awarding diplomats for reaching agreements they don't actually want. This I learned upon meeting a veteran Chinese diplomat at the United Nations who was assigned to negotiate with the Russians over some land dispute. I casually asked him how the negotiations were going. "Wonderful!" he said, his face lighting up.

Longing to pick up some inside information, I asked, "How so?"

"Twenty years of talks," he said, grinning. "Twenty years, and no agreement on land in dispute. No agreement on mechanism for resolving dispute. No agreement on agenda for talks. No agreement!" China had possession of the land, and so his bosses were pleased by the lack of movement. I left wondering where we could find such a fine individual in our Foreign Service, for here was a special diplomat.

TAKING THE EASY ROAD IN ROUND ONE

Our diplomats and especially our politicians are prone to procrastinate. They are reluctant to make a controversial decision ever, and especially until (or unless) they must. This came out in the spring of 1981, when we had the first round of our annual SALT II taffy-tug.

Logic would lead one to presume that Reagan would instantly scrap our adherence to this unratified treaty, and be done with the issue. But Washington never works in such a straight way.

Instead, the new Secretary of State, Al Haig, worried that scrapping SALT II would prompt problems with the Allies and Congress. Sure, he had criticized the treaty as Supreme Commander in Europe, even giving critical testimony before the Senate, and he ran against it during his fleeting presidential bid.

Still, he fretted. No arms negotiations were then under way, and no one in the new administration was too keen to get them under way, at least before the Reagan economic program and military buildup were begun. Haig wanted to avoid fights with the Allies (on top of those he was having with the White House staff). His State Department advisors claimed, correctly, that there was no *practical* reason for abandoning SALT II. No weapons we wanted to build were being restricted by the treaty. Haig was backed, during the crucial 1981 White House meeting, by a CIA presentation done by William Casey's deputy, Bobby Inman, which claimed that the treaty helped harness the Soviets. This case was not made convincingly, but no one around the table besides Haig knew enough to counter it, and he had no reason to do so.

The easy move was to punt for the moment. The administration would temporarily adopt an "interim restraint" policy wherein we would not undercut SALT II as long as the Soviets followed suit. Thus would the treaty's provisions take effect even though it was not adopted legally. No one thought where this new policy would lead, but like Scarlett O'Hara, we'd think about it tomorrow.

Later I would often reflect on how easy it would have been for us to have rejected SALT II then and there. That's what Reagan had pledged to the American people. That's how the Democratic Senate had felt. And that was the right thing to do. SALT II was against U.S. national interests, point-blank. Reagan should not have us abide by a "fatally flawed" treaty.

Such a clean break may have evoked a one-day adverse story, at the most; coming on the heels of Reagan's firing of the air traffic controllers, and it could have come off as another decisive presidential decision, so welcome after all of Carter's waffling. It could have been a one-day positive story.

But that was not to be. Those in government delay until they can delay no longer, and even then cut and trim. They resemble the proverbial city council that, when divided over whether to build a new bridge, eventually decides to build the bridge halfway across the river.

Yet our initial SALT II decision was not castigated as a cave-in, for Reagan had fashioned a *tough* new interim restraint policy, befitting his new team of tough hombres. We would not undercut existing arms accords "so long as the Soviet Union showed equal restraint." Haig and Gromyko privately agreed to these terms in September of 1981, and the President publicly announced them on Memorial Day 1982.

This new policy played pleasingly. It showed how sensible Reagan would act as President, despite his wild words as candidate. It seemed so reasonable and yet was shortsighted and self-deceptive. Shortsighted to trim the cat's tail one inch at a time, and deceptive since the Soviets had displayed no "equal restraint," and would not do so.

They had not violated SALT II by then, because of the high limits it set and the brief time since it was signed. Still, they displayed no "equal restraint" in what really mattered; their strategic nuclear buildup proceeded apace, mostly within but later beyond the SALT constraints. As Henry Rowen, the CIA's top analyst then, has since written, "The number of known Soviet systems deployed in the first half of the 1980s . . . was twice that of the U.S." On key measures of strategic power Soviet production rates had ranged between two and five times greater than ours since the SALT treaties had been signed. They built seven times more missile-carrying submarines and produced 340 strategic long-term and intermediate bombers, to our 6 during these years.

There the issue lay for a spell, neither receiving nor deserving much attention. Someone would occasionally ask why Ronald Reagan was respecting Jimmy Carter's "fatally flawed" treaty. Replying to this required the agility of an acrobat, but that's life in any administration.

Then something changed; folks became more sensitive to Soviet cheating. As the dialogue with Senator Kennedy illustrated, with the discovery of the Krasnoyarsk radar, compliance—once primarily a concern of the right—became a centrist issue. Congress then required a yearly presidential report on Soviet compliance; this was not truly a congressional initiative—I spent hours helping to make it happen—but it passed with a Senate vote of 92 to 0.

The administration then had to craft the report. When I arrived at the Arms Control and Disarmament Agency early in 1983, there was a lot of heaving going on. Slews of staff from who knew how many agencies had been thrashing about over a report on twenty-plus alleged Soviet violations, a pathway to nowhere.

I told then National Security Advisor Bill Clark, a fine man and a good NSC chief, that we in ACDA would do the first draft on six main issues. He seemed relieved, but he was the only one. Everyone else resented this bureaucratic grab. Still, we proceeded.

I spent much of that summer cooped up in the ACDA conference room with the top staff slogging through issues while going through jars of gourmet jelly beans. There was blood on the walls as we worked—these are not easy issues, and folks in ACDA disagreed violently about them—but finally we finished. Clark then circulated the draft for others to pick apart. (It came out remarkably intact, even a tad improved.)

The timing was odd in one respect. As we were finishing, the intelligence community found the Krasnoyarsk radar. Back at the jelly beans we went to deal with this newest and largest compliance issue. But here we could not describe any Soviet response to our allegation, since there was none. Shultz had elicited no explanation from Soviet Ambassador Dobrynin when initially protesting the radar, and Moscow refused to hold a special session in Geneva, as expected in such cases.

We decided to complete our report anyway. So we crafted two or three of the best explanations for the radar available to Moscow—all plausible, some even nettlesome to refute. One ACDA expert speculated that the Soviets might claim the radar was built for space tracking, but others dismissed this as too weak an explanation. Exercising the awesome authority vested in me, I decided, "What the hell?" and included it in our report, though listing it as the weakest possible response. Little did I know that the Soviets would choose this as their sole justification for Krasnoyarsk. In a nutshell, we could have written a better brief for their case than they concocted.

No Pattern of Compliance

Even before the rise of arms control, the Soviets were known to break treaties. They had violated several "nonaggression pacts," including those signed in the 1920s with Estonia, Latvia, and Lithuania—independent states recognized as such by Moscow and others, all three full members of the League of Nations —yet were annexed by the Soviet Union after Stalin's 1939 Nonaggression Pact with Hitler. (Here, incidentally, is the one international agreement Moscow scrupulously followed at the time and ever since.) In the immediate postwar era, the Soviets violated Yalta and other accords. Such has led two scholars, Professors Jan F. Triska and Robert M. Slusser, to conclude in the pre–arms control early 1960s that "Soviet treaty violations have been on a scale and a character for which it would be hard to find an adequate precedent."

This pattern of violations continued in the arms control era, as they have violated provisions of the 1925 Geneva Protocol, the 1963 Limited Test Ban Treaty, the 1972 Biological and Toxin Weapons Convention, the 1972 SALT I Interim Agreement (SALT I), the 1972 ABM Treaty, the 1974 Threshold Test Ban Treaty, the 1975 Helsinki Accords, and the 1979 SALT II Treaty.

Not every provision of these accords has been violated; this would be impossible for anyone to manage. But too much should not be made of this fact, for it is no defense of a man accused of adultery to list the times he slept with his wife. Al Capone never violated *all* the laws of the United States; indeed, he never violated most of them, as this too would be impossible for anyone to manage. He was, however, guilty of violating important laws, as the Soviets are guilty of violating important provisions of their treaties.

And probably like Capone, the Russians did not go out intending to cheat. They merely preferred to build weapons and facilities rather than comply with the provisions of the various agreements.

Soviet indifference toward compliance has itself been verified.

In his best-selling *Breaking with Moscow*, Arkady N. Shev-chenko, the high-ranking Soviet defector, described his Foreign Ministry responsibilities on the 1972 convention on biological and toxin weapons:

> While the military strongly opposed any agreement on chemical or biological weapons, the political leadership . . . felt it necessary for propaganda purposes. . . . The military's reaction was to say go ahead and sign the convention; without international controls, who would know anyway? They refused to consider eliminating their stockpiles and insisted upon further developments of these weapons.

The upshot suited everyone. As Shevchenko writes, "The toothless convention . . . was signed in 1972, but there are no international controls over the Soviet program, which continues apace."

The casual way Soviet leaders view treaty adherence is matched by the casual way most others view their adherence. The millions of words European leaders heap upon arms control yearly lack any mention of Soviet violations. Not one European government has ever found one Soviet violation of any one arms control treaty. Nor do they seem terribly distressed by Soviet infractions of other accords—the United Nations Charter, the Helsinki Accords, the Universal Declaration of Human Rights, and the International Covenant on Civil and Political Rights—to which European states are themselves party.

Third World states are worse. Their lack of concern over Soviet violations takes extreme forms. My favorite example—which Donald Lowitz, our gifted Ambassador to the forty-nation Conference on Disarmament, told the President in the Oval Office one time—occurred when a flustered Indian delegate answered his speech on the dismal Soviet compliance record by blurting out, "If you are going to stress verification and compliance, we'll *never* have an arms control agreement." Even the best minds of our negotiators become scrambled upon entering this topic. In 1986 a reporter from the *Sydney Morning Herald* asked a top negotiator, "Why continue negotiating new agreements when the Soviets violate old ones?" The answer: "The problem with dealing with the Soviets . . . is that they cheat. But he says this does not mean you can't do business with them. . . ." Right. But can the business you do with them accomplish anything if, as he says, they cheat?

The American public is likewise ambivalent, with large majorities believing both that the Soviets cheat on agreements and that we should conclude new agreements.

The President's report proved Soviet cheating on SALT II in three main ways: encrypting their telemetry (scrambling the signals) so as to impede our efforts to verify the accord; building a second new type of land-based missile (each side was only allowed one); and exceeding the overall limits on strategic nuclear delivery vehicles.

This report was solid, as it had to be. The single biggest sin in government is sloppiness, and even a little sloppiness kills credibility. In the administration's early days, Secretary Haig ordered a report on Soviet-Cuban-Nicaraguan subversion in Central America. His was an excellent idea, but Haig wanted it too fast. It was written too swiftly to allow sound scrubbing. Ninety percent or more was perfect; 10 percent or less was wrong. Yet the press jumped on the wrong parts and discredited the whole endeavor.

With respect to our compliance report, we were pleased to learn that—despite the forty-thousand-plus individuals now on the payroll of the United States Congress, including battalions of recent MIT graduates flurrying around their senators—no factual error was found in either the classified or the more abstract unclassified versions.

Still, Congress griped about the report. Conservatives complained that we treated only seven key issues; they counted more than twenty violations and suspected we were engaged in a "cover-up." Liberals accused us of excessive rhetoric about minor violations. They, along with the traditional arms control community, conceded that the Soviets found "loopholes" and stretched the "spirit" of the agreement but were wont to admit that they engaged in out-and-out violations of anything serious.

This was the view of President Jimmy Carter (whom I had first gotten to know in most unusual circumstances; on the day he left the presidency, I accompanied him and his top administration members to Wiesbaden, West Germany to greet the American hostages just released from Iran) after spending an afternoon on this issue in Atlanta. Sure, the proof might be there, but Henry Kissinger had convinced him that the Soviets break only the "spirit" of agreements, not the letter, while the Chinese uphold both. That's what he found, too.

Interestingly, on this score the oft naive Jimmy Carter joined the realist Winston Churchill, who, despite his general insight, had moments of misjudgment. The great man told the House of Commons on February 27, 1945, weeks after Yalta: "I know of no government which stands to its obligations, even in its own despite, more solidly than the Russian Soviet government."

Despite the Carter-like qualms in many quarters, a general consensus formed that, yes, the Soviets were violating SALT II, along with the ABM Treaty. The debate then turned on the importance of such violations.

Administration opponents considered their importance slight. On this they were somewhat shifty. During the opening of the Senate debate on SALT II, the three provisions the Soviets subsequently violated had been highlighted as among the treaty's key elements. Back then, President Carter became so carried away with the importance of the encryption issue that he said publicly such a violation might even lead to a nuclear showdown. In an astonishing April 30, 1979 press conference, which must have driven his staff up the wall, Carter said rather grandly in response to a question on encryption:

> The Soviets know that if we ever detect any violation of the SALT agreement, that that would be a basis on which to reject the treaty in its entirety; there would be a possible termination of the good relationship between our country and the Soviet Union on which detente is based; and it might very well escalate into a nuclear confrontation.

Star SALT II witness Paul Warnke claimed in 1979 that the numerical limits and the ban on more than one new missile were critical elements. The Senate Foreign Relations Committee report back then also singled them out; SALT-seller Senator Joseph Biden offered a nonbinding amendment to emphasize his and the Senate's insistence on these points, particularly on the encryption provision. Yet during the first of the annual Reagan spring fetes over SALT II, Carter, Warnke, and Biden summarily dismissed these as peripheral provisions.

The critics' general point—that these violations did not alter the overall U.S.-Soviet strategic balance—was easy to rebut in public, though it was basically correct. In debates with Warnke or on television, I said that my not paying taxes would not alter the overall financial posture of the U.S. Treasury, yet the IRS would come after me for not paying. Otherwise the institution of tax collection would wither and die.

Similarly, Soviet violations affect the institution of arms control, which would die if the Soviets could pick and choose which provisions to follow and which to ignore. Just as U.S. citizenship is a package deal, with rights and obligations, so treaty making is a package deal. There are provisions we like and others we do not like but have consented to in order to have an agreement that, on balance, helps us. If Moscow merely adheres to some provisions while we adhered to all, this would change bilateral arms control into unilateral disarmament. Besides, if certain provisions did not matter much, why did we insist on them? And why did the Soviets violate them? They mattered enough to us to include them in the contract and enough to the Soviets to contradict them.

But our opponents had a point that Soviet violations to SALT II did not affect the strategic nuclear balance since SALT II itself did not affect that balance. And the critics were right that the Reagan administration changed the ground rules on compliance from focus on security to focus on politics. The key question went from "Is the nation's security harmed by Soviet violations?" to "Do the Soviets cheat?" Before Reagan, "adequate verification" had been defined as our ability to detect major violations early enough for us to respond in time to preserve U.S. security. During the Reagan years, the standard became our ability to detect *any* Soviet violation, regardless of its military significance.

Having basically won the argument over *whether* the Soviets cheated, the administration landed in the Kennedy line of inquiry: Why then proceed with arms control? Good question, with no crisp answer. To acknowledge Soviet violations is to acknowledge the vacuousness of arms accords. No matter how wisely negotiated and how scrupulously verified, a treaty may not reap its promised benefits if the Soviets cheat on it. So why proceed? There's an old adage that goes, "Fool me once, shame on you; fool me twice, shame on me."

We ducked that question—we had to duck it—and faced the more practical question of what we would *do* about Soviet cheat-

ing. Another tough one, but necessary to address. For to acknowledge Soviet violations is to be propelled into action.

The answer used by President Reagan, Secretary Shultz, and
others was that we were insisting upon better verification for
future agreements. This sounded good but wasn't right. Not only
were we proposing draft treaties in START and on chemical
weapons that had worse verifiability, but this response confused
verification with compliance. Our verification arrangements
proved swell on SALT II and the ABM Treaty; we found and
documented their violations. Our detection was not the problem;
their adherence was.

The more accurate and obvious response was to end our interim restraint policy on SALT II. Clearly their cheating meant
they were not practicing "equal restraint." According to our own
policy, we were thus no longer bound to SALT II.

So runs the logic of the issue, but not the politics; for by 1984
and 1985 the SALT accords had assumed soaring symbolic salience. They were the sole existing arrangements on strategic arms
and the only ones on the horizon. Since the Reagan administration could not achieve a new accord, the prevailing argument
went, why trash the existing ones? Without them, the world
would be hurled into a "new round of the arms race" with "unlimited competition." The Pentagon sought no military programs
beyond the SALT II limits, and besides, things might become a
whole lot worse without the treaty. Soviet forces would sky-
rocket once unshackled from the SALT constraints. So it was said
in the halls of Congress and on op-ed pages throughout the land.

These debates permeated Washington, stirring the President's
staff to do what comes naturally in such circumstances, to throw
a meeting at the problem. Thus in the spring of 1985 we assembled once again in the Situation Room for another in a caravan of
meetings over SALT II.

With the President presiding, Bud McFarlane opened by re-
minding us how we had concluded long ago that SALT II was no
good. It had not improved any after the Soviets began violating it.
He then asked about the military consequences of our leaving the
treaty.

Joint Chiefs Chairman General Jack Vessey reckoned not
much. He correctly deemed this mostly a political and not a
military issue, and said that others around the table were better
at politics than the Joint Chiefs. He quickly added that the Chiefs
had no funds for new programs to offset Soviet violations.

Vessey tossed this out nonchalantly. Little did he know—little did we know—that this assessment closed any possibility for a serious U.S. response to Soviet violations, whether to offset any military advantage they accrued or to teach Moscow a lesson. The General's remark proved the death knell of a tough compliance policy during the Reagan administration.

Secretary Shultz next presented his rather abstract and somewhat contradictory thoughts. It would be a grave error for us to scrap SALT II, even though the Soviets did not seem much constrained by it. Still, we had to respond forcefully to their cheating. How, required more study. But remember: given the congressional problems we faced fielding new strategic weapons, we needed arms control more than the Soviets.

None of us knew what was the bottom line to all this, but we were sure about Weinberger's position. He wanted us out of the interim restraint policy and said so strongly. Casey seconded the motion before detailing the Soviet strategic buildup during SALT II, while Attorney General Ed Meese rendered his judgment that we had no legal requirement to stay with the treaty (no one ever claimed we did) and advocated putting SALT behind us.

I appealed to Reagan's common sense. All of us around the table had opposed SALT II before taking office. It seemed senseless for us to abide by a treaty we opposed when it was unratified and unratifiable, violated, and expired. Paul Nitze, leader of SALT II opponents before this administration began, then seconded Shultz to stay within the treaty. As usual he had come to this conclusion after considerable number-crunching; his calculations showed that there was nothing significant we could do militarily beyond SALT II. Again, no one had ever said there was.

When these arguments were laid before the President, he posed questions and pondered. Actually this was all role playing. The brilliance of our presentations, indeed the merits of the arguments, had little to do with his decision. That had been ordained before our White House session ever began.

In fact, the decision became inevitable when Gorbachev agreed to have a summit in the fall of 1985. Reagan was delighted at the prospect of such a stellar event and would not risk endangering it or its "atmosphere." In our session that day, the critical comment came when a White House aide said simply, "Do we want the Allies and Congress dumping all over the President just as he's about to meet Gorbachev?"

So once again the SALT II decision became an easy one. Once

again was it deferred. The White House put the best face on this dodge by announcing that the President wanted to "go the extra mile." We would retain the interim restraint policy but raise the stakes even higher. The President laid down three tough conditions for our future adherence—no further Soviet cheating, no continued Soviet strategic buildup, and no more Soviet stalling in Geneva. Moreover, the President would bring up compliance directly with Gorbachev, and the Pentagon would report on what military moves were needed to offset Soviet violations. Everything in government needs an acronym to be official, and we were blessed with a particularly good one here—RSVP, the Response to Soviet Violations Paper. Although taking delight in this, we never expected the report to be as much of a dud as the summit chat.

The President did raise the issue with Gorbachev that November in Geneva, but he did so sheepishly. Maybe deep down he figured the Russians cheated by nature, so what good would his harping do? Anyway, Gorbachev fired back that there were no Soviet violations. And it was left at that, as the two pledged to accelerate progress in Geneva—where Soviet negotiators merely resumed oral readings from Tass, *Pravda*, and Gorbachev speeches at the table—and to increase the frequency of Shultz-Shevardnadze meetings, though they were not to meet again for some ten months. So much for summit pledges.

But not for SALT II, which continued to bedevil and bewilder the administration. The public debate never subsided, though the issue required no further decision until the spring of 1986. There then arose what we call in government a "decision-driving event."

The Navy launched a new Trident submarine for sea trials, which, under SALT II's terms, would require us to dismantle two Poseidon submarines. By then the lumbering Pentagon had completed the RSVP study.

Actually we had already discussed draft copies of this report, which turned out to be a real downer. No one could have guessed that it was written under the watchful eye of the toughest hawks in town—Cap Weinberger, Fred Ikle, Richard Perle, and Frank Gaffney—for it was a real puffball.

Admiral Poindexter realized this as well and, much to his credit, wanted to put some bite in it. He tried, but as with so many of his attempts, his efforts went for naught. The Pentagon didn't want to do anything but reinforce its existing budget requests. Each military option we conceived in the Poindexter meetings had, they claimed, already been considered and rejected by military planners.

Truth be known, each of our options had its individual disadvantages—excessive cost, production difficulties, impossibility of deployment, whatever. But most important was that the Pentagon staff did not wish to reopen old budget fights. Deals between the services had already been cut, plans had been laid, and any change in priorities, even under order of the Secretary of Defense or the President, was most unwelcome. The best outcome we could reach was to propose a "compliance supplemental," asking the Congress for new money to respond to Soviet violations. But even this approach raised the same old problems. Would the Congress give "new money" when it was refusing to fund original budget requests? If so, what would the new money go for? If it went for the original programs, Congress would automatically turn us down again. If it went for new programs, we had to explain which ones and why. This wasn't easy since the Joint Chiefs of Staff did not want new programs; they wanted the ones they had originally proposed.

I found the Joint Chiefs implacable in these views while discussing the RSVP report with them in the ultra-secure "tank" in the heart of the Pentagon. We held an incongruous session one day; the Director of the U.S. Arms Control and Disarmament Agency argued for the United States to scrap an arms agreement, and the Joint Chiefs of Staff argued strongly for us to remain in SALT II.

This was quite a reversal of expected roles and quite different from the fears generated by ACDA when it was established in the early 1960s. Then, Congressman Craig Hosmer warned that the agency would attract "nutball people"; former Secretary of Defense Robert Lovett said it was "going to be a natural magnet for those rather uninspiring groups that have slogans like 'Better Red Than Dead' and 'Surrender and Survive' or the give-up groups." Senator Barry Goldwater said the United States was "developing a new mother-love type of agency," one, according to Congressman William Bray, that would be "studying reasons for the Free World to surrender to the Kremlin." Senator Thomas Kuchel said his mail indicated that "thousands of Californians remained firmly wedded to the following fantastic fairy tales: that ACDA can and will disarm the United States . . . that the law establishing the agency constitutes treason, and so forth." And as recently as November of 1983, the Chairman of the House Foreign Relations Committee defended the agency by saying, "Let me state categorically that the President does not have authority to transfer jurisdiction over our armed forces from the Department of Defense to the Arms Control and Disarmament Agency. . . . Let me also state categorically that there is no authority in the act for the Director [of ACDA] to call out the Armed Forces of the United States."

In any case, the lily-livered arms controllers urged the military brass to come up with more mighty options. All we managed to present to the President were options to dry-dock the two subs, put three-warhead missiles (then held in storage) into silos containing single-warhead missiles, and boost research on chemical weapons (how this made it on the list, I never figured out; such research could be done apart from arms control). None of these options had much military bite; none had much military support; none had much military rationale.

Thus this rather thin report went in to the President. More pressing than RSVP—how we were to respond militarily to Soviet violations—was what we would do about dismantling the two Poseidon submarines, as required by SALT's provisions.

Hence, the fate of SALT II could no longer be kicked down the road. Or so I thought, as we gathered in the White House for yet another mini–NSC meeting. The arguments were strong, passions ran high, and in the end we decided to build the bridge halfway across the river.

Actually, that spring of 1986 the President called two sessions on SALT II. The first came at the tail end of our bombing of Tripoli in order to put Libyan President Qaddafi back in the box. Weinberger furnished the meeting's high point when informing the President of the raid's success. Don Regan, never one to let another person's dramatic report go without comment, warned that the Libyans might attack American consultants still living in Libya. Cap quipped that he had long tried to trim the number of consultants in the business.

Back on topic, Poindexter reminded the President that he had originally established the interim restraint policy to create an atmosphere for *mutual* restraint (this surely put the best light on a cobbled-together, shortsighted policy). No such atmosphere had been created. We kept our part of the deal; the Soviets did not keep theirs. They failed to show "equal restraint" from the start and failed to meet the three added presidential conditions (no more strategic buildup, no continued violations, and no more stalling in Geneva) over the previous nine months.

Weinberger was clearly more intent on scrapping the interim restraint policy than on promoting the military options, such as they were. He gave a nod toward the RSVP report by mumbling about keeping submarines around or shoving some Minuteman III missiles into Minuteman II silos, but his body language said, "Let's not."

JCS Chairman William Crowe reiterated the Joint Chiefs' age-old arguments. The first priority was to assure congressional support for the Strategic Modernization Program (SMP).

Shultz was gone somewhere, so Deputy Secretary John Whitehead represented the Department of State. Unfortunately, as happens, the intelligent Whitehead lacked enough time to grasp all the nuances. State wanted to forgo any option that would cause us "to violate" SALT's numerical limits. If the President chose moves that put us over these limits, Whitehead said, we would be the first to break this, the heart and soul of the treaty.

When my turn came, I took his argument on. First, we were not talking about the United States "violating" anything. Under consideration was our interim restraint policy, which we were as free to leave as to adopt in the first place. Moreover, this heart and soul of the treaty, the overall numerical limits, had already been violated by the Soviets. Even the State Department had agreed that the Soviets had violated them.

Losing ground on the facts, Whitehead resorted to principle. He reiterated State's usual argument: regardless of the merits, Congress and the Allies would hit the roof if we left SALT II. This had merit to it.

As is often the case, the State Department and the Joint Chiefs of Staff locked arms. Admiral Crowe nodded conspicuously when Whitehead warned that scrapping the interim restraint policy might prompt Congress to scrap elements of the Strategic Modernization Program.

William Casey turned the focus back on the Soviets. The President just *had* to show them that we meant business; they had better start abiding by treaties or else. Casey made the telling and original point that the military options before the President were so weak because our military planning, unlike theirs, had long been constrained by SALT II. There were no major military steps we wanted to take outside SALT since the military had previously not deemed it possible to take any steps beyond SALT. The long-range program had been tailored to fit into the treaty terms.

I tried to be upbeat among this scrapping crowd and said that the President was to be congratulated as the first to face up to the compliance issue. This put us in a bind, however. To harp upon the problem for five years and end up doing nothing about it was the worst possible outcome. Better not to have raised it in the first place, for at issue here was nothing less than the President's credibility, I contended, credibility vital in realms beyond arms control. There could no longer be any doubt that the Soviets undercut the "no undercut" policy of 1981 and met none of the three conditions he laid down in 1985. The President had gone the extra mile in what was becoming a marathon. Now was the time, not to change policies, but to implement our original policy; we would no longer abide by SALT since they showed no equal restraint.

The President cringed visibly when I pointed out how SALT II was becoming "the Reagan treaty" more than "the Carter treaty" since by then he had lived under its terms longer than Carter. As to Whitehead's comments about public reaction, a subject that always interested Reagan, I figured the American people would not want us to abide by a lousy agreement that the Senate did not and would not ratify and which the Soviets had violated.

The President took all this in. He then mentioned that he had heard, from whom I never learned, that the two Poseidon submarines in question (the ones that had to be dismantled for us to stay within the SALT limits) had little life left in them anyway. Reagan said he wanted to move the public focus off SALT II (why, then, not just cut the cord? I wondered) and move along to a new and better treaty. If we ended up scrapping the interim restraint policy, he mused in a rather detached manner, it might be better *not* to accompany it with defense increases. The people would thereby realize that we were leaving SALT because of Soviet violations and not because we wanted to begin a big buildup.

Whitehead felt the tide flowing out and so he fired all his ammunition. Despite the violations, SALT still provided restraint; without it would come an "unconstrained environment" (Mac Bundy's argument). The Soviets had not broken all the SALT limits (the Al Capone argument). They could escalate the arms race absent SALT (Warnke's fear). None of the violations changed the military balance; and so on.

Reagan came alive, as he frequently did, at the mention of the arms race. He told Whitehead that the Soviets had greater reason to avoid an arms race than we did because of their sorrowful economy. He had made this very point to Gorbachev. If they ever chose to race with us, we would outrun them; Gorbachev got the message. (No one asked the President how much faster the Soviets could race with strategic programs than they had been, or if he could imagine Congress funding a military race on our part, in order to leave the Soviets in the dust.)

A few more jabs back and forth, and the meeting closed. As was his wont, the President ended it with a story or a joke that left everyone feeling good, however confused in thought.

Before our second NSC meeting a month later, reams of papers were written, loads of staff meetings were held, and scores of "talking points" were drafted and negotiated for "the principals" to go at it again. As the stakes were raised, more people got in the act. After reading about the first NSC meeting in the press, fifty-two Senators wrote the President to advocate that he stay with SALT. Thirty-four Senators wrote asking him to end interim restraint. As Poindexter later pointed out correctly, the first group consisted mostly of Senators who often opposed the administration on contentious defense matters, while the latter consisted of our stalwart champions.

The Allies read about our sessions, too. At least inspired if not prompted by the State Department, they kept their cards and letters coming. The day before our second session—remarkable, the timing—in came a letter from Prime Minister Thatcher telling "Dear Ron" that it would constitute an "important act of statesmanship" for him to stay with SALT.

Around the table we gathered once more to play our parts, but this time with some strange twists and turns. Weinberger reiterated that SALT II restrained us and not them, though this time he did not even feign support for any military options. Shultz had returned from abroad, which did not help the atmosphere in the Situation Room, as he and Weinberger were then at the nadir of their long, entangled relationship. They sparred back and forth in a most contentious way—I'll spare the gory details—as the President watched with serenity and the rest of us with incredulity.

Moving on to substantive arguments, Shultz said he deemed it unwise to break SALT II's numerical limits. "There is a certain magic to the numerical ceilings," he stated, reinforcing his point by observing that the Soviets had dismantled more launchers under SALT II than had we. Shultz agreed with the Joint Chiefs: the key thing was to get our Strategic Modernization Program funded. Anything that furthered that goal was good; anything that harmed it, like leaving SALT, was bad.

Crowe naturally echoed Shultz's restatement of Crowe's position. He urged that we do nothing to damage budget prospects on Capitol Hill. This he then fleshed out. Increasingly over the years, the Joint Chiefs have steadily moved from focusing singularly on military factors to advising the President on congressional relations. Once in the Joint Chiefs' tank, I said flat out that the President could gain such advice from his own congressional relations staff, political advisors, Capitol Hill leaders, from an army of Washington insiders, and the like. But he could obtain a hard military assessment on an issue from only one source, the Joint Chiefs of Staff. Thus they should stick to their comparative advantage rather than venture in an already overcrowded area in which—judging by the fate of military budgets over the years—they were not terribly proficient.

But here Crowe again fretted about the congressional reaction. We just had to get the SMP funded, he said; it already took into account Soviet violations (how remained a mystery to me).

Bill Casey was, as ever, less cautious. Soviet violations meant we should take whatever actions we wanted, regardless of the damned SALT constraints. We should take forceful action to show them that we could respond with vigor.

Casey referred to a chart that the CIA and ACDA had worked up showing that in the coming years we'd have to dismantle more warheads under SALT than would the Soviets. He recommended to Reagan, with whom he had a Dutch uncle relationship, that we immediately announce an end to the interim restraint policy. We could actually exceed the SALT II limits, however, later that year when putting cruise missiles on more strategic bombers. This approach would put the Soviets, Congress, and Allies on notice.

Secretary Shultz then objected to the CIA-ACDA chart since some of the systems scheduled for dismantlement "under SALT II" were old systems that would be dismantled anyway. I said the

Secretary of State was right. But that argument also refuted Shultz's previous point that under SALT II the Soviets had dismantled a lot of missiles. These too were old and may well have been dismantled anyway. This back-and-forth, on substance for a change, showed how tricky it is to use hard facts and figures to decide such issues. Statistics can prove most anything.

The President was still groping for a way to finesse SALT but was not getting much help from us. Ed Meese suggested, as before, that we put SALT II behind us: the treaty was bad, and we should look forward, not back.

Still, no one was helping the President find a way out. Rather, all of us wanted to squabble. Shultz objected to my saying that the State Department did not favor doing anything about Soviet violations; it strongly supported the SMP. I responded that *everyone* supported the SMP. We supported it before we knew of Soviet violations and afterward. The question at hand was whether to do anything different because of their violations.

Paul Nitze, who seldom spoke in such sessions, also went after me for misrepresenting State's position. The department did not wish to continue to abide by SALT II—Shultz looked puzzled when Nitze said this—but merely wanted a sound response. Supporting the SMP was it. That was all we needed, all we could afford to do, since it would cost us loads of money to violate the numerical limits. (The cause of the meeting, whether or not to dismantle the Poseidon submarines, had long been forgotten by then. Not dismantling them, which would have put us above the numerical limits, might easily have cost less than dismantling them.) Nitze saw no point in alienating the Allies and Congress over a new approach that furnished no concrete benefit.

Weinberger and Nitze then somehow went at it over the merits of the ABM Treaty. They squabbled about whether the President did or did not want to scrap that treaty, too. The only person who could answer this, the President, listened to all the bickering and said nothing. There he sat with a look of resignation, probably still trying to find a way through the SALT maze, not worrying for the moment about the ABM maze.

He interrupted this latest, useless spat by returning to the subject at hand. The American people did not want a big military buildup, he felt, but they did support more modern systems. Maybe we should keep the overall numbers down but modernize within those limits. Reagan said he liked the idea of dry-docking the submarines—lifting them out of the water but retaining them on hand—which would have caused us to exceed the SALT II limits without any military benefit whatsoever. Missile-carrying vehicles without missiles, submarines docked on land, are not of much strategic utility. Here was a "bridge halfway across the river" option if there ever was one.

So what to do? We advisors were more intent on conducting our intrafraternal fights. The President was more concerned about public reaction. Poindexter and Don Regan were concerned with keeping the President on schedule. Thus did we end the meeting. Instead of a story this time, the President broke the good news that Helen Caldicott was retiring from disarmament activities after fifteen years of "service." This, I quipped, was worth at least one Poseidon submarine. Maybe two.

As is often the case, we left the White House without a clue of what the President would decide. I felt guilty about our comportment and the dubious information many of us had imparted to him.

Judgments differed, as they always do on arms control, but here facts differed, too. What was dismantled during SALT II differed from what was dismantled *because* of SALT II. And we did not know the facts about the two submarines in question. The President came to believe they would have been retired anyway. The Joint Chiefs of Staff were indifferent over their fate. Navy personnel directly responsible for these two submarines told me, in my office before the second NSC meeting, that the boats had another eight to ten years' service left in them (which differed markedly from what the President had apparently been told).

Who was right? The President, who presumably had access to the best information in the world? The Joint Chiefs, who have responsibility to give the President accurate information on military matters? Or the staff operators in the Navy, who should know about their own equipment?

I tried but couldn't sort it out. I could never get to the facts and was bothered that such a big decision was based on sand.

The President was thus caught in a bind. Everyone acknowledged that there was little we could do militarily to respond to Soviet violations. Yet we had to do something, if only because we had made such a fuss about their cheating and everyone else was making such a fuss over our policy toward SALT.

The key questions remained the same. How much sense did it

make for Reagan to continue adhering to a "fatally flawed" treaty the Senate had never ratified and that the Soviets were clearly violating, after it would have expired anyway? Then again, how much sense did it make to infuriate some in Congress and most of our Allies for no clear military benefit?

While the President cogitated, others pressured. The notion promulgated in seventh-grade civics classes—that his advisors offer the President their counsel and leave him to decide—is a far cry from how Washington really works. This tells half the story; we do offer our best advice, but then we muster forces to (using a gentle euphemism) help him decide. In short, we pressure our boss.

At our urging, a group of anti-SALT Senators visited the Oval Office. They mostly reiterated the same arguments Reagan had heard from us. But Senator Dan Quayle added a new and, as it turned out, effective twist. He said that for the President to keep SALT longer would establish "the Reagan precedent." Any future president—a liberal president, as he hauntingly put it—could hereafter conclude any agreement with the Soviets and have us comply without following the constitutional procedure of gaining the Senate's advice and consent.

When Quayle said this, Reagan sat up and ground his teeth, a telltale sign of aggravation. Shultz glowered. Quayle's was to prove the most effective argument; it might well have given us the winning margin. And, as Henry Kissinger likes to say, it had the added advantage of being true. After all, SALT I was held in force after its expiration date, also without congressional assent. The Senate's constitutional powers were steadily being eroded.

Some strangely advocated that they be eroded more. During a conference I attended at the Carter Center in Atlanta, Jimmy Carter recommended that future arms control agreements *not* go through the Senate for ratification. He recounted the pain of gaining the requisite two-thirds Senate majority for the Panama Canal Treaty (and initially for SALT II). Carter advocated treaty adoption either by a majority in each chamber of Congress or by presidential fiat "as President Reagan has been doing with our treaty."

Perhaps because of his legendary passivity, Gerald Ford agreed with his fellow former president, who sat beside him on the dais. To this day I regret not having objected then. I guess I was too stunned or too weary after having objected to a host of other foolish ideas throughout the day. The counter-argument is obvious, best stated by John McCloy before the Senate Foreign Relations Committee, who told how the Founding Fathers "intended that the making of treaties (which were not too popular) should be a difficult process." International agreements were considered important in themselves and became the "supreme law of the land," overriding domestic legislation. Thus the Constitution writers lifted the two-thirds requirement from the Articles of Confederation, where treaty ratification was subject to nine of the thirteen states, and put it into the Constitution, giving the Senate this power.

Meanwhile the SALT champions were mustering their forces, too. The State Department fought with an intensity rarely displayed in its dealings with the Soviets or others around the world. (State's "diplomatic entrance" features a flower garden filled with pansies and bleeding hearts.) In this case, the department was fierce. Cables of alarm streamed into the White House from our Allies. The same governments that mustered no enthusiasm for SALT II when it was signed showed an intense adoration of it after it had been violated and had expired.

Even the State Department's intelligence bureau, normally quite responsible, entered the policy fray with dire predictions. Were we to abandon SALT II, it reported right on the eve of a White House session, Soviet leaders would certainly write off any chances of doing serious business with this president. They would end any prospect of a 1986 summit, maybe scrap the arms talks, and be forced to take military steps such as adding many more warheads.

The bureau wrote no evaluation on the possible effects of *not* altering our policy, especially after the President had laid down three conditions that were clearly not met. Might the Kremlin not interpret his lack of follow-through as a sign of presidential weakness? That the President's word meant little? That their violations meant little? Might Ronald Reagan's continued adherence mean that the United States was simply incapable of *ever* leaving an arms accord?

It is rare to have such an intelligence estimate proven untrue so quickly and so unmistakably. But that's what happened here. Not two days after the President announced an end to the interim restraint regime, the Soviet team in Geneva presented a new, more serious arms proposal. Surely their initiative was not made *because* we abandoned SALT II; but then again, it was not pulled back after the President's announcement, either. It proved, to me anyway, that they cared as little about SALT II as some of us had long suspected.

After the second Situation Room meeting, Paul Nitze was dispatched to "consult" with the Allies. He presented the President's "tentative decision" to scrap the two Poseidon boats but to end the interim restraint policy forthwith and to exceed the SALT limits by the year's end (when we would place air-launched cruise missiles on more bombers), basically Bill Casey's option. European leaders told Ambassador Nitze that they welcomed the first part and objected to the last two, an expected reaction.

What was unexpected—by me, at least—was the absence of any substantive reason for their stance. Prime Minister Thatcher made a stab at substance when she spoke of the need to respect international law. This was but a stab since our interim restraint policy was not part of international law; it was solely a presidential policy. Other Allied leaders never even made a stab. They feared an adverse public reaction in their countries.

Sure, their publics were upset that we were leaving SALT II, for the people had not been told by their leaders about Soviet violations. At that time the United States Information Agency's polling data showed that an overwhelming majority of the French public would not want the United States to abide by an arms treaty the Soviets were violating; likewise but less so for the British. Interestingly, only the Germans overwhelmingly wanted the United States to adhere regardless of Soviet adherence. Most important, these polls revealed that only the slimmest percentage of Europeans knew anything at all of Soviet violations.

Moreover, the question struck me: Why should the President pay much attention to advice from the Allies on matters like this, and at times like this? SALT was an issue between Moscow and Washington; the Europeans were not party to it, nor did they have much to say about the strategic forces of either side.

And as I told Shultz—much to the horror of some State Department officials listening to my argument—the Allies had not been particularly supportive of matters then important to us. All but Britain had refused our planes overflight rights on their way to bomb Tripoli, and they criticized the attack afterward. All had been opposing our stance on Nicaragua for years, had passionately opposed our military action in Grenada, and were uncomfortable with our approach on the Israeli-Arab dispute. We did not need to pay the Allies in arms control policy, I submitted, for the honor of protecting them and hearing their criticisms when we acted in our own security interests or in the larger interests of civilized peoples. So much for Allied reaction to SALT II. At least this was my view.

Congress was a different matter. We had to heed our own legislative body. But Congress is a many-headed beast. Reagan's natural friends and supporters on Capitol Hill were petitioning him to end the treaty. The President's natural adversaries, who opposed many of his defense moves, were urging him to stay with it. Why not reward friends, not enemies? This line apparently made an impact upon Reagan. (Left unspoken was the more telling argument that the swing Congressmen and Senators, the ones needed to gain approval for controversial defense programs, generally supported staying in SALT II.)

Fortunately, the third button normally pressed on issues like this—that the reaction in Moscow would be adverse—was not persuasive then. U.S.-Soviet relations had turned chilly after the first summit. Moscow stood by Qaddafi after our attack and accordingly canceled a springtime Shultz-Shevardnadze session. Leaving SALT II would serve them right, our side argued, since they had shown that they cared more about backing a renegade regime sponsoring state-supported terrorism than about making progress on arms control. So the winning argument in 1985, that getting out of SALT II would ruin the superpower atmosphere, could not be used in the spring of 1986. There was not much of an atmosphere then to ruin.

Our campaign seemed to be gaining ground, but not before the situation took some tricky bounces.

The President would not announce his "final" SALT decision, the White House said following the Nitze consultations, until after the upcoming economic summit in Tokyo. Upon hearing this news, I feared all was lost. The Allies knew the President's tentative decision and didn't like it. Some in the State Department would surely inform the Allies that only they could dissuade him. And Reagan, who had a hard time disappointing anyone face to face, would be an easy mark for a gang-up in Tokyo.

Yet that was not to be, for there was no gang-up in Tokyo. As in the Sherlock Holmes story "Silver Blaze"—where Holmes solves the case by noting that the dog did *not* bark in the night—here it was key that no Allied leader barked in Tokyo. A few dutifully raised this issue with Reagan among a list of their concerns, and left it at that. Most did not even go that far; they simply thanked him for the consultations.

To be fair, though, the Allies were sandbagged. They figured that the pro-SALT II forces had won this round, as they had the previous rounds. Scrapping the two submarines kept us within the SALT II constraint, for the moment, at least. Ambassador Nitze told them that we were ending the interim restraint policy immediately and would exceed the limits by the year's end, but these were words and not deeds. So SALT seemed safe for the moment.

In retrospect, it seems evident that Reagan dodged left and moved right, but neither they nor we could know this then. And none of us could tell—as with so many actions by that amazing man Ronald Reagan—whether any of this was in the least bit deliberate.

Nonetheless the President left Tokyo believing the Allies were indifferent to the fate of SALT II. They did not care much about it, at least nowhere near as much as his fretful, fussing State Department had assured him they would.

Reagan also left Tokyo once again aggravated with Moscow. On the eve of that Western economic summit came the Chernobyl nuclear accident, which the Soviets, even under Gorbachev, handled in their usual secretive, insensitive, and maddening manner. Commentary, including an editorial in *The Washington Post*, made the analogy between Soviet secretiveness in cases like this and in arms control. This line of thought momentarily took the steam out of arms control.

When the final, final moment of final, final decision came, that too (as Claudius would say) fell right. It came when the President returned on the eve of the long Memorial Day weekend. Congress was out of session, so SALT II's most ardent supporters were not around for floor tirades and television appearances. By the time they would return to Washington and try to make a fuss, most found that their constituents couldn't care less.

But the big question remained: Would the President do it? Would he bite the bullet, which he had shied away from doing nearly each springtime of his presidency? None of us knew for sure, though we felt—as I then told Senators Quayle, Wallop,

Wilson, and the Democrat Hollings as we approached that final moment—that we had set everything in motion to make it come out right. We left nothing to chance, and events were breaking right.

At last, the President decided he would do it. What finally did the trick? Who knows?

To me there was one big intangible—intangibles are always underestimated in decision-making—that did it. President Reagan had simply grown tired of SALT II. He was just fed up with it all.

Reagan had discussed SALT's flaws during his entire presidential campaign, presided over wrangles about it during his entire administration. Nearly every Senator had written him about it, and many had come to see him on it. He was given an ungodly number of cables about it over the years. He had to listen to his advisors fight about it regularly. He had been buttonholed about it incessantly. He had to read reams of news articles and scores of op-ed pieces about it. He had gone through piles of "Dear Ron" letters from the Allies pleading about it. And, as some of us warned him, he would face the prospect of this springtime exercise twice yearly from then on out if he did not cut the cord now. Some new weapons system that might incrementally break the SALT limits would come along each six months or so. He could not have cherished that prospect.

Hence the ultimate factor in this decision, as in so many made by Reagan, resided in the gut. If not him, then who? If not now, when?

He could not have wished for better timing—far from the November elections or any high-level meetings with the Russians— or better conditions to do something he had hankered to do for ages. And, best of all, he'd be finished with SALT! Just as Macbeth opens one of the final scenes with the cry, "Bring me no more reports; let them all fly!" so the President closed SALT with the plea, "Bring me no more SALT decisions; let them all fly!"

PLAYING IT OUT

The decision was duly announced that Memorial Day weekend. Unfortunately, the President had again failed clearly to cut the cord. Utter confusion reigned, perhaps unmatched in the annals of such a controversial presidential decision, over just what he *had* decided.

Quick out of the box, as always, were key congressional players. But they scrambled about, unsure what it all meant. In the liberal camp, Senators Kennedy, Pell, and Gore initially praised the President's decision; ordering the submarines dismantled showed he was staying within the SALT limits. Meanwhile their ideological teammate, former ACDA Director Paul Warnke, condemned the decision just as vigorously; the President's announcement to end interim restraint now and his intention to exceed the treaty limits later killed SALT II. On the conservative side, Senators McClure, Wallop, Quayle, and Wilson welcomed the decision warmly, for the same reasons Warnke opposed it harshly. Yet the more moderate Majority Leader Robert Dole blasted it harshly, for the same reasons Kennedy, Pell, *et al* praised it graciously.

This congressional reaction was not terribly damaging—a Reagan arms control decision lauded by Ted Kennedy and Claiborne Pell could not seem too reactionary—but it was terribly confusing.

The press did not know what to make of it, either. Peter Jennings opened his ABC broadcast that evening (May 27, 1986) by intoning, "The President decided to continue to abide by a major arms control treaty with the Soviet Union" and ended by saying, "The message from the White House is very clear" (when it was anything but): "the President will abide by the treaty for now, but he is not in love with it."

The newspapers, with less of an excuse for error, having had more time to ask around and more inclination to read the White House release, fared no better than ABC News. Some papers even changed their big message between editions of the same day's newspaper. The first edition of *The New York Times* on May 28 headlined, REAGAN DECLARES U.S. IS DISMANTLING TWO NUCLEAR SUBS with the subtitle "Move Continues to Keep U.S. in Step with the Provisions of 1979 Arms Accord." By the second edition, the subtitle told how the decision meant the United States would be getting out of SALT. On the very next day, in the same newspaper by the same author, Michael Gordon, the main story had become REAGAN AND ARMS TREATY: A SHARP SHIFT IN POLICY, which the previous day's headlines had not indicated.

The foreign press was also bewildered. The London *Times* headlined U.S. SCRAPS SUBS FOR SALT TREATY, while the *Manchester Guardian* went with REAGAN TO ABANDON SALT TREATIES. The *Financial Times* stood midfield between them with REAGAN

THREATENS TO IGNORE SALT UNLESS SOVIET "VIOLATIONS" END. Most accurate of any foreign press was none other than Tass, which honestly admitted its confusion and headlined correctly WHITE HOUSE DECISION: A STEP FORCED UPON IT.

Editorial opinion, on the other hand, was not in the least confused: it was mostly hostile. *The New York Times* thundered forth the following Sunday, when circulation nearly doubles its daily paper, with a lead editorial and three of its four op-ed pieces clearly condemning the President's decision (the fourth was merely a mood piece about Memorial Day).

Each op-ed piece contained factual errors—I counted twenty-three in all on the page—and a number of harebrained opinions. For example, the *Times'* own editorial—which previously pontificated piously about the sanctity of constitutional processes when decrying Reagan policies on civil liberties and such issues —found only one positive element on Reagan's handling of SALT II; he had been "right to adhere to the treaty without asking Congress to ratify" it, the *Times* said with utter disregard of constitutional requirements.

Senator Albert Gore was given the main play on the *Times* op-ed page that day. He praised Moscow for having "already destroyed more than 1,000 missiles in order to comply with SALT restrictions," a strange figure for an American to use since Soviet spokesmen had previously claimed in public to have dismantled only 540 systems under SALT. Various Americans kept raising that number as time passed; by Thursday, during a debate with me, Paul Warnke lifted it to 1,200; by the following Sunday, when Robert McNamara was given nearly half the *Times'* op-ed page for another savage attack on the President's SALT decision, it was upped to 1,366. None of the American critics mentioned that these missiles may have been so old and of marginal utility to have been dismantled anyway. Meanwhile the stolid Soviets stuck to their 540 figure (during their June 5 press conference).

On that initial Sunday *Times* op-ed mugging, Flora Lewis took first prize for the most bizarre argument, namely that Reagan could not make a decision—"This is another characteristic administration waffle on arms control, putting off real decision [sic]"—in a column criticizing the decision on a page filled with tirades against the decision. James Reston contemplated the American belly button in this confounding way: "Mr. Reagan . . . reassured the hawks but infuriated the doves" by claiming that the treaty was fatally flawed (ignoring that Reagan had done so in this decision as well), "but once he was in the White House, Mr. Reagan said he'd abide by the treaty anyway if the Russians behaved. This infuriated the hawks and immobilized the doves." Not once did Reston so much as mention Soviet violations, though that was the main reason of the decision.

The New York Times was not alone in its harsh treatment. The *Los Angeles Times*, which had opposed SALT II when it was signed, incongruously championed it after it was violated and expired; IT'S ABSURD was the headline of its lead editorial, the first of many opposing the President's stance.

Congress needed no such op-ed prompting to jump further into the act. Bills and resolutions began flying in both the Senate and the House. By then, even Senator Edward Kennedy caught the drift of the President's decision. Thus on June 2, he took to the floor for some stellar hysterics, made all the more ludicrous in retrospect:

> Six years into the Reagan administration, the prospects for nuclear arms control have never seemed bleaker. No issue has higher implications for the future of our country or our planet, and yet no issue has lower priority on the administration's agenda. The rabid right is spoiling for a new escalation of the arms race.

His thundering address ended in undiluted hyperbole:

> The Chernobyl disaster is the handwriting on the wall, a sign of what lies ahead if we proceed on the present course. There is still time for Mr. Reagan to play his greatest role as President—the role of peacemaker. It will be sad—and a threat to the peace as well— if he chooses to exit from the White House in the role of Rambo.

A bill was drawn up in the House by Foreign Affairs Chairman Dante Fascell. It originally urged the President to abide by SALT's "numerical limits" as long as the Soviets did likewise. But on the eve of the committee markup, some sharp staffer spotted a problem: the Soviets were already violating these limits. So Fascell altered the language to force us to stay within those parts of the treaty the Soviets chose not to breach. This bill had six substantive provisions, each one containing at least one substantive error, and made no mention of Soviet violations, even though Fascell and other Democrats readily admitted the Soviets were cheating.

And, as happens, administration critics outflanked the Russians. Not only did they continue claiming that Moscow had dismantled twice the number of strategic systems the Soviets themselves claimed, they also asserted that Reagan's decision ruined the prospect for new arms agreements. Robert McNamara's op-ed piece, "15 Years of Arms Control Demolished," ran several days *after* Soviet negotiators presented some new and important moves in Geneva. Moreover, the critics lamented our shattering the "framework" for an arms agreement *after* the Soviets had themselves abandoned the SALT framework; rather than adopt the SALT focus on the overall number of strategic systems and missiles, they bought our START framework, which focused on warheads and throw weight.

Were there any accountability in this field, the McNamaras, Gores, and others would be discredited for being so clearly wrong. But, alas, there is none.

During all this fervor, some of us tried to set things straight—I called Peter Jennings, among others, to say that he had gotten the story bass-ackward—though this did no noticeable good.

So we mustered our forces for the final battle that fall of 1986, when the United States would actually exceed SALT limits by deploying the 131st heavy bomber with air-launched cruise missiles aboard. This normally mundane military move would, we knew, take on momentous political import. Those on the other side knew this as well. Paul Nitze told a group of reporters soon after the May 27 decision that the Navy wanted to cut up another submarine (which meant that the cruise-missile deployment would not cause us to exceed the SALT limits). This was neither sanctioned nor correct; certainly it was unhelpful to an administration castigated for not getting its arms control act together.

At last the big moment arrived. But, in the wondrous world of government, it was no longer a big moment at all. The Iran-contra affair had erupted like a tornado, sweeping aside everything in Washington that fall.

Strange how these things happen. The final Situation Room meeting on SALT II fell on November 25, 1986, the very day President Reagan had announced that funds from the arms sale to Iran had been diverted to the contras. After that bombshell, Attorney General Ed Meese faced a wild press in his most notable press conference.

Within two hours the President ambled down to that now famous White House basement to meet with us again over SALT. Actually, the meeting's most dramatic moment occurred before it began. I arrived a few minutes early, in time to see one of the nice NSC secretaries whisk away the nameplate of John Poindexter at the foot of the table facing the President and replace it with the hastily written nameplate of his deputy, Alton Keel. Admiral Poindexter, she told me with the nonchalance of Ophelia's grave diggers, had departed a few hours before.

I could not believe what I was seeing as President Reagan sauntered in the room seemingly without a care in the world. After casually asking Meese, "Ed, did everything go okay?" he opened the meeting, as always, with a funny story. Meese was also nonchalant; he nodded to Shultz, who smiled back. Could he not have heard that Meese more than hinted to the world that Shultz should either support the President or leave the administration?

Weinberger, as always, held two pencils in his hand, a feat of dexterity seldom seen anywhere let alone in the upper reaches of government, and buried his head in his heavy black notebook, which must have contained every fact and figure ever known about SALT II. Shultz looked exhausted and acted most accommodating, obviously feeling himself vulnerable at that moment. Only Don Regan appeared different. Before and during the meeting, he buried his head in transcripts of television broadcasts from the news the night before and that day's flash announcements. His fate, which was inexorably if somewhat unfairly tied to the Iran-contra affair, interested him more than the fate of SALT II.

Cap kept the mood cheery by telling the President that the cruise missile–equipped bomber—the one that would have us exceed the SALT limits, once it flew—had already been painted three times while awaiting the President's final okay. The plane stood outside the hangar, set to take off anytime the commander-in-chief gave the nod.

Shultz, not wanting to take on another of the President's close friends, said that he firmly agreed with Cap. The plane should fly. We should stick by the May 27 decision, forget the SALT constraints, and deploy the plane forthwith. The Allies, he informed us dead-panned, had become more concerned about Reykjavik than about SALT II since last spring.

Even after his top advisors spoke with one voice at long last, the President strangely got cold feet. How to explain this is beyond me, but he told us that making this move now might hurt some of "our friends over there," evidently in Europe who were facing elections soon. (Some were *always* facing elections, truth be told.) Couldn't we show that we were keeping our weapons more in line with SALT than the Soviets? This he posed, even after his aides reminded him that we had left SALT II last May.

The meeting proceeded for another hour—I made many of the same points as before—but again we were role playing. Life had gone out of the issue. Don Regan, looking up from his television transcripts for the first time, announced forcefully that a decision paper had to be prepared by noon the next day, as they would then be heading off to California for Thanksgiving.

The President continued in his dandy mood. He regaled us with tales of the legendary Satchel Paige, who according to the ex-sportscaster could wine and dine and do other things all night long and then go out the next day to pitch both games in a double-header.

The last word was Acting NSC Advisor Keel's: "On yet another issue, Mr. President, your security advisors agree fully." After all the shouting, all the hysteria, all the hoopla, all the confusion, SALT II died with a whimper. Everyone was shouting about something else by then.

CHAPTER 7

TOWARD A SAFER WORLD

THE SOLE SUMMIT I missed during the Reagan years was the one I most wished to see. Not that it would have been the most fun to be a part of; that honor goes to Reykjavik, which was the least desirable kind for the United States to have. Summits should not be free-wheeling, à la Reykjavik; but when they are, they become more fun for the participants.

However, the Moscow summit was best as it highlighted America's main concern—human rights—and may have helped most where today's changes are greatest, within the Soviet Union. What's happening in Moscow, once a numbingly boring topic, has now become riveting. The changes there are of such scope and happening at such a pace as to constitute a "great awakening," to use Jonathan Edwards's phrase, and accordingly to demand fundamental policy reformulations on our part.

This comes as awkward, if not unsettling, to a conservative. Indeed, skepticism of Soviet motives and castigation of Soviet moves have been among the hallmarks of the conservative movement since the early 1940s. Now that mooring is no longer so fixed.

The astounding events in Moscow—who could have believed that Soviet groups would be formed to honor not Stalin, but the victims of Stalin? that the brutality of the communist system would be traced back to Lenin and then farther back to Marx?— fit nicely with the adjustments needed in U.S. defense posture, diplomacy, and arms control. Indeed, changes there compel us to make adjustments here in order to usher in a safer world.

Those changes there first hit home to many Americans when Ronald Reagan premiered at Red Square, where we now go before peering into that future and better world.

. . .

The " '88 springtime in Moscow summit" was another amazing performance by that amazing man, Ronald Reagan. It was Hollywood on Red Square, with the leading role played by the citizen-politician who built a career on anticommunism; the man who during his first presidential press conference said outright the Soviets reserved the right to lie, cheat, and steal for their cause; the man who denounced the USSR as the "evil empire" and "focus of evil in the modern world."

Yet there he was, the one to rack up the all-time record for the most meetings (five) with a Soviet leader of any U.S. president. And there he was, giving a nice cuddly hug to the head Bear himself, the Soviet General Secretary Mikhail Gorbachev, right at the wall of the Kremlin.

Who could have imagined it? Only those who knew Ronald Reagan as a man who, though of too little learning or intellectual curiosity, was fully capable of adjusting—a man who ultimately puts direct personal relationships above abstract ideology.

Thus did he make a major contribution to improved U.S.-Soviet relations and to American security. In his own haphazard manner, seeming like human tumbleweed, Reagan pointed the way to a safer world. It is a progression that might have developed anyway—given the economic, political, military, and technological trends of the times—but breaking the ice began on Reagan's watch.

The reversals in this "summit of reversals" boggle the mind, beginning with a dramatic turnabout on human rights. After total silence on it at Reykjavik, tiptoeing around it in Geneva, and skipping over it in Washington, President Reagan roared about human rights where it was most incendiary to do so, right there in Moscow.

His previous "quiet diplomacy," which often slid into "no diplomacy," turned into "megaphone diplomacy." It was long overdue. Standing under the Soviet flag, in front of a mural of the glorious Russian revolution, and beneath a mammoth marble bust of a scowling Lenin, Reagan told Moscow State University students that the key to progress is "freedom of thought, freedom of information, freedom of communication." He praised glasnost but said straight that it had much farther to go.

Lenin—who once said, "As soon as we are strong enough to defeat capitalism as a whole, we shall take it by the scruff of the neck"—scowled as Reagan took totalitarianism by the scruff of the neck. The President told those Moscow students that they lived "in one of the most exciting, hopeful times in Soviet history. It is a time when the first breath of freedom stirs the air . . . when the accumulated energies of a long silence yearn to break free." Yet liberty, he warned, must be institutionalized to be assured. *Glasnost* would obviate the need for *glasnost* when the State no longer had power to open or close the spigots of freedom.

Gorbachev, too, was amazing that late May and early June in 1988. Russian reversals were as mind-boggling as Reagan's. Could one have imagined the booted-out "mayor" of Moscow and fervent reform-pusher Boris Yeltsin telling Dan Rather live, on the air, that Soviet second-in-command Yegor Ligachev should be expelled from the Politburo? Could one imagine Gorbachev responding, also on the air, by denouncing his longtime close pal Yeltsin and defending his reputed rival Ligachev?

Talk about an administration not getting its act together! Don Regan's dealings with Nancy and Shultz's skirmishes with Weinberger paled in comparison.

Sure, Reagan had his off moments. Excusing seventy years of Soviet repression as bureaucratic snafu was a doozy. And he should have pushed harder for greater freedom in Poland and less Soviet military aid to Nicaragua. Then again, Gorbachev made mistakes. His whining about the lack of progress on arms control— "We have missed a chance to take an important step forward" —seemed as silly as his call to "bang our fists" for such progress.

No wonder Gorbachev was frustrated. Reykjavik highlighted his main concern—arms control, particularly SDI; the Washington summit swirled around Gorbachev, the phenomenon; while the Moscow summit was all Reagan and emphasized our main concern, human rights.

Actually all four aspects of U.S.-Soviet relations—human rights, arms control, regional issues, and bilateral issues—are spun from the same cloth. How Soviet rulers treat their own people affects how they treat other people. President John F. Kennedy once said, "A nation that is afraid to let its people judge the truth and falsehood in an open market is a nation that is afraid of its own people." And a nation afraid of its own people must be even more afraid of foreign peoples. Less repression at home leads to less aggression abroad.

Human rights directly affects arms control. Greater *glasnost* should lead to less Soviet military spending. Given a choice, people consistently prefer butter over guns, especially in a country like the Soviet Union, which is lacking in both butter and the kind of a threatening neighbor to warrant having many guns. Greater openness in society leads to greater openness on military expenditures and military exercises. It leads to better treaty compliance, since a government that keeps faith with its own people is more inclined to keep faith with foreign powers. Besides, having violations discussed internally can be embarrassing.

Change in the Soviet Union works entirely in our favor. *Perestroika* and *glasnost* are the best things the West has had going for it in ages. These changes can, over time and if spun out, make the Soviet Union less a dagger at our throat than a thorn in our side.

Despite the unruly impression of Gorbachev's rule then, he too triumphed during that Moscow summit. Westerners who constantly nudge us to "do something" to "help Gorbachev" should realize that we already *are* doing so—not by an economic bailout but by a political boost. Gorbachev's dazzling worldwide image, at least partially due to the kindliness Western leaders show him, gives him an enormous advantage over any conceivable successor.

More specifically, Reagan's presence in Red Square was of huge benefit to the Soviets as it set the outer limits on the right of American policy toward the USSR. Having Reagan pay his tributes there delegitimized commie-bashing, perhaps forever. No one can legitimately "run against the Reds" again, as Reagan did in 1972, 1976, and 1980. Those who tried in 1988—Jack Kemp, Pat Robertson, and Al Haig—fell flat on their faces. And no one can enter the Oval Office, as Reagan did in 1981, with fists clenched and dukes up toward Moscow. After the 1988 summit, U.S.-Soviet relations had to fade as a contentious political issue here; indeed, it was scarcely mentioned in that year's presidential campaign, though it had dominated nearly all previous campaigns for forty years.

Moreover, Gorbachev's taming of Ronald Reagan legitimized arms control. No one could run against the process per se after the last winning candidate to do so wholeheartedly embraced it once in power. Indeed, Reagan left office considering the INF agreement among his greatest achievements, touting the prospects of more arms accords and giving the kiss of life to the very process he had once deplored.

This transformation unsettled many conservatives, who unkindly thought that Reagan's stance toward the Soviet Union was like the month of March: in like a lion, out like a lamb. They continue to fear that the arms control process, and especially its product, lulls the nation and thereby undercuts popular support for defense.

This, the right's most tenacious assault on arms control, appeared early on. In May of 1953 Secretary of State John Foster Dulles warned that the Soviets might make "concessions merely in order to lure others into a false sense of security." The Congress and Allies then "might feel that the danger was over and therefore did not need to continue to spend large sums for defense."

Herein lies another arms control myth, as devoid of proof as the liberals' claim that arms control saves money. It is hard to imagine the country being lulled when conservatives keep sounding alarm bells about the perils of being lulled. And it hasn't happened. No major American weapons system has been stopped or seriously constrained by the terms of an arms agreement. Nor have congressional allocations for defense fallen with the rise of an arms agreement.

Quite the contrary. Arms control seems to raise defense spending. As I mentioned earlier, SALT I was accompanied by a slew of accelerated strategic programs and SALT II by a presidential commitment for a 5 percent annual real defense growth. Between those SALT accords, and absent any new arms control agreement in the mid-1970s, the United States experienced seven years of real decline in military spending.

In the 1980s Congress began slashing defense spending long before the INF Treaty seemed possible. After soft-line presidential candidate Walter Mondale pledged in 1984 to boost defense spending by 3 to 4 percent annually, hard-liner Reagan presided over real military spending *declines* during his last four years in office.

How about public support for defense? Conservatives commonly claim that this slips when arms control rises, but the evidence here too tells otherwise. Polls in the 1980s showed popular support for more defense spending falling sharpest when prospects for an accord seemed darkest, during the last year of Reagan's first term.

While the lulling argument has no evidence to support it, the arms control process does help blur the deep differences between our values and theirs, even after the advent of *glasnost* and *perestroika*. Such a blur is bad, as values and interests shape international relations more than personalities or treaties. A British historian once lamented that Russian officials wore coats and ties; if only they wore dashikis or turbans, he felt, we could easily *see* they were different. But because they looked like us, we assumed they thought like us and were like us.

But they're not. Gorbachev never loses sight of his principles or goals, which boil down to a more efficient and, yes, more open communist system, but a communist system nonetheless. He seeks a hardier communist state, not a weaker one or an end to communism. He is for strengthening that system, not scrapping it, as he told the Central Committee: "We cannot remain a major power in world affairs unless we put our domestic house in order."

Hence his resistance thus far to taking the steps China took to transform its economy, including major cuts in defense spending and military assistance abroad. As CIA Deputy Director Robert Gates (now deputy National Security Advisor) made public in October 1988, the CIA had detected no slackening of Soviet weapons production since Gorbachev's rise. In fact, the Soviets' research on new, exotic systems continued apace while their long-planned systems kept rolling off the production lines. Nearly all major Soviet strategic weapons will be replaced by newer models before the mid-1990s; by then they will have added a new strategic bomber for the first time in decades.

As for aid to the outposts, Gates disclosed that in 1987, under Gorbachev, the Soviets and Cubans poured nearly $1 billion into Nicaragua; sent more than $2 billion worth of military equipment into Vietnam, Laos, and Cambodia; and dispatched more than $1.5 billion in military equipment to Angola, twice its 1985 level. Cuba continued to reap around $7 billion in Soviet handouts every year. "At a time of economic stress at home," Mr. Gates declared, "these commitments say a great deal about Soviet priorities."

China, in contrast, trimmed its overseas flings while putting its Mao Tse-tung torn house in order. It cut military spending in half, from around 12 percent of GNP to some 5 percent, in part by laying off one million soldiers and cutting military procurement by about one-fifth. No such dramatic move has been made in Moscow.

Nonetheless, West European statesmen scramble to "help Gorbachev" by falling all over their capitalistic selves to grant loans, guarantees, and economic assistance. Least subtle are of course the Germans. When Chancellor Helmut Kohl paid his first visit to Moscow in October 1988, he brought along two dozen eager German business tycoons. (I know of no other head of government who brought business leaders with him to a summit meeting.) The Germans then gleefully signed sixteen contracts with the Soviets, including one to build a high-technology nuclear reactor. They also arranged a $1.7 billion loan agreement and helped the Soviets secure nearly $300 million on the German bond market.

They would have justified their actions—had they felt compelled to do so at all—by claiming they were helping Gorbachev's reforms. Actually such economic aid *hinders* his reforms. It allows the Soviets to forgo making the wrenching changes, particularly in the two prime areas of price reform and abolishing state monopolies. Gorbachev continues mostly to exhort the people to work harder instead of instituting incentives to encourage harder work. Leaders in the USSR, as elsewhere, will undertake real reform only if they must. If the West bails them out, the "must" vanishes. The greatest incentive for change in the communist world (as perhaps anywhere) is failure.

From our security vantage-point, such assistance is shortsighted. The West has no interest in making Russia stronger, only in making it freer and less aggressive. Injecting large amounts of marks and dollars when the Soviet military still gobbles up large amounts of rubles can only hurt Western security.

A THREE-PRONGED APPROACH

George Orwell once said, "We have now sunk to a depth at which the restatement of the obvious is the first duty of intelligent men." This applies to our situation here. Although America can try to put its finger in the dike to stem the flow of Western funds to Moscow, it seems like a losing battle.

More promising is an effort to put our own foreign policy house in order by adopting a three-pronged approach. First, we can move to protect the country by, among other things, working toward a carefully-crafted SDI. Second, we can initiate better diplomacy. And third, we can create a new (or revived) approach to arms control and defense planning.

TECHNOLOGICAL INNOVATION: SDI

SDI constitutes a major historical legacy of the Reagan administration. Former White House Science Advisor Jay Keyworth had it right when he said:

> There never was any single initiative by the Reagan administration that was so thoroughly created and invented in Ronald Reagan's own mind and experience. It was his decision. It was his creation.

Any other chief executive would have had the program hashed and rehashed by his staff, thereby permitting the bureaucracy to gum it to death. No other president would have been as romantic, even visionary, as to launch and push the concept the way Reagan did.

Contrary to popular belief, SDI did not spring out of Ronald Reagan's head full-blown in March of 1983, when he introduced SDI at the tail end of a rather mundane pro-defense address. Rather, it had been rumbling about his brain for years before he entered the Oval Office.

A key moment came on July 31, 1979, more than a year before the Republican convention that nominated him. That day Reagan visited the North American Aerospace Defense Command (NORAD) in Colorado and underwent an "ah-ha" eye-opening experience. As he told advisor Martin Anderson on the way home, "We have spent all that money and have all that equipment, and there is nothing we can do to prevent a nuclear missile from hitting us." Warming to the point, he went on to say (as related in Anderson's excellent book, *Revolution*), "The only options we would have would be to press the button or do nothing. They're both bad. We should have some way of defending ourselves against nuclear missiles."

Thus a "policy memorandum" was written for him at the Reagan for President office that set out three basic approaches to national defense: "a) Rely on Soviet good intentions, b) Match the Soviet buildup, and c) Develop a protective missile system." The memo writers naturally preferred "c" and told how "that idea is probably fundamentally far more appealing to the American people than the questionable satisfaction of knowing that those who initiated an attack against us were also blown away." Questions of cost and technical feasibility were raised, "but there have apparently been striking advances in missile technology during the past decade or so that would make such a system technically possible." In sum, "the development of effective protective missile system might" be needed in the 1980s. The memo ended by informing Reagan that Dick Allen had thus enlisted some experts, including "Eugene Rostow, Henry Rowen, Ken Adelman," and others to work on this project.

Knowing nothing of the NORAD visit or much about Reagan's thoughts at this time, I nonetheless was then crafting an article for *Policy Review* entitled "Beyond MAD-ness," which advocated reinvigorating a missile defense program "as a means to address and redress" U.S. strategic problems. "It is ironic that the 1970s opened with high hopes for strategic arms control, which soon culminated in the ABM Treaty. The decade ended with low expectations for arms control and serious consideration for scrapping the ABM Treaty." The "serious consideration" was, truth be told, confined to a select few.

One of them, however, was Ronald Reagan. It fit in nicely with his basic abhorrence of nuclear weapons, which we were later to witness (to our regret) at Reykjavik but which also had been percolating in his mind. This notion first slipped out in a speech to the Japanese Diet at the end of 1983. Part of Reagan's long-shrouded nuclear disdain may have come from his suspicion that there was something to the biblical prophecies of final judgment. On his final day in office, Reagan mused that "we have begun to see the prophecies of some of the things that the Bible says would foretell it . . . natural disasters, changes in weather and violent storms and earthquakes and things of that kind." Previously he had made much of the fact that in the Ukrainian Bible, the word for Armageddon was Chernobyl.

Who knows what led Reagan to his beliefs? Surely not even Reagan. In any case, those beliefs in turn led Reagan to SDI. He launched the program dramatically but not terribly effectively, at least not in a way to maximize support. Reagan had long wanted to launch SDI in the worst way possible, and that's just about how he did it.

Reagan's strategic "bolt out of the blue" came on March 23, 1983. It shocked everyone—Congress, Allies, even the Pentagon. Secretary Weinberger, then touring around Europe, attempted a long-distance intercept against the SDI launch. But he failed.

So Reagan gave the speech and thereby put up a target itself easy to shoot down, namely a leakproof SDI that would shield us from all nuclear weapons (in its most extreme presentation) or all incoming ballistic missiles (in less extreme, though still exaggerated, form). Alexander Hamilton once said that absolute security is "a deceitful dream," but the President did not see it that way.

I remember the rampant confusion, even within his administration, during SDI's initial year. At an NSC meeting on the defense budget in the fall of 1983, Secretary Weinberger pleaded for a full commitment to SDI; infused by then with the passion of a convert, he argued that SDI made deterrence obsolete. Secretary Shultz interrupted to say, correctly, that such talk was downright dangerous. We and our Allies were then battling the nuclear freeze movement here and the antimissile movement in Europe by arguing that deterrence had worked for forty years. We should make it work for at least forty more, he added.

Although SDI may become a technological innovation, it is no conceptual breakthrough. The idea of defenses is old. And debate over defenses is old, originating in the 1930s over air defense. In 1932 Stanley Baldwin, then both former and future British Prime Minister, declared defense impossible since "the bomber will always get through." Fear of air attack was severe, as prominent British writers such as B. H. Liddell Hart warned of "three-quarters of a million dead in London" after an air war, which would mean "the end of Western civilization."

Such dire discourse prompted some toward appeasement and others toward rearmament. In 1934 Winston Churchill said that "the crash of bombs exploding in London and cataracts of masonry and fire and smoke will apprise us of any inadequacy which has been permitted in our aerial defenses." He thus urged air defense: "What are 50 million or 100 million pounds raised by tax or loan compared with an immunity like that? Never has so fertile and so blessed an insurance been procurable so cheaply." Air defense, it turned out, worked well; Churchill was right. It saved London during the Battle of Britain.

The same debate now swirls around SDI. Critics trot out self-styled scientific "experts" to proclaim that it can never work, though even the best "expert" scientists can be woefully wrong. To wit:

- Thomas Edison once forecast: "Fooling around with alternative current is just a waste of time. Nobody will use it, ever. It's too dangerous. . . . Direct current is better."

- Simon Newcomb noted in 1903: "Aerial flight is one of that class of problems with which man will never be able to cope."
- Lee De Forest argued in 1926: "While theoretically and technically television may be feasible, commercially and financially I consider it an impossibility, a development of which we need spend little time dreaming."
- Admiral William Leahy, President Truman's Chief of Staff, said shortly before the Manhattan Project proved successful in 1945, "The [atomic] bomb will never go off, and I speak as an expert in explosives."
- And one scientist concluded in 1932: "There is not the slightest indication that [nuclear] energy will be obtainable. It would mean that the atom would have to be shattered at will." That expert was none other than Albert Einstein.

Worse than wrong, expert scientists can be political. Those who blithely claim that SDI won't work repudiate the essence of scientific inquiry, which after all is to discover whether something will or will not work on the basis of hard evidence rather than ideology or politics.

But the key question boils down to: Work to do what? SDI cannot accomplish Ronald Reagan's goal, the complete banishment of nuclear weapons from our world, or even total protection against a barrage of incoming missile warheads. But to say something cannot work perfectly is not to say that it is perfectly useless.

SDI can help with our main nuclear problem, namely nuclear weapons aboard ballistic missiles. It cannot help shield us from those aboard airplanes or cruise missiles or those in a terrorist's suitcase. Nor can SDI save us from an all-out Soviet missile attack.

Nevertheless, Reagan was on to something. His perfect defense was right as SDI's goal, though not its prospects. Most presidential goals—to end the scourge of drugs, to rid us of inflation, to stop unemployment, to prevent crime—can never be realized, however important it is to strive for their realization.

Critics who mock SDI because it can never be leakproof apparently prefer a totally leaky defense. Mocking SDI for "only" achieving effectiveness of 60 or 70 percent, they thus wish to leave us with zero effectiveness. And, of course, they cherish arms agreements, as if there could ever be leakproof arms control.

Scientists and politicians who oppose SDI often speak with forked tongue. Many oppose sufficient research to tell if SDI can work, convinced beforehand that it cannot. Most claim that it would be destabilizing even if it *did* work and spin out grandiose theories on arms control and strategic stability.

Yet few critics have the candor to oppose SDI research altogether. They cannot explain why we should spend our increasingly scarce defense dollars on something that would be dumb or dangerous, even if it worked. For instance, in 1988 presidential candidate Michael Dukakis called SDI "idiocy . . . a magic gizmo" and said that he "strongly opposed the President's Star Wars program" since it "is a fantasy." Then why did he advocate spending $1 billion per year on such an "idiotic" program?

Rhetoric aside, can SDI work? Yes, in three ways. First, it can further discourage the Soviets from launching a nuclear attack. It can thus reinforce deterrence. As to an *all-out* attack, no rational Soviet leader would dare such a thing, since our remaining nuclear forces would then wipe out the USSR. As to a more *limited* Soviet attack, one designed to hit prime targets here, SDI would help enormously. Simply put, *some* U.S. defenses would complicate *all* Soviet targeting. They could not be assured of hitting what they needed to hit to make us surrender. So, the reasoning goes, they would never be tempted to launch in the first place.

In the terms of the trade, SDI could preclude a successful Soviet first strike, precisely the goal arms control has tried in vain to achieve for nearly twenty years now. SDI effectiveness of any reasonable level—50, 60, or 70 percent—would accomplish this goal. Obviously, the higher the better.

Edward Teller, the genius nuclear scientist, made the point with perhaps greater clarity:

> If there are no defenses, the damage to the United States in case of a nuclear attack will be decided in the Kremlin. What they decide will happen. What damage they want to inflict will be inflicted.
>
> If there are defenses, even incomplete defenses, then the damage we shall suffer will not be decided by those in the Kremlin. They will not know what kind of damage they can inflict. They can only guess. If they don't know, they will have a much harder time deciding to attack in the first place. And as we develop our defenses, it will become harder and harder to inflict damage.

Second, SDI can work to help prevent an accidental or unauthorized attack. Accidents can happen, leaving a president today with the Hobson's choice of either sending condolences to Americans or sending retaliatory missiles to Soviets. This is exactly the thought that popped into Reagan's mind on his way back from NORAD.

Were our sophisticated warning equipment Reagan saw in Cheyenne Mountain to tell of a real nuclear attack, the President could then have a third alternative, besides expressing sorrow or firing back. In graphic terms, he could push the button of defense, to kill the weapons coming at us.

Third, SDI can work to help prevent another country besides the USSR from attacking us with nuclear weapons on ballistic missiles. This was one justification for the ABM system in the mid- to late-1960s, which ironically has become ever more valid as crazy leaders have come to power and especially as ballistic missiles have spread like wildfire. Middle East countries are acquiring them with haste and have used them with effect; ballistic missiles were fired during the Iran-Iraq war. Without too much technical expertise, they can increase the range of these missiles so as to endanger those beyond their immediate neighbors. As a long-term project, the United States should develop some protection against a future Idi Amin or Khomeini or Qaddafi getting his grimy hands on such deadly wares.

These are the soundest reasons for SDI. These are the reasons the Pentagon has been researching strategic defense long before Reagan's 1983 speech. (Ironically, it was funded at higher levels *before* the SDI speech than during the two years following.) These are the reasons SDI should be deployed if the research succeeds in the future.

Yet that now seems more in doubt, as the Bush administration lacks much oomph for the project and critics continue their barrage. Indeed, the virulent reaction against SDI reveals the hypocrisy that permeates this field. There were no howls in America when the Soviets began researching, deploying, and modernizing *their* strategic defenses; the outcry came only when we began highlighting research for *our* strategic defenses.

This utter hypocrisy resembles that on the deployment of our INF missiles in Europe. The public clamor began not in 1977 when the Soviets began deploying new, triple-warheaded SS-20s to threaten Europe and Asia, but in 1983 when NATO began deploying a handful of less capable missiles to protect our Allies there. French President François Mitterrand put it best when he asked, "Why are all the protesters in the West and all the missiles in the East?"

Such hypocrisy blinds some traditional arms controllers to what they would otherwise find attractive about SDI. Its ultimate goal, as promulgated by President Reagan, is for the eventual elimination of nuclear weapons, which is the traditional goal of extreme arms controllers. Its more immediate (and realistic) objective is to reduce the effectiveness and salience of nuclear weapons in world affairs, which is a goal all can and should share.

Moreover, SDI can reduce or even eliminate opportunities for a successful Soviet first strike, which has been the prime arms control objective. It can also help prevent the possibility of "nuclear winter" in a way no arms treaty possibly could. The environmental devastation wrought by a nuclear attack could be mitigated by precluding many, if not most, blasts on U.S. territory, especially in urban areas where the frightful nuclear winter scenarios have most validity. Knocking out a nuclear weapon in space is far preferable environmentally and in every other aspect to having it detonate on earth.

In sum, SDI and arms control share the big-picture goals of bolstering strategic stability by buttressing deterrence and limiting damage should deterrence ever fail.

SDI should also have gladdened the hearts of arms controllers since it indisputably helped bring the Soviets back to the bargaining table. It has since been the engine driving them to negotiate over deep reductions in categories of strategic arms. As the Marxists like to say, "it is no coincidence" that Moscow summarily rejected offers of deep reductions under Presidents Nixon, Ford, Carter, and Reagan until after Reagan unfurled SDI. Such a stance is logical, as SDI *can* help bring about deep reductions (if such is in the works) by discounting the effectiveness of ballistic missiles and by furnishing us with some insurance against Soviet cheating.

But no such logical arguments for SDI have made a dent in the arms control community. Most members stand foursquare against it, primarily because SDI calls into question that jewel in the crown of arms control, the ABM Treaty.

Why this adoration? Surely no treaty takes precedence over enhanced U.S. security. If technology advances and certain world conditions change (such as the spread of ballistic missiles), our security will be better assured through strategic defenses than by a treaty essentially banning such defenses. The ABM Treaty should then be scrapped and defenses built.

Nearly as emotional, though stranger, is the community's attachment to Mutual Assured Destruction (MAD), which contends that peace is maintained by our ability to obliterate them and their ability to obliterate us. George Orwell once quipped about something being so silly that only an intellectual could believe it. Certainly that sentiment applies to MAD, which came from intellectuals like Robert McNamara.

The former Secretary of Defense presented his version of MAD with typical McNamara precision. For deterrence, we had to be able to respond to a Soviet first strike with sufficient force to wipe out between one-fifth and one-third of the total Soviet population and between one-half and two-thirds of its industrial capability. McNamara's strategic analysis, which evolved from 1964 to 1967, was cut from the same cloth as his adopting precise "body counts" and percentages of territory pacified in Vietnam, which likewise evolved then. Interestingly, the Soviets seemed to have taken McNamara quite seriously; they calculated that this criteria required a 400-megaton nuclear strike, which their military planners call "One McNamara." And it was McNamara who said in 1965 that "the Soviets have decided that they have lost the quantitative" strategic arms race and "are not seeking to engage us in that contest. . . . There is no indication that the Soviets are seeking to develop a strategic nuclear force as large as ours." Over the past twenty-five years he has made other wrong assessments and many bitter comments. So distressed has he become by the prospects of SDI, for instance, that he actually believes the Soviets would "be justified in shooting the [SDI] system down, even in peacetime."

In any case, MAD is based on the notion that greater safety lies in greater danger, that vulnerability contributes to peace and invulnerability to the risks of war. This approach was enshrined in the ABM Treaty (which Thomas Schelling, one of the fathers of modern arms control, called "incompatible" with arms control "philosophy" since it did not increase stability). No country in history has left itself vulnerable to its enemy as a matter of deliberate national policy. It is one thing to recognize whatever vulnerability exists at the moment. It is another thing to prolong that vulnerability when alternatives exist. That is unreasonable.

And morally objectionable. Reagan was right, MAD represents

"a sad commentary on the human condition." How ironic it is that liberals, who pride themselves on their moral motives, advocate such a bloodcurdling approach, namely that all is well as long as we can launch enough missiles to kill a hundred million or so Soviets. Their favoring a mini-strategic force, just enough for "minimal deterrence," would force a president to "launch on warning" or "launch under attack" in a crisis, thereby risking unfathomable destruction on the basis of computer information. The minimum strategic forces needed for minimal deterrence would deprive a president of options besides those of the Hobson's choice, surrender or devastation.

Such a stance is likewise shortsighted. Over the long stretch, public support for defense will flag if administrations request more and more missiles to target more and more Soviet sites. That, however, has been the trend. Indeed, the Strategic Air Command has long measured the effectiveness of our strategic forces in terms of "DE," or damage expectancy—not the damage expected to America (which best be minimized), but the damage estimated to the Soviet Union (which SAC strives to maximize). Nowhere in their statistical computations does directly protecting America figure in.

Already Americans are growing skeptical as resistance mounts to more missiles. In the entire postwar era, no strategic program a president proposed was rejected by Congress until Reagan asked for two hundred MX missiles. He sliced it down to 100 under the auspices of the bipartisan Scowcroft Commission, but Congress in turn sliced this in half. Only fifty MXs have been deployed. Likewise, Democrats on Capitol Hill will never realize their plan for five hundred Midgetman missiles, which are simply too costly. Funds for our protection appeal more than funds for their devastation.

SDI, while abhorrent to liberals, has been fetching for conservatives. Again, Reagan, that instinctual genius, hit chords that resonate among his natural flock. SDI offers hope to conservatives that they may recapture the good old days of American invulnerability. SDI could, they believe, reduce if not completely remove the corrosive psychological and political damage done by our severe vulnerability today.

Moreover, SDI smacks of isolationism, which unhinges the Allies for the very reason it delights conservatives. The notion of America sitting fat, dumb, and happy behind an impenetrable shield strikes a positive chord among conservatives. And, perhaps above all, SDI embodies hope—the emotion that has so buoyed arms control for so long—but it places the hope squarely in our hands rather than in Soviet hands. With SDI we need not rely on anyone else, much less the Russians, to help remove the nuclear specter.

We can do it ourselves. And we can do it by capitalizing on our strong suit, technology, rather than by competing in their strong suit, brute force. Ex-Governor Pierre DuPont put it best by saying that he would rather rely "upon American ingenuity than Soviet integrity any day."

If SDI fouls up or slows down the arms control process—even if it jeopardizes an agreement like the ABM Treaty—so be it, add conservatives. Indeed, so much the better. For all these reasons SDI has gone from a long-term Pentagon research program to a conservative article of faith.

Yet the U.S. military never shared that fervor. Despite initial encouragement of SDI, they now are drowning in a sea of budget woes. SDI will invariably suck up funds that could go to tanks, ships, and planes.

Historically, military institutions consistently resist change; those in uniform were most skeptical of the value of aircraft, intercontinental ballistic missiles, and cruise missiles. When I worked there in the mid-1970s, Pentagon civilian leaders rammed cruise missiles down the throats of the reluctant Joint Chiefs, who maintained (in a tautological way) that there was no "military requirement" for the new technology.

Consequently it took the Joint Chiefs four years to write any military specifications for SDI, and even then the specs were not compelling. They called for an SDI capable, in its first phase, of stopping half the Soviet's heavy ICBM warheads and 30 percent of all Soviet warheads launched in a massive assault. There is nothing terribly consoling in these figures.

The Soviet military seems keener on SDI, perhaps because it never bought MAD. They considered vulnerability something not to embrace but to eschew or escape. Soviet civilian chiefs considered defensive systems morally superior to offensive ones. In 1967 Soviet Premier Alexis Kosygin said:

I think that a defensive system, which prevents attack, is not a cause of the arms race but represents a factor preventing the death of people. An antimissile system may cost more than an offensive one, but it is intended not for killing people but for saving human lives.

This perfectly foreshadowed the views of Ronald Reagan, who never tired of saying that SDI put nuclear weapons, not people, at risk.

Even after signing the ABM Treaty, the Soviets did not embrace MAD. Indeed, they *increased* spending on strategic defense and continued to express horror over vulnerability. This came from centuries of Russian history. Soviet programs reflect a historic penchant for defensive systems, as Moscow now operates and generally modernizes:

1. the only missile defense system in the world, the Galosh ABM system around Moscow;
2. the sole antisatellite system, their co-orbital system off the SS-11 rocket;
3. a massive program of civil defense, with amazingly deep underground bunkers for hundreds or thousands of top leaders;
4. a large air defense system, with some ten thousand interceptors around the country; and
5. research, unabated by the ABM Treaty, on ballistic missile defense.

All this adds up. Since signing the ABM Treaty, the Russians have spent more on strategic *defense* than they have on strategic *offense,* even though they have continued the "production of rockets," in Khrushchev's fetching phrase, as "a matter of mass delivery, like sausages that come out of an automatic machine." In contrast, U.S. spending on strategic defense has been one-sixth of that on offensive weapons during those years. All told, they have devoted up to fifteen times more to strategic defense than we have.

Hence, the big point: The Soviets are not against SDI; they're just against *our* SDI. They do not seek a world without defenses, only a West without defenses. They know that if SDI is built, they may have to change their programs to overwhelm it, with more offensive power; to go around it, with more air power; to be able possibly to attack it, with an antisatellite weapon; or to match it, by proceeding faster and more fully with their own SDI.

None of this would be easy, for a variety of reasons we need not go into here. Suffice it to say, however, that Moscow's easiest (and most successful) counter against SDI is to suffocate it in the crib. That has been their approach, as Moscow launched an all-out assault on SDI.

The Soviets harped on how SDI would spur an "arms race in outer space," even though approximately ninety of their one hundred yearly space launches (about five times our number) go for military purposes. Space was first "militarized" by the Soviets with the advent of ICBMs. Both sides put military intelligence satellites in space, satellites that are essential for arms control verification and strategic warning. No one interested in stability wants to scrap such beneficial systems.

Moscow also claimed that our SDI program was intended for offensive use. This pitch caught on here, even though it is ludicrous. Nothing is, or could be, better suited for an offensive capability than the tried-and-true ballistic missiles with their devastating power, pinpoint accuracy, and reliability. The United States would be crazy to spend loads of money on SDI for more offense when we already have more than we need.

Furthermore, the type of SDI being researched cannot be an effective offensive weapon. Interceptors fired from space could burn up before they hit the ground. Those fired from the ground in the United States would lack enough range to hit targets in the USSR. Besides, much of today's SDI research goes for precision guidance to hit fast-flying and small warheads in space; none of this would be needed if SDI were designed to hit targets on earth. Finally, the Soviets' accusations lands them in a gigantic contradiction: if SDI is for more offensive capability, then how could it (as they contend) violate the ABM Treaty? That accord places no limits whatsoever on offensive systems.

Soviet allegations that SDI violates the ABM Treaty contradict their previous stance, enunciated by their Minister of Defense, Andrei Grechko, who said in the early 1970s that the ABM Treaty "imposes no limitations on the performance of research and experimental work aimed at resolving the problem of defending the country against nuclear missile attack." Accordingly, Moscow built its ABM system and researched directed energy and laser programs. It was Soviets, not Americans, who pioneered work on X-ray lasers of the type now championed by Dr. Teller and developed at Lawrence Livermore Laboratory.

Given their past efforts and our recent interest in SDI, who's ahead now? Each side has advantages: we are far ahead on computer and sensoring know-how and on command-and-control capabilities, but we have had severe setbacks in space. In early 1986 came a cascade of catastrophes: the Challenger space shuttle blowup and then the successive failures of the Titan and Delta rocket launches. The Soviets are ahead on reliability for launches and heavy lift capabilities into space, as well as on ground-based lasers, particle beams, and terminal defense.

This is the current standing. Still, the future lies with us because of the depth and breadth of our technological base. SDI's success hangs on the very sciences that are most promising in the West today: guidance and sensor technology; optical systems; laser and particle-beam technologies; miniaturization of components so that satellites can be smaller, cheaper, and more survivable; and distinguishing decoys from real warheads.

And we can put things together better than the Russians can. We excel at systems management, the consolidation of disparate capabilities into one workable package. So, given the rapid advance in such realms today, it is rash to rule out a bright future for SDI. "What is now proved was once only imagined," as the poet William Blake put it. Sure, SDI is betting on the come, but then again that's how much of science works and how America works; we see a problem and set about to solve it with our legendary doggedness.

Yet critics claim that even if SDI could be made to work—to accomplish the three goals laid out above—the Soviets would initiate countermeasures. But that may be tough for them to do. It is surely easier for American critics to concoct countermeasures in their armchairs than for Soviet producers to make them in their factories. It is said, for instance, that they could (at a minimum) increase their missiles if we built a missile defense. Granted, such is not impossible, but it is not inevitable, either. How much more could they do? At what cost? With what objective?

Or, it is argued, the Soviets could attack our SDI system. Again, although this is possible, we could always take steps to made SDI systems safe from such an attack—by hardening, dispersing, proliferating, moving, hiding, or arming them—in essence, the same way we protect any prized asset.

All this awaits resolution, as SDI's future lies in doubt. So for that matter, does the Soviet attitude toward it. Will they *ever* move into what the Reagan administration called a "cooperative transition" from offense to defense? That depends upon what their real goals are.

If they seek simply to threaten us, there is little hope for a cooperative transition toward SDI. But in this instance there is also little hope for productive arms control. This may turn out to be the case, especially as they reap psychological and perhaps geopolitical benefit from being able to intimidate us and our Allies.

If, on the other hand, their prime goal is to protect their own nation and people, then a cooperative transition can come about. For each of us, the United States and USSR, indisputably can move to a safer world if we do so cooperatively rather than antagonistically. Both may come to realize that today's predicament of holding the nuclear gun to each other's heads is insane. Each now survives at the sufferance of the other, which is uncomfortable (to say the least) for both. Moving toward greater reliance on defense, and less on offense, will enable America and the Soviet Union increasingly to hold the key to their own survival.

THE BIG QUESTION: ARMS CONTROL AND SDI

However SDI develops, it certainly has had a sweeping impact upon arms control to date. This relationship is hotly debated, with SDI supporters (like me) claiming it has helped, and critics that it has hurt.

Even within the generally pro-SDI Reagan administration, differences appeared. The revealing moment here happened in 1987 as an exceptionally contentious NSC meeting closed. We stood up to leave when the President sat back down to share a thought. "We just have to make progress" on these matters, he said with unusual gravity, or else we might someday face the prospect of nuclear holocaust. Life on earth would be ended, he went on emotionally. Even the living would be better off dead. Whatever prompted this miniburst, I cannot imagine, but it came and was heartfelt.

Secretary Shultz said he heartily concurred. The President was absolutely right, he intoned, looking around at us, and this was precisely why we needed a new strategic arms agreement so badly. Secretary Weinberger perked up to say he too shared the President's sentiments, which was precisely why we needed SDI so badly.

Here, in microcosm, was the ensuing national debate, which

too often disintegrates into a contest between two delusions—
that a treaty with the Russians would deliver us from nuclear
terror or that an impenetrable shield would do so. If a choice had
to be made, though, I deem SDI the better bet. In a technical face-
off between silicon and plutonium, the former will win out. Besides, the very least that can be said for SDI is that, unlike a
strategic arms accord, it is not a *proven* failure.

During the Reagan years, the arms control vs. SDI argument
was posed in terms of a "grand compromise." This is likely to
become a huge issue in the Bush administration as well, so it
deserves a moment's contemplation.

Pounded into the public consciousness has been the notion
that only a grand compromise could break the "arms control
deadlock." What this consists of differs according to its proponents, author Strobe Talbott and Senator Al Gore being among
the more prominent. Generally, though, it involves our conceding to limitations on defense for their agreeing to reductions on
offense. More particularly, we would agree to extend the ABM
Treaty for a number of years and somehow to restrict SDI testing
and development in exchange for big cuts in the Soviet strategic
arsenal, especially in their first strike weapons.

To me the grand compromise makes scant rational sense when
you get below the grand conceptual level to practical considerations. Its underlying premise, that with less offense (fewer missiles) one needs less or no defense (SDI), is dead wrong. At lower
levels of offense, strategic defenses (SDI) become more important,
not less. Why? Because SDI can be more effective if the number
of possible missiles arriving is reduced. SDI also then becomes
more appealing as insurance against Soviet cheating. (The lower
the overall nuclear arsenals, the more important any such cheating becomes.) Then too SDI becomes more appealing to protect
us from Third World countries, which would be increasingly inclined to acquire nuclear weapons if the two superpowers radically reduce their nuclear stockpiles. History bears out the
overall point: while the United States and the Soviet Union had
small strategic arsenals, neither side wished to ban defenses; only
after both increased their warhead numbers did the ABM Treaty
become attractive.

On pledging to adhere to the ABM Treaty for a number of years
(ten was suggested at Reykjavik), a dilemma arises. Why should
the United States reinforce a treaty that the Soviets are violating?

Besides, this notion too becomes convoluted since the standard for withdrawal is already high, affecting the supreme national interest. For us to agree *not* to withdraw, even if our supreme national interest is thereby affected adversely, is ludicrous. By definition, that "supreme" interest should prevail. No nation should adhere to a treaty *no matter what.* We shouldn't continue complying in the face of gross Soviet cheating, an outbreak of war, or spectacular technological advances.

To revisit history for a moment, we already tried one "grand compromise" and it failed. Why get burned again? The ABM Treaty and SALT I constituted a grand compromise that was made explicit by our chief negotiator. Ambassador Gerard Smith stated publicly that if the Russians would not agree to deep offensive reductions within five years, we might abandon the ABM Accord. Five years later President Carter proposed deep reductions, and the Soviets brushed him off with a rather rude *nyet;* yet we did not abandon it. So much for that experiment.

Political factors, diplomatic and domestic, constitute another argument against the grand compromise. For herein too lies a contradiction: either the SDI testing and development restrictions proposed in this grand compromise have a bite, or they do not. If *no*—if extending the treaty or redefining its terms does nothing to harm SDI research—why would the Soviets agree to slash their land-based missiles in exchange? The fellows in Moscow are no dummies, willing to give up offensive military might for our giving up nothing on defense. Fine if we can get it, but those championing the grand compromise know we cannot.

If *so*—if extending the treaty or redefining its terms *does* hurt SDI research—it may constitute a huge sacrifice for us. SDI research is still in its infancy and thus needs wide running room. Adding development and testing restrictions to those already set in the treaty would sap momentum from SDI research. This too has historical proof: after the ABM Treaty was signed and despite testimony from then Defense Secretary Melvin Laird that the United States should "vigorously pursue a comprehensive ABM technology program," Congress cut this program by a factor of seven between 1971 and 1975.

Unfortunately critics did not have a monopoly on foolishness over SDI. The ideas they put forth, like the grand compromise, were matched by ideas emanating from the administration.

Among them was the President's own notion of sharing SDI

with the Soviets, which sprang forth during the President's 1984 debate with Walter Mondale. Though some of us tried, no one could budge it afterward. So there in Reagan's mind it stayed, only to emerge before an incredulous Margaret Thatcher or a disbelieving Mikhail Gorbachev, who responded that Reagan was unwilling to share even dairy technology with the Russians. So how could he believe the United States would share SDI? Yet Reagan was not deterred by this or any other counter-point.

Sharing SDI became yet another spectacular Reagan reversal. The man who entered office so suspicious of the Soviets and so determined to limit technology transfers to the Soviet bloc that his administration banned the Apple II computer later advocated handing the Russians the most sophisticated technology in the world—technology we might not hand our closest allies, technology that stands on the cutting edge of our most advanced sciences.

Such contradictions never seemed to bother the President. Nor did the pitch that sharing SDI might negate it. If the Soviets received SDI, they could figure out how to thwart it. Reagan heard these points and always came back with a rejoinder. His willingness to share SDI, he said in several meetings, would prove the Soviets had nothing to fear from SDI. "The whole world would benefit by having it." The fact that SDI was not an "it" but a complex system of sensors, tracking devices, computer facilities, satellites, guidance systems, missiles, power stations, and the like never sank in. "Let's share it once we get it," he would say. Neither side could then launch a nuclear strike, and "these things" (nuclear weapons) would gradually disappear.

After hearing him say this enough times to realize that it really *was* his view, we underlings had to devise ways of squirting perfume on such a scheme. So we altered the operative phrase from "sharing SDI" to "sharing the benefits of SDI," though we never figured out precisely what this meant, either. In the fall of 1986 we resorted to the tried-and-true approach (used before on the "no nukes" notion) of burying it under a mound of conditions. SDI sharing would not occur *until* the Soviets agreed to a) leave the ABM Treaty, so that either side could deploy defensive systems; b) eliminate all offensive ballistic missiles; and c) implement a specific plan for sharing SDI's benefits reciprocally. These conditions stayed on the administration's position papers, but they never came out of the President's mouth for they never entered his head.

The one argument we did *not* use was the best, albeit the most cynical one: Such sharing might be inevitable. We probably will share SDI, though not intentionally. The West has honed its skills of sharing our most advanced high-technology equipment with the Soviets—from the KH-11 satellite system, whose manual found its way to Moscow, to the cruise missile, whose technology found its way into the Soviet arsenal. In part, they steal our technological advances, and in part we or our Allies sneak such to them. The same may well occur with SDI, once again making Ronald Reagan strangely come out right.

TROUBLES EXPAND

The temptation to feed a president appetizing ideas overwhelms most mortals. It overwhelmed the President's Science Advisor, Dr. Jay Keyworth. After doing some superb pioneering and missionary work on SDI, he left the White House flinging a grenade over his shoulder.

Dr. Keyworth saw the President's ante on sharing SDI and raised it one. He left the President this final thought: Why not design SDI with many buttons? Then any number of world leaders could push the one marked "protection" in case ballistic missiles are launched anywhere.

What woes followed Keyworth's letter! Interagency groups worked this problem for months. Much top-level time in government is spent putting bad ideas back in the box; we managed to kill this one, but only after long and hard effort.

Meanwhile we faced a wider sea of troubles. Early in 1987 the need was felt for a new U.S. arms control initiative. I use the passive tense intentionally; it is rarely possible to trace exactly where or why such a felt need arises. We had gone through such exercises before, particularly on the fashionable idea in 1984 for a "build-down" of strategic forces. Like a comet, it shone brightly on Capitol Hill, faded fast, and then vanished altogether.

Part of the push in this instance, in 1987 may have come from Defense Secretary Weinberger, of all people. Cap was then trumpeting SDI's successes and pressuring the President to approve more SDI research than allowed by the ABM Treaty's traditional interpretation.

For every government action there is a counteraction. The State Department wanted something new for our negotiators to do in Geneva, just as Cap wanted something new for our scientists to do in their labs. The President may have wanted something new, too, since he knew the clock was ticking. Time was running out on his chances of ever concluding a mega-agreement, the kind he thought just beyond his grasp at Reykjavik.

Besides, upbeat reports were then coming into the White House from Geneva. The Russians, our diplomats cabled, were poised to move out. Not that they had made any substantive moves; they merely seemed to be buckling down to business.

So top administration officials manned their battle stations and swung into the ready-for-action routine. A list of options was drawn up, and two White House meetings were scheduled.

The first session was routine, though I found it aggravating. Perhaps my reaction was due to fatigue. I had been on a trip to Geneva and European capitals when the meeting was called. I dutifully departed on an all-night flight aboard a C-5A jumbo cargo plane from Bonn, Germany, to Bangor, Maine, where I had to awaken an Air Force doctor because of an eye infection. I then flew on to Dover, Delaware, where I caught a small Air Force jet to Andrews Air Force Base. We landed at 4:30 A.M.

Or perhaps my irritation was due to a rare spat with Secretary Shultz, who for some reason told the President at the opening of the meeting that someone in my agency had leaked a damaging story to *The New York Times*. I took strong exception at the table to this careless and needless comment, for which Shultz apologized afterward. No doubt he was fatigued as well.

Sparks flew wildly at the second session in mid-February 1987. These were dark days at the top of the administration, and it showed. Secretaries Shultz and Weinberger went after each other so vehemently as to make such meetings nearly painful to watch. During this session, someone handed me a note saying it was going to be a long, long remaining two years in office. Even the President looked askance at such behavior.

Eventually we turned to substance. The State Department had concocted an "option c," which would allow our negotiators to discuss with the Soviets precisely what kind of SDI research was permitted by the ABM Treaty. Ambassador Paul Nitze publicly championed this approach. He filled it out with precise ideas about power apertures and allowed levels for lasers, particle beams, and so on. Given unlimited time, energy, resources, and expertise in an administration, the idea might have had merit, were we negotiating with the Canadians or British.

But to do so with little time left, no real knowledge of where SDI research would go, and the Soviets across the negotiating table—this made scant sense. It was a quintessentially State Department idea, as it would absorb loads of time and effort, give the appearance of progress, and respond to Soviet desires without our knowing what was in it for us. Suspicious minds in the administration took option c as the first step to restrict SDI, but they had no proof of this (except the way such ideas usually end up). No agency besides the State Department was supportive.

And even State's representative, Secretary Shultz, was not supportive. At least he wouldn't say that he was. After NSC Advisor Carlucci introduced the topic and summarized option c, he asked Secretary Shultz to give his views. Shultz wouldn't. He said he was *not* for that option or any option, at least not in this meeting. Word of the previous NSC session had leaked to the press, which meant that even in the Situation Room he could not give the President confidential advice. So he just wouldn't say anything.

Everyone sat there stunned. Someone said it was hard to have a productive meeting if the President's principal advisor wouldn't give him advice. We sat for an awkward moment until the never reticent Weinberger piped up, "Good, George. I'm not for option c, either. Not because we shouldn't discuss it here, but because it's a terrible idea." Cap then massacred the proposal, with others piling on afterward.

After this played out, the President hushed the crowd—all but Secretary Shultz, who had been hushed from the start—and said he had been thinking hard about all this. He had a look on his face I had first seen years before, a pensive but strained look that conveyed how tough it was to do the kind of thinking he had been doing.

This was a sure sign of something interesting being birthed. In 1980 the same look preceded his telling Al Haig that an idea had struck him while horseback riding at the ranch: "Wasn't the UN started to deal with this kind of thing?" he asked, referring to the takeover of American diplomats in Tehran. "Well, then, it should solve it!" Haig gazed at him, waiting for more. "Why don't I call in the UN Secretary General, this fellow Waldheim, right after I get in office? And tell him to solve it. Just solve it. If he won't, within a week or so, I'll call him back in and then tell him, well, to leave. Just get that place [the UN] out of here, 'cause it's no good." Haig, looking aghast, managed to get the then President-elect back in the box through a nice blend of flattery and logic. There might be other ways to solve this thing. Why not hold off until after the inauguration? When we're both in office? We could talk about it again then.

So I, at least, was forewarned by Reagan's look. Why not, he asked this time, develop the idea of sharing SDI technology, combine it with the total elimination of nuclear weapons, and do this through an international body? That way, SDI would exist for everyone, not just for us and the Russians. No one would want or need nuclear weapons any longer. We could turn a page of history.

As he proceeded down this path, I lifted my finger, figuring it was better to do so before he headed clear out of sight. "As one of your representatives at the United Nations for two years, I learned that the UN couldn't handle such responsibility, at least not responsibly." Before I finished, the President broke in to say that he wasn't talking about the UN. He was talking about some new international organization.

Even then the idea had loads of problems, I replied. To eliminate all nuclear weapons was impossible. It would make the world more dangerous even if it could be done. Again I used the example—by then the others must have been sick of hearing it—that Europe had endured two conventional wars during the first half of this century (World Wars I and II) and hadn't liked either one. In the second half of the century, after the introduction of nuclear weapons, there had been none.

I lacked time to walk through the argument on the role of nuclear weapons for "extended deterrence," our protecting Europe against even a *conventional* Soviet attack. One scholar, Jeffrey Record, has shown that before nuclear weapons came into existence in 1945, a major war had erupted in Europe on an average of nearly every dozen years. Hence there was "a major war taking place somewhere in Europe for 152 out of the period's 345 years" before the advent of nuclear weapons.

On this occasion, the President was not laid-back. He understood that argument, he responded rather firmly, but it wasn't clear that nuclear weapons had kept the peace. Maybe other things, like the Marshall Plan and NATO, had kept the peace.

I responded that the President might be absolutely right, but this was a proposition no one wished to test. Back and forth we went.

Meanwhile his key Cabinet officers sat mostly as spectators to this verbal match. Secretary Shultz reiterated that we couldn't discuss such sensitive matters here since they'd leak out. I responded all too sharply that the President asked for our views; I at least would give them.

I did, though it didn't help. After more banter, the President unveiled his full thoughts. Why, we're just fiddling around in Geneva! Nothing ever happens there, with all these numbers going back and forth and all that. Our fellows over there should change what they're doing and present this scheme. That way we might get somewhere. Throwing caution to the wind, I said that what they were doing in Geneva was just fine. We had no need to do much more or change it.

Thankfully Frank Carlucci jumped in to break up our face-off. He asked others how the Soviets might react to such an idea. Paul Nitze said they'd wish to stack such an international body with people Moscow controlled. Though technically correct, Paul was missing the big problem here. The President was meshing his two worst ideas—sharing SDI and eliminating nuclear weapons—and placing responsibility for them in the worst possible place, in an international organization. But at least Paul had spoken negatively.

Shultz kept sulking as Cap started talking. The President's idea, he said, would "electrify the Europeans" and enable him to seize the high moral ground. Realizing I had said too much already, I blurted out, "Electrify the Europeans? It would electrify them all right. Just like Reykjavik!"

The mood was sour. Something was eating at Shultz. For all the abuse heaped upon him at times, all the pressure, the difficulties of operating in this untidy administration, aggravation of pitching daily battle with Weinberger (with whom he had worked for years, always uncomfortably), Shultz's demeanor was normally exceedingly polite. The same could be said of Cap Weinberger.

What disturbed me most, however, was their reluctance to be frank with the President. This need not have been—Reagan never took criticism or disagreement personally; he actually welcomed straight talk—and it should not be. Each advisor has a sacred duty to talk straight to power, even (or especially) to a president. But such duty usually yields to the inclination to please; or it yields to the intimidation of the Office of the Presidency. Roaring tigers in the White House waiting room became pussycats once ushered into the Oval Office for a meeting with The Man.

Our meeting was not unique in lacking frank advice to the President. Not by a long shot. A few years before, likewise in the Situation Room, out of the President's creative mind came a new angle on INF. How dare the Russians object to our stationing missiles on our Allies' territory, he exclaimed. Why, they had been stationing similar missiles on the territory of *their* Allies for years!

Shultz looked impressed and said he had not thought of the problem in those terms before. That's a good way to look at it. Weinberger joined in the praise; indeed, the Soviets had no right to do so. How hypocritical they were! Before everyone went too far congratulating one another, I raised "a point of information." The Soviets did *not* have such missiles deployed on their Allies' territory. There were no SS-20s in Eastern Europe. There never had been.

Someone replied that the Soviets *could* have them there; that's what the President meant. I let it pass whether that was his meaning but commented that they never would place SS-20s in Eastern Europe. There, the missiles would be more vulnerable to NATO attack and to problems in East Europe itself. The missiles were much safer on Soviet territory. Moving them westward would be foolish since they could hit any place in Western Europe from Soviet territory.

Over time, discussions within the Reagan administration became better since the meetings became smaller. And the participants became more knowledgeable. During the first year or two, in 1981 and 1982, we mostly met in the lavish Cabinet Room. Those sitting at the table then stuck to their carefully crafted "talking points" while their staffs lined the walls waiting to catch any deviation, which the Cabinet officers knew and feared. Even uttering a kindly phrase like "That's a good point" to a rival colleague might be risky.

That dread ended when the staff was excluded. Yet keeping the meetings tight invariably excluded some who knew most. This administration was not, in case anyone had not noticed, top-heavy with foreign affairs expertise. Some officials did not even realize their own limitations; Don Regan, the Chief of Staff during the administration's most active period in arms control, once told *The New York Times*, "I don't take kindly to this criticism by people who have not examined my record. How much more experience do you have to have in foreign policy than I do, to believe you are qualified?" This from one incapable of distinguishing *our* position from *theirs*, red from blue, at Reykjavik, either then or since.

Advisors ignorant of a field or topic should not feign knowledge. They need to find out, tell a president the facts, and convey their best judgment. And they need to correct a wayward president to assure quality decisions.

We eventually convinced the President to shelve his scheme for a new international organization to eliminate nuclear weapons and share SDI. We stopped the White House from sending the idea out to various agencies for study (announced during our meeting) since this would surely leak out. That would have added to the erroneous but spreading suspicion that Ronald Reagan had become the nation's "Uncle Charlie," still titular family head and owner of the business, but no longer really up to being either. Secretary Shultz and I, when we spoke privately after his staff meeting one morning, decided a quiet talk with the President would work best to put such thoughts back in the box. It did.

Despite the fact that SDI is burdened with overpromises and associated with foolish ideas, it remains sound in theory and technology. But will it, as advocated here, be deployed in the future?

Hard to say. Opposition to SDI is fierce; resistance to scrapping the ABM Treaty is fiercer; Allied skepticism over how SDI would affect "extended deterrence" cuts deep; costs may be high; and uncertainties abound.

SDI's effectiveness will forever be questioned. Nothing in the strategic business is for sure. No one knows how strategic nuclear weapons would actually work in a war. If, God forbid, that were to happen, even a deployed SDI will by then have failed in its primary mission—to help assure that such a war never happens.

The future national debate over SDI should weigh the risks of both deploying *and* not deploying it. What if the Soviets deploy a defensive system and we abstain? What kind of damage is done to the American psyche by unending vulnerability? What are the risks of having *no* protection against a precisely executed or unauthorized or unintentional Soviet—or Third World country—attack from ballistic missiles? Conceivably the formula for success over the past forty years may not be the same for the next forty or four hundred years. Somehow, diminution of the nuclear threat must come, and SDI can help that happen.

When could the "go" decision come on SDI? By the turn of the century after a reasonable amount of research has been completed. But its deployment should be planned and even anticipated now, for this type of encouragement is needed to give SDI its best shot. Such a challenging research program needs the prospect of deployment down the line to attract and then motivate top-notch scientists now. To hold off a final "go" decision until *all* research is completed is to hold it off forever. Research on such an effort is never truly completed: scientists can always learn more.

What shape would it take? It should be designed to preclude the possibility of a decapitating attack against key U.S. targets and to provide insurance against an accidental or Third World country launch. Protecting our leadership, command-and-control, and port facilities, along with a number of silos, would remove a Soviet limited-nuclear option. Subsequent SDI stages can build on this to help limit damage of a moderate to heavy attack against American territory.

A combination of a ground-based ERIS system and close-in ground-based HEIDI system now, with spaced-based kinetic kill systems a bit later, might do the trick. Or the Pentagon's new rage, oddly dubbed "Brilliant Pebbles," may prove even wiser. But that's what a well-funded and politically pushed research program is for—to tell us how best to do what we *should* do. If Americans can, as they do, spend $400 billion yearly on insurance of all sorts, we can allocate a mere 1½ percent of that in research for a type of insurance that helps protect America.

RELATIONS WITH THE RUSSIANS

Back to our three-pronged approach. On top of a new attempt to help protect the country by SDI should come a new American approach to diplomacy and a new (or revived) approach to arms control and defense planning.

The latter two will both depend upon and help fashion U.S. relations with the Soviets. So before diving into them, we should consider one critical question: Is the Cold War over?

For forty years U.S. security and diplomacy have been dictated by a fairly hostile relationship with the Russians. Even a tried-

and-true conservative like myself must admit that this may now be changing.

Mikhail Gorbachev is indubitably the most captivating figure on the world scene today, partly because of his personality but mostly because of his mission. Gorbachev is the first General Secretary to hitch his welfare to that of his people, by showing he knows and cares about their daily life, both intellectual and material. Stalin was said (at the time, anyway) to care but not to know, Brezhnev to know but not care. Above all, Gorbachev has removed fear as a central element in Soviet daily life; nothing else he does can equal this truly historic accomplishment.

Outsiders commonly concentrate on Gorbachev's economic woes. And with good cause, since things there look and are dismal. No one is clearer on this than The Man himself. In his book, *Perestroika*, Gorbachev says:

> In the latter half of the 1970s . . . the country began to lose momentum. Economic failures became more frequent. . . . Elements of stagnation began to appear in the life of society. . . . The gap in the efficiency of production, quality of products, scientific and technological development began to widen. . . . A sizable portion of the national wealth became idle capital. . . . There are glaring shortcomings in our health services. . . . And there were difficulties in the supply of foodstuffs, housing, consumer goods and services. . . .

And so forth. So out of kilter are things that rents in the USSR have not been raised since 1928. The cost of bread hasn't changed since 1954, the cost of meat since 1962. Farmers commonly feed their pigs bread since it is cheaper than grain.

Nonetheless, Gorbachev has yet to tackle the twin evils of that economic system, government monopolies and nonconvertible currency. The ruble is not convertible either into hard currency or into decent products. To illustrate the point, the main cause of fires in Russia today is home television sets. It is said, and it's true, that communist workers make phony products while their managers give them phony wages. The sprawling Soviet superpower cannot compete with a tiny city-state like Singapore or Hong Kong on any product.

Though he recognizes the problems, Gorbachev has shown scant ability to solve or even alleviate them. Since he assumed the top post, Soviet economic growth has been lower than during the much maligned "stagnation years" of Leonid Brezhnev. Were the Soviet people asked the Reaganesque question of whether they are better off today than they were four years ago, when Gorbachev took the top post, they would resoundingly respond, "no" in material terms.

He could thus be held accountable, even though the obstacles he faces are genuinely awesome. While there are thousands of treatises in the USSR on the transition from capitalism to communism, there are none on the transition from communism to capitalism. And that's what's needed now.

His attempts at economic revitalization are widely applauded, however. Adapt or die, say the South Africans. Reform or the system will die, says Gorbachev. Specifically, he has said that socialism "will die unless we reform the political system" and that *"perestroika* is our last chance. If we stop, it will be our death." On this, everyone there stands with him.

The Soviet leadership and people know they are losing ground to the West. They fear slipping into irrelevance on the world scene, on top of inflicting even more misery at home. In 1960 Nikita Khrushchev boasted, "Our per capita output in 1980 will be much greater than that of the U.S." Now it stands at around a quarter our level.

All this means suffering by the people. Soviet sources figure that some 40 percent of the entire population and an appalling 79 percent of the elderly now live in poverty. As Brzezinski points out in his new book, *The Grand Failure,* South African blacks own more cars per capita than all Soviet citizens, and life expectancy of a Soviet citizen born these days is lower than that of a Mexican.

Recent information suggests that the Bear is sicker than we had imagined. The size of the entire Soviet economy still seems to be around one-third ours, rather than the one-half many Western analysts had assumed in the 1970s. And the Soviet growth rate seems to have been slower than we estimated, not the 2 percent previously thought, but staying flat for the first half of this decade. This leaves per capita GNP actually declining over the past ten years. To these miserable figures should be added a worrisome budget deficit estimated at about 11 percent, more than twice America's constantly lamented level.

Although grave, I do not consider the economic mess job-threatening to Gorbachev. History and ethnicity could well be.

Glasnost is unleashing a torrent of woes about past wrongs that is being heaped on top of current woes. This is momentous. For as an old Russian adage goes, what is written with a pen cannot be hacked out with an ax.

Truth has long been recognized as a key point of vulnerability in that society. After a visit to Russia 150 years ago, before the advent of communism, the Marquis de Custine wrote, "One word of truth hurled into Russia is like a spark landing in a keg of powder." In recent times history has become the soft underbelly of communism, which turned time upside down. According to Marxist theory, the past is up for grabs; the present is in flux; only the future is certain, as it will unfold into an idyllic workers' paradise under communism.

No one believes such rubbish anymore. But people now wonder if anyone *ever* believed it. And why? What happened in the past? And why?

Early in 1988 Gorbachev told the Central Committee that he could "understand the impatience of the public wishing to take a look sooner at the closed pages of our past." Yet to do so is perilous. Questions in history lead right to questions of legitimacy.

What kind of system for seventy years hoists up leaders like Stalin, who massacred untold millions of his own citizens (more than Hitler, according to popularly published Soviet articles) and the bulk of his own officials and soldiers? In the 1930s Stalin slaughtered around 100 of the 139 Party Central Committee members. He had more Soviet army and naval officers executed in two years (1937 and 1938) than the Germans killed in the first two years of World War II battles with the Soviets. Throughout the USSR today, citizen groups are attempting to locate the killing fields where Stalin's henchmen tossed bodies into unmarked pits; interest is keen on estimating the total number of victims, which could rise above the 20 million figure appearing in the Soviet press.

And what about leaders like Brezhnev? He collected cars, the showier the better, and laurels for himself—some 220 orders and medals, including the gold decoration of a Lenin Literature Prize. For Soviet citizens to take a look "at the closed pages of" their past is jolting. It would be like our coming to believe that America's Founding Fathers and their thoughts—the Declaration of Independence or the Constitution—were no good. What Gorbachev does to Communist party infallibility when saying that the Party has "no monopoly of truth" is akin to what Luther did to papal authority. And when the Hungarian Prime Minister says, as he did in April of 1989, "The model of a party state has hit a dead-end street and has proven to be incapable of making further headway," that only adds to the withering away of the Marxist state.

Alongside the dagger of history exists the danger of ethnicity. Eruptions have taken place throughout the Soviet Union; in late 1988 the CIA counted some six hundred "popular disturbances" due primarily to ethnic tensions and affecting more than half (nine of fifteen) of the Soviet republics. These nationalistic groups have latched on to the potent ecology movement by linking preservation of their culture with preservation of their lands; this adds immeasurably to their force. No longer can anyone consider the Soviet Union as, in the words of its national anthem, an "unbreakable union of free republics joined together by a Great Union."

These ethnic woes reverberate in the Soviet bloc, where the crisis, long in coming, will be long in unfolding. These once dormant provinces of the mighty empire have become among the most unstable of places today. Future historians may compare conditions in Eastern Europe now with those that led to fervor across all of Europe in 1848. Long a sleeper issue, Eastern Europe is awakening with a roar.

For across Eastern Europe, but most clearly in Poland and Hungary, the workers demand less communism. Contrary to the situation in the Soviet Union, where Gorbachev must motivate a lethargic populace, in Eastern Europe the leaders strive to reign in a restive peoples. Turning Karl Marx on his head, they see capitalism as the final stage of socialism. Marx wrote: "Of all the classes . . . today, the proletariat alone is a really revolutionary class." But today's proletarian revolution is not to usher in a Marxist state but to push it out. Labor leaders and intellectuals across Eastern Europe know that they have "nothing to lose but their chains," and this they know without having to read the Communist Manifesto. On top of the resentment from the imposition of an alien ideology comes fury by the neo-colonies in Eastern Europe feeling culturally superior to the neo-colonialists in the USSR.

Brezhnev clones, who still rule in some states of Eastern Europe, nervously hear echoes of Czech reform leader Alexander

Dubcek emanating from Moscow. In fact, during a 1987 trip to Czechoslovakia, Gorbachev's spokesman was publicly asked what was the main difference between the reforms of Gorbachev and those of Dubcek. The spokesman delivered a two-word answer: "Nineteen years."

Such talk makes the old fogies who still rule in Eastern Europe's gang of four regressives—East Germany, Czechoslovakia, Bulgaria, and above all, Romania—exceedingly nervous. For instance, when asked about Gorbachev reforms, Romania's strongman Nicolae Ceausescu said that just because a neighbor painted his house is no reason you should do likewise. And the East German government bans some Soviet publications, deeming them slightly subversive, and called the West German television showing of the Soviet film *Repentance* anti-Soviet propaganda. The clock is ticking for them, caught as they are between the greater integration of Western Europe (quickening as 1992 approaches) and the greater disintegration of Eastern Europe and the entire Soviet bloc.

What does this mean for Gorbachev? A tough row to hoe, for sure, and just when he is most vulnerable. Any one of a score of possible setbacks, either at home or abroad, could bring his colleagues to fear that things are getting completely out of hand.

The more they feel their leadership's loss of control, the more they will feel Gorbachev is dispensable. For those in the Kremlin are notoriously risk-averse. They can tolerate change, but only managed change, change they can control.

Nikita Khrushchev learned this lesson the hard way. He became dispensable in 1964 for a variety of reasons, including efforts toward *glasnost*. Khrushchev recounts in his *Memoirs:*

> We in the leadership were consciously in favor of the thaw, myself included, but . . . we were scared—really scared. We were afraid the thaw might unleash a flood which we wouldn't be able to control and which would drown us.

Those in the Kremlin can feel another flood coming. They look out and see trouble all around; they realize, as Machiavelli said, that "there is nothing more difficult to carry out, nor more doubtful of success, nor more dangerous to handle, than to initiate a new order of things." Especially since many of them probably prefer the old order of things.

They see Gorbachev successful in dealing with the West, which is a cause for pride especially if it bring loans, guarantees, and technology in its wake. Yet the same style that appeals in the West may not appeal across the Soviet Union. Gorbachev's vivid colors seem out of place in the gray Soviet soil. The personality of the man does not match the personality of the system. And when a leader does not fit the system, something gives. Rarely is it the system.

Hence my personal feeling for some time that Gorbachev may be down or out within a few years. If down, he will be worn down and shorn down. He may come to realize that, as Czar Nicholas II said, he does not rule Russia; ten thousand clerks do. Gorbachev once told an American group that his attempts to reform that bureaucracy were similar to shooing fifty crows from a clothesline; minutes after shaking them off, one hundred crows return.

Were Gorbachev to be ground down, he would follow a long line of Russian leaders that includes Catherine the Great and Alexander I who entered office as ardent reformers and then resigned themselves to keeping their desks tidy. If Gorbachev is driven out, he will follow the likes of Khrushchev and Alexander II who launched reforms and lost their office (the latter also his life) as a result.

What does this mean for us? Good tidings, if we play our policy right. Their being immersed in a sea of troubles means calmer waters for us.

Again, to borrow the communists' favorite phrase, it is no coincidence that the Reagan years closed with peace breaking out all over—from the Iran-Iraq war, across to Cambodia, Afghanistan, the Sahara desert, and through central and southern Africa. Our sending arms and aid to those combatting communist cliques raised Moscow's price of retaining power throughout its far-flung empire. Hence the communists' flight. And hence the death of the Brezhnev doctrine—decreeing that once a Marxist regime, always a Marxist regime—and life to the Reagan doctrine—that the United States lends moral, political, and military aid to insurgents fighting communist regimes in the Third World. In short, the Soviet Union is no longer on the march; it is now on the run.

NEW DIPLOMACY

How to handle such good news gets tricky. Despite good tidings of the Reagan summits, U.S.-Soviet relations will never be (in that marvelous Chinese phrase describing their relations with North Korea) "as close as mouth and lips." But they can and will improve if and as Soviet reforms unfold.

Meanwhile we can help bring this about by clearly identifying three American goals for better relations with the Soviets, pushing them, and conditioning our moves on their progress. Taking a page from Chinese diplomacy—conceived and executed so well with its "three obstacles"—can help us overcome our greatest diplomatic shortcomings. These were perceptively identified by one who should know, longtime Soviet Foreign Minister Andrei Gromyko. Americans, he said, "mistake tactics for strategy. Besides, they have too many doctrines and concepts proclaimed at different times, but the absence of a solid, coherent, and consistent policy is their big flaw."

We can correct this "big flaw" by presenting the Soviets with specific steps needed to improve the relationship. We could dangle carrots of freeing up U.S. trade restrictions and of being willing to cut them in on more diplomatic dealings (such as in the Middle East). If all goes well, we could entice the Soviet Union with a willingness to include them in European and Western institutions—like the European Economic Community, OECD, IMF, and World Bank—if they meet our conditions and adopt necessary political and economic reforms.

America's "three obstacles"—more than three becomes confusing—could include the following.

First, tear down the Berlin Wall, a veritable gash across Europe, and reduce Soviet military presence in Eastern Europe far more than currently announced. For openers, the Soviets could remove more men and arms from Hungary, which has no foreign "threat" (besides Romania) and borders no NATO nation. They could dramatically cut back in East Germany, where they now station more troops than exist in the entire United States Army.

While this obstacle may seem extreme, it merely takes Gorbachev at his word. He has said, "We favor socialism, but we do not impose our convictions on anyone. Let everyone choose for himself." Fine, then begin with East Europe. That's where the

Cold War began—to say nothing of the two world wars this century—and that's where the Cold War must end.

For our part, we should seek a type of Finlandization or, better still, Austriazation for Eastern Europe—free internal system with minimal accommodation to Soviet security concerns—that we abhor for Western Europe. Our objective is the objective of the people in Eastern Europe, to fashion a civil society with a variety of political, economic, cultural, and labor institutions that are free from Party control. In the near term, our (and their) objective is, in the words of Polish philosopher and *Solidarity* activist Adam Michnik, "to live freely in a country that is not itself free."

The second American obstacle involves requesting the Soviets to lower their military spending below a wartime footing, to under 10 percent of GNP, say, and to slow if not stop military aid to states in our back yard. Exact figures may be tricky for us to compute, especially on total Soviet defense spending. Still, we seek a "civilianization" of the Soviet economy, with their initial cuts made where they most threaten our interests.

Our third obstacle plays into *glasnost.* We should request that they open up both information and emigration. They should make Western books and magazines available to their citizens and allow those who wish to leave the freedom to do so.

Such demands too may seem extreme, but the Soviets are *already* legally obliged to allow such liberties under the UN Charter, Helsinki Accords, Universal Declaration of Human Rights, and International Covenant on Civil and Political Rights —all of which Moscow voluntarily signed.

Such demands, too, take Gorbachev at his word, as when he told the 1988 Communist Party conference that he would like to improve "political freedoms that enable a person to express his opinion on any matter. . . . Comrades," he continued, "what we are talking about is a new role of public opinion in the country." Since then, he said that the country was "going through the school of democracy afresh. We are learning. Our political culture is still inadequate. Our standard of debate is inadequate." His goal was to make the Soviet Union "one big debating society," which in a way happened during the Spring 1989 nationwide elections. Our demands in this third category help reinforce Gorbachev's stated goals.

Highlighting these three obstacles—on Eastern Europe, Soviet military forces and military assistance, and human rights—

would not end all America's problems with the Soviets. But they would certainly help, if achieved. They could help transform the Soviet Union into a country less bent on (or even capable of) aggression abroad or repression at home. This would help the United States, help the Soviet people, and help the world at large.

Nevertheless, this is a diplomatic approach, and diplomacy has its limits. It cannot solve most international problems any more than arms control can solve most defense problems. George Marshall once said, "If man does find a solution to world peace, it will be the most revolutionary reversal of his record we have ever known."

There are no ultimate solutions to most international problems. No Middle East peace process can completely eradicate the strife that has plagued that region since the days of Jesus and before. No political, diplomatic, or military action will end racial strife in southern Africa for all time. French President Charles de Gaulle rightly observed that diplomacy cannot solve problems, only alleviate them. In life, that should be sufficient.

ARMS CONTROL REVISITED AND REVISED

In the third prong of our overall approach—after SDI and a more focused diplomatic stance—comes, of course, arms control. Here the recommendation is to go back for the future, to take a field turned counterproductive back to its basics.

Mine is a call for a return to traditional diplomacy, though one conducted by military experts more steeped in security matters than traditional diplomats. Gone would be the formal, quasi-public discussions in Geneva over arcane strategic matters. Back would be a focus on the big picture of greater security with fewer nuclear weapons.

Replacing the elaborate arms control ritual would be what in March of 1933 Churchill called "private interchanges." He illustrated the dialogue as " 'If you will not do this, we shall not have to do that,' and 'If your program did not start so early, ours would begin even later.' " Churchill believed that

a greater advance and progress towards a diminution of expenditure on armaments might have been achieved by these methods than by the conferences and schemes of disarmament which have been put forward at Geneva.

He was right then and would be right now. For here too is an approach that has been tried and that has largely succeeded, as we will see.

The case for this approach of "arms control without agreements" rests on three propositions. First, the existing way will not work. Second, this way has, can, and is likely to work. Third, it is inevitable anyway.

First, the bad news: START, conventional arms control, and a chemical weapons ban cannot deliver anything remote to what they now promise. They may deliver nothing good at all.

No arms agreement in these areas can be comprehensive. So each opens itself up to the "balloon argument," namely that military capabilities pushed down by an arms accord in one area will pop up in others. Reductions in tanks and artillery will heighten competition in air-delivered weapons; cuts in air-launched cruise missiles will cause expansion in sea-launched cruise missiles or in bomber capabilities; and so forth.

No accord in these realms can be well verified, either. As explained previously, the strategic weapons now coming on-stream —cruise missiles and mobile land-based missiles—are exceedingly tough to verify. In June 1989, Chairman of the Joint Chiefs Crowe said the "verification questions that remain on START" are "like horsemeat—the more you chew them, the bigger they get."

Contrary to public expectation, the ground-breaking verification provisions in the INF Treaty still fall short of sound verification for START. As also explained in chapter 6, a treaty totally banning all chemical weapons defies *any* verification; such substances can be made in fertilizer plants and transported in perfectly harmless vats to become deadly only when mixed with other harmless substances.

As for a conventional arms accord, measuring the precise numbers of troops or tanks is daunting. Small weapons are tough to verify, as we learned from INF. Despite our intelligence focus here over the past seven years, we still erred badly. For we had no idea the Soviets deployed *any* SS-23 missiles in East Germany, until they told us so. We had long figured a total of 24 to 36 of these systems deployed anywhere, whereas they actually had 167.

Fortunately, the Bush administration staved off new negotiations on short-range nuclear weapons, for a while at least. During

NATO's gala 40th birthday summit in Brussels in May 1989, this contentious issue was virtually resolved, even though no leader would openly admit it. The Americans and British had wanted modernization but no negotiations; the Germans and Russians wanted negotiations but no modernization; the outcome will be *neither* negotiations *nor* modernization.

This upshot was practically inevitable. For the only country that could conduct such negotiations, the U.S., didn't want them. And the only country which could deploy such modernized systems, West Germany, didn't want *them*. So neither will have either.

Yet that summit raised false hopes for vast conventional arms control in Europe. President Bush dazzled the NATO gathering with a spanking new proposal, pushing up the completion date for such an accord while heaping upon it yet more obstacles. Bush apparently hopes to end forty years of Soviet conventional superiority via a treaty drafted and agreed to in six to twelve months' time, although the full Western proposal would not be presented to the Soviets for several of those months.

As intractable as MBFR was, the current Vienna talks are even more arduous. The already unwieldy negotiating process has been enlarged by inviting more countries to the table, including the ever-contentious France. This makes for trouble. As George Kennan once quipped, the failure of any negotiation is related to the square of the number of participants. France squares it again.

Morever, the talks' geographical and military scopes have been enlarged since MBFR, with more territory and weapons included. Now NATO has acceded to limits on aircraft and manpower, which are the toughest to categorize and verify, and which will necessarily impinge upon British and French nuclear capabilities (though they contend they will resist such restrictions).

It is unlikely that any of these arms negotiations will result in greater stability. Sophisticated arguments can be (and have been) made that our security would be hurt, not helped, by the START proposal *we* offered late in the Reagan administration, let alone the one that could come out of Geneva after much haggling. President Bush's National Security Advisor, Brent Scowcroft, joined experts John Deutch and R. James Woolsey in concluding that START could push us to "a new kind of triad: vulnerability, wishful thinking, and a hair trigger." Not terribly consoling words, but true.

And none of these would necessarily, at the end of the day, save money. Here the argument is more tentative since the particulars become more critical. Still, logic and history dampen hopes for any "peace dividend" arising from arms control.

THE GLIMMER

The one exception to arms control's vast wasteland these days lies in a rather novel notion: the United States and the Soviet Union could jointly turn the INF ban against a key category of ballistic missiles into a worldwide ban. By signing others onto obligations we have already assumed, we could thereby work to halt missile proliferation, just as we have long worked together to halt nuclear proliferation.

That there is a dire problem here is no longer in doubt. CIA Director William Webster figures that around fifteen Third World nations could be producing their *own* ballistic missiles by the turn of the century. They "have capabilities well beyond the battlefield and can strike in minutes," he has said. "Once fired, they cannot be called back." Nor defended against, which could trigger a foe to strike fast and hard in a crisis. That constitutes the very definition of danger.

So why not expand the INF ban of ballistic missiles with ranges between 300 to 3,400 miles—the nub of the accord Reagan and Gorbachev signed in December of 1987—to all countries? U.S. and Soviet diplomats could introduce a joint draft treaty in the forty-nation Conference on Disarmament in Geneva, where it might even carry appeal. For unlike the Non-Proliferation Treaty, this accord would not be discriminatory; we'd not ask any country to forego anything we had not already foregone.

Thereby prohibited would be missiles capable of carrying chemical and conventional arms, as well as nuclear weapons. Hence would this move help reduce the dread of more chemical warfare and eliminate the nightmare of marrying poison gas with ballistic missiles.

Why would other countries buy on? Some out of sheer superpower sway. A few out of moral suasion; it is, after all, the right thing to do. Most out of fright that otherwise their arch-enemies would get these bloody things. Conceivably arms control can contribute where neither side has a weapon and each would rather not acquire it than end up—as is commonly the case—with both obtaining it.

we would not have ended up with fifty highly capable, highly warheaded, highly vulnerable MX missiles deployed in the worst manner imaginable.

If my premises are correct—that traditional U.S.-Soviet arms control is conceptually bankrupt and practically blocked; that sound verifiable accords on strategic, conventional, or chemical weapons cannot even be written up by the Americans, let alone negotiated out with the Soviets—we should face the music and change our act. Rather than go for an agreement without real arms control, we should seek real arms control without necessarily going for an agreement.

We should adopt an approach of reciprocal though individual moves. The United States and the Soviet Union would thereby design programs to enhance their own security and then discuss those policies with each other, ideally coordinating them. Adopting this less formal approach keeps top officials from being lost among the trees and helps them see the forest: how to reduce the risks of war, the number of nuclear weapons, and so forth. They could more clearly see and build strategic systems that would be most survivable, sensible, and affordable rather than those that would be easiest for the other side to verify or mightiest to use as a bargaining chip in Geneva.

Under this approach, we could skirt the age-old quandary over which systems or capabilities to include and which to exclude in the talks. This would keep our leaders from lunging for the capillaries in security deliberations with the Soviets.

More widely, this approach would slay today's pactomania, which leads the public to hope (or even believe) that parchment brings peace. It would likewise stop all the nonsense adorning arms control today—the daily temperature taking on the talks, the back-and-forth accusations over who is stonewalling now, the endless banter that "the ball's in their court" after each teeny step, the *People* magazine tidbits of who's up and who's down, who's in and who's out, in the unending Washington battles on arms control. And with less rigidity, parallel or reciprocal U.S.-Soviet actions could be more easily modified should conditions change.

Again, history justifies this tack. Informal arms control has been far more successful than formal. Like the individual startled to learn he had been speaking prose, many may be surprised to learn we have been relying upon informal arms control.

Examples abound, but one looms above the rest. That is the nuclear curse—not the weapons themselves, but the *curse* itself. By now it is universally accepted that nuclear weapons are distinct from other kinds. This may not be true in quantitative terms—nuclear arms can have less blast than conventional munitions—but it is surely true in qualitative terms. Their potential power makes them most frightful. Officials have come to consider their use totally out of the question, except when the nation's very survival would be at stake. Even then they would be used with a sense of resignation and doom rather than of anticipation and victory.

So deep has this sunk into the world's collective conscience that it is hard to believe it was not always within us. President Harry Truman slept soundly after ordering the atomic bombing of Hiroshima and Nagasaki; Americans cheered themselves hoarse when hearing the news. Not long after that, British Prime Minister Clement Attlee flew to Washington to urge Truman to abstain from using nuclear weapons in Korea, even if we started losing on the battlefield. So began the concept of limited war and the reality of the nuclear curse.

But it still had not taken hold when Dwight D. Eisenhower entered the White House, for he chatted casually about nuclear weapons before television cameras:

Now, in any combat where these things can be used on strictly military targets and for strictly military purposes, I see no reason they shouldn't be used just exactly as you'd use a bullet or anything else.

The President's casual talk on how nuclear weapons were *really* no different from other weapons created no fuss then. That same statement would trigger a veritable eruption (if not calls for impeachment) now.

As one measure of the curse's power, it has become virtually impossible for the military to design war games that "go nuclear." Whether played by top-brass military or at the highest civilian level—no matter how dire their predicament on the battlefield, with "red team" tanks storming for the English Channel —"blue team" leaders resist pushing the button. This has diminished the utility of such war games to the experts for their training. Although frustrating to them, it must come as reassuring to the rest of us.

Below the nuclear curse, informal arms control has had impressive success in non-proliferation. Parkinson's most astute law tells that the success of any policy is measured by the catastrophes that do not ensue. This happened here. The literature of the 1950s brimmed with doomsday forecasts of a world laden with many nuclear weapons states. In 1963 President Kennedy warned publicly of a world with fifteen to twenty states brandishing the bomb by 1975. When he spoke there were four such states; China made it five the next year. Very few have joined since then, India obviously in 1974; but the total is nowhere near Kennedy's predicted fifteen to twenty.

The proliferation taboo preceded the Non-Proliferation Treaty of 1968. Singular successes started much earlier. In the late 1950s Canada, West Germany, Switzerland, and Sweden toyed individually with the idea of building the bomb. And most of them did more than toy. The Swedish and Swiss militaries each made firm decisions to go nuclear, and they had their publics with them. Switzerland, in fact, held two plebiscites. The first proposed rejecting the nuclear option; this was overwhelmingly rejected. The second required another plebiscite before deciding to acquire nuclear weapons; this was also turned down flat.

Nonetheless, over time the nonproliferation norm took hold. It has been reinforced by successful talks between the United States and our Allies, and between the United States and Soviets. With the Allies, we draw up lists of items too sensitive to export; we share intelligence; and we exert diplomatic pressure when countries take steps to proliferate.

We hold twice yearly private talks with the Soviets. We discuss, not when to begin the next round or when to adjourn it or what to discuss, but real ways to keep the bomb from spreading. The Russians evidently value these "private interchanges," which take place in relative obscurity. When they walked away from the table in 1983 and ended START, INF, and MBFR, they continued our nonproliferation talks on schedule.

A third shining example of this type of arms control bears on the safety of nuclear weapons. This is no small matter. To assure that nuclear weapons could not be detonated by a madman or by accident—in essence, to assure the President keeps a hammerlock on their use—in the early 1960s U.S. technicians devised "permissive action links," or PALs. In layman's terms, these are combination locks that must be dialed correctly to make a launch possible, with the correct combination relayed from the White House. If a few mistakes are made in dialing, the devise is unable to operate for hours; this prevents anyone from trying repeatedly to break the code.

Through private interchanges in 1963 or so, U.S. officials shared the notion of PALs with the Soviets and may have pointed toward the right technology. In any case, the Soviets seemed to have adopted a similar device, making catastrophes less likely on either side.

Less dramatic but no less important examples exist. Both sides have generally tailored their strategic arsenals in ways that best preclude the need to "use 'em or lose 'em" in a crisis. This serves the security concerns of each of us. Both countries have likewise emphasized secure and reliable command-and-control systems. On our side, NATO has spent sizable sums of money to help assure that nuclear weapons do not constitute the only possible response to aggression in central Europe.

These are among the real accomplishments in the past. An impressive list. In addition there are several instances where this type of informal, individual, and reciprocal approach could have been helpful, even with respect to the two weapons that dogged both the Carter and Reagan administrations: INF and ASAT (antisatellite weapons).

In the mid-1970s the United States (and NATO) could have warned the Russians not to deploy their SS-20 force "or else" we would deploy our Pershing II and cruise missiles. Who knows what would have come from this type of informal offer? Had they believed it and bought it, we and they would have ended up where we will end up, without any INF systems. But they would have arrived there without expending billions of rubles, and we without spending billions of dollars, to say nothing of being spared a staggering amount of acrimony and aggravation.

Similarly on ASAT. Had we both frozen this technology in the mid-1970s, each country warning the other that it would modernize only if the other did, both sides would have been better off. Neither the United States nor the USSR welcomes threats to its satellites, which are critical to strategic safety.

Leaving might-have-beens, we can conceive of some to-be-dones. The Bush administration should institutionalize security discussions between our Secretary of Defense and the Soviet Defense Minister, and between our Chairman of the Joint Chiefs and their Chief of Staff—discussions that the Reagan administration began, though sporadically. Such deliberations should avoid technical trivia and nuclear numerology and instead fix on military doctrine, crisis prevention, crisis management, and crisis resolution. They can and should hash out today's mega-issue: how to move toward more defense and less offense.

These Soviet-U.S. executive talks should be conducted in sync with congressional-executive talks, in a way to Americanize the process Churchill outlined. In a parliamentary system, the leader can inform a foreign leader, "If you build x, we will build y," and deliver on it. An American president cannot, unless Congress goes along.

Hence, to adapt this approach to our system, a U.S. Defense Secretary would tell the Soviets the nature of an informal deal and then tell Congress *both* that he had told the Soviets *and* that he means it. This would give the members fair yet firm warning that if the Russians do proceed with x, he will then be back to Congress to request y. Besides being sensible, such an approach is eminently sellable; it would strike most members of Congress as a reasonable way to assure American security. Everyone could hold hands so that later nobody could point fingers.

This could be done, for instance, with stealth sea-launched cruise missiles (SLCMs). Neither side would develop or test this weapon, which is destabilizing in that it cuts strategic warning time, unless the other so proceeded. We could handle any new ASAT system in the same manner, as we could any new land-based missile with more than one warhead. One could go down the line on strategic weapons. The possibilities are vast, if the concept is bought.

In the realm of conventional arms talks, we'd best jettison the type of green-eyeshade activities now ensuing in Vienna. Instead we could focus on more productive activities, such as taking steps to make a surprise attack across the East-West dividing line more difficult for either side. Western states should take Gorbachev at his word when he stated in his 1988 United Nations address that Pact forces will henceforth be deployed as "clearly defensive." This requires removing their vast arsenal of bridge-crossing equipment, for instance. Defensive Pact forces have no need to cross bridges into Western Europe.

After specifying three or four concrete steps to implement this "clearly defensive" posture, we could institute on-site inspections of key military points—railroad junctions, storage sites, air fields, and various other installations—to help assure such actions are taken. Even without such steps, NATO has scaled back the alliance's biggest annual military maneuver; in 1989, for the first time since 1967, the United States did not send over massive reinforcements in the REFORGER exercise.

Meanwhile, naturally, each side should cultivate its own garden, thereby doing its part to approach arms control's goals. We can (and should) continue to reduce the number of nuclear weapons, as we have done so dramatically yet surreptitiously over the decades. None of these cuts—25 percent of the total number of our nuclear weapons since 1967 and 75 percent of their total megatonnage since then; furthermore, removal of 2,400 nuclear weapons from Europe—could have been achieved had we made it a matter of formal arms negotiations with the Soviets.

Rather than move into new negotiations on nuclear weapons in Europe, as both the German and Soviet governments wish, we should handle the situation by ourselves. More battlefield nuclear weapons should be removed from Germany. Even the current NATO military commander, General William M. Galvin, says the United States can safely take out another one thousand nuclear weapons from Europe which would then leave around 3,000 there, compared to some 7,200 in the late 1960s. These reductions could be made after other nuclear systems there are modernized. As long as the total number of nuclear arms deployed there declines, the German public should be mollified, if not satisfied.

We can keep improving the safety of our nuclear stockpiles, too. It is chilling to think back to the 1950s, when a seventeen-year-old GI with a rifle would guard a prefab warehouse in Germany filled with nuclear weapons; thank God we passed that era. Research is now under way to develop safer types of nuclear weapons, those that emit no radiation and cannot detonate under high impact such as a midair plane crash. This is the type of research that really *does* make the world safer.

NATO can, in the coming years, change the mix between nuclear and conventional weapons. As explained in chapter 4, conventional munitions can now fulfill missions long assigned to nuclear forces, such as attacking hardened facilities like bunkers, bridge pylons, and other targets behind enemy lines.

Such changes are coming, which brings us to the third advantage of this new arms control approach of fashioning evolving, parallel policies with the Soviets mostly absent formal agreements: It is inevitable anyway.

For forty years, the West has been waiting breathlessly for an end to the Cold War. According to one scholar, Dr. Burton Marshall, top U.S. officials or opinion molders have declared a turning point in U.S.-Soviet relations on fifty-four different occasions in recent decades. None of them turned out to be definitive or lasting. But the fifty-fifth may be.

Sure, the possibility still exists that Moscow might lash out while communism gasps its final breath. Or Gorbachev could take Henry IV's deathbed advice to his son Henry V and declare war so as to "busy giddy minds with foreign quarrels." But I doubt either will happen. While less predictable today than ever before, the Bear is just too sick, and Gorbachev is just too practical. He too can see that communism is on its deathbed and communist states everywhere are on their backs. The high-water mark of the Soviet empire passed in the 1970s; what lies ahead is shallows and miseries.

Since Americans heralded the demise of the Cold War on fifty-four occasions when there was scant cause, it is not hard to understand their anticipation today when there is good cause. It may be difficult for our government to manage the devolution of the Soviet empire in a sensible way. We can take consolation, however, in the knowledge that it will be far tougher for them to do so.

The logical consequence of the unmistakable decrepitude of the Soviet empire and the resulting Gorbachev reforms is a cutback of Soviet security spending, on the amount dolled out both to Soviet outposts and to Soviet forces. The Soviet leader announced the first steps in this direction during his ground-breaking December 1988 UN address, when he trumpeted the demobilization of five hundred thousand Soviet troops and the removal of ten thousand Soviet tanks from Eastern Europe.

Subsequently he stated publicly that Soviet "studies show that we can cut" military spending "without lowering the level of security and the country's ability to defend itself" and gave more specifics. Around half of his five hundred thousand troop cut (which amounts to 12 percent of total Soviet military manpower) would come from the western part of the USSR, where they are most threatening to NATO. Of his tank pull-back from Eastern

Europe, slightly more than half (5,300) will be of the "most advanced" types of tanks. All told, Gorbachev claims the Soviets will dismantle nearly 20 percent of their tanks; more than 25 percent of their artillery pieces; and nearly 20 percent of combat aircraft.

This cut in forces enables Gorbachev to cut defense spending, which he announced early in 1989 to the tune of 14.2 percent overall and 19.5 percent in Soviet military hardware. Because certainly we don't know (and probably he doesn't either) precisely what the Soviet military now spends, there remains room for skepticism in Gorbachev's green eye shading. But given his record and temperament, we should not put it past him to implement this.

For he has a strong popular wind behind him. In the spring 1989 elections, the Soviet people unmistakably spoke for slackening the military buildup, most evidently by defeating at least four generals and two admirals running for office. A Warsaw Pact commander lost by nearly three to one to a young colonel advocating slicing defense, just as the commander of the Soviet Navy's key northern fleet lost to a junior commander in a major naval port filled with naval personnel. Other winning candidates around the country widely mentioned defense cuts among the changes they supported. Naturally, many party stalwarts did not, but then many of them lost; some 20 percent of Communist Party members who ran were defeated, including the mayors of Moscow and Leningrad.

They too felt the wind blowing. A more recent poll by a leading Soviet sociologist published in *Literaturnaya Gazeta* showed that an astonishing 71 percent of the 200,000 plus respondents named as the first thing the country should do to improve life is to curtail severely its military spending.

Right after these historic elections, Gorbachev announced an end to student draft deferments, which paves the way for a U.S. style "all volunteer force." Moreover, Western intelligence sources indicate that Moscow has scaled back submarine production and cut the size of its Pacific fleet by forty ships over the past four years and its operations over the past year.

Even with the announced ground forces cut, the Soviet bloc retains conventional superiority in Central Europe. As mentioned, Gorbachev today has more Soviet divisions in East Germany than exist in the entire U.S. Army and more troops in one country, Czechoslovakia, than the U.S. has across Western Europe. Besides, the Soviet military-industrial complex still cranks out enough tanks each *month* to equip one new tank division. Since Gorbachev assumed power, the Soviets have deployed more tanks and artillery pieces than Britain, France, and Germany combined have in their armies.

Still, Gorbachev's announced moves are not bad for starters, especially since it now appears that he will remove forces which have spearheaded the Pact's notorious "short warning threat" to NATO. Such moves may engender some resistance within his military—Marshal Akhromeyev's retirement, announced the day after the UN speech, may indicate as much—but Gorbachev can resort to the best of all possible sources for inspiration in this, namely Lenin.*

In the 1920s, the great founder of the Soviet state slashed Soviet military manpower by 90 percent, cutting it from 5.3 million men in 1920 to 562,000 five years later. Ending the civil war and beginning the New Economic Policy allowed Lenin to make these cuts and even to relegate those remaining in uniform merely to a homeland militia.

Gorbachev also has more modern precedents. Immediately following World War II, between 1946 and 1949, Stalin cut the Red Army from somewhere around twelve million to three million. Between 1955 and 1957, while Khrushchev was consolidating his power, the USSR unilaterally reduced its forces by 1.8 million men (more than three times Gorbachev's level). And in 1960 Khrushchev announced another unilateral move since he realized that such cuts would be doomed if they became a matter of U.S.-Soviet or NATO-Pact negotiations. In his words:

> To keep its army at its present strength without making any unilateral cuts in it until we succeeded in convincing our partners that they should agree to mutual reductions . . . our Soviet state and people would lose . . . because national funds would be spent completely unproductively.

Interestingly, Gorbachev too made his moves unilaterally. To

---

* In another way, too, Gorbachev must go back to move forward. His *glasnost,* regardless of how stunning it appears to us, still falls short of allowing the degree of political freedom in Czarist times; between the revolt of 1905 and the revolution of 1917 were extensive political reforms in Russia with embryonic multiparty competition, a freer speech and press than allowed even now, and an independent judiciary that made critical court decisions against the government.

have waited for NATO–Warsaw Pact arms negotiations to succeed would have prevented him from making such reductions any time soon, if ever. To make the point most dramatically, Gorbachev thus announced cuts that were *forty-three times* what the hordes of Western diplomats ended up requesting in the MBFR talks in Vienna, which for nearly fourteen years accomplished nothing. In terms of forces in Central Europe, he cut by a more modest but still astonishing *twenty times* what the West was finally seeking.

Gorbachev later offered some interesting comments: "When we speak about defense sufficiency of the armed forces," he told a Western group early in 1989, "one should keep in mind that this notion is a changing one. Its contents will depend on how the West conducts itself." Gorbachev then laid down the gauntlet for the type of less formal arms control advocated here. "Our *perestroika* will come to pass, but we expect *perestroika* from your side as well," he told the visiting Westerners.

As to cutbacks in those massive Soviet expenditures to communist outposts, nothing has yet been announced. But this may come on the heels of the settlement in Angola and with the exhaustion of the Soviet treasury. Besides, there is nothing in Russian history or the Russian psyche driving the Soviets to retain support for far-flung countries like Cuba, Nicaragua, and Ethiopia, which costs Moscow more than $8 billion yearly. Such massive aid to such nations is relatively new, a Soviet innovation of the 1960s and 1970s. As such, it could conceivably be diminished even more easily than cuts in the Soviets' own defense forces, which were huge under both the czars and commissars.

Over time, though, one can easily envision Moscow reducing aid to the outposts, along with removing some of its forty-plus divisions facing China and even slowing its strategic buildup.

What does all this mean for Western security? Only good things.

Commentators are quick to conclude, as Hotspur did, "Out of this nettle, danger, we pluck this flower, safety," even though we are not out of danger yet. We should hold back the hosannas until we know we *have* won the Cold War, which may not be knowable (or even happen) for a good number of years. We should realize that there will surely be bumps and diversions along the way.

Meanwhile, we must cope with runaway Western sentiment

that the Soviet threat is passing, if not passé. Support for increased Western military spending has evaporated and will continue to evaporate unless Gorbachev resorts to some outlandish action, à la another Afghanistan, which is most improbable. Hence Western political will is lacking to support more missiles or new and terribly pricey strategic bombers. Strategic defense, executed deliberately and coolly, can gain support, but only if (as I expect) SDI research pans out and is accompanied by cuts in other strategic programs.

In a nutshell, real arms reductions are coming. They will result not from negotiations in Geneva, but from deliberations in Washington and Moscow. Budget cutters will do what arms controllers have generally failed to do. In fact, they are already doing so, with U.S. defense spending declining by more than 13 percent in real terms over the past four years and announced Soviet cuts of the same magnitude over the next year. We should now let nature take its course, watch the improvement of strategic stability and the draw-down of conventional forces and nuclear weaponry outside of what happens around the tables in Vienna and Geneva.

Why, one may reasonably ask, would Gorbachev reduce his conventional forces (for example) unilaterally rather than multilaterally in the Vienna talks, where he can get something from NATO in return? Simply because he *knows* that he will get something from NATO in return for more *unilateral* cuts. No one glancing at the mood across Western Europe today can miss the tremendous benefits he's already reaping from the limited conventional cuts announced thus far.

Besides, such a process is as natural as the formal arms control process is artificial. When two nations move from being fierce enemies to strong adversaries to mere rivals, they commonly lower their armaments—not through arms control, but through downgrading the threat. This has happened repeatedly in history —with the United States and Canada in mid–nineteenth century, the British and the French in the early years of this century, and China and India during the fifteen years after their 1962 conflict. It is happening now between Russia and China.

If, as I contend, formal arms control has little to contribute to this quasi-inevitable process, at least it can step aside and let the goals of arms control be realized without the formal process blocking their realization.

The toughest part of adopting the informal and reciprocal approach to arms control is the general absence of American dexterity and patience in foreign affairs. Alexis de Tocqueville caught the truth 150 years ago in *Democracy in America.* He wrote that our system:

> can only with great difficulty regulate the details of an important undertaking, persevere in a fixed design, and work out its executions in spite of serious obstacles. It cannot combine its measures with secrecy or await their consequences with patience.

The approaches recommended here—on SDI, arms control, and diplomacy—demand dexterity and time, dexterity to be laid out carefully and executed appropriately and time to be adopted and to work. Meanwhile they would come under attack—SDI for the reasons given; the diplomatic tack for being confrontational or overly demanding; and the arms control approach for sundry reasons.

Each has problems associated with it, some of which have been addressed here and others that I have failed to anticipate. But what approach does not? As Dr. Samuel Johnson once said, "Nothing will be attempted if all possible objections must first be overcome."

Of the three, the new approach on arms control is most vulnerable to attack from all sides. Conservatives can picture it on that proverbial slippery slope, the beginnings of unilateralism. If we make significant changes only to find that the Soviets do not follow, this approach would have been misinterpreted and should then be discarded.

Liberals could castigate the approach as constituting semantic subversion, claiming it is not "real" arms control but a sneaky way of killing real arms control while co-opting its good name.

To them, I answer that they are confusing the means with the goals. What matters is to find the best way to approach the traditional goals of arms control. If that be via formal agreements, fine; the Non-Proliferation Treaty and INF Accord, formal treaties both, *have* contributed to arms control's goals. But except for an expanded INF treaty, one turning the bilateral pact into a multilateral one, that well now appears empty. Generally over the years, even decades, formal agreements have not led us to its goals, and today's conditions hold out less promise than before.

Most debilitating will be criticism of informal arms control by the politicians and press for sapping spice out of international affairs. What they fear would become the reality: no flourishing beginning of formal arms negotiations; no leaks of this minuscule move or that; no end game; no signing ceremonies.

In a word, no headlines. Just as it is impossible to organize a parade for proximate justice, so it is impossible to arouse much enthusiasm for informal arms control and prudent defense planning, one tailored to the threat rather than to the demands of an accord.

While political and diplomatic types in the White House and State Department would resist, the rest of us could rest assured that we were making progress toward a safer world. "The commonest error in politics is sticking to the carcasses of dead policies," said Lord Salisbury.

After some time, historians can and surely will look back to ponder what caused the arms control hype of our era. Surely hope lay behind it, a hope that later may be transferred to SDI and to the obvious warming of relations between the Soviet government and ours (which can only follow the warming of relations between the Soviet government and its own people).

And surely historians will see that tension and antagonism lay behind the arms control hype. When the U.S.-Soviet relationship was strictly antagonistic, formal arms control came to be regarded as its barometer. It was treasured, not for what it accomplished in the way of its goals, but for what it indicated in the way of U.S.-Soviet relations.

Once the superpower relationship turns less antagonistic, as is happening now, formal arms control will lose even this utility. So, in perhaps the ultimate irony, future historians will come to view formal arms control as just another accoutrement of the Cold War.

INDEX

ABM (Anti-Ballistic Missile) treaty,
37, 101, 102, 145, 184, 188, 203,
204, 210, 225, 226, 227, 231, 250,
263, 312, 313, 321
disagreement on, 29, 277, 299, 304–
305
interpretations of, 213
justification for, 303
and MAD, 308
and SDI, 48, 53, 71, 73, 80, 81, 85,
304, 307, 309, 314, 315, 316
Soviet violations of, 29, 150, 252,
266, 268
wording of, 99
Abrahamson, James, 135
ACDA. *See* Arms Control and
Disarmament Agency
Acheson, Dean, 193, 250
Acton, Lord John, 246
Afghanistan, 25, 43, 58, 60, 100,
102, 122, 125, 129, 131, 134, 142,
153–54, 183, 187, 206, 214, 218,
228, 255, 328, 347
genocide in, 140–41
Africa, 43, 155, 206, 328, 331
See also South Africa
African students, in Soviet Union,
151, 152
Air Force (U.S.), 38, 171, 172, 196–
197
Air-launched cruise missiles. *See*
ALCMs
Akhromeyev, Sergey F., 60, 137, 230,
345
background of, 58–59, 109–10
status of, 201

tactics of, 48–50, 51, 52, 54–55, 56,
57, 104, 174
Alaska, 37, 38
ALCMs (air-launched cruise
missiles), 35
Alexander I, Emperor of Russia, 328
Alexander II, Emperor of Russia, 328
Allen, Richard, 126, 255, 299
Amin, Idi, 303
Anderson, Martin, 298
Andropov, Yuri, 256
Angola, 60, 102, 129, 131, 141, 186–
187, 296, 346
Anti-Ballistic Missile Treaty. *See*
ABM Treaty
Antisatellite system. *See* ASAT
Arabs. *See* Israeli-Arab dispute
Arbatov, Gregory, 50, 51
Argentina, 68, 335
Armageddon, 163–66, 246, 299
Arms Control and Disarmament
Agency (ACDA), 32, 169, 181,
186, 191, 257, 262, 271–72, 276
Army (U.S.), 224, 344
Articles of Confederation, 280
ASAT (antisatellite system), 170–72,
340, 341
Asia, 37, 56, 57, 60, 78, 155, 206, 235,
236, 237, 238, 303
Asian students, in Soviet Union, 151,
152
Aspin, Les, 82
Atlantic, 150
Atomic Energy Commission, 181
Attlee, Clement, 338
Augustine, Norm, 223

ABOUT THE AUTHOR

Nominated by President Ronald Reagan in January of 1983 as Director of the U.S. Arms Control and Disarmament Agency, Kenneth L. Adelman served in that post until December 1987, when Reagan and Gorbachev signed the INF Treaty. Previously he was deputy U.S. representative to the United Nations (from 1981 to 1983) with the rank of Ambassador Extraordinary and Plenipotentiary. He had been assistant to the U.S. Secretary of Defense from 1976 to 1977.

Now a nationally syndicated columnist with the Tribune Media Services, vice-president of the Institute for Contemporary Studies, and national editor of **Washingtonian** magazine, Ambassador Adelman also teaches Shakespeare at Georgetown University and security issues at Johns Hopkins School of Advanced International Studies. He frequently speaks on world events and was a consultant for CBS News and for the BBC during recent summits.

In past years, he was a founding member of the Sherlock Holmes Club in Washington; participated on the Zaire River Expedition, a three-month voyage down the Congo River on the 100th anniversary of Stanley's trip; and translated for Muhammad Ali during his heavyweight bout—"the rumble in the jungle"—in Zaire.

He lives with his wife Carol and two daughters, Jessica, fourteen, and Jocelyn, twelve, in Arlington, Virginia.